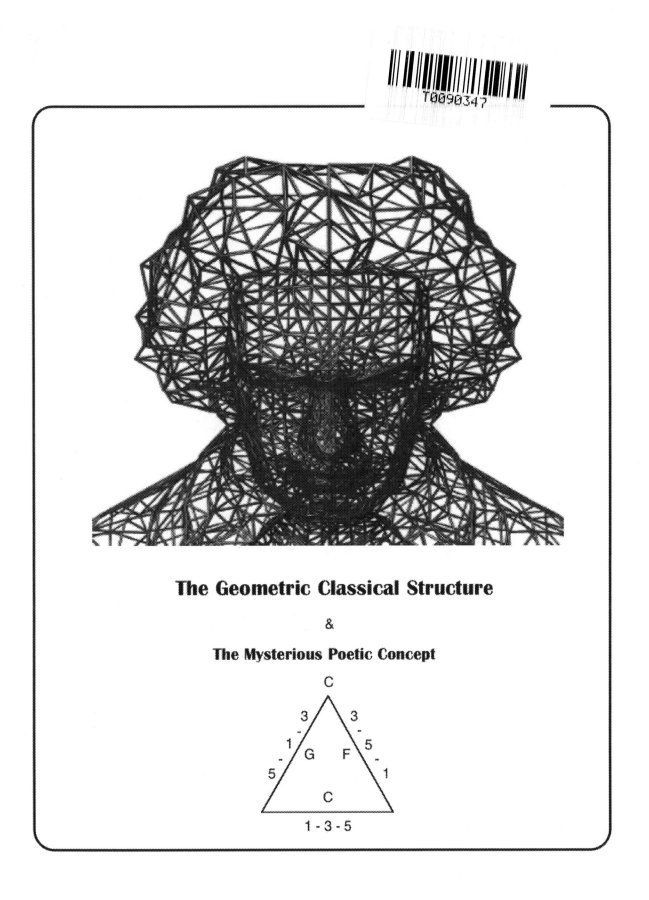

The Geometric Classical Structure

&

The Mysterious Poetic Concept

The Classical Method

Piano Classical Improvisation & Compositional Theory and Harmony

By

Robert Kaye

authorHOUSE

AuthorHouse™
1663 Liberty Drive
Bloomington, IN 47403
www.authorhouse.com
Phone: 1-800-839-8640

Published by AuthorHouse 5/21/2013

ISBN: 978-1-4208-0311-2 (sc)
ISBN: 978-1-4772-6155-2 (e)

Library of Congress Control Number: 2005900018

This book is printed on acid-free paper.

The " Classical Method " in which I spent the better part of over ten years, has yielded me the following; It's to my best judgment, the method that I discovered by ear, as well as by experience, is the method once used by the great composers themselves. I did not quit pursuing until I reached the pinnacle of sound that I had been familiar with and playing since childhood. Nevertheless, It's not by any means that there aren't any more theoretical material or further studies that one can acquire, but it's the piano method from where all the theoretical, conceptual, improvisational, compositional and orchestrative elements thrived and was induced from. And this is, the first book written on classical improvisation. This subject was not even relevant for discussions in the past, meaning in this century or during our lifetime.

It's said that Chopin almost wrote a book of his theoretical works, but after my studies I can understand why in his short virtuous brief life he did not. It would be a lifetime of authentic rich material in which he encompassed over his life times compositions. Another words as long as it would take him to write his piano pieces, it would have relatively taken him that long to write his ideas and approaches systematically as he discovered each piece of music he gave birth to." The depths of Ideas are judged by a life-time of work". And it would have taken any great composer very deep and thorough anguish to relive one's experiences. Not to mention the time it takes to write the book. Most of the great composers died very early with no time to spare, much less spend it writing a book. Although I'm sure there are studies in the circulation. It just so happens, it did not surface around me or in my life-time.

So I took it on myself to discover in the span of 10 years of compositions the revealing criterial anti-dote. Also one can use enough theoretical elements and a lot of creative imagination at a young age and produce a vast piece of body of works, and only if all the conditions and requirements are completely met and present.

Secrecy is also a factor. Most composers did not reveal their theories. Although they did teach those that were serious, honest, willing and not a waste of their time. Liszt taught all his students free of charge his entire lifetime. He himself was taught free by Beethoven's student, Carl Czerny.

In my lifetime, we grew up trying to achieve the impossible. For instance; Jazz gigging, playing in clubs and restaurants and acting this is normal, when the music was not even published in the open. There were no teachers or classes in schools or colleges to teach us this chart oriented quick burst of gigging. This music that is all over the record industry but yet its hush hush in the streets. You had to make copies of the books that only a few whom had traveled to New York or had coincidentally run by them. The direct sources were the players themselves. I heard that over and over, growing up. And that's the only way one could achieve in further educating themselves in this era of music called Jazz.

As the century closed; We now know the legacy of this new art form, have a better grasp of how it was achieved, and can find it with its predecessors in concert halls, in books, on college campuses and in the classrooms.

And during, or after all of which we experienced the song-writing era. The new stereo commercial FM sound. A product from a voice of survival. The aftermath of a revolution. The new medium. A voice for the new generation. In which I found myself reminiscing back to the late sixties and early seventies culture. During the civil rights movement. Where songs were the dominant media outlet. Jazz and classical venues went out of business. Rubinstein, Horowitz & Van Clyburn had retired. Sara Vaughn was no longer employed. Orchestras were gone.

I remember one of my first relationships during high school. With a friend named Maggie M. Just as soon as all kids decide to move on to other girlfriends. Rod Stewart day-viewed his first hit of " Maggie May ". My new girl friend this time was my size. A petite ballet' dancer. In which young Elton John just wrote " Tiny Dancer ". At the time I ended up in the basement of my piano teacher. I was 17 years old. Some of my guests that came over to Jam during a free moment were such as, a keyboard player that had played with Jefferson Airplane. The horn player was an Emerson, lake & Palmer employee. And then Frankie Valley and the Four Seasons followed with " My Eyes Adored You ".

And then again many dates, flashpots, light shows, roadies, trucks, buses, airplane offers, PA's, road grind and a new band to settle down with. A new relationship formed on a farm setting this time with J. West, she was much older than I was. That's when Dotty West and Kenny Rogers released " What are we doing in Love " .

There were many more. Soon afterwards country mixed with rock. And new forms of songwriting genre's were being formed. This was a direct link to my generation and our culture. Enriched with the songwriting radio commercial element during and after a revolution. Great timeless songs that will forever be on the radio.

However ; The theoretical elements of the original method in which classical composition and from where the original and indigenous musical art form had evolved was relinquished. Not to mention the fact that machines have taken over the idiom of today's society as well.

I have also found myself reminiscing on the days of practicing piano impulsively, days in days out. Only to wind up surprisingly rewarded by being invited to a "Grateful Dead" concert, sitting by the stage and having Jerry Garcia come over to give his regards. Or merely having a record player to figure out how to play my parts for this song before going on the road again.

The Beatles music had not been published in notation yet. Nor any other in the song or band era as the Allman Brothers songs. Only the jazz standards were but with a quiet twist. And mostly hand written. And were I grew up, it was illegal to have in one's possession.

We picked up songs that were on the radio to perform by ear only. Played the same clubs following the Allman Brothers and The Martial Tucker Band..Soon afterwards the culture normalized again. And the other venues opened up again. Both jazz and classical. I sat in with musicians that had played with Art Tatum or I was gigging with individual members from Johnny Carson's band. Other greats from what seemed a by gone earlier era. And reminisced about those days. I found myself interested in what other gigging musician's approach to music education. Corky as it seemed to my friends next to me. I took lessons from them. My curiosity of what they were using in regard to their approach as a working musician. And over the years. It was those little bits of information that I had picked up from those that have studied from the likes of such diversities as, for ex: Lenny Tristano to Sergei Rachmaninoff's students. These bits of nuggets I picked up over the years from curiosity culminated the essence of this book. Not one source gave me all that I needed to uncover this method. It took every bit of all from many different directions. And years to sort out, absorb and further uncover by everyday playing and studies.

I started using the walking bass line with my left hand on piano's for solo jazz gigs. At that time no one had played that way except the organ players did from time to time, because of the heavy deep bass one can substitute with the hammond organ. I myself didn't want to commit with a bass player or a drummer, because of my background and studies. And the commitment one would have to relinquish any further studies. Soon afterwards everyone started playing the bass with the left hand on the piano. Dave McKenna opened the flood door there.

I've gone through two marriages by now and I'm living next door to Charlie Rose whom is holding my infant daughter in his arms. He would ask me if I new this and that musician for his up-coming shows.

I found myself playing with big bands in Hollywood functions, restaurants, private parties. Other Jobs were plentiful again. I got more offers than I could keep up with. On any given night we would have as many as multiple singers or acts sitting in. I would be handed a 20 page chart to play at the gig with no rehearsals.

I also played in 5 star restaurants or played the lobby of hotels such as the Hilton inn, jazz and classical. Occasionally I would be informed that IBM have rented the restaurant or this major corporation rented the hotel with CEO's from different European countries are present for the night and would like you to play further into the night. This was after I had already played for three or sometimes four or five hours. Try to find your keys, or your car in the parking lot after you've poured your heart out and squeezed every ounce of your brain for hours on in already. And then play further into the night for a few more hours. It's those days and nights that I had to come up with a method to improvise and play on for a few more hours with my tuxedo drenched in a sweat and a creative lather. My body was broken down already for the night. There was a saying among jazz musicians. It was called; " I busted my $hit ". That's what piano player's would say. Or "Clamming up". That's what horn player's would say.. I had to rely on my brain to finish the night.

After twenty years I had to go back in my mind and dig up what I had used to achieve or accomplish those unexpected nights. There are no room for mistakes in front of the public eye. Some nights you could hear a pin drop. One had to sound perfect as music should be or it was more noticeable in front of dignitaries, celebrities, government officials. etc. You dreaded the coughing, if it ever began. Professional singers used to sit in on the spot. And I had to play in their key instantly. I had learned to swap harmonies and melody lines and re-arrange to offset my chest getting tight. I could time when at a distance pace I would start having chest pains. keeping a smile all along. Those are the moments when your life is literally on the line and a method or an alternative had to ensue for the sake of commitment and return. This book is the acclamation of where this method came from. And how it was achieved in spontaneity. Thus taking more than ten years to document a previous 20 year carrier. Experience will ultimately speak for itself.

After playing professionally, the rock hits from the 60's and 70's, top 40 radio, disco, southern rock, country and country rock from the radio. To Duke Ellington and George Gershwin, Cole Porter, Johnny Mercer, Jerome Kern, Harold Arlen, Hoagy Carmichael, Rogers & Hart, Parker & Gillespie, Tatum & Garner. To Bach, Beethoven, Mozart & Chopin. That's pretty much a full circle of what the musical field has yielded up to date. So I got a pictorial view of every angle of where all these composers were creating as well as how it is handled on the piano.

And the greatest of the classics of all music, have been published and forgotten. As if it fell in through the cracks at one time, and a day from an even further back era, And now lay dormant somehow, as if it didn't really exist. And so, it is to my best and solitary seclusion, that I have entitled myself in this ode. It hasn't been long since this systematic method of the classics has been dormant in my opinion. We can still find those photographs of our loved ones dressed in outfits that look like a uniform of some sort by today's standards. Rich, poor, white or black we still have those photographs tucked somewhere to remind us.

This era of communication, civility and the controversial standardized, adversarious juxtapose, revealing itself, with antiquate enlightenment. At-least in our day and time. With the motion of music and its intellect, we can still find those pockets of elements of total originality. And how they were achieved. As scarce as they are not.

I have taken on myself to reveal what was once the norm in this form of studies. And have written the first book on classical improvisation. Of what once was considered for composition only. I say it's for both. And I created this method, formula's, patterns and theories to reassure that improvisation is for classical composition as well. Seems common sense to me. My lifetime wish to play and create anything I wanted in the style of Bach, Mozart, Beethoven and most of all Chopin at the piano instantly and creatively on daily basis.

An art form that has long been forgotten. A poetic and geometric truth. Musical poetry. Mystical or mysterious, humanistic, spontaneous, compulsive, combustive, creative, multi facet, improvisational structural composition. The most powerful art of all communications. Something the great composers were very familiar with. Having improvised classical music live themselves since childhood. Improvised and composed with poetic jurisdiction on daily basis. A Composition a day. Quickly achieved. A rare entity indeed. The creative daily element of an artist. The long and arduous path to the immortal truth. An educated and well calculated spirit within a method confronting the agony of everyday boredom in reprise with exaltation of the highest creative artistic achievement for the profound humane truth professing virtuously in prodigal construct. " The Classical Method "

R.Kaye

Henry Steinway in New York 2000

R.Kaye 1980's 1990's

1980's

1970's

Artimus Pyle of Lynyrd Skynyrd in Nashville

Grammy recipient Joe Vento's Big Band in LA

London 1960's

1950's

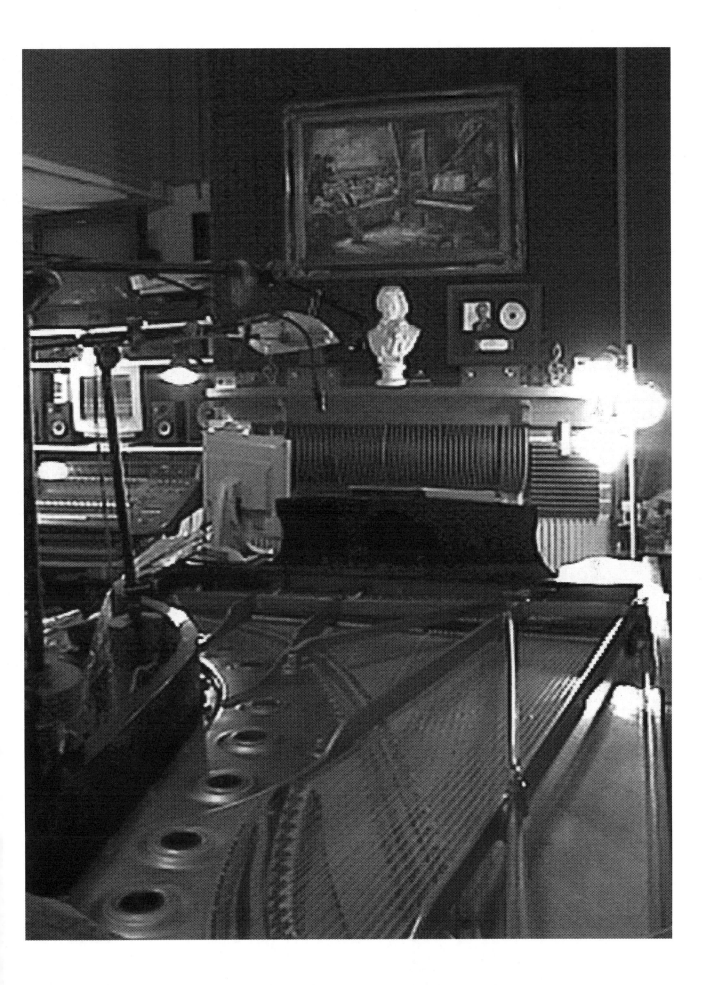

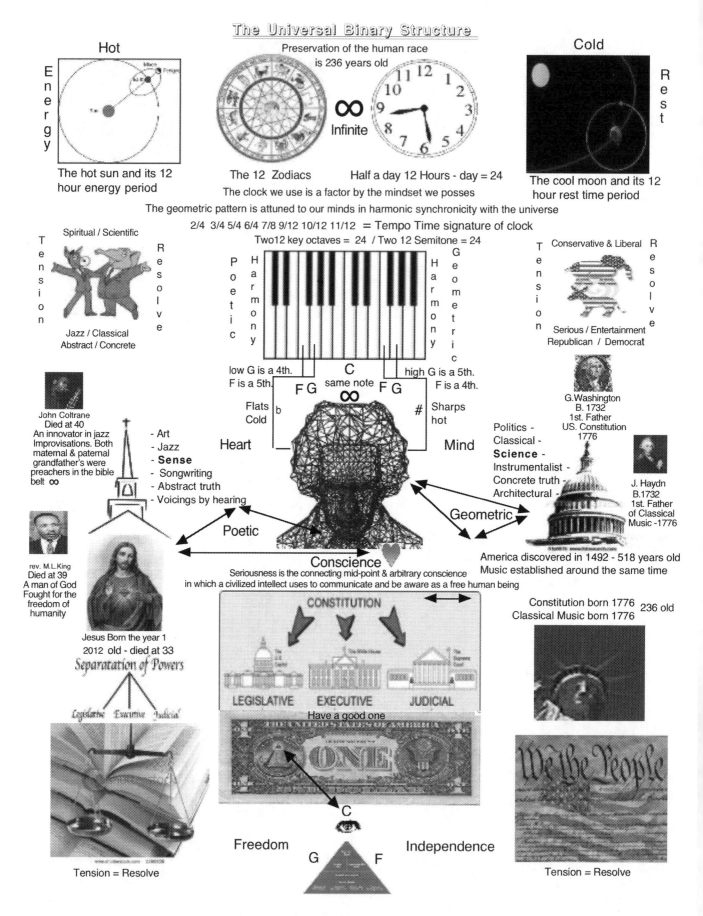

The Universal Binary Structure

Hot

E
n
e
r
g
y

The hot sun and its 12 hour energy period

Preservation of the human race is 236 years old

∞ Infinite

The 12 Zodiacs

Half a day 12 Hours - day = 24

The clock we use is a factor by the mindset we posses

Cold

R
e
s
t

The cool moon and its 12 hour rest time period

The geometric pattern is attuned to our minds in harmonic synchronicity with the universe

2/4 3/4 5/4 6/4 7/8 9/12 10/12 11/12 = Tempo Time signature of clock

Two12 key octaves = 24 / Two 12 Semitone = 24

T e n s i o n — Spiritual / Scientific — R e s o l v e

Jazz / Classical
Abstract / Concrete

P o e t i c   H a r m o n y

G e o m e t r i c   H a r m o n y

T e n s i o n — Conservative & Liberal — R e s o l v e

Serious / Entertainment
Republican / Democrat

low G is a 4th.
F is a 5th.

F G   same note   F G
∞

high G is a 5th.
F is a 4th.

Flats
Cold   b

Sharps
hot

Heart

Mind

John Coltrane
Died at 40
An innovator in jazz Improvisations. Both maternal & paternal grandfather's were preachers in the bible belt ∞

- Art
- Jazz
- **Sense**
- Songwriting
- Abstract truth
- Voicings by hearing

Politics -
Classical -
Science -
Instrumentalist -
Concrete truth -
Architectural -

G.Washington
B. 1732
1st. Father
US. Constitution
1776

J. Haydn
B.1732
1st. Father
of Classical
Music -1776

rev. M.L.King
Died at 39
A man of God Fought for the freedom of humanity

Poetic

Geometric

America discovered in 1492 - 518 years old
Music established around the same time

Conscience

Seriousness is the connecting mid-point & arbitrary conscience
in which a civilized intellect uses to communicate and be aware as a free human being

Jesus Born the year 1
2012 old - died at 33

Separation of Powers

Legislative Executive Judicial

Constitution born 1776   236 old
Classical Music born 1776

CONSTITUTION

LEGISLATIVE   EXECUTIVE   JUDICIAL

Have a good one

ONE

C

Freedom

G   F

Independence

Tension = Resolve

We the People

Tension = Resolve

Understanding my: METHOD: *Theories, Patterns & Formulas*

My Theories transform in the mind as Improvisations: ∞

1. ***Abstract*** *thoughts or contemplation. When proven, or used correctly, they become **Concrete.***
2. *The body of rules, ideas, principles, and techniques that applies to a particular subject, especially when seen as distinct from actual practice.*
3. *An idea of or belief about something arrived at through speculation, conjecture or experience.*
4. *A set of facts, propositions, or principles analyzed in their relation to one another and used, especially in science, to explain phenomena.*

Theories : *Imaginative posits invented in **one** piece for application to nature.*

Theories gives you the key to proven solvent mathematical equations that circle eternally. Using theory is mathematical harmony. Using geometric mathematical patterns musically is using harmonic poetry in time and motion, which sets the passage of time as eternity. Exercising the freedom of **Religion** with **Science** in virtue by shaping time with music. **Geometrical** and **Poetical**.

Classical & Jazz – Are two of those ***binary elements*** that allow one to circle eternally forever ∞ with infinity. And somewhere in the middle, ∞ ***They eventually meet at a serious point and can switch***. ∞ And there are many styles and forms of **jazz** and **classical** music within. So

Can you Prove my Theories: ? ….

Jazz : Is the art of improvisation. Straight or abstract.

Straight jazz is tonal harmonies with rhythm. Abstract jazz is non tonal with rhythm.
Without Rhythm ; The structure of straight jazz is classical.
Without Rhythm ; The structure of abstract jazz can be anything.
The art of jazz improvisation consists of the playing of a natural and physical ability with spontaneity. Layering, using overtones, harmonics. It's the creative form of composing. Playing on a tempo. Cocktail and solo piano. All in the improvisational form. **Jazz is an abstract expression of freedom**.

Jazz is also an interactive art of other Instruments in an improvisational form. Jazz relies on rhythm and technique with other instruments, using the song or chart format which plays on the rhythm or the beat. The pulsating rhythm is half of the style. The 12 bar blues, fast or slow.

There have been masterpieces written much like the classical way of writing long pieces, but all in all, and it's safe to say. On the majority; Jazz is the art of improvisation. Take away the recording industry, the coffee shops, the restaurants, any entertainment venue and you've taken jazz away at whole.

Jazz specializes with the flattened and sharpened split wide sounds and voicings. The walking tenth's, dissonance and improvisational overtones are only heard from good sounding instruments, which explains where and when jazz was born. It's derived from working people who can easily use this art of improvisation at night as a means of secondary income, here again at night, which aims towards entertainment or cool venues, Las Vegas.

There are only a few who have carried on and excelled to big band composition, which is close to orchestration or the same…

Chopin composed his ecossaise's when he was 16 years old. And later his " Butterfly " etude also, and all are stride piano.

And in today's trend; **The creative playing provisions in jazz music has vastly expended through evolution**. Which is usually **a modern abstract harmonious compositions created from voicings**. The form that's used today consists of **improvisational voicings on an already composed chart or song, arranged and prepared in a "modal" modern pentatonic state**, underlined with the blues in which all work for the rhythm or the bass.

Improvisation can take heed from suffering, melancholy swashbuckling in a truthful plain of euphoric ecstasy. This is where the feeling comes in. **Jazz has the feeling**. That's mostly what jazz is about. As early as one of America's premier composers; Duke Ellington. He had this feeling in multitudes. Evident in his piano playing. **A humanistic sensual form of expression that can also be applied to classical**

improvisation. As in sacred music. The church and its crucified truths. Mostly around the baroque era and early sacred classical. Palestrina, Vivaldy, Bach, Mozart, Beethoven, Chopin. Also have the feeling. The church and its crucified truths. This is why I use these composers for reference over and over. Also, they all seem to have something in common between them, they all performed live on daily basis at a young age and could improvise if they ever needed to. Just happens, their music is our favorite, and it's the best, as well as **they were masters of their instruments**. Just as an accomplished jazz great is. Just a note here; There was a time when jazz greats were distinguished between ordinary jazz musicians and not so great jazz musicians. As George Duke or Duke Jordan were jazz greats. But as time went on, the difference was no longer distinguished. But those of us that lived through it, we know, and remember.

All in all, **jazz has the feeling**, (Romantic). **And classical has the power or technique**, (Geometric). And Chopin may very well be in the center of it all. Which seems to be attuned as poetic in turn seems to reflect Bach's music. In turn it goes in full circle. And where seriousness meets midpoint and in the subconscious binary mind. ∞

John Coltrane's grandfather was William Blair a preacher ∞. Thelonious monk toured as an evangelist playing the organ. Both born in the **Bible Belt** and became innovators of improvisations ∞. Indicative of the spiritual era of that time. (The civil rights movement) ; As well as " Dizzy ", John birks Gillespie who got his music degree from the bible belt also ∞. And the other giant innovators of jazz were Parker, Davis and Hancock. Both lived along the Mississippi river in which it flowed up from New Orleans where Ferdinand "Jelly Roll" Morton claimed to have been the creator of jazz at the French quarters of New Orleans, and where Chopin was played on daily basis. ∞ And from which the spiritual black movement arose there from the multi cultures and was not suppressed for a period of time. Not a coincidence just plain old factual, truthful explanation and where the binary influences surfaced and were acclaimed from non other than education and the religious spirit itself ∞. Again Chopin seems to be the central figure and the link between classical and jazz. His music was science and emotion in one ∞. **Feeling and power in one**. Tchaikovsky said Chopin's music was like flowers and bombs all in one. Here again the same binary analogy surfacing over and over. Everything makes sense like it should. One other note to mention here is that Winton Marsalis who may very well become one of Gershwin's contemporary is also from New Orleans. This is also where Louis Armstrong eventually represented all of jazz as its ambassador.

Jazz has taught me to be aware of the **spiritual elements** aside from **education** ∞. The spiritual element is evident in the improvisational field.

I also live at the **Bible Belt** or what's left of it ∞. We could be in revelations as it seems. I've driven down wide streets of solid giant oak trees draping over nothing but grand houses after houses buildings after buildings of religious grand classical pillars and the connotation of worshiping businesses as far as the eye can see. It's an indelible sight to ponder with memory. I'm gathering it's the central offices of the Baptist religion. Its not called the **Bible Belt** for nothing. The most spiritual and innovative jazz musicians came from these areas. And as a working jazz musician a few decades ago, I was handed down the element of spirituality from an existing mentor in which I'm sincerely grateful to and was told it was handed down from Charlie Parker. This is a transformation that to my surprise gave me the assurance as well as the confidence to improvise freely and with spirituality that to this day, I maintain in regard. And can gig at any time I wish, not knowing what to play ahead of time, but trust in myself of the spiritual experience and the love and enjoyment of it.

Of-course I no longer get out much anymore, but here we see that the great classical composers of the past most definitely had their spiritual element in their every day creativity also. This is the element that I think has for ever been neglected as well as been misunderstood throughout history in regards to how classical music was treated at its inception.

This is, the first book on classical improvisation. First published in 2004. I went against all odds to create it. I was told, I would never work again, if I didn't follow as all others do. There is no such thing as classical improvisation. The old saying from show business: If you don't do as I say, you will never work in this town again. And the bottom line is of-course money and kids are paying for the industry. That kind of thinking is very real of-course. And most people have no say so. They do as they're told. This book is even banned in my local area from fear itself. I am banned, come to think of it, from fear itself, for crying out loud. And on the other side of the coin of-course sometimes it's a blessing to be just as any other free person minding his or her own business. But people do as they are told. For example: when you want to borrow money, you're at someone else's mercy, and are fortunate they lent you the money. Or if you're in need of a car, borrowing can ruin one's bank account, but one has no choice but to pay the over budgeted car for the small payments that go on forever and the ability to have something just so the gas mileage is taken in consideration. Or the ability to purchase a small electric car, for ex; " the electric smart car " which looks like a cute cookie, is more than the price of a used / new GT mustang, but if you have bad credit it can be purchased. This is the unfortunate situation that we're all caught up in.

I like to think, perhaps i am fortunate, in the fact that, I can strive for the truth, because it's all we have when we don't have much time for anything else. And i achieved it complete in part by my spiritual jazz and classical backgrounds among the obvious other financial independence with rest and freedom. It's very simple, the big question I asked myself, that started it all for me, and the for-telling obvious question for any-one playing from night to night in the improvisational field of entertainment, exhausting themselves to the point of playing anything the ear asks for with a piano. And can see the past restrained and disciplined era in a binary trait with the serious point meeting at hand over and over with curious indentation. And the obvious question would be: **How could the great composers write one composition a day ?** Or in Mozart's case, one symphony or piano concerto a week or two? He even wrote a symphony in four days. Or in the case of Bach being escorted to jail; While in jail he wrote the equivalent of three compositions a day. Being served three meals a day, one would think he made use of a free meal..

It had to be by the confined restrained proper structural knowledge, an accomplishment early by age and a methodology used as well as by the practice of it for fluent classical improvisations on daily basis at a free hand and at a drop of a hat, replacing the radio for the enjoyment of music. And by the honest raw physical ability applied from note to note in real time. I have proven Chopin's poetic style to produce a complete composition in one take (Nocturne in A, All Berceuses, Ballads) from improvisations. Or Mozart's style; A sonata in one take, (Sonata no. 8 on Video) or Bach's 2 hand weaving improvisational frugal method in one take. Beethoven's innovational transcendental and geometrical builds. Perhaps are the median here,.... And can be carried or achieved either way... All my music has been for the most part from Improvisations. My videos on U-tube are the proof made in one take, instantly for this book. Just as the great composers did from day to day. With no preparation of the composition. **It's a feeling in the moment created for the relief from boredom**. This is the prize one can achieve if deciding to apply oneself in this ode. Composition is Improvisation & Improvisation is Composition in my definition and art of a method. And I have brought attention to this with scholars and changed the traditional way of thinking. With no relief from altered rejections or insults inherited within the traditional way of thinking or applications.

From the spiritual side, It's an out of body experience to think one step ahead and make decisions instinctively in a sublime subconscious level. As in jazz, interacting between others, as in a trio, bass, drums and piano. Or quartet's, quintet's, septet's etc.. All have to rely on the other to instinctively make an honest decision what to play next in spontaneity. All out of body, sincere, honest, experiencing the same spontaneous reaction. All jazz musicians experience this, think and play one step ahead of time while being in the moment live. Knowing a precognant moment ahead of time, or at the same time in the moment. As of picking up the phone at the same time as someone else. Or knowing when the phone is going to ring.

Another trait of this issue is conducting an orchestra by a composer and a non-composer. The conducting composer always conducts on the beat as apposed to non-composers which are usually more experienced and taught to conduct ahead of time and not on the beat, but following the score and in the moment, inducing feeling, triggering passages, to prompt sections of the orchestra ahead of time and is the proper conduct, for a worth while clearer musical passage, and a majestic powerful experience. I find that somewhat interesting and in similar parallel also. Most conductors are dynamic Interpreters of music.

The other angle of this can be described by what was once called the eighth wonder of the world, I believe? It's been so long ago, but I'm referring to George Shearing. How can this man play as well as any other who can see. This is an arguable issue. Blind people can put themselves in this zone and can very well be used to describe this out of body bigger than life experience. Herbie Hancock said George Shearing was his mentor growing up. So there, we're in the midst of this issue again.

Art Tatum the king of jazz piano was another blind. And Winton Marsalis whom is the popular jazz artist of this era also used Markus Roberts whom is blind. Just to mention here again that Stevie Wonder is blind also, and he's in that circle of the best songwriters of all time. This is not a coincidence. I've watched my mentors when they closed their eyes and went into a trance that forced the music out of them, in which I myself tried and found it not only works, but works beyond understanding, in which I use to this day in public as a show motif, and the confined private space against public distractions. I have a short video of it, I sometimes post. Jazz can be played with the eyes closed and with feelings. Mysteriously.

I've also studied Lenny Tristano's method from one of my mentors growing up, whom still teaches at our local university. Tristano is also blind and also played publicly on daily basis, and his method used to help me play at the time, was epic in figuring out my methodology. Lenny used to say can you see the position. As to say, you people are blind. Can't you see what's in front of you? And this is also used in targeting the standards for playing at gig's. The length of this melody line from one note to another. Distinguishing between melody notes geometrically for memory. This is one of the traits in which I tried for use in classical theory, in which proved to be the method that I think the great composers had in their minds, at whole and for the majority. The shape of the 5-1-3's, one looks like this and the other looks this way. Learning the structure from shape and sound, as opposed to notation. Some do learn from notation but the notation has its own patterns and theories for reading only, for the neatness of ledger lines. Its purpose is primarily for the notes to end up in the middle of the staff for clarity of reading, only. Its not for the purpose or reason of sound. Another reason; For the purpose of using certain orchestral instruments issue. Or a type of genre' in-which uses certain distinct instruments in a certain key. I'm documenting it's a false pattern because of the enharmonic keys or notation rules. It's used to produce its surrealism, minimalism complication instead of simplification. It goes beyond 12 keys. Beyond 24 keys. Which is odd in geometric use with our minds. I believe we're programmed in twelve increments beyond our understanding. Or an educator in this early field mentioned he uses 24 keys, meaning the use of the minor keys also. I call the minor keys a mode. In-which I've created target notes from the beginning of this book to use the major and minor keys, but only see 12 keys because there are only twelve keys in the piano. The modes themselves are derivatives of the keys and can be applied to add more keys, but that doesn't make the piano with more than 12 keys in sound. With all do respect to those who use improvisations in that manner. So the word Improvisations can be generalized at whole indeed. Or for that matter at hand, this educator can also be correct. In-fact one can switch keys on a notated staff and change any piece of music in as many keys as asked for. Double sharps or double flats or triple. Meaning there are numerous ways to use music, once it's notated. And so that's were you see some compositions by Bach or Rachmaninoff created from just that, just the same. Bach has written so many pieces of music he did not hesitate to use any angle in trying to explore his fertile field or approach of composition. His last composition was the spelling of his name. That was the rule and idea for that composition. This can be a whole new method of approach in creating just as well. So you see, there are several ways to create with. I do the same also. But there are only one path to follow for the harmony of **geometry** and **poetry**. And **poetry** is what the mystery is about, as well as **geometry** is what education is about. Thus both create harmony within your **heart** and **mind**. For the exploration of composition is **science** in-deed and worthy to use for ideas. But the fluent **tonal** draw comes from the natural and structural **geometric** and **poetical** methodology that only those that have experienced the spices can know and understand the difference in the path to follow, and use at will. Draw what sound you're hearing instantly, harmoniously, and in complete charge of. Not have it in control of you without reason. The players. Those that gig on daily basis. Art Tatum played live, so much, he created his own runs and rules as well. The musical concept is a maze full of ideas, hurdles, open and shut doors and cases, and only those that have been down the maze several times or lived it in their sleep can enter the maze and come out from the other side without hitting walls or dead ends.. It comes from both. " **Science and emotion** ". " **Tonal and atonal** ". " **Explanation and magic** ". " **Government and god** ". " **Technique and feeling** ". " **Reason and reasoning** ". I sometimes play in a sequencer with the keyboard turned down. You can play your theories out of your mind without the sound turned up, but let your mind hear it inside your head, and only follow the rules from this book and trust yourself to create music without the sound turned up. This is also mysterious and surprising. Or just jot down notation on a staff, theories that you know. For example the diminished rule of thumb chart and expand with notation. It is scientifically proven so there should be no hesitation but harmonies and rules of engagements to follow. If using this book as a guide or structural path to follow.

Notation is a must in re-playing on a piece of music, but it is not the path the great composers I mention which are my favorite used to improvise with on daily basis as their common or standard path or method.. For one, again, the enharmonics will throw it off into its own format and will fray one from the proper path of creative virtues and correct mathematical and geometric patterns and most of all the poetic path at will. Or song-writing. Most songwriters don't read music. Paul McCartney said he does not want to know a lot about music for it will diminish his creativity. And on the other side of the coin the other best songwriters like Carol king and Burt Bacharach read music and can play their instruments rewardingly very well. And are very interesting to watch. Have learned the ropes of were to go for the creative element. And I feel Paul McCartney is very well trained in music more than he cares to mention as well. But he's been around long enough and exposed to the best this world has to offer and makes this very point of this issue I'm trying to address and points out very clearly from experience. In my opinion he has tapped in this mysterious side farther than anyone else. In the song-writing recording field. He lived it as he was inspired by the age and time and all the proper reasons that caused him to snap in this grid. As the great composers or great jazz pianist were in the right place at the right time to engrave themselves as proprietors of that profession.

Songs are short abstract musicals that are derived from the truth. Abstract truth that is. And with rhythm and a beat they will touch the heart, entertain, and gain power. And most of **all the singing is tonal**. So the culmination of all make it a binary poetic statement and one of its kind, that will stay in the mind circling geometrically, poetically for comfort, recollecting, reminding, sentimentality engrained in memory, melancholic, ∞ etc.. <u>Songs contain both binary elements ∞</u>. With good vocals that is.

Some classical composers and jazz composers can make their instrument sing. Classical is concrete geometric and jazz is abstract and emotional. <u>Science and sense</u>. Between the two you can have the complete package. The binary element. As in the great composers skills. They inherited both elements ∞.

But over time and in some composer's music you can hear the change. As in Liszt or Alkan's, or some Rhachmaninov, or Stravinsky, or Prokofiev, or Schoenberg piano works. Aside from Liszt's early 27 preludes or etudes, which got lost by the time he started composing. Although, not to bash these great of the greatest pianists / composers, which still cannot have their shoes filled by anyone of this age.. But some have stated that their music tends to sound like exercises and scales, abstract, surrealism, or always leaning on rhythm or synchronicity to surpass or help save or balance out. As apposed to **<u>tonal instinctive immortal ideas that come from a higher power that live forever</u>**. As if they were preparing the Miles Davis quintet to complete the rhythm cycle of composition with the congenial American quartet and its original art-form. And anything but that will lack the complete cycle of musical power. And become just short of the fab four I mention over and over. Bach, Mozart, Beethoven & Chopin. This mathematical system in which someone had bestowed on us, looked at from the keyboard, as apposed to, from the notation table. An A flat is the same note as a G sharp by looks and sound, but it's not the same note by a notated definition. These are enharmonic notes. Or enharmonic keys for notation only. I'm addressing this as a completely different approach and being distinct by pointing it out. Where others in the past have not, through classical and jazz and song-writing. But the final notated score should be the same. The notation is standard and should comply at the end as usual, as always. But only at the end of the creative process, and not during. That's the difference. You learn that from experience and playing on daily basis. But others and scholastic pedagogues will never admit to that, for they have to communicate by the proper path of education, which serves the students only in playing, just playing, as in interpreters. Here again, not to mock the great interpreters, for today there are some that interpret the composers music better than the composers ever would. Just to be clear here. Take Mitsuko Uchida the greatest interpreter of Mozart. Had spent her life specializing in playing Mozart. What a gift from God as they say. For the interpreter and the composer ∞. This type of work takes time. One has to decide to become an interpreter or composer for the work is a lifetime from either side. ∞ Glen Gould is another. Rubinstein, Horowitz …. Etc.

And so the difference between jazz and classical composers is **classical composers are by themselves**. They are loners, because it does not serve the recording industry or the format of jazz as it is today. Or once was. Nevertheless it's the same issue being discussed here. **The sublime instinctive state of mind.** In which some educator's call crazy as hell to attempt or use live. But just for the sake of truth and education, lets go down this road.

I personally have had this e-mail from one of the reviewer of this book, whom is a PhD and whom have called me crazy as hell and have had his students attack me for the sake of not following the traditional present way. Or actually, he's trying to elect his constituent. Race & politics etc..

The students today graduate into rock band members, drafted as athletes do in sports. It's one way to insure a marketed industry and all of its luggage surviving even if the times have passed it by. So most likely it's the other luggage that is the culprit and sought after. Not the music. Sex, drugs and Rock & Roll. And this is very dangerous indeed. Maybe they seem to have a grudge against my way or approach of a method. As apposed to reading one piece of music and relying on improvising from the piece being read. Using the theory of that piece to improvise. Another words, that's fine and dandy but the piece will circle back around and round and soon, the piece will get stale after a while and bore you. Unless you're Art Tatum maybe. I did this for years playing in public. Carried a stack of books from restaurant to hotel to club to whatever. After an hour or two the notes will blur and you go into a forceful mode to memorize quickly, and improvise to keep one's mind interested as well as to continue to play something that interests the listeners. And in some places it would get so quiet by the audiences that you could hear a pin drop,. This is how one survives hours into a gig. It's called pacing, and you see other pianists with their books coming in after my shift and do exactly the same. Actually most just played through without mistakes and did not rock the boat. But others were very interesting. There are only so many that interested me. And they were my mentors. Art Tatum was a master of this type of Improvisations. And he's Blind.

Reading a piece of music and improvising on it is the most common way to use. This is nothing new. None of these students or this particular PhD figure have ever experienced any of this professionally by the way, might I add. And It's quiet obvious. For failure is important in live Improvisations. You learn from failing in front of people. If you don't ever experience this then you do not play professionally. You might be an Interpreter. And I don't recognize the name of this PHD as one of any Interpreters of music. He later told me that no one will ever hear his music. So this is a grievance of a way to become recognized. People work, pay taxes and die unrecognized. This is a sham for anyone with a dream in music… So attack my work at its inception and see how much work it takes to prove it after already learning one concept that is traditional. Therefore this will eliminate any extra work for this person whom is a teacher. Eliminate a nervous breakdown. And the students have no idea that there are only a few that really delve in music completely, they think everyone can be and the world is filled with gifted artists. Ugh, unprofessionalism and kids can really cause a stink !. The bigger they are the nicer they are. And the opposite is obvious here..

We live in a different world today with digital music, as apposed to living with an analog live world of entertainment of the past. The entertainment era has vanished. It's all marketed business of money making digital machines. As in the stores of scanned and computerized systematic flow. The sensuous aspect of trading and communicating is replaced by calculators and scanned codes. The checkout counters at Wall-Mart are managed by Spanish speaking employees. There's no need to speak any more. Machines have replaced it all. This is were the crazy era comes in. With all respect to Spanish speaking people of-course, for this is not attacking them but the system that uses this controversial technology for the sake of money.

And at the present we are going through a transformation of the first black president elected in history and race hysteria is being manipulated indeed. But for the first time, the politicians aren't getting assassinated. This is a miracle in itself, and there's still a lot of manipulation to iron out though. And this particular PhD reviewer is from South Carolina. Whom insists on writing South Carolina down publicly. Just below the Mason Dixon line. He's actually from up north himself. So here's the binary element again. And the primary motive that has nothing to do with the subject of music..

I've gotten two other rotten reviewers also. One from Vanderbilt university in Nashville, but was covered long ago by adding an o at the end of my first name (Roberto). Obviously there are professionals in Nashville and Hollywood that know how to accommodate these issues or situations as they incur accordingly. Hollywood is skilled in that sort of thing without a blink.

And the other rotten reviewer is from Kansas university, by someone not willing to show himself in which I'm guessing is from up north also but disguising as a southerner by print, just the same as the others. Here again the binary issue. It's meant to look like something else. By the way, if you're wondering why Kansas university. It's because it's called KU. My name is Kaye and these people are attacking the K. To them it stands for race also. Or someone is drawing a line midway across the country. So I'm told afterwards. And so this is what its about. Race and not education. **Race is the primary issue in my lifetime here in the US**. And election is the issue presently. Warren Buffet just said its two race car drivers. One white and one black, trying to show who can drive the craziest against the other. Its time to throw the steering wheel out. And face the binary issue at hand, decipher, analyze, do the math and stop this corruption.

Nevertheless, I'm in the middle, or right on the line. ∞ I've lived right on the Virginia line in North Carolina for many years. Which runs parallel to Nashville and Kansas. This is the **Bible Belt** after the civil war. I also live in **The triangle area** ∞ as its called here just bellow this Mason/Dixon line. It's up to me to divide these incidences into a binary systematic resolve and with poetically good conscience. Binary is two and conscience is the middle ground element that gives it the third element with the seeing eye on top. The tonic, as its called the eye of providence. In which my daughter lives in this town called providence located in this same area, on the line, and try to turn and make good sense of this issue as we go into this political transformation. A disgruntled reviewer is obviously incapable of doing so without gaining his own 15 minutes of fame of someone else's work. Or as I call it, turning one on the other. Apparently a classical composer cannot get along with another classical educator. I've seen this in my past over and over. Oh and the ignorant ones are the classical musicians. ! How about that. Did you get that? As if it means anything in music. This is why the government stopped the funding for the arts. In-fact after this incident they cut the salary of teachers. This is not good. Coincidences? You be the judge.

First of all, hate does not work. So it has to be solved with the goodness of both sides from a responsible intelligent approach. Obviously this is childish and someone is in need of attention. I've been sabotaged in the past so many times that it has become second nature, second rule at this point. In-fact the present cover for this book just got sabotaged by someone at the publishing company as we speak. Or one page with sensitive information got cut out at the end of this prologue. You learn to face obstacles constantly. I've had my scores sabotaged many times over the years. In Hollywood by intentional orchestra players, brain washed as of its their duty, but only once. I've had my scores stolen at church gathering ceremonies just as it began. One learns to play by ear from these types of obstacles. I've had my instrument tools stolen even as far back as the marching band in high school, by the other opposing team's fans. These things make the jealous fifteen minute famer happy. There have been so many of these nurtured sabotaged events that one see's ahead of time but keeps to himself. You learn to think ahead of time also, you hear what you're about to say in your mind before it comes out of your mouth. What's the use?

Even a young black design consultant at my publisher told me he likes the second half of the book. The Jazz part. And that I would not be able to sell it without prostituting. And I believe his name was Robert also. The insanity is bottomless.

And i honestly am so glad that the current president is black, that for the first time in my life of a tragic everyday past, I have the freedom of speech. The white and black man ∞ has finally got their tongues back in their mouth and can speak with intelligence and without guilt, and with eternal values at will. The honest and humble man that is. Although I've grown up with many honest poor farmers, white and black that keep to themselves by being extremely religious, and just are very rare people in this day and time. ∞

As Chuck Close, the great modern artist said, during the civil rights movement revolution, it was our duty to cause trouble. That's how this change was brought about. ∞ So now we have a means of a binary genuine understanding by **science** and **emotion**, by **black** and **white,** by **republicans** and **democrats**, for the first time in my lifetime. And so will the US forever be divided or united into this binary **north** and **south**, **white** and **black**, **hot** and **cold**, **jazz** and **classical** type of a binary system for mankind to follow in assurance for its preservation? One thing for sure, if it does or does not, ∞ today it's working for the first time. The politicians aren't being assassinated as they did in the 1960's. Aside from the injustice, in which is evident here, for I'm trying to feed my daughter and put her through school in the midst of this irrelevant nonsense perpetrated and deliberately aimed against the innocent. There goes my money. Or is it there goes my American dream .. And the irrelevant get what they want.

I remember when I was a teenager the parents of some of my friends would whisper in my ear, the political parties will switch from one to the other eventually within time. I did not really understand much at that time. But now I'm writing about this dichotomy indeed. And understand the relevance of this important manifestation. This systematic dichotomy that's engrained in our hearts and mind. Lincoln was a republican where in-fact today he would inevitably be a democrat without a question...

I've worked with builders when I was a teenager that have told me they would build me an A frame house for $1200. It appears that the people that are around me since childhood, understood my position better than I did, until now, where everything is unfolding before me. I did figure out the pyramid and the pure tones in relationship to C as the seeing eye though.

I've visited professors at universities and showed them some of my theories. And was surprised that they hadn't a clue of what I was presenting to them. Which leads me to believe that my work is completely new to them. These professors are well into composition, having composed symphonies themselves. Some have been honored through out the country. As if its cheerleading events. Put your money in the pot and receive a trophy for your membership. I wouldn't say anything about this, but when you get attacked, you lose your sense of friendship and respect for the con game.

I've also been offered several degrees and or diplomas. With and without the internet. At this point everyone wants to put their name on my work, which is absurd indeed.

Also at this time, the biggest ponzy scheme ever was perpetrated by a man that has pictures of bulls on his walls. Has a yacht named bull. No one could take him down and his scheme until all the money was stolen and done with. So there, for those that think real life is a happy endings. This is the results. And this man may very well be innocent. The market may just be in trouble. Who knows?

Classical music mind you was referred to as a woman by Beethoven. No one learns the word bully more than classical musicians. My whole life is a product of an object of a bully. A bully wants all the attention his way and no other. They start yelling and not making sense but want things their way despite. This is what is in store for anyone trying to achieve the impossible. My own father and uncle's are of this character. It also seem to co-exist with alcohol.

Beethoven said at his last breath, the comedy is over. He tried to sue promoters in his day and tried to state that his music is for an educational value. Write that on the promo, he would say. And during Liszt's time, Beethoven's music was called brain damage music or the result of brain problems.

Presently, It does seem that we're going through revelations, because of all the technological gadgetry, and the religious negligence and abuse. Therefore it's a new era or the binary issue is finally in place and working even at this early late stages. And of-course corruption is another issue.

In the music field, you would think all is stable and the music is in charge of it all. But that's not the case. In one day, we went from show tunes, Broadway theatric musicals to radio oriented songs and mixing and engineering. In one day we went from rock to disco. And I remember it in a South Carolina club in the 70's. The disco ball went up and we were told to play 60/40 rock- disco, just like that. Signifying the end of a flower revolution, and the end of the hippie era. In one day we went from a decade of the epic of country to pop, witch is from the 90's until 911, and it ended just like that. In one day we went from jazz to hip hop, because of a younger defined and targeted music buying marketed plan that can make more money, as well as technological breakthroughs.. Etc.. It's all because of the powers to be deciding in a moment or an instance. Sometime its political, sometimes its financial, sometimes its technology, sometimes its race, generation to generation ..This is how fluctuating this business is. And most think it's almost always for the sake of money. That's the bottom line. And so

On the other side of the coin, this book was also inspired by an educator from a conservative school. I guess old conservatory is not new conservatory. Conservative means white and democrat means black nowadays. Not to mention the powers to be using educators and their kiddy's whom are in a band now and are a business for someone to make money with, to attack me for not taking their offer of playing with bands or just being a normal ordinary good boy and being dumbed down or bullied as a nobody as apposed to trying to get to the bottom of this great art. And creating something serious to talk about. Or with all honesty, playing creatively like Chopin, Mozart, Bach and Beethoven on daily basis. And writing it down for future perspective. It's the creative element of these great styles and serious profound music that keeps one going, searching for honesty truth and knowledge on daily basis. And after a while it's evident that the seriousness is epic. Seriousness means good music. Powerful music with intentions. That's an adult overview. And is resonated from both fields. Jazz and classical. Somewhere in between they both switch to seriousness.

On the other side of the coin, I've also had great response from other PhD's whom think like I do. Commend me and reassure I'm on the right track. Completely different. And if you notice in today's time, the teachers no longer post their music nor want anything to do with the public eye and exposer. This is alarming and has everything to do of what I'm stating here also. Boy, turn down someone in the present day of instant communication and watch your carrier go down the tube. You'll never work in this town again. Or losing one's tenure. Taking advantage of children just coming out of music schools, and old has been teachers that think they have a chance of becoming someone great without working for it, with just having a lot of hot air. And that's were critics come from, And that's what this is all about.

Often students start teaching right out of college. My sister's daughter is a violinist in high school. She's already teaching others. Very proud of her.

Students have no idea what's in store for them nor can they use their overbearing education for anything concrete, other than teaching the same old over-kill information to someone else. Make sure you learn the nomadic scales. Or for that matter the diminished scales. Which are the west Indies idea. Yes, you'll end up using all of this material to teach someone else. Not to mention it takes years to sort out or get a taste of some of it, before one just gives up and moves on to making money any way possible..

This book is the only one for that matter, for example that say's not to use the diminished scales, among other way's to look at useful positions. It's my experience to play freely. And using the diminished scale will alter you down to a slow halt in playing. This is completely my opinion. And among many different other scopes. Another example: I like to see a melody line in major, as a vertical. And a minor as a horizontal, because of the infinite line that will circle the earth in its own right. Well the schools use a completely opposite portrayal. Exactly the opposite. This is just my way of seeing the overall picture. Again, are the schools describing all in all through the tonic of 1-3-5. That could very well be the explanation, as I'm describing this whole method through the 5-1-3 approach. Jazz students occasionally will describe this approach as the Lydian mode. This is true and false as well. There's a big difference in studying the fundamentals of music and the specialization of composition, for the serious pianist. Also generalizations can alter the meaning al-together. As well as time and politics, and so at this point in time, it will have nothing to do with music. Some people have been calling it crazy times. Ye, but not as bad as the past. The living is at the finger tips. We have luxury over-night deliveries etc.. at our front door step. The object is to recognize the worthiness of this era and capitalize on it.

I've always been told that if you want to be like your mentors, you have to learn from them or a working musician doing it everyday. And that's what I did, other than maybe studying orchestration, film scoring, editing for motion pictures and other valuable professions. For example UCLA and other well known proven outlets. In the midst of silicon valley. Quick access to courses to pick up certain important information to use quickly, that's very much in demand. As in technology, hardware, software etc.. You end up in many learning institutions that want you to exhibit your work to upcoming students getting ready to graduate or performing for music classes. Playing with music graduates was always fun also. I used to usually always ask if they have a Steinway to perform on. That is always a good incentive to follow.

I've always been told that I can teach, maybe some can, but I'm not one. If you have food on the table why give your time away. I'm speaking of the past, of-course. Today it's completely different for me. In the past, I have had offer's from music industry offices. Hundred's of thousands of dollars mentioned, but have turned it all down to keep pushing forwards in my work. Which does puzzle anyone not understanding my main goal or motive.

I Have rubbed elbows and dined in Hollywood with such greats as Elmer Bernstein, Neal Hefty. Knowing these people from playing their music night after night. Or Lenny Niehouse offering me half of his sandwich during break at a recording session at Capital Records in Hollywood. Or an orchestrative copyist giving me his chair in front of the orchestra as it's being recorded. These are the friends I remember the most. Those that have done it for many decades professionally and successfully. ***The bigger they are, the nicer they are***.

And the music industry will prosper in certain areas and dwindle down after a certain time. It's all a frontage and a gamble to content with. There are no assurances to kick back from.. Although the unions do keep one working on daily basis, and try to accommodate. That's in the big cities only of-course, and not below the Bible Belt.

I've learned to produce myself completely. With no help from anyone else. This is sad. As all the great composers on the other side of this coin also never owned a home or had any money or wealth. Bach never had his music published or played in his lifetime. Other organist would pack up and get out of town when they heard he would be visiting them. Mozart copied his own music. And sold it to others in their name. Even the lacrimosa he died in the midst of, it was to be named under someone else's name. Chopin wrote for himself only. Beethoven moved from month to month to different dwellings. And these are the greatest ever in music. Dizzy Gillespie would say: Maaaan No one showed me $hit !! I can relate to that statement.

There are stories of Mozart not having enough time to write out his sheet of music to perform, so he puts up a blank sheet of paper in front of him and improvises with the chamber orchestra, in which he just composed the music for, and while the ink is still wet. Or young Chopin, just a toddler being called in for the duke whom have just returned from battle on horseback. Screaming in trite for the little boy who improvises in baroque to the duke to calm his nerves down, all along screaming at the little Chopin who looks straight up at the ceiling with no respond scared in timid and out of his wit, mind and body.

In jazz you strive for sounds as in voicings and reach by feel of fingering brilliantly following a chart as the theory, with the rhythm or bass to play on. Or without following the rhythm improvising in abstract form continuously. As apposed to in classical you use methodological theory and play from the brain and not by feel of fingering or voicings. Because it's the structure that's being manipulated, improvised and being constructed automatically by my methodological path that's creating the composition, and in both classical and jazz in an eccentric sublime subconscious. **In jazz you can play with eye's closed, by feel in Abstract form. In classical you can play with ears plugged, straight from the brain using my method.** Or notated without a keyboard. Without listening to it. But it has to be seen with the eyes. Because its geometrical patterns and target notes are foreseen. In Jazz, one can plug ears also and play from the mind but my scientific theories and target notes have to be used as well. Which is the classical method indeed.

So I've applied my methodological classical theoretical structure as the theory to follow in jazz this time. And it has yielded something new. Spontaneous jazz compositions in the style of for ex: Tatum, Morton or Chopin or even Mozart and Beethoven. This is something new and unexpected. Yet the sound is similar to playing jazz from the root 1-3-5. But It is not. **It's playing from 5-1-3. And not looked at from notated harmonics.** And a bass player is not needed. A composer composes by himself. Sounds the same but is created from improvisation from another position; (5-1-3). I was only trying to search out classical music. And so it leads me to believe that if the great composers where alive today. This is how they would play jazz.

And also without the truth and honesty and the spiritual factor, it cannot be achieved. <u>One has to have the confidence, be brave with the spiritual truth to trust oneself to achieve and create subconsciously on daily basis.</u> It's an out of body experience in which a higher power is in charge of. And we simply are the in between who channel it.. Just a couple of notes here; incidentally when I was younger and lighter in weight. Whenever I gigged fluently, I used to dream of out of body flying experiences on daily basis. And others said they also did. It's common knowledge. Somehow this is something beyond our understanding and most likely deals with physics. And I've also just had this dream again, so it continues depending on your health and body weight status and how much you can play with good light weight feeling. In which I call **" play mode "**..

Another note: The video on my web sight or on U-tube of the improvisations on one of my compositions; The Impromptu in the back of this book is the only video of anyone improvising an impromptu of a waltz that, has been written since Franz List. Out of the million video's around the world. Mind you, I was taunted a fraud and that there was no such thing as an impromptu of a waltz improvised. Impromptu means improvisation on a composition in classical music. Much the same as jazz following a chart form, but in classical. So there you have it. Educators, engineers, producers and God knows whom ever, trying to tell you it cannot be done, or there's no such thing. This only strengthens my point and validates my studies. And the other videos of myself live are all spontaneously created. With no preparation or following any music. This is the first that I've experienced in my lifetime. Waking up everyday and creating a clean composition in an instant is my goal and achievement. Just the same as creating jazz from my past on daily basis. But this time I switched it to classical. It's that simple to achieve as the great composers did on daily basis.

The videos I have posted are complete improvisation on my method as I felt that day. And the whole video is improvised in one take and can be notated now for an orchestra and all else. I should add that whatever the day brings could change the different piece of music. One day it's a nocturne in the middle of the night. And the next it's a sonata in the morning. The next is a scherzo or a waltz. At a drop of a dime the mood can change to another form of a piano piece with exactly the same theoretical structure. Ramsey Lewis just said; **" *Jazz is an expression of the feeling you have at that moment.* "**

I try not to repeat a creative moment. If I practice something, then the second time around I change its style to keep myself amused and interested in it continuously. Or your mind will shut it down to a stale state. So nocturnes, sonata's, etudes, ballads are all the same but a mood that forms the music at that moment. Something I found out by surprise. And of-course **Strength and feel good is the factor**. Beethoven and his music is the iconic cymbal for seriousness and strength. Hummel is another, his compositions are so daring that no one will attempt to perform them still today. (Hummel also had his own method). Liszt used his strength in performing. Part of his showmanship was reading a piece of music spontaneously and commenting on it. As well as turning it up-side down and reading it that way for show. The stronger you are, the farther you can pull yourself out of your body to form the music. And the longer you have the decision to make in a split second and at the speed of thought. Physics and the physical ability are epic, and very mysterious indeed. The definition of **Physics** is : <u>The science that treats of motion, matter, and the energy, and their interaction.</u> Another definition is <u>- Discovering the deeper structure of reality</u>… Another is; <u>The art of healing</u>… Look how diverse these definitions are for such a mysterious subject or topic. **The Physicist** is: <u>a physical scientist</u>.

When I decide to sit down and improvise, I'm almost always deciding at peak strength. **It's the euphoric feeling that creates the composition**. I'm only using my feel good moments to play with, however long they last, depending on how much I've exercised. It's not something prepared to play with. **It's the feel good that triggers the composition to be created spontaneously**. That's not to say that in front of a lot of people you don't get pumped up to perform your skill. A man knows how to push himself for strength as an athlete does. If doing so, or performing without any rest, as I have done many times, you will suffer a long rest afterwards. Rest assure relinquishing those feel good moments for a long while. Also when I was young I didn't know how to control these feel good feelings. This is where some turn to stupidity without control. You have to grow into it. Learn by experience and time. Its an element that has to be mastered.

Restaurants are the premier atmosphere to create the feel good feeling with. Classy restaurants are ideal for the whole experience relying on the feeling. Feeling of elegance, superior, charm, extra-ordinair. It's the atmosphere that creates the music in this venue. It's a feeling that triggers the creativity, and the joy of being there and doing it. The calmness, the purity, the restraint, prestige, discipline, showmanship. etc..

All the videos I have on U-tube are created by the feel good feeling of the body and never prepared ahead of time. Except of-course the Finale' Nocturne impromptu in the back of this book used for show and reference. The theory is the structure used, and always giving new material by the physical feel good of the body. I had no ideas what these video's of those moments were going to sound like. On one I used my " diminished rule of thumb " completely, and the video came out to sound like Rachmaninoff to my surprise. That was the part that I remember was the daring moment that I thought I would crumble in if I tried since I'm recording for public view, and am taking a chance in which might ruin the whole video, and had no idea that there were going to be an explosion of composition. I thought the good part was going to be the beginning and end baroque session part in which I attempted on other improvisational sessions before and enjoyed, but of-course it no longer was of interest for me. I actually flubbed those that I thought would be.

After all this time working on this subject, I too will think negatively from time to time, because of the physical condition my body is in. Is it in shape and happy? Or is it going to fail me? Even I, from time to time will go back to fear mode, hesitant and almost harm myself from reaching this subconscious level for the sake of not ruining a video session. Or I simply forget to take the chance listening to others telling me it cannot be done. And forgot that I created all these theories, patterns and methodology to rely on. Remembering is the key here. There is reason here.

Carl Popper said " **Our deepest insights come from pure reason** ". So for me it's the physical ability, as well as it's for little bodies of young kids. They say you're once a man and twice a child. So if one understands the limit of their own body, then they will be able to judge the outcome.

There is also brain tiredness which can cause fatigue, and should be accounted for. And feel good means plenty of room to remember. It's how much do you have in your body to attempt at. So these things seem to thrive around happy accidents, as artists, the painters often say when they paint a picture, in which they call a composition. They also say that sometimes, their pictures fail as well, to my surprise. Some click and some don't. This is also something to touch on here. Now we're entering the brain issue here.

I have had sessions in which I thought I was going to create something great, but turn out to fail completely. And that is due to old age only, but there is also **The mind factor**, very important. It's almost as if you are either on the tracks or derailed. There are no in-between. Our minds are programmed as <u>a **clock that ticks on a railroad track**</u>. This is a state of mind beside the <u>physical feel good of the body</u> of-course, or <u>the brain tired issue</u>. The mind and how it works is a mystery. Usually when I find a new theory to play with. The first experiments are the creation of great music as I'm experiencing it also, **It's the journey that keeps one attuned and interested**. This coexists with living also. Fresh. Live. Also after a while theories become stale, if not used properly and with confidence or on track. So if you're recording yourself, and you're a songwriter, those are the moments to look for. Before you expect them. Try to catch yourself in those moments.

You often experience the " **Mind click** " from producers in the studio telling the artist to play another take, or movie directors using at least three takes for each shot. It's because of the " **Mind click** ", as I call it. Our minds are like a **Train ticking on a track**. You want to be aware of this in creating, and not be confused with the physical ability aspect or brain tired issue. I usually catch the train on the second take, after I go through the motion of setting up the sequencer controls for example. If it's a difficult passage of-course it can take several takes. But the " **Mind click** " issue is usually on the second take with me. Some jazz musicians call it " **getting in** ". The Mind and the body working together in conjunction.

When taking the train on the track, by playing and singing a song, for example; As the body gets older, the performance can be described as a rubber band elastic effect, by feeling the body falling behind on the tempo. You feel, as well as hear, the elastic effect. Chopin's method is contrived from this instinct. He created the most beautiful style out of a physical condemnation. Or some say John field created the style from his 12 Nocturnes. And Chopin took it to this mysterious elegant and excelling virtuosity. Incidental elasticity, Instinctive piano music. "Rubato" is just that. Same as a drummer dragging. Drummers drag as they get older. This is the " **mind click** " falling behind or off the track, as the body regresses. As rust is on the track the train is traveling on, thus holding it back from rolling freely. If you continue to play and work around this rust, then you learn to disengage your body at certain areas to allow the geometric mind patterns to continue multiplying in harmonies as the theories or piece of music is unfolding in live mode. Or allowing the body to catch up with the " **mind click** ". I've learned to let go at certain areas before the stomach gets astringed and can cause a throbbing pain to completely derail the train. And sometimes it derails for month's if kept going and not taking action at these conjunctures. If you practice this disengagement then you can work around it. Often young kids who don't understand this can comment or spot these disengagements and know by sense that something is wrong with the player, as he's not the excellent performing type. Because some of the timing is not quiet perfect or up tempoed as it should be. Even Beethoven was made fun off early on in his career, as he was described as banging on the piano. Or played his own sonatas by banging them out. But this does not mean to quit composing or playing. All the great composers, composed or played to the day they died. **" Give and take ".** Management of the **" mind and body "** is what is being manipulated here. Rubinstein played well into his nineties, playing Chopin's polonaise in Ab. This is remarkable of this performer, for he had learned to manage and manipulate his body, for the love of performing, to the day he died. Of-course one has to concentrate on only one task to deliver, be it performing or composing. All time is spent on one certain area only. And that is how to be productive through-out a life-time or a career.

There are plenty of stories of such artists as Errol Garner walking in a studio sitting at the piano and mesmerizing the whole staff speechless, motionless before they realize to turn the recording equipment on.

I have also done that in a studio early on. The staff of a studio are not prepared, unless you get them prepared. But how does one know when these feel good happy important moments, or accidents are going to happen? One does learn after a while.

You often hear of other artists that say they had time for just a small piece of music at the end of a long recording session, and to their surprise played something off the wall in which became their music to get recognized over, or sold more than any other.

I remember one incident when I talked to a keyboard player at his gig one night in between sets. And somehow I derailed him in the process, so by the time he was on again it was so noticeable that the rest of his band members looked at me while they were singing the song and eyeing with mental seriousness until he clicked back on track again to normal. This area is very mysterious indeed... the **" Mind Click "** .

When you play live, sometimes you think you're having a great night, when it is really dragging. And some nights you think you're awful but it turns out to be great. One never knows. But you learn from your experience. Professionalism. And the evident factor to eliminate is health of-course. The health at an early age can make up for it all. This is why Jimmy Hendricks, Janis Joplin, Charlie Parker, Mozart, Chopin etc.. could not live up to their expectations after this certain age.

This includes songwriting of-course. Feeling good is what writes songs, once you grow up, then the feel good goes away. That's when working from the brain comes in. **" The Classical Method "** So on the other side of the coin; If you try to learn music from songs, you will confuse yourself and be disappointed. Because songs are a creative hearing abstract that come from the lyrics, from a feeling, from an accident, from another song, from a number of sources. You sometimes take a part from one song and from another song and patch together from a feeling you experienced previously that stuck in the mind indelibly and that's how importance and relevance comes in from song-writing, not necessarily structure. As all the great composers have done as well. The bucket drawing is endless. So if you're trying to learn the musical concept from this format. It would be like trying to scoop the water out of the ocean with a bucket. I might be exaggerating a bit but not far from the truth. Songwriting is magical, and doesn't necessarily follow a pattern or formula or theories. Although people do it, and you can hear a song that sounds like another heard already, which is copying at that point. Especially with machines nowadays. Not only that but, it takes all members of a band to play the power of a song. Or Willy Nelson's delivery of a Beatle song will not be as powerful as Paul McCartney's or john Lennon's delivery of the same song. And vice versa be it a country or bluesy song.

And some can make a great statement of a song all by themselves, as of James Taylor, Glen Campbell, or George Benson or Daryl Hall. The Beatles, they have a gift of playing their instrument with freshness and enjoyment that is exciting to watch, creative with appeal, contains a substance of a spark and different, happy full of joy and young energetic, harmonies pre arranged and a correct message to communicate with the masses. The teenage world lurking and luring for it. Their singing is tonally creative every time and the song is an abstract mystery. Their range of styles covers all genre's. From classical to jazz to Latin to Indian music etc. And sometimes all in one song. And there is the good side of learning songs or playing these happy moments as a benefit; One can learn notation from these heart felt melodies. **The melody can guide to follow the notes in learning notation or intervals**, or sounds that just so happens are the make of this entity. Training wheels for beginners, if you will. The feeling is enormous and can trigger a learning curve instantaneous. **This is very useful to learn from.** But all in all learning structure or the musical concept is learned from the brain. **Scientifically**. There is a reason why this passage harmonizes with this passage. There is a reason why 3 positions make up a 12 dividend of a triangle that three keys will harmonize in eternity harmonically. Generating energy that utilizes time with infinity. An infinite harmonious **Geometric** or **Poetic** path to use. ***Flats and Sharps***. ***Hot and Cold***. 12 hours of **Daylight** and 12 hours of **Nighttime**. " ***The clock we use is a factor by the mind set we posses "***. *The geometric pattern is attuned to our minds in harmonic synchronicity with the universe.* **Heart and mind. Science and Sense**. **Abstract** songwriting and **Classical** architecture. The binary element that we all posses. The keys are laid out in **Black** and **White** on the piano right in front of us. So here, here.. We're finally here at last. Classical Improvisation...Working from the brain: ......

Classical Improvisation : is the art of Composition.

Can also follow chart form and improvisational format. As in an impromptu. Baroque can be played in a punctual counter punctual improvisational form. But it's rarely done. So it's safe to say classical music is the art of composition, which I say is also derived from improvisation. Used with my method and theories and notated in lengthy compositions or orchestrations. Because it's also the raw form of creating.

Tonal structure; Once it's created, it can be revised to a more difficult form to enhance for performers. Once it's revised and nurtured to a more in depth composition, then it gains priority over works that are raw, and it's no longer an improvisational composition. That's not to say there aren't written improvised classical compositions. Just listen to Brahms's compositions for one. He used to improvise classical music in brothels. Similar to cocktail piano. Using the in-depth descending fourth's in parallels. His entire style took up from this technique. Brahms's technique is made to surprise the composer as its being applied, played or written for the sheer joy of new ideas and accidental harmonies keeping one attuned and intuitively tolerating small upright pianos that are hard to get good sounds out of, much less keep in tune. Therefore the method he uses compensates these hurdles. And concentrates on bass and harmony as apposed to melody and scales or traditional theoretical structure. I do not go into Brahms method because after all else, we now can look back and see that Beethoven's power, can out perform Brahms's method, therefore I have not mingled with it much. And it is also physically demanding, as of one bullying the piano by playing very rich and full. It was also derived from the thorough-bass method at whole. Brahms was not popular during my childhood. He became known, or popular only in the late sixties, believe it or not. He himself thought Mozart was the best composer. Some say, his method is the more complex following Beethoven. He was dubbed as the third Bee of the three. Bach, Beethoven & Brahms after-all. He does think deep and carries on in an innovative complex ideas. Rachmaninoff resembles Brahms at times. Public opinion dubbed him as writing Beethoven's tenth at the premier of his 1st. Symphony. His piano pieces will surprise any one of the diverse styles and dichotomy he uses. ∞ Δ He was the beginning of abstract form and he uses classical and romantic as well. Subjective and objective, following Bach, Beethoven & Chopin. You can hear all of these composers influences in his music. And that's how it should be. I would describe him as a composer's composer.

So lets take Chopin's style for example: I've drenched myself my entire life to get this elegant "poetical or explosive classical" style mastered. It is without a doubt an improvisational piano style. Very mysterious indeed. And very rewarding if you are a pianist. It does require a good, full and emotionally in depth grand piano, and perfectly in tune. And the knowledge of the theories in this book, in which I struggled to uncover and connect together working hand in hand and heart and mind. As well as the years of playing professionally that culminates the mastery of an instrument. Does mysterious and master coexist somewhere in heaven or in between ? This thought and approach is also used in the pure classical style with improvisations, as well as baroquing. The pure classical style is derived exclusively from the fingering of the piano. It is the piano that created it. So how can one not say it's from improvisation? Baroquing is also first improvised, then tracked for additional harmony tracks. This is the original way of working with classical music as a whole. And proven by the great masters that came before us that gave us the gift of this earth.

But over time, the improvisation of classical music has dissipated. Which in-turn classical composers vanished. The reason being after WWII as the Jewish and the blacks were being persecuted, everyone's response was the complete opposite other direction, in abstract survival, until today, were we have balanced the political system evenly, in dichotomy. And it's still a struggle from day to day. But we are in time, were if you add the date you're born and the years of your age, you will get 111. (That is in this year of 2011- 2012 of-course). This is geometrically significant with time in this universe and in relevance with the strength of the dollar bill. The currency used through-out the world to bring all in one fair and free conscience. The freedom of man. The brain. **Science and sense**. Here again.. And so I'm going back to what has been missing for generations due to the most violent and severe century ever recorded. The 20th. century. And all the maniacs that possesed it. Filthy rich, drunken hippies, and ungodly rulers, etc…

" **Classical music is the art of tonal structural composition** ". The creative composition in classical music is usually virtuous and written for interpretive performers. Which were born here in-after. If you'll notice I do not talk too much about Interpretive performers or usually referred to as: " concert pianist " in this book. It's because they live a perfect life. Most of them will live to a ripe old age. With the exception of the great Glen Gould. He lived until fifty years old. Interpretive performers will only use their time for playing. And playing designated pieces and nothing other. And some will teach or conduct. But they seem to realize that life is short. And a performer concentrates only in performing for the sake of their health, profession and the enjoyment of the limelight. As well as selling great records. And they should be thanked for bringing live the correct way of playing the best music has to offer. The virtuosity that cannot be gotten from any other. Without these performances, we wouldn't get the exact picture of a great composer. This field is still yet thriving also. For excellence is a rarity indeed. Hard work from birth is the question. For example : Hummel's music is still somewhat daring to bring to life.

Interpretive performers are also wonderful to pick up tid bits from. Only a few will play on until a ripe old age. Daniel Barenboim said*; "classical music is similar to going around a mountain and forgetting the other* *side". " There is always something different about it ".* This is the creative artistic interest that keeps one attuned to it.

{ There is no " writers block " in Classical Music }. It's derived from a well thought out eternal theories that have the factual proof of mathematics. Or concrete structure proven to work.

Classical music carries the full spectrum of sound. It cannot be compressed. It's the only music full of its dynamic range. It's the only type of music that builds up to a point of loudness with its arrangements, harmony and all its glory higher than any other music. All other music are limited to stay under the bass, drums, or singers.. etc.. Classical music has no limit or ceiling other than the hall itself in which the orchestra musicians themselves are the equalizers or attenuators, or compressors, or engineers in live mode. The pianist themselves control the ceiling. It's the only music form, that has this powerful trait in it. This is something that no musician will turn away from, if confronted in honesty. It's equivalent to; lets say: The greatest athletes, or greatest painters, etc.. Is anyone aware or afraid to admit of this? The swelling most likely occurs in classical music. The swelling of innards or your organs during classical improvisation is an evident factor. If you notice in jazz, it's an ongoing mainly relaxed or paced type of improvisational playing. The walking bass takes the brunt. Hardly any swelling of music or of the physical body, most of the time that is. But it can be traitorous in soloing for instance, that's why jazz is improvised by the A-B-A, A-B-B-A figurative type of arrangements. As the soloing gives room to breath for the players, one at a time. As of someone has tagged this art form for the benefit of the physical body… And the big bands of yesterday and its swinging sensual saxes accented into well written compositions, in my opinion is the closest to as good as music gets compared to Mozart's harmonious happy classical string sensations. It's as humanistic as it gets. No machine can duplicate this. And the many Instruments that fill the stage arranged and arouse the seriousness and power of this great profound music. Just to mention here also, somewhere in between these binary dichotomies there is a spot where these two great styles of music meet. And switch. Or where songwriting, which has both tonal and abstract, or classical and jazz, meet this seriousness. And switch from entertaining to seriousness. **" The binary element is the trait that posses the formal objective that rewards any great art ".** **" Infinity is timeless and defies gravity ".** ∞

And the American jazz Pianists, quartets, quintet's, septets come afterwards and offer the magic of modernism. And its virtuous physical improvisations performed live. **The American art form** that closed the tumultuous 20th. century for the rest of the world in virtue. Completed the dichotic cyclical eventful time in history, and during my childhood or generation. And have already gone through its renaissance once by definition. *(I remember Eubie Blake mentioning eating only chocolate, one week long ago, as I was also eating only chocolate that same week, while working at an all black apartment complex, during a jazz renaissance that we jump started after the Vietnam era, or the hippie flower revolution movement. He chose to communicate to me in that manner one day long ago.)… Eubie Blake was born in 1887 and died in 1983. He was a rare stride pianist, who helped create* **The American art form** *in its heyday. Played off and on to the day he died.*

Improvisation: is so fluent and spontaneous that jazz musicians will have a solid lengthy recording careers without often writing anything but having recorded many hours or a lifetime of music.

In the jazz world, the best pianist many think is Art Tatum. Art Tatum never wrote anything. This is the greatest jazz virtuoso in the history of the piano. Can you imagine jazz existing without the recording industry. Tony Bennet, Frank Sinatra, Mel Tormay, Nat King Cole, Ella Fitzgerald recorded or released literally thousands of records. Jazz is a recorded medium. Or I like to use The count, The king, The duke, The earl. The same goes for the classical composers, Bach, Mozart, Chopin. What if they didn't write down their music, just improvised. There weren't a recording industry back then, maybe that's why? But Bach's oldest son improvised and did not leave much in music compared to his brothers. So it's the composers that were aware of their well-being, careers and legacies.

And here is a great example in which one can answer of anyone's question of why don't the altruistic considerate aliens from other planets intervene or speed up our industrial and technological grasp throughout civilization. It's because we wouldn't have gotten the full potential capability that mankind would achieve if tampered with in these certain areas, as in the great composers of the past. **We have to do our own homework to learn it properly.** Had the great composers have had all the technologies we have today, they would not have written in ernst and left behind the body of works for mankind and others to treasure and learn from, admire, and marvel in and use as an example. Nor would we've had Einstein, Newton and the others. These people were created by the less use of technology. Although having to learn everything primitively without machines, they would have then welcomed the technology to use afterwards. But have they had the technology ahead of its time, they would have undoubtedly bypassed their accomplishments. Most suffered a shortness of age in doing so. So I guess one can think of it as a sacrifice for the future of mankind to follow.

One does get visited from time to time to be reminded, that they're one step ahead of us. And that's another whole book that I don't have time to write about. But other's are in the field and are doing so for the first time in this new era and time of revelation and consciousness. And where this book is being manifested, urged, directed and given the opportunity to be written in return.

My field of experience. The inclination that has possessed me since childhood. I remember telling Frank Colletti (The pianist) at the Beverly Hilton lobby in Hollywood about what I'm trying to do, connect music together somehow that will go on forever. I had no idea of what I was talking about only to feel my way to the present day. From figuring out the beginning date of music (1492) to comparing it to the constitution and the epic of Classical music. (1776). One unfolded after the other. And continues to do so… Having said all that…Lets continue in mundane form.

Is it a coincidence that the television set was created after WWII, when the nuclear scare came about, when everyone now has nuclear weapons? Or the color television set was created at the end of the race era, (1972). Or the computer was created just before the wall and communism fell. Coincidence? Is this the answer in benefiting from all these new technological gadgetry as the world population increases? Or are they inevitable and foreseen ahead of their time? For the relieve or release of tension between human beings? Are we getting smarter or dumber as we grow older together in these technological times? Is it a coincidence that music was created the same time the continent of the United States was discovered? Or classical music was created the same time the declaration of independence was created? 1776. Thus launching this <u>binary form of structural government</u> for the preservation of mankind. Coincidence? It's inevitable that one came before the other. In the proper order. As of a creator was in design all along. And with no rush or hurry, but the inevitability or certainty of these events to take place at the proper time and order to achieve a structural binary grand design of scientific and spiritual form of communication or profound creation for all mankind to thrive from with certainty and the preservation of, for all to follow and be free from within.

How about the story of John Adams and Thomas Jefferson. Both died on the 4th. of July. Adams said; Jefferson lives, at his death, when Jefferson had just died, Adams not knowing as he dies. Coincident? North & South. Republican & Democrat. July 4th. The birth of a Nation.
The two men that set the binary document and gave birth to this Phenomenal. Unbelievable ! One was a northerner, and one was a southerner. Their lives were the incepted true original dichotomy of a nation, as they wrote the constitution. And they mirrored each other to the very last moment of death, not knowing themselves how even they represented the foundation, as of someone was refereeing the creation of truth, balance, example of the infinite immortal consequential outcome of a systematic declaration of and the preservation of the freedom of man and the human race. The assurance and preservation of, for all mankind to follow. A systematic geometrical binary structure. Set by the work of secrecy of the original masonic eye.

Experience is of wine. It cannot be achieved with a short cut. It has to ferment in time… No serious work is ever achieved quickly. Berlioz took his entire life to complete his great symphony in which he never heard the final draft. Almost all the great composers took their entire life perfecting and completing any given piece of their earnings. Beethoven wrote his sonata's for himself only. He used much of them for his symphonies and other works. I'm sure they would have loved to have "copy and paste commands" with the computer, for printing the orchestral parts instead of writing it by hand. Beethoven's copyist eventually had heart problems. Bach went blind from copying. Mozart's hand was as curled as a liver or kidney would get as he sits at the dinner table to eat from day to day. But the point here is; Certain tasks are best left alone for better outcome.

It is painful to accomplish improvisation in the style of Mozart or early Beethoven or Chopin. This is why Mozart and Chopin were children and giants in their period. It's the most difficult to play. Because of the Classical Technique. It has to be perfect with accurate delivery. Mozart used both hands to climb the scales most of the time. As the violin does by sound. Two fingers, one from each hand exploding up the scale and picking up speed in motion reacting to the composition. As a frisbee does in take off. The depth of it is questionable comparing it to the modern pianos and what they can accomplish. But that's another matter. As simple as Mozart kept it, it is inherently difficult because of its forward bounce demand or humanism. But the reward is the orchestrational part.

The classical style fits the violins like a glove fits in a hand. If you use for example the Vienna symphonic library. You don't have to work as hard if you have already written the part in the classical style. Or lets say, trying to make a virtual orchestral sampling software sound real or as good as a real orchestra. Well if you have inputted one of Beethoven's concerto's, will anyone question or talk about the samples or how the orchestra sounds. No, because the hard work is already accomplished. It's the classical style in virtuosity.

And although baroquing can drain you just as quick because of its steady exuberant tempered expressiveness, Similar to jazz. Steady pulse which has the tendency to drain one if not careful to reserve the well-being of health. Take Glen Gould for example, he loved Bach's music and played it as the best interpreter. And he died at fifty years old. An exemplification of the style. Although baroquing can be restrained also for improvisations, cleanses the soul from within. Ah the sacred goodness of the divine. That's the beauty of it. And on the other side of the coin it can be the most difficult to perform and has to be prepared ahead of time without any question. Both hands take a separate monophonic part to form a polyphonic composition. That has to be practiced. This is why Bach is the father of music. And Rachmaninoff is the father of the Concerto.

And finally Chopin's style. It is my favorite, for it is almost made for improvisation of the piano. It is, piano music. It allows one to elastically stretch the tempo at will and according to the music. This is very rewarding for health as well as for creativity in a spontaneous motion. And as all the rest, one does get mentally spent in it as well. For it's best to change styles from day to day, to keep the mind interested and searching for something new, continuously.

One does have to practice these theories in this book to achieve compositions on daily basis. But at least the styles can be switched to keep the mind interested.

The older one gets the less the body can handle of-course. And the younger the body is, the deeper, the more tasteful and mysteriously, this powerful music can be achieved. Mind you, this is the only music that one can build up the creativity of it spontaneously, as well as bring out raw power as it is being formed. Because the structure is what is being manipulated. Not tempo or voicings. But the structure itself. Tonal music has no monopoly on time. Composition organizes time as its form emerges. That is why Mozart wrote directly into concert score. No other music is looked at or written this way. Especially if improvised. The better the health is, the more power one can ingrain out of it instantly.

Performing a song alone while playing the piano maybe the only other way in building up a crescendo. And hitting a loud or powerful phrase. But its limited because a song is short. And it has to be written ahead of time. So classical music is the only way in achieving this power, spontaneously as it's being created, leaning on how much energy your body can deliver. And how well your physical condition is at the time.

I work myself mentally as an athlete does. This type of preparedness is necessary and good to motivate the body and mind ahead of the improvisational session.

I admire those with work ethics. This is necessary. The health of the body is the key to a great improvisational session, hands down. This is of-course after one has drilled themselves in the theory and have memorized the most important passages and practiced them on daily basis and understands the path to follow and how everything can produce creative passages on constant basis. And has had a taste of these theories to use them at will. Again the older one is the less it can be achieved, but this book, is the primer and reminder after one gets to rest for a period of time and forgets of-course. And from time to time this rest period is very necessary. The body is an organism not a machine.

Beethoven used his body religiously from day to day. By only playing for a certain period of time everyday. And walking by the piano without touching it until the next day. If you want to produce music, this is the only way to handle it on daily basis. If you break this cycle or pattern, it will hurt you and delay everything. Listening to music is also a hurdle in trying to achieve composition. Or investigating a model for example. An electronic instrument. Listening to all the sounds in it to learn it. Or listening to television commercials. All these are timely distractions that will delay your mind in settling down to work in music from day to day.

- From a physical perspective of anyone over forty; Playing less means playing better or more.
- From a mental perspective or getting spent; Being aware in that playing more means less.
- From a knowledgeable and sharpness perspective; Playing more means more new music, deeper thinking and having your game at hand instantaneous. This is the youth element at hand indeed.

The body is an organism that has to be treated like one. And of-course diet and sleep are the other essential elements and factor in playing.

Feeling good is the key to a prosperous improvisational session. The less one plays the more one achieves. This is after being accomplished of-course. This type of schedule does take time to achieve. And one has to be on top of their game. Similar to golf or other sports played on daily basis. In music, writing down a composition, (notating) is time worthy and does throw one off the game of improvisation, creating or playing. But then again this book is the reminder to get back on top of one's game.

When you add a theory to your repertoire, you then have to use it with all the other theories that you have been using before. And that state of mind is very dangerous and can derail one to think they can not understand or one can very easily be discouraged from it. This is only experienced for a short period of time until one grasps the idea of it and goes back to normal state of mind, but this time with more power to use. Or have arranged the theories back in correct order again to work properly. So it is necessary to think in student mode until it sinks in to add to one's repertoire. **And the confidence is back to epic level**.

Another example from a territorial point of view is: **Breaking in sounds**. Every theory has its own tension or sound. Going to new territories means to explore shaky grounds. Forcing yourself to enter new territories. Or force your muscles to play something different. Your ear or body will want to differ or buck it, and play the usual. But you have to force this new territory to happen until it becomes familiar and becomes standard with all your other accomplished theories or repertoire. Once you learn these new grounds then you can move on to more new sounds. This experience separates the novice from the beginners. For ex: The great composers as Bach, had been on more grounds or arrangements than any other person and can use all of them together at will. This is what separates the great composers from the ordinary ones. Of-course after Bach's time came the dynamics of the grand piano in-which added more complexity, from that approach, or how do you judge complexity with the changing of instruments or style of music. Or how do you judge muscles against bronze in the music field? The strength of playing a dynamic instrument against the advanced complexity of arrangements, theory or ideas? Fertility against taste perhaps?

If you start exploring or experimenting at a young age also, you begin to accumulate your own style per say in a shallow description or better yet you begin to create your own character or what I frankly call a thing. Because no one really understands what it is you're working with everyday, it is more evident that everyone has their own thing. You nurture your thing from a young age. And one better yet creates their own characteristic or style. Or thing again. You build your thing from day to day. And no one understands other peoples thing but their own. If you develop a relationship with your thing from day to day, then you begin to rely on yourself from time to time. Only you understand your thing and where it's at from day to day. You sometimes have to rely on your thing to pull off situations that occur unexpectedly. You sometimes gain exhilaration if you're respecting your thing and building trust and admiration to create euphoric substantial moments that catch everyone by surprise. You learn to gain trust in yourself in which one so desperately needs for creating something completely new on the spot. Or **gaining experience by understanding that loosing concentration from reaching resolve of composition is an abstract from comprehending or gaining the clear and complete thought or structure**. Excitements, hurdles or breakups keep the inexperienced confused and from reaching this zone or level of composition.

Practice is essential and rewarding. " **Patience is the virtue of excellence** ".

Composing <u>not from improvisations</u>, but direct <u>bar by bar</u> is the other way of achieving composition and most of the time more powerful because of the choices that can be used. Making a composition extremely hard or melodically complex is a filler and the way to great powerful music also. But it is slower and cannot be achieved without this practice or improvisation, preparation or being accomplished for composition. It is also slower for anyone old. It can drain the body and consume the time an old body has to feel good with in just a few bars written.. This is why I created this method. To offset the waste of time for one. And to play classical music as jazz is approached on daily basis.

Or playing in public. I often play in public or in front of people today, in music stores etc.. and have a grasp of how powerful to make it. Most of the time one has to tone it down to keep an elevation of uncommon civil unrest from occurring. Power has to be respected. Or it will destroy one. You learn these things from daily occurrences. And it's good to feel the situation or room or other people around you and weigh the prospect, or run it in one's mind ahead of time to see if the outcome will be comfortable. I almost always give way to others. The instrument used is of-course the other factor in improvisation. With structure you can accommodate what type, or style you can play. With modern keyboards, one has the choice of baroque, no sustain pedal. Or strings with synthesizers. Or vibes using a jazz approach on the modern electric pianos. Or very rare, Chopin's style on grand pianos. There are no limitations on this type of music. If you create the structure, you decide what style to play, or improvise. And I do not have any racial problems with this method. It delivers a binary Improvisational compassionate outcome.

Theoretically from the beginning to now, it's all the same to a composer in regard to theory. It's just evolved from style to style, form to form. The theory is the same.

When I want to study a style of music I listen to it ahead of time, just to get the muscles flowing in that type of style first and then its very simple to use the theory and play from that type of preparation.

An example of this is one day I found myself in a conservatory school listening to a concert pianist just getting ready to go on the road and perform his list of pieces for us. Shortly after listening to his presentation, I offered to show the listeners how a composition is created from improvisation. I sometimes get someone's phone number and ask for a key to be given and a style of a composer and I would improvise the given information and create a composition within, on the fly. That day I just listened to the performance of this concert pianist and he ended up with a Prokofiev piece as the finale'. Well after I asked for the key and the phone number to use from the listeners. I went straight to the style of Prokofiev to improvise. Because the previous pianist had filled the hall with Prokofiev's music and all our muscles and geometric brain energy waves were still vibrating in that style. So it was very simple for me to just improvise in that style. I hardly had to try. It just flowed automatically without hardly any effort. I could have used another style, but one learns in those certain moments you just are better off to go with the flow as they say. I could have played jazz in the same situation. Again it's all the same in regard to theory. It's just a style to another style.

The theories are all the same, and are the brain for just music. They can be used for any style respectively. But society is different. It has put boundaries and racial differences between styles. **If you look at the evolution of the musical styles as a racial gain, you will lose the theoretical element**. It's all proven math that has to be learned and memorized at first with sensible education. But don't mistake real life and its diversities. It can cost you yours. Try to see through if one is talking about music or using music for their demands. Be it what. Separate the issues of politics and its social forms. Because ordinary people will tend to use music and the social issues in that manner. If you want to study music, you have to separate the issues and concentrate only in music. Even though there are truths in discussions.

For example; The Beatles body of work today belongs to M. Jackson. So if you're talking to someone in the business about the Beatles. He will be understanding it from the Jackson camp point of view. The difference is night and day. Another Example:

If you're in need of a manager, make sure it's either your family, where you have trust, or somebody older where they understand politics. I had a manager in the 1970's who was much older than I, that told me all the events that are occurring in the news today in regards to the gulf war. He depicted every bit of it way back in 1970's. He died unfortunately years ago, never saw his predictions, but amazingly had it all right.

Take for example, the string machine synthesizer, It's almost inevitable that classical theory is used to play it. It's hardly playable using jazz theory alone, and very limited. On the other hand if used with classical theory, the result is symphonies, among other classical styles. You hardly hear anybody improvising with a string machine in the symphonic form. It's because the change of times.

Bluegrass music uses improvisations also. Is it classical or jazz? Is it live or Memorex? It hasn't been classified yet because of its touchy issues maybe? Or just being misunderstood.

If the piano and the 12 key musical concept is the primary source of music and instrument to compose on, and theory is the proven mathematical formula in which to use. And the indigenous and original theory has been uncovered during the beginning of the music era. (during the great composers era). It does not make it for classical music exclusively. It makes it the primary theory to use for composing using the 12 key concept. If you deny yourself the learning of it, you have denied yourself from composing, period. That is not to say that you can't use modern jazz elements of theory and write material. Jazz is just approaching it from another direction, which is achieved possibly by ear. Much the same as song writing is. Which can use the leading tone, the maj 7th. And breaks the eternal mathematical cycle. But it's a full sound. In-depth folding in this book is the maj 7th usage. (chapter four). In which great songwriters like Burt Bacharach, Roger Nichols, Carol King, Brian Wilson, Stevie Wonder, and the Beatles capitalized on. And in Nashville the first guitarist to use the maj seventh's was Charlie Daniels.

I've documented chapter four for classical exclusively. But show on the first page the songwriting path as well. Octaved triads as opposed to un-octaved minor and major 7th's. And do show from another perspective the songwriting folds in the back of the book from page 160-173, but without the bass notes. Here bass notes of chapter four and the thorough bass method is taught in schools today as the method to learn. Surprisingly: P. McCartney, Brian Wilson, Roger Nichols are all bass players. This is the cream of the songwriting crop. This is not a coincidence. Or better yet, how about the <u>Beech Boys</u>, <u>Burt Bacharach</u>, <u>Beatles</u> and the <u>Brill Building</u>. We see the cream of the crop in binary code form again. Coincidence? You be the judge.

Song writing is the art of writing by ear. Some days it happens and some day's, it's called a writers block. You have to wait for it to come to you. And a song is a short theoretical progression. Sometimes created from the melody line. Or sometimes created from the harmony progression. Sometimes created artistically from the lyrics. Or any artistic imagery or feeling. From the heart. (I've used my heart to write a lengthy nocturne in the style of Chopin in empathy and out of respect, which poured out before I realized what was going on). (The heart also works in Classical or other styles. Just to point out here). For the most part the song's hook is what makes a song memorable. There are chorus hooks, lyrical hooks, melodic hooks, alliterative hooks. Most of the time there are two forms of songs structures: Verse-Chorus and Verse-Bridge.

And today the machines have come in to indefinite structures. As in tracking with computers and exclusive plug-in studio work. I call the modern music as <u>" Songwriting tracking and engineering collagen concept "</u>. Or <u>a mosaic or a montage</u>. Leave it to the kids to create the new sound or concept. A great sounding scientific engineering process that locks in to extreme abstractions, where it's too complicated and a lengthy process for others to duplicate or repeat, as a great artistic abstractive creative painting cannot be repeated. That is the only draw back for these times with songs. Therefore the traditional songwriters from the traditional songwriting era will have their songs played and performed only, by other artists. A traditional great song will stand the test of time. As a traditional good piece of music written down or penned or notated as it's referred to, will also. Written music will live forever, because others have the score to play it.

I have a list of songs that are my favorites in the span of 40 years. And it's a list that can be written on one piece of paper. Good songs are just not that many. That's how rare short and true song writing is. The quote from Duke Ellington still stands in songwriting as well. He said " There's good music and bad music " Its that simple, and this also applies to songs as well.

A good example of a good song is what Daryl Hall is presenting currently of his " live at Daryl's house " show. He shows how a good song is treated and recognized by anyone serious, experienced and loves music. He invites those that have those 1 or 2 songs and re-invents them with his formally trained band members. It helps to surrounds oneself with great musicians. He shows how a circle of great musicians hone or sculpture a great song with the live aspect of performing. Playing live is essential and rewarding. It happens unexpectedly, as well as its being controlled and in complete control of by seasoned trained professionals. Hall & Oats have always used the best musicians in New York. Those that housed Saturday night live weekly. And cannot be discussed without mentioning the late T-Bone Wolk influence and how dangerous studio work and achieving a great sound is. T-bone was a specialized songster that new how to fill in-between riffs and passages that excited and elevated a song. This is the inception of this type of sculpturing as the recording electronic amplified studio industry is created. And T-bone will be missed, but his riffs and feelings in all those recordings will be recognized and will live for-ever on the radio. Also good songwriters often double from guitar to piano to bass for the draw of composition as Daryl Hall does. As well as Carol King, Paul McCartney, John Lennon, Brian Wilson and so on. These songwriters have many songs because they were confined to an office or studio without much touring which helped them accumulate these many great songs. The Beatles were actually shut in. They couldn't perform after Beatle-mania. They were together for four years only after their fame and recognition.

XM radio is also recognizing good songs as the tally has accumulated by now from decades of songs. Finally, that's how rare and true and powerful great songs are, and the time period it takes to have an accumulation to recognize. Hall also just commented that great songs cannot be gotten at any time wished. It happens once in a lifetime. Although businesses will try to use formulas to try to duplicate on artist. But true songwriting and good songs are as rare as an endangered species is. 1 or 2 great songs will knock the wind out of the sail of anyone after the hard work is applied to them. I often used to say, you can acquire cancer if you apply yourself wholeheartedly with taste in any piece of music. It will kill you, if you don't be-careful. That's why a young age is important in music as well as old age is important in wisdom and understanding. One can do it without understanding at a young age with all the physical ability, but understand it at a later age and lose the physical ability to do it again. It can be referred to as a double edge sword. There is good and bad in everything. No one has it perfect all the time. But if you follow those that come before you, you can achieve. This is why I'm writing this down for others to understand at a young age, and take advantage of the time one has. Its ok, if not all has sunk in yet. It still can be achieved. Mysteriously, in song writing that is. Where in Classical: there's still only one Mozart, one Chopin. The wondrous children, whom learned it all at a young age. Master chess players of music. Vanished before the age of 40. Again Bach went blind, and Beethoven went deaf. Did that prolong their lives? You be the Judge.

What a time to remember. Bacharach, David & Sager were possibly the heart of American formal recording industry and songwriting at its height. And Lennon and McCartney were the great team that started it all. (There is a page in the back of this book on songwriting after the wholetone generation that further discusses this topic. Page 176)…

On the other hand Bach has written over 1200 pieces of music and all are great. Mozart, Beethoven, Chopin, all are the best. Brahms burned the majority of his compositions equaling even more in volume comparing to Beethoven for the sake of good and precise pick of taste and quality.

A good song or a good piece of music can be compared in analogy to a frisbee. A song takes off slowly and builds up speed and elevation or dynamics and gradually descends back down like a frisbee. A song does it all in 3 to 4 minutes. A long piece does it of-course in a much longer period of time.

Songs have to be nurtured as wine has to be fermented. You have to beat it out of you. As a sculpturer does. I have written a song in 10 minutes or in ten years. Chris Christopherson said " **everyone has 1 or 2 good songs in them** ". Another words you can spend all your efforts on a couple of kids and turn them out into something great. Paul McCartney said " **The songs write themselves**". This is immensely helpful for anyone starting out.

Songs are complex as well as simplistic. Which is Mozartian or better yet Beethovian somewhat in a more direct subtle response. Elton John said " **you have to write quickly if you want to be marketed in a commercial industry** ". And he is the classic iconic figure who understood marketing at the inception of the stereo field and its invention. He's the most recognized and known commercial figure worldwide with Paul McCartney today, as we're closing the songwriting era from the sixties and the seventies. Here's a good example of taking advantage of the quick side of songwriting. The other half is the recording and engineering. It's the recording industry as well, which is time consuming and costly. And therefore the simplicity and quickness of songwriting comes in handy again as well. And once again, the best work in songwriting is always accomplished at a young age. This is not a coincidence. The young mysterious physical ability is epic and foretelling and happens unexpectedly. And the music business demands and pays for singer-songwriter performers. And some of the rock stars from the sixties or seventies for example Joe Walsh or Peter Frampton or Frank Zappa are so well versed in engineering that they hold the highest status in that field as well. Tom Scholz of the band " Boston " is an inventor in this field of studio technology. Graduated with a bachelor's degree and a master's from MIT.

Music is given away today, somewhat, and the tickets to a concert are the bread makers. It costs so much to record in professional studios, that only the top, cream of the crop or those that are picked for bread winners will have their songs engineered by those that I call sacrifice their lives for it. **Engineering is the science of songwriting in the commercial advertising world. *It is both, that make up modern songwriting successful.*** Yes one can engineer at home with machines now, but the big sound and the time spent by experienced and state of the art equipment are only delivered by these well known but a few studio figures that quiet often work harder than the songwriters themselves. And the Cd's that are produced by these great songwriters are only a few. Do the math. It averages out to one song a year, written and engineered by any of the best songwriters. This is with a staff of people producing them. Yes it's a treasure but only to a handful, or a few. The business of songwriting is not as easy as one thinks, now that the era has past by, and we can see the aftermath... And so this is partially what led me to this method, after all ...

The theoretical method I use is broken down to target and sight. You don't need to think of no's, name of position or scales etc. Even though math and names are involved. And has to be learned and practiced correctly. You target by sight which is easy, providing one learns the pre material. And that does take years to learn. And that's how the great composers did it.

Honestly speaking, I do not expect anyone to seriously take up my method for its early and time consumption. And its unconventional way of learning the musical concept as well as students spend their hard earned money and will not relinquish their education in the time limit one has to spend today to learn and use publicly and re-learn again. This is one angle in which might have been why no great composer had left their notes for others to follow. But I would imagine secrecy is pronounced foremost and inevitable. As a great gourmet' recipe is kept. Or to whom, do really want to be composers as opposed to players.

But the great composers also gave away their approach to anyone who was serious. So they were honest to those that were serious about their music. And wanted to be composers, instead of bad reviewers.

This method is not easy and require many years of formal training to pull off. As well as the fingering and reading skills required alongside. It is very difficult even for skilled pianists. So one can imagine what non pianist may think of it. That's why there is only one Beethoven, as the saying goes...

I do not use the traditional figured bass or thoroughbass methods from the baroque era of descriptive analogy. (6/4, 5/3, vii or º). Because I believe the key lies in the keyboard and not the symbols or notation staffs. Notation is good enough for symbols to communicate with as it is. We are in the 21 century folks. Why are we still using symbolism to communicate with? It's because the music students are not all experienced pianists. And there has to be a method to communicate with-in the school systems around the world. That's why. So the initial path has been paved over and covered early on. Notation itself should be plenty good enough to communicate with, as everyone does. Not descriptive analysis from the root. It's very good to know descriptive analysis from the standard symbolism of the books used in schools. Don't get me wrong. Knowledge is power. But it can take more time. If its not necessary, why fool with it? Is it to teach others that don't play the piano? I don't use any of the literature definitions I learned in school. It hardly helps in writing or spelling. I wished I learned music in those classes. They were supposed to help us learn how to think maybe? I still think I could have learned music to think with instead. Although my mother would tell me not to think, I remember since I was a child. But that's another story.

I use this book's Method and retain it to memory with practice. Retaining target notes and the triads as symbols themselves. Other symbolisms will deter your memory and vision. Using 5-1-3 or 3-5-1 will give you the exact key, scales, harmonic degrees, the 1 or circular 4th & 5th. targets. ***I also use only 12 keys to mold in my hearing's mind.*** (C,Db,D,Eb,E,F,F#,G,Ab,A,Bb,B,) Notice all normal key's with the flats and one sharp; F#. This is the only way to clearly hear all the keys and every note on the piano and know it by taste. Or looks. And at the speed of thought without confusement. There's still unsettled thoughts though. Can this method be used as compositional improvisations? Or improvisational compositioning? Can composition be improvised? I immediately have had doubt-sayers that eventually returned on their thoughts.

I use this method for other music and it works just as well. It's called classical because that was the era of when music matured or was educationally created. It's music for all. It's the scientific aspect of music. And there is only one way to digest it. Classical music happens to be a style of it that was incepted from the keyboard. So it gained prevalence or indigenous connotations of-course, but its standard music for all. It's the language for musicians. As it's the language of English for all to communicate with.

I've spent a week playing eight hours a day trying to connect one theory to another. Sometimes targeting one finger in which leads to the next position month's later. Sometimes going on a hunch by ear. Sometimes in sleep subconsciously, sometimes walking by the piano and striking a chord that hits a geometric harmony that leads to an entirely new direction that gets worked on for weeks. I myself not understanding why until a time later. But going on intuition and what I once played long time ago. And the repetition of the sound engrained in my head since childhood. This is hard work. Not to mention the years spent instilling all the styles not just the classical style in my repertoire.

I've gotten negative callers while being interviewed on the radio in saying that they are not of any contention or ordeal pertaining to classical music for it arouses kings and that is the foreshadowing of slavery and demise. So actually what they are being taught or conditioned by saying in analogy; That classical music if compared to great art. As in Rembrandt, Michael Angelo, Da Vinci or Shakespeare. Are bad work and should be banned out of existence. This is the modern attitude towards serious music. Have we lost our sense of well beings? Is it the end times? Are we sick as a society? Is education being taunted again for the sake of money, the power hungry and recognition? Where is jazz today? The other educational field in music. It's in schools yes. Finally. And we put it there. After a hard battle. And I have the scars to prove it. But we lost the war. It's no-where to be mentioned on 100 channels of television. So we return to where it all came from. At least I am. And am using my life-time experience in capturing what had been lost since WWII.

And now we're losing everything al-together, if some of us don't step up and do something about it. Soon it will be nothing but machine music with a push of a button by 10 year old's that we have to be forced to worship, admire and promote fearing the alternate consequence of losing ones job. This could happen if we don't speak up and define our culture and the way we're being treated.

This is my method that I documented in order to write and play like the great composers on daily basis. I alone fought all odds and continue to do so for the sake of serious music and education.

There is good and bad in everything. Except in an injustice. This is what the holocaust survivors have taught me.

And no wealthy king or queen have ever worked hard to the point where they are of a historical art or a musical figure. Their occupation does not allow them to be, for one. The meek and the poor or the have nots will gain the earth and all its richness. We the people, the first words on the Constitution.

Beethoven used to say; There are plenty of princlings, kings and queens. But there is only one Beethoven.

And should one remind our young misled friends that most of these great composers I mention, never owned a home or could pay for their own rent to the day they died. And the baroque era changed to the classical era due to the sustain pedal on the new piano's that were invented. Haydn didn't get paid by a wealthy slave driver to create it. He was already taught and well into organizing his theories and studies to a serious term. He was the primary radio of his day and time, for those that can afford to hire him. He himself was homeless at a young age.

And when the piano changed again, the next had even better harmonics and well resonated tension, and changed the style again up to the modern era of romanticism from a well built harp boards and repetitive action that created the whole-tone generation. No one paid anyone to create a style of music as the youth are sometime brought up to think and infuse. You simply cannot create great composers of music. No matter how much money you throw at someone. No one with plenty of money will ever work as hard as any of these great composers, That is a fact ! And is true for jazz greats also. There is only one Coltrane, one Bird, one Monk, one Hancock, one Tyner, Corea... And they changed the world. Many died for their work young. No wealthy person will kill himself for his work. He doesn't have to. Doesn't that make sense? And I haven't seen any king or queen of this era ever assault any one or demise a poor soul for that matter. The British kingdom denounced slavery in 1838, way ahead of everyone else in the world. And we no longer live in an era of privacy, therefore the strain of the wealthy is neglect and abandonment by the whole masses. Isolation from everyone. Also wealth doesn't belong to the wealthy any more but others that manipulate.

Look at your life as it is in real time and point at the culprits that hurt you. Could it be, non of them are any of these people? No one that suffers for his work will ever hurt another. It's the corrupt that don't work for their work, that do all the damage. Those that are in the right place at the right time. In the right place to collect vast amount of money. The lottery winners. The ones controlling everything. We will never see them. That is always the case. Once they're discovered then they are exposed.

You cannot create great composers or innovators quickly. This type of thinking is the same ideology as the past generation of folks used to think that Elvis Presley wrote all of his songs. That's why he's the king. This is a marketing philanthropy aimed to instill and diminish by paralleling the serious, the educated with the commercial or those in the right place at the right time as of its equal for the sake of money. Kindly put, **stealing**. As anyone can become a Rembrandt if paid. This is hog wash. And can only fool the young and the ignorant. Or whom ever pay the real slave masters. As Glen Gould predicted.

I myself am simply bored with the stale harmonies or short pieces of music that one plays over and over to promote for money. I know there are better sounds to be gotten from the piano. And do not repeat a written piece of music on daily basis. And mixing and engineering is harder than writing after one is skilled in writing. Mixing and engineering is listening to something over and over. It can drive a person bonkers ! Its cutting your life in half for the sake of engineering. That's why I'm sticking with this music. Not because I'm higher standard. That's hogwash. My mind will simply shut down from boredom or pain by playing material over and over. I've played every style of music professionally. I will not, ever, memorize anything anymore for the sake or benefit of others. A slave driver can only get so much out of someone. And yet I get accused of being a racist and all the exact opposite or as others call dis-information spred. Over and over. This is the present day 20th. century which has beens hanging on for power, and that will, eventually fail them. As we're seeing.

I've played all of the musical genre's and forcibly, might I add. And unwillingly. Until I literally started throwing up in convulsions from the smell of beer and cigarettes mixed in night club carpets. You cannot get blood out of a turnip. Of-course we all were blind at one time or another. Until it all came crumbling down with the computer... The Berlin wall along-side.

I remember when we weren't allowed to mention anything about foreign leaders, other countries or anything out of our own culture when we played live during the cold war scare. And in one day, the kids were on chat lines with the entire world population online and communicating with each other, as the computer was invented. And I still remember when I mentioned to my neighbors that Elvis didn't write his songs. I was greeted with odds. And a disappointing conclusion. As the entire farm population were marketed to think he did. And that's why he was the king. This was a major surprise to me. He was undoubtedly one of the best singers, after he made his money and up-graded his songs and show, of-course. One of the greatest entertainers ever. A giant of a figure that is rare today by-the way. Just to mention the truth here..

Song sheet music wasn't printed until late sixties or seventies. And before songs, there were tunes. We've made great strides since, but these ideologies have now been **twisted** to educate or condition the young to even worse posture which is nothing but the same as before but from another angle. Their objective is not to indulge in seriousness. Or condemn education and knowledge any way they can. Therefore all are under control once again. This is the mainstream thinking, where all the money is being made. The top one percent as they say. And the limousine riders today are all of a well contracted well calculated marketed generation of a new culture wired with a cell phone to a satellite computerized marketed commercial spree. He who hurts gets the rewards. Climbing the corporate ladder. Greed is good. And honesty fair and religion is voltaire. Things don't change much from the old times to the present. The world is pretty much the same. Only the obvious gets a new twist. <u>Twist</u> is a nice word for a lie. **Spin** is even better. These are common words used today on mainstream media in compensation to the greed and lying of the real everyday reality. (*Just to mention here the rock star Dee Snyder of the band* " **twisted** *sister* " *has successfully or artistically mirrored or for-shadowed his own life and profession to incline an image of society today. This artist is a living proof of the times we're living under. He for-saw ahead of time what has become of our society. His family could not be any more serious or normal than the best of them, but yet the looks on the surface is so* **twisted,** *affirming the image of society as we're experiencing. And behind every successful man there's a good woman. And a blessed smart family. As what this family had successfully college educated their children to learn, understand, be aware of the* **twisted** *facts or times we live in from the street smarts of the rock revolution or the* **twisted** *times we've been through and the* **twisted** *times we're facing.) ...* Δ ∞

And to everyone's surprise the billionaire Warren Buffet just commented on television how he receives social security without even asking for it. He clearly states that the system is for the rich by means of corruption, and not education or honesty. The more money one has the more power he can gain. If a wealthy man comes out to expose this corruption, then what does that say for the others.

The great performers themselves never indulge in this nonsense. For it's the surrounding low totem pole in music that create all this trouble and they are the hidden upper totem pole of rulers of society. There is an old saying in show business; " The bigger they are, the nicer they are " I've always found that is the case and true. After all, no one that works hard has the time to conjure up nonsense. No one great will waist his or her time in that. Which proves who is really in charge of it all. No one in the music business, that's for sure.

Thank God there is something real or of true intrinsic value. Math is real. No matter how much one tries to spin it around. Real art or science cannot be twisted or spun into vague despondent continuity. *I think seriousness or formal predication is the center point median, in arbitrary conscience, in which at one, any intellect uses creatively to communicate with and be aware for survival sake, as a civilized human being. Thus harboring both sides and elements of the human species as infinite, as freedom is.* <u>Education, if lost will be the demise of any civilization</u>. The founding fathers were not kings. They might have had slaves. **But they were the writers of a well and carefully written document that concluded the ideological era into an ever present conscience and subtle justifiable means of a structural understanding that serve humanity for the sake of the betterment of mankind and a free mind for the rest of the world to exercise.** And I've simply tapped in the musical harmonious and spiritual equation sector of it. Which is mysteriously uncovered. Have been cut off or relinquished since WWII. And now being also primed by the very people that it was created for perhaps to eventually help. *The black spiritual conscience. Race, and the struggle for education, civility, human right, justice, the pursue of happiness, joy, eternal values, wisdom, and the evident factor of all; Freedom for all.*

I've created a scientific methodology that uses theories, patterns and formulas to bridge the geometrical, architectural, classical mind to the poetical, metaphysical, imaginative, judicial, theoretical, emotional heart in an eternal binary conscience of one. This entity of time in which this year adds up to 111 if you add your age to the year you're born. And the " one dollar bill " signifying the monetary issue for the world to meet in a one consciences effort to free the masses from tyranny, oppression, dictatorship or communism. The first black president elect. For the first time ever throughout history. Recovering the banking systems as we speak. Strengthening or building the dollar. And he himself comes from a binary white mother and a black father.

So maybe one can understand what the young generation are trying to say by phrasing it in another way perhaps; As in **Generalization can blur definition**. As in <u>people and objects can be concrete</u>. And <u>language and numbers can be abstract</u>. This is a reverse analogy indeed and can confuse by just merely

Robert Kaye

generalizing. Or merely describing "**Nature however beautiful; Is not art**". But "**Art is natural beauty interpreted to human temperament**".

Here again the answers lie in good conscience somewhere in-between the binary issue given through science and art. Related to the constitution and our free form of government, in which I document further on the last page of this forward. Tempering intuition with science.

Strauss and Rachmaninov were the last of the great serious composers. Both died right at 1945 and 1947. End of WWII. Not a Coincidence. Stravinsky, Prokofiev, Schoenberg, Berg, all the surrealist came after WWII. This is not a coincidence either. Perhaps signifying the change. And American composer; Walter Piston has written eight symphonies after he returned from WWII and they are very tasteful. They are of the modern scoring western music as it's called. It surprises me extremely. He should be noted as possibly the best American composer. But no one really cares. Is it because, it's not serious music? Kind of odd if you ask me. But maybe it's time to bring back the seriousness. The computer has certainly spilled the beans. And there is plenty of work still ahead. We are still relatively young as a civilized society. The knowledge will continue**. For the future will tell on us again and again, if we fail to act. Or fail to learn the lessons from the past.**

Classical Music emphasizes clear beautiful melodic structure with clarity and expressive restraint. It uses multi thematic phrases, accents, harmonies, resolves, intimacy, delicacy, strings, bounce, divertimento, exposition, expression, recapitulation, clarity of line, proportion, pauses, moments of acceleration and slowing as themes are introduced, transited, juxtaposed and developed. Rhythmic flexibility imburge it with rhetorical sensibility, akined to speaking or story telling. The pause that conclude an excerpt is the exact discontinuity, rhetorically native, it's a moment of rest. An inhalation before the narrative theme. Esoteric purity, balance, lyricism, elegance and good taste are the hallmark. (*I thank Dr. Robert Greenberg for these nice descriptive words from his lectures. And also giving me the date of Joseph Haydn's birthday. It hit the mark remarkably well with my studies.*)

Classical music is simply complete and where all music styles and form originated, from the obvious instrument; The piano, which is the Orchestra. Tastefully and perfectly balanced to the highest priority. Most of all, one has access to all the keys all the time in structural form. It does not need any compression or attenuation or any other engineering. It cannot take any. It's complete from top to bottom. As mentioned; *only big band complex, arranged and charted swinging saxes, bop or even modern quintets or quartets of the past era can come close and meet classical music*. But jazz ultimately gets limited because of the steady rhythm. As Baroque can be. Not to mention the un-natural physical shape it demands. *Where classical has the in-between breaks and relief that one can rest in at a moments decision. And this is great for improvisations*. And new in my book. For Jazz, aside from the abstract form of-course, its continuous rhythmic pulse again limits it. Just as it would, if classical music used rhythm also.

jazz without the rhythmic pulse is abstract classical. Which is Schoenberg's method and theories. In which he brought with him or created after WWII as he escaped from the Nazi's. And is used for scoring, for motion pictures. Or used by Leonard Bernstein. That's why Schoenberg was based in Hollywood. Someone said he couldn't get anyone from the motion picture industry to pay him enough for his orchestrations. In-which in my opinion he was great at. Obviously worked hard enough at it that he wouldn't give it away for a low amount of money. Makes sense…

And the last great jazz setting which brought attention from the aspect of the small trio or quintet setting, was Winton Marsalis with the late great short lived and much under rated and the last of the breed and era; Kenny Kirkland. This was when Winton was in his teens. Which is the age of improvisational performance. If used correctly and virtuously. i.e., Charlie Parker as Mozart and Chopin as Cannonball, Coltrane, Tatum, Waller, Schumann, Mendelssohn, Schubert, Gershwin and Bellini … All were masters of music, deceased around the age of forty. Glad Marsalis is aware of this and have adapted with age.

Improvisation can be open for more creative advantages. Its theory can be eternally useful with its physical ability. Because these mentioned above used their ability continuously. It killed them. Because they learned the theoretical formulas at a young age. And sacrificed their body. If they only stopped at 40, then they would have survived. But needing money, and not having history to learn from, is the results.

Haydn was already in his forties when he was finally accomplished and composing. Late, but he created the style and handed it down to the young as it killed almost all of them. He himself lived on well into the late seventies. It took Haydn his youth to create the classical style. It was inevitable as the sustain pedal was created.

Most of the terminology in music today were not even used back then, or existed. Non of these great composers even had a college degree. How ironic. Early on, they taught each other as the jazz musicians taught each other during their inception of jazz music. Rossini stopped playing at 37 and he lived another 37 years afterwards writing classical songs. Which are nothing compared to today's demanding songs and engineering. A physical nightmare.

The age factor is very important here. The composers named above, wrote at a young age. That's why they stand out from other composers. Their music is full of life and virtuosity, because they were young and strong and not weary of physical ailments. Chopin's etudes are even difficult to play even if you practice them continuously to perform. Piano concertos are the same.

Age is everything if you want to be somebody. Know your body, you are not a machine. You are a living organism. One minute you can play this passage and the next minute you cannot. You are human, if you don't have the proper nourishment or rest, you are unproductive. **One must have the proper rest, strength and nourishment to produce**. There is no other way. Physics is much more complicated than one is aware of. Ordinary people are not apt to this. **Passages of music are involved in physics**. I don't know how, but I just know from experience. Especially in classical music. Or an interpretive performance.

If you notice an orchestra musician, they are very aware of dynamics. Very delicate and at attention. Most take cortisone to maintain their status and remain employed. Where jazz musicians can relax. They are laidback and pacing themselves for a long night.

You write music, or play for yourself not others. Others do not know your body and what it's capable of. Only you do. Kids do not, they are not old enough to understand. **Everybody know their own body like everyone knows their own computers**, sort of speak. **If you don't work for yourself, then you will suffer the consequences mentioned above.** And today the opposite can work for you if you know how to use it as well. For example if improvisation can kill you. Well today it can work for you with the help of Computers. And can give you a playing field to work with. As opposed to the past ages. This is the modern innovations in music today. The new door opened which I'm using for my benefit....

Alcohol or substance use, only shortens the health of-course and confuse as they cover up momentarily. So understand the truth.

There is one incident that I remember in the 1960's. I once performed in the auditorium piano before school started. The teacher wanted me to repeat the performance for the school shortly afterwards. Being a child I went along with everything. After she filled the auditorium, I then could not repeat the zeal performance in which I had just a few minutes prior. I did not know why, and the teacher definitely did not know why. So the incident was dismissed unexplained. In those unexplained moments, I remember since I was a child, I always thought that its because of me, maybe I'm crazy. I do not understand this. What I did not understand is how one could monitor or read their body. And how much strength was left or the physical and mental ability drained. You learn this if you become a serious pianist. How does a child or even someone in his twenties understand this?

One movie comes to mind is "shine" the story of the hard working classical pianist. Who lost it all. Today I know that my little body at that time had only enough energy for one performance, especially in energetic dynamic classical pieces that need strength. I grew up my whole life not understanding why one minute I could and the next I could not. You have to know these things if you want to understand.

Another aspect **is the mind getting spent**, as we call it. **If you play a lot, your mind will get bored and will lose its interest and quit on you**. But if you keep yourself amused by switching a style of music continuously, or key, **you will offset mind spending** and still maybe then will be faced with physical drainage if continuing, depending on age. You do not have to work aggressively on one style or one piece of music day after day, even though that's how you force yourself to finish something. This is the great characteristics of classical music. One has the advantages of subtle and discontinuity. Pause and the multi thematic phrasings. Never the same. It's the most any creator can asks for. Never boring. You have to know what and how much you need to play each day to use your body and mind productively. Accommodate changes and adapt as you get older. But on the other side of the coin, working on notation on daily basis is as common as someone going to work as any other. It's a job. That sometimes is a blessing. As it becomes very easy from that out-look.

Playing before the age of forty can also be dramatically and emotionally confusing. Because music is attuned to body, motion and works with your muscles. And sometimes your muscles demand the next phrase to play. This is where the **"Songs write themselves"** comes in. Or knowing how to play by heart as it's called. This area is mostly and profusely mysterious. Other than when someone already had been exposed to a particular type of music that can be recalled by sound and played if possible. If not just heard. Songwriters hear their songs orderly and sometimes another person helps pull out the song for them. I used to play anything I wanted. Sometimes execute songs or tunes publicly in which I've only heard a few times on television and execute it perfectly in front of an audience with no prior preparation. Or to switch key's without a thought in a split second. These are the miracles that have given me the confidence and self esteem and inventions in creating this method from experience. There is **Telepathy and subconscious** involved also. This is part of the mystery. Obviously the great composers that I use all were public performers also. And wrote on daily basis. They were extraordinary improvisers in classical music. Which is taught false or wrong today. And I'm slowly changing it.

Bad reviewers will never be able to use this method themselves, because they need to use symbolism to communicate with others. They chose to teach or play and not to become composers**. Without suffering for it. It cannot be achieved otherwise**. Playing by ear I pronounce no one really knows what it is other than one's muscles help astringe or gel or infuse what to play next. Obviously the heart or love, help induce this state of mind also. Drugs also seem to free the nervous system from other obstacles therefore releasing it with relaxation. But drugs will not work after the age of forty. And they will deter the physical ability which is crucial in classical strength. And in the long run, meaning long pieces of music, **drugs will kill you**. Therefore they are not an inducer other than a relaxer. Which is a harsh price to pay for relaxation, even before forty. So the state of mind remains a mystery. And is only apt from a good shape and form of a physical and bodily health. And waiting for this state of mind can be time consuming. But it's the luxury that a young physical ability has. And shall not be wasted while it exists on daily basis.

Sight-reading are the years within these confounds also. Where the body is at strength. And plenty of energy and mental, physical and literal demands are met. This is the area where Mozart is considered and printed as the best composer of all. His ability to write directly to concert score quickly, and the ability to improvise, read, compose and understand what he's doing in a euphoric state of mind, all at the same time. It's the age ability with all of its confines of the very literary and physical sense. Balanced, lyrical, elegant with good taste. He was the youngest accomplished composer of all. That makes him and his music stand out over others. His father gave him the best education money can buy at a very early age. The great composers themselves from the best countries in Europe. It's what he wished to have had as a child. He was a composer of his own rights also. You can also look on the other side of the coin; The old and experienced will be able to write deeper and more meaningful ideas if allowed. Maybe not up or forward moving continuously, or spunky. Which means if you understand your body and know how to squeeze it for strength and ability, then you can use it to a certain degree.

When I first realized that my body could not accommodate my gigs at the age of thirty five, I was devastated. I thought it was the end of music. But slowly I learned to use it with caution, and control the pain. The object is to stop right before the stomach becomes astringed or strained. I was coached by others that came before me to control it. Or catch it ahead of time, and that can give one breathing room to use the body on daily basis. Of-course concerts and aggressiveness is no longer in the picture but at least being able to control or manage the physical body is a productive metaphor.

Theoretically my body is completely shot. I've had every organ fail on me over the years. But remain in tact and I've found many work arounds that enable one to use it productively. Dieting and planning is continuously at work. Certain winters, one has to gain weight to foresee the future with proper nourishment for certain tasks to be completed. As for example after writing this book, notating a 439 page orchestrated composition and completing a CD, programming, mixing and engineering it at the same time. And then preparing for dieting, for play mode to take place for next season. " **The object is to survive the composition** ". Each hour of the day is calculated and monitored as well as counted for sleep and mental ability. And computers are used for publishing as well as play back for bodily preservations. Over the years you learn the nourishment of food and how it can alter one's ability and strength providing a euphoric capability. Of-course that's never consistent, or on daily basis. And the older one gets, the slower and less one can achieve. But it can be achieved, as **Haydn exemplified, as the most evident and accomplished warranted long living, serving and respected example.**

This method I created is my answer to it also. I have no doubt in my mind that the great composers all had their own books to follow. And every one of them burned it at the time of their death. We're lucky to have Beethoven's deaf scratch pads remaining, but has been altered somewhat by his shady friends. Here again that's why they burned almost everything.

It's Impossible to maintain everything to memory without the many pages to refer back to. Along with the target notes, approach, tricks, and helpful mnemonic reminders that's kept to memory …

The pieces of music one writes becomes as someone's kids. You get so involved in it, because of the long time spent in it, that you cannot judge it from others. It becomes part of you. As a painting becomes also. You cannot tell the difference or you get confused on where it sits. You get so deep in it that you cannot judge it against others, until some time goes by. Again the fermentation period here. The same falls in engineering. Your ears will fool you after working on something for a stretch. You have to let time go by and start with fresh ears as the saying goes. I've had my ears infected from head phones use, day after day. Again; **The fermentation of time in music is very necessary and important to make a valid judgment of the work itself.**

Listening to movie soundtracks or electronic motion picture music of today can be confusing. Because it can confuse you on form of sound. For example; A major or a minor. A 6/4, diminished or sharpened & flattened ninth's are all standard recognized sounds that one eventually gets familiar with. But the new way of composing with electronics can fill the ear with confusing elements to throw you off into the unknown. I lost my bearing for a number of years, as a keyboard player, as keyboards were invented during the 1970's. So it's important to learn basic theory and its positions and try or taste them to have a feeling of what this is and to advance to playing and using it to identify with the normal sound of use. **Have trust in yourself**. **You would be surprised how you can tell what key a piece of music is in**. *By the fingering sense of sound*. Or the type of music in which you know what key it uses just by listening to it and identifying from experience. And that only comes from time passing by. **Time lived is experience and important in music. As time in music is important as the fermentation of wine**. So older composers or writers should be revered a treasure to the young coming up. Not because of popularity but the education spent in a lifetime.

It's no accident that Mozart sounds like JC Bach or Haydn. Or Hummel sounds like Mozart or Chopin sounds like Hummel or Schumann sounds like Chopin, or Czerny sounds like Beethoven,. **Information handed over is as valuable as a secret kept**. And it is not accomplished quickly without experience, practice, the right approach and with time passing by. But diligent work and knowledge, recognizing **Time is virtue. And virtue is excellence !**   " *Information is not Knowledge* "   A. Einstein

The Age Factor & Health

When I was young, I would lose my mind whenever I would stride something above my age, or accidentally play a complete improvisational piece, complete and perfect. I didn't understand why this would happen? Is it a chemical imbalance? Is it just me? This thing we call music is so powerful, that it can embarrass just as well as impress someone. I didn't understand the spiritual aspect aside from the educated line, or vice-versa? Trying to accomplish something by the lonesome self in music is not simple. I had one mentor would tell me; that no one understands you, do they? I would add to that that I don't understand me either. This is how and what a young pianist really goes through. A mirror to that would also be someone from the old age of record companies giving someone too much credit to have to live up to. Right away the Elvis mode, Mozart's, the Jimi Hendrix's, the Charlie Parker's etc. From both sides of the field fall short by a tragic end. I now question this point, where I didn't understand nor could handle at a young age.

Lets say you get out of school at 22 years old. You then only have 10 years of prime real estate of your body to accumulate material with. An athlete's best years are from 20 to 30, the same as a musician. What you do in those years determines what kind of success you'll have. And how much you accomplish. After 30 years old, everything slows down to slow motion, while the wage of living increases. If you spend ten years to learn 12 key's and 12 chords, or looking for a method, or playing cocktail piano. You would have lost your prime years. That's why I wrote this book. It's a quick correct path to learn the necessary tools to use.

W. Bach, one of the sons of J.S. Bach himself was considered a genius in his day. Because he learned from his father the essential elements of theory. But he did nothing but improvise as he traveled and drank in ecstasy. Today nobody knows or cares that he even exists. On the other hand his brother C.P.E Bach has over 700 pieces of music to his name. Our local radio station is named WCPE after him.

All of Bach's son's surprisingly ended up on the second string of composers, as I refer to them again. And the reason being the age factor. Bach wanted more than anything to give his children an education. So he included in his contract that the court would grant him a clause to educate his sons. By doing that he actually took away some of the primary years in which a composer needs to be accomplished. And those years have turned out to be the prime factor in deciding the strength of his sons music and what classified them to be in the second string composers as opposed of the first string. i.e. Bach, Mozart, Beethoven, Chopin. Of-course I'm classifying these categories and comparing them to the giants of the past. Despite what anyone would defer. R.Strauss was another whom was thwarted towards going to gym class in school, and it did give him extra years to live out as a result.

Mozart was the youngest of any composer to be accomplished. Therefore that makes him the best. And rightfully so. No one would argue this point. Unless they have another agenda to unsurface. Infact all of these 1st. string composers are assimilators. Meaning they used other composers styles, and created the most fertile meaningful tasteful serious profound lively music of anyone to this day, because of their age and accomplishments. And time not wasted. And their output was enormous, considering the fact. Bach himself wrote his most important work being the Brandenburg concertos in his prime age of around thirty. They were never performed in his lifetime, nor did anyone even know that Bach would eventually be known as the father of music. He was criticized for sticking to the baroque style when at the same time everyone were changing to the classical style because of the sustain pedal in the new pianos.

Outsiders or critics have no idea how long it takes for a composer to be accomplished and producing music. All the other first string composers attempted to write like Bach but failed. And vise versa. This is how hard and long it takes to be accomplished in one's own way of working with music. **And the age factor is the crucial element to any one in the music field**. Age is everything here. What separates these first string composers from the rest is their age in learning and accomplishing their studies. It just so happens Mozart, Mendelssohn & Chopin were the youngest to be accomplished and they died at the same time. Never reaching forty years old. Neurobiologist Dr. Eric Kandel, a Viennese Austrian said: The plasticity of the brain is so enormous when you're young that one can learn different languages very quickly, but only at a young age. Here is the definition of plasticity: the quality of being easily shaped or molded. The adaptability of an organism to changes in its environment or differences between its various habitats. Bach was slightly late because of his father and mother's death. But he replaced them with the divinity of the church and excelled back to what his father and uncles taught him and never got a college education in which proved to be the factor. And he also was blinded at his later years in which was the cause to save him some years to live out, as well as Beethoven loosing his hearing in which it also added some years to his life at the end. We see all these factors after the fact. And judge by the music. **Time in music is the fermentation of the process.**

 I had no way growing up. Or even we had no way growing up. You tend to go with the flow and rear off your plan for your life to succeed. For example: We lost a whole generation of sober musicians during the Vietnam war. The draft and the civil unrest caused a piece drug flower revolution that took music to the rock stone age. Roger Waters of the band " Pink Floyd " described it clearly after all. He said suddenly he realized that, what his mother has been reaffirming all those years ahead for preparation into college and then your life would begin. Suddenly dawned on him that there were no later on when life began. It was now or never. That is a revolution in the midst of. Caught all of us by surprise. The structural life style broke up as we were just in the brink.

 The jazz musicians went out of business and many people think that's better. But is it? Is it because many people never had a chance for an education? And that's the only way for them to fit in society? Democracy or the majority ruled. It's the welfare of the majority. The people. The standard society is in at the time. That is the culprit and not race. Because the classical musicians also went out of business. Rich man, poor man. Although the propaganda campaign would like you to think it's race. **But the point is the whole country went in one direction and changed your path of education**. Of-course today everything is by design. And there's less of a chance of something like that happening again, but who knows.

 Incidentally the great guitar player (Brian May) of the rock band " QUEEN " has a doctoral degree. In today's time there is no revolting or loud messages of society, so its only kids getting in a struggling rock market. When the market pays. It draws reel people in it as apposed to just kids. And In time of survival and war, education takes a back seat. Life is a crap shoot.

 When I used to play clubs, comedy clubs etc. I often asked questions, and the reply I got was, its all a crap shoot. Life is a crap shoot. From politics to a rock star. For ex. When president Ragan was shot. Immediately afterwards; General Haig announced on television the infamous words; (As of now , I am in charge). From that moment on, everybody knew who Alexander Haig was. It's being in the right place at the right or sometimes not so right moments. It's all a crap shoot.

 By the way during the Vietnam era, it was Henry Kissinger whom went with president Nixon to China secretly to resolve the Vietnam war. Here you have the secretary of state of the United States in a crucial revolutionary time being an <u>Austrian intellectual</u>. The **binary trait** at work here again. An Austrian Classics representing **Science**. And an American political intellectual representing **Abstract**. This is the infinite dichotomy in politics resolving one of history's most urgent tumultuous climax during war time. By the use of **binary code**. This is the method I'm introducing here through music also. The use of theories in building structural form, creating composition or structural government with the use of **abstract** and **formal** art. Or <u>poetical intellect</u>. **Reason and Reasoning**. This is why Henry Kissinger is highly regarded as the best secretary of state to serve that particular office. General Haig touched on the subject also, before he recently died. As I'm unfolding my theories and documenting the thought. This is called a big <u>**one**</u> in everyday laymen terms. The one dollar bill represents it by the very geometric structure of the Masonic pyramid with the all seeing eye on top. Which represents structure and the military in which where, I myself reside. On the **Mason / Dixon** line. Here again, **binary code** at work. In-fact the very spot where all capitals exist are in the middle of any state, just drawn in the center of any populated area, thus splitting it in two. As well as the first president of the United States on the one dollar bill. Whom was born the same year **Joseph Haydn** was and in which created classical music in 1776. And **George Washington** with the birth of the Constitution in 1776. **Binary code** again. And after the Vietnam war, China now has this binary political system installed in its early stages and exercising as well as Russia. And the Dollar is monitored on daily basis for the connotation of a bullish market set against crude oil, commodities and high interest rates. As well as Google, Amazon, PayPal and Wikipedia adventuring for the first time throughout the world in $ dollars.

 If you only have between now and 35 years old. Why play the crap shoot game of life. Understand what you are in store for. And make the right decisions. Know where you are going, despite temptations. Take the road that doesn't lead to gambling. Because the odds are a million to one. I've always heard that it takes ten years for any business to succeed. And so today Nashville is even called a ten year town. Or was being called that during the Bush administration. It appears to be shut down at the moment.

 If I was 20 years old in school, studying. I would not hesitate to accumulate compositions while I'm still in that age zone of (10 - 30). Its not just paper you will be accumulating, but books, or volumes of your music. Which now can be inputted by any musician of any age in the computer and turned into CD's. When you accumulate your work in volumes in front of you from day to day, then it's real. There is something to be said about that. Even if nobody will know who you are. **Your work will live forever**. And you have quite an impressive material to sell. There is a big difference between the great composers and the ordinary one or two book composers of today. And child prodigy is nonsense in my opinion, seeing all the great composers came from families of education. They just were taught by teachers, which were their parents, at a young age. Common sense. It's sad to see that almost all the great composers died at around 40 years old. But today we now have a longer expectancy of age. We can use computers to extend our age and further our studies, if it's painful past 35 years old. But nothing can replace the years from 10 to 30. Those are the prime real estate years. In careers in music. You have the following options:

1. To become an interpretive performer. (Concert musician) and possibly have a few CD's at end of career. Possibly become known.

2. To become an improvisational performer. (Jazz musician) and definitely have a few CD's at end of career. And possibly become known.

3. To become a composer. And accumulate a vast amount of material to use. For CD's. for publication, for education. And the amount of material is the factor and what will eventually make you known. (without a gamble). Even if it's for posterity. If you try to be all, you will only partially achieve your goal, and just be ordinary. So on the other hand; You can compose in all genre's. Jazz compositions are very rare. Because "Jazz is the art of Improvisation". (So its actually songwriting). And there are more halls to use nowadays than before. Schools are mainly for use. Song writing is waiting for song's to come down, and its time consuming. There is nothing wrong with these great genre's, but classical compositions has concert halls and orchestras all over the world to use. And the music is mathematically eternal for composing. Which leaves you less time to waist. And gives you material on day to day basis. Continuously without a block. And it's the only type of music in-which one can shake the earth's axis with if prompted at the right age. We now have engraving programs such as (Finale' or Sibelius,) to quickly teach us notation. Which is an instant publishing virtual environment. And if you become a lifer in this venue then you will want to learn such Programs as "Logic" for full studio and notation environment. In my opinion; **" The difficulty of reading music, aside from physical deterioration, is a discouraging myth that was instigated and purged from the denial, realization or comprehension of the building of composition " " The build is the relief and key of knowledge to the interpreted and written composition "**. *The freedom of the mind !* My definition of Composition is; **" The Exaltation of the highest creative achievement for the profound humane truth professing virtuously in prodigal construct ".**

To be somebody in this world of music, you have to know your body. How to diet. You will use your body eventually more than an athlete. Because music is more intense in regard to sitting in a chair and not moving about. And you have to be your own physician. When I used to play jazz in Cafe's or an exclusive gig for the owner or a subjected specialized dwelling, you wind up playing day after day, or appearing at a short notice with unconformity, these are the days that you simply will lose your left hand. And it will vanish on you, from pain, if you abuse it, or over use it. This is more after you are 30 years old. When you are over the hill. In classical you practice the piece of music over and over until you can play it in your sleep. Thus giving you a different perspective and control. You manage to pull off the interpretation, if you know how much strength your body has. A slight difference from the two styles of music. You learn to monitor your body constantly. After a while you will arrange the date, set the time, play by organizing an exercise and eating habits. You learn to live with pain. You learn to live with starvation, so to achieve a productive working body capable of producing music. Which is the bottom line. You learn to play on an empty stomach or might chance a leakage which will set you back weeks or month's if neglected. You will find out that **non musicians are in another world of living**. From decade to decade you go through stages of bodily and physical ailments. You learn to control your organs. I often say, **what I improvise depends on my organs**. They are in charge of how the music is formed and when to let off and when to pick it back up. **This is also a luxury if you know how to improvise**. Actually, if you're over the hill, **this is the only way to compose or play period**. You no longer can read music. Unless it's privately because of bodily ailments. Or that's all you do with a big figure type of a body maybe with daily practice. You no longer can perform. Unless again, it's the only job one has and is kept in shape and practiced on daily basis exclusively. And it starts getting painful. So all the time is being wasted in that approach. Time is wasted which is the bottom line here.

Improvisation is the only path to follow in playing at will on daily basis of a creative enjoyment if desired as opposed to the others which are repetitive music on daily basis. This is the other side of the coin. And **composing is the luxury**. And if you're under age, then you're in contention with the great composers. That is very rare. One out of millions. And this is the epicurean reverent objective of my work and writings, theories, patterns and formulas pronounced and implied in thorough and diligent comprehensions…..

My everyday life and computers, is more important than other peoples demands. Although in the commercial field of business, yes it is the opposite. No one cares about how you feel, they just want to be entertained. The body is like a car battery. If you kill it completely, it will kill you back at the age of 50 on. If you give it time to re-generate, it will serve you again. **Moderation with non-abusement**. If you spend a week in a gym exercising strenuously in anticipation of a great musical performance or workout. Then you have exactly that same amount of time in witch to play, compose or perform. **No pain no gain.** And it is in comparison to a frisbee again. **The amount of time exercised is the amount of time produced**. The frisbee flight is of the same amount of time in the air as of how much power or thrust you deliver in its throw.

We live in a bullish monkey world. You are conditioned to think for instant drinking and smoking is the norm. At least during the years of my growing up. You have to follow and become like others to be accepted. Your own family sometimes drives you off of a cliff there unconsciously. Or a big event, as of the flower revolution did. Even president Johnson had hair down to his shoulders during the flower revolution. The world runs on money, monkey world. Don't be a follower, even if all the major radio stations are.

Chopin, Beethoven and others never owned a home. Beethoven moved on the average 11 times a year. And look where they are now. In every music store growing as the world grows. I'm not Beethoven, but I can say I moved 3 times in one month before. From apartment to apartment, house to house. At that time I did not know what was going on. That's why it's worth mentioning.

I've bought pianos from the salvation army outlets cheep in time and had ended up leaving them at the last dwelling in which I've also left my bed and anything else at the time and moment. I've lost all my records that I've owned while growing up. Anything owned is temporary, you have nothing to show, as one finds out by surprise. This happened over and over, not just one time. And to my mentors as well, as I find out to my surprise also.

Early in my youth, in junior high school. I've slept in the woods with no covers, coat or anything anticipating the bus early in the morning to take to school. As well as in high school, I've slept on the busses in the neighborhood with no coat or covers until the driver usually woke me up to drive his bus to work.

These are just some of the concurrences that one experiences. It's nothing new or unusual. And I will not mention the incidents from the adult stage of this ambivalent life style for its best forgotten for its serious reap and outcome. But I can mention that after having strokes, chest pains, arm numbness and weaknesses, angina blockages, one tends to shut down the mind completely until recovery. And that tends to cause forgetfulness in many fields. For example even painting. I have a hobby of somewhat amateurish jurisdiction, which is painting on canvas. Well, painting as music has to be learned all over from time to time, if one suffers the extreme chest pains or body ailments. Notation, as well as theories, as well as scales. Everything. This is one of the issues why my notes accumulated into this book. It's for, infact in-need to remember with. **A seasoned composer can turn his mind off completely at will from experience**.

Also serious music has the tendency to accumulate severity in the average human emotion and may cause instability and social unrest in human beings.

After 35 years old. You will notice writing music on paper by hand is not by all means like writing words on paper. Music is very painful to write by hand because your body is going through the piece of music, then you have to live the piece of music as you're writing it down. It feels as if you're playing, reading and writing all at the same time. Very painful physically and mentally after 35 years old. Especially if you've gigged weeks at a time. From club to club. Or hotel to restaurant week after week. Your body has had it. The object is to write quickly or eliminate playing passages over and over. That's the hurdle. Playing something and holding position until it's written down. That is fine under 35 years old. But after that it's torture for serious music that is. Therefore this method can also work in a direction of eliminating the holding process by improvisation in a program and there after notating it. And then one can add more layers once the initial score is complete, if so desired.

I accumulate improvisations in the summer time for a later date to notate. As a squirrel stores nuts for the winter. Occasionally I get asked to convert scores for oboe, flute, guitar or clarinet. Once the initial piano score is notated then it can be transcribed or orchestrated completely or for any instrument very quickly in a matter of minutes. Or giving the orchestra their parts in a matter of minutes. This is the power of the computer today. I improvised a 45 minutes sonata in 45 minutes one summer, it took 9 month's to notate, and one day to orchestrate after the initial notation period was completed.

In my mid fifties presently, I usually prepare three to four days rest and building nourishment for the primary day to come, to sit down and compose. Aside from paying bills and meeting choirs which are time consumption and a factor within also. And occasionally I treat myself to a piece of cake or something to look forwards to. And create a euphoric session from the food itself. Thus bursting out a short piano gem from time to time. That is rare though. And I don't quiet do anymore for the fear of diabetes does strike at an older age, and very painful and timely to content with. I take three to four days to rest and build up steam again, sometimes there's three to four days of constant composing. It's the nourishment in one's body. And how it is spent. Diet correctly and repeat the process.

Haydn would write a few bars only as he woke up each day and hand it over to his orchestrator. That is a luxury even from back then. Having servants take the heavy part. He would accumulate symphonies still in his seventies and live on. He understood his body. And took care of it. By knowing when and how much to write and or play. Eight bars a day adds up to symphonies yearly by daily basis as one lives a fruitful life of serious authenticity and a genuine standard. And opening the day with a creative riff or episode on the keyboard is a vastly enriching life to experience and enjoy. Giving birth to greatness on daily basis.. And all at ease confined within the subconscious of an unbound license of artistical truth and profound virtuous freedom.

∞ ∞ ∞ ∞ ∞ ∞ ∞

" God is Consciousness "
<u>The Religious Emphasis</u>
" Telepathy is signature of the Devine "

" *Whoever undertakes to set himself up as a judge of the truth and knowledge is shipwrecked by the laughter of the Gods* ". A.Einstein

Johannes Kepler - describes science *as* " *Thinking God's thoughts after him* ". " *God is Geometry* "

An honest Individual always learns his work. A thief always steals and cheats. Most great artists have religious connotations in their backgrounds. That's why they are great. A thief can't talk too much, or to anyone because he will give too much away and get caught. So he works in the shadows. Not out in the open. An honest individual will express his mind, his music, his art, his secrets,..... An honest person is productive, especially in the music field**. <u>An honest person is not scared, but sacred</u>**. There's a dichotic meaning between scared and sacred indeed. ∞ For honest people are scared, in-deed. Scared from others no doubt. ∞ An honest person is often also poor, where a dishonest person is rich. ∞ After one lives a while they learn the gloomy side of life. **<u>Praying means confidence</u>**. This is important in <u>performing or improvisations only</u>. Confidence is what everyone needs to look ahead without distractions, in the field of music. We are scared humans. A child or an adult. Humans still have the in-between thoughts that creep up at night or against a will and scare us. For children, the monster lies under the bed, or for adults the struggle to achieve against all odds. I've had more attempts against me, in an everyday working life struggle than I care to recognize. We humans are a scared species. This is an animalistic instinct. And is this where praying comes in? Prayers give us confidence, the bravery or the serene, divine intervention to go up against all odds, with contingencies. The calm, the brave, the imaginative substance needed. Sacred music is what started it all. Music originated from prayers and the church. From the monks chanting to the creation of the staff. Music was and is the creation of prayers.

There are 12 Key's in music. And 12 semitones. There are 12 hours in a watch. There are 12 month's to a year. The year when time according to the birthday of Jesus started it all. Which is the calendar year 1. It's what we use, all over the world. It's when time began for us on paper. Obviously there is something there. And it's religious musical and mathematical all in one. If we use the same fractions as the clock has in the octave of the piano conformed to time, then some one has programmed our minds to this mathematical entity. The physicists are also just now realizing string theory deals with these numbers also.

A jury has 12 jurors in it, also. Same as the clock and the piano. So does that mean that we have a programmed conscience already programmed in all of us weather we like it or not. This also reassures that any guilty person cannot live with himself or her conscience. So alluding one is harder than one realizes. Or lying before anyone is very easily detected. Music serves in more ways than one. Have we realized this yet?

Notation was formed in the churches of Europe. So its safe to say music started in the church. Classical music of-course. Which is taken in seriousness. Bach, whom is called the father of music was raised in the protection of the church his entire life. Joseph Haydn, the creator of the "Classical form" and "Symphony" was protected in a castle and paid to entertain in the "Classical form". **<u>In my experience, you mature through life spiritually, and with music unconsciously</u>**. " **<u>God is a greater intellect than humans</u>** ".

For example; The most important part of you of-course is your hands. I have managed to crush all my fingers, at one time in a garage door. Just happens the kid that lives down the street asked me if I wanted to play basketball at the house of the couple that were at our living room the day before in which I played to the German lady Beethoven. Coincidence my fingers were crushed completely the very next day in her garage door? A spiritual accidental coincident. Had them sown back together at the hospital. And she insisted in taking the stitches out eventually. Today I have smeared finger prints.

Another incident; Hit with an ax on hand and sent to the hospital again to get sowed back up. Hit by the kid that my buddy brought his record over and somehow we ended up scratching it on purpose. Coincident? A spiritual accident.

Split an artery with the other hand and gone to the hospital to get it sowed back up. Split one finger permanently, broke one finger by accident, almost cut one finger off with the band saw in school shop class. (by the way, the bone is milk white).

And today I've been diagnosed with melanoma cancer. And the majority of my thumb has been amputated. Had lymph nodes removed with four surgeries in which will stop me from ever being at the level I once was. In-fact some of the very theories that I created will be something of the past. But I'm glad I did it when all was well, for they have been proofed.

All these incidents are added up and realized in later life. Unconsciously all are hands accidents. I don't think it's coincidental. There is a spiritual element there. **Coincidences is God's way of manifesting.**

Society today is very vulnerable because of modern technology. The use of satellite, cell phones, computers, invades one's privacy and makes our every day lives much more vulnerable. Of-course it can work the other way also. But on the overall, the whole world can end up in your living room on daily basis. It gets old after a while. It has made everyone nervous in opening up or having an open mind for communication between one another. Fear and frenzy. So here is where praying comes in.

Praying is essential for me. It is of-course mysterious also. Praying is my best friend. God is my best friend. I appear to create unimaginative material subconsciously with the love of God. The relying on the greater powers. Relying on God for help seems to be the reward at the end. Unexpectedly happening. This is the secret aligned and affected by the surrounding factors. Crazy as it might be, But in this country it serves for piece and honor. It serves for the good, the humble and the honest. And that is the bottom line, and my experience since childhood. Even in Russia, Saint Petersburg, the religious community has produced many giant composers. That religious community has made history.

Einstein speaks of the search of those mighty universal laws from which the picture of the world can be obtained by pure deduction. There is no logical paths leading to these laws. They can be reached by intuition based upon something like an intellectual love of the object of experience.

God is conscience. **God is grounding**. And God works in mysterious ways. He sort of sets you out to work for him not knowing what is really going on. But only finding out later what has happened. We each have a job for the great creator to fulfill. But we only find out later in life when we see and understand more of the surrounding we're involved in. And what was the job that he had us perform for him.

The same is practiced in Hollywood, on the sets of movies. You get the picture of what is asked of you to act out and only later you find out what the skit is really about or how it was used. Sometimes everyone on the set is surprised by the outcome. As if someone greater or a greater power had channeled through the artists to fulfill a communication to benefit mankind and for all to see.

This country is in its 235 years of the preservation of the human race for all mankind to follow and be free, by using its binary, Initial primary principals as an example; Science and Religion. Republicans and Democrats, Structure and Emotion. **Government** & **God.**

____From the invention of electricity by Benjamin Franklin, who never became president. To the separation of church and state and reverend Martin Luther King whom was assassinated.

" Before we can have reason, we must have ourselves " – Keneth Pike

Experiences ....

Making the choice of music and business is important. When all said and done. It's the music and how good it is and how much of it that's going to make you or break you. Most bands or recording song artist, end up with a career and 2 to 3 good songs to their roster to be remembered by. **The Beatles are the only band that stands out at the top of my head that had many great songs**. And they jumped across all boundaries of genre's to do it. This is very dangerous in-deed. After certain tours their plane was shot at. Ringo was targeted in Canada, because he was found out to be Jewish, and we see what happened to John Lennon. They are the first of the song writers as I remember. In the right place at the right time in history when the radio, TV and the recording industry were just starting out. Never again will it be repeated. Today it does not matter anymore, it's all a working business and funneled to make money. So there is a chance to get noticed with bad music also, or not get noticed at all, which seems to be the latest. Even the very studio where the Beatles were recorded is for sale today. And was the same studio that England's greatest English composer of the 20'th century was recording. Sir Edward Elgar. Whom was on the English money and now has been taken off.

In the long run, nobody will remember. As you grow up, you get caught in the moment and get carried away or lose track and perspective. It's only when you look back after life has gone by, you see and understand the difference in music and how to judge each piece of music. **Today, we as the entire world need a department of education in music.** This is the first time in history that the culture is no longer in control of the music or the description of it. People like Johnny Carson, Steve Allen, Beverly Sills were musicians themselves when they were on television, so they would understand the level of musicianship in an individual and place them on the air justifiably in all genre's or style of music. The truth was out in the open. Today, some-one said music can create a world war.

Today it's hidden on purpose. Or there are no one who is brave enough to go up against the money machine. Fearing they would be replaced. **We are in-need of an authoritive figure to judge the**

commercial media and its production. There is no accountability in anything any more. It's the wild wild west sort of speak, again in the media industry. Especially in this culture of confusment regarding push button technology, a hundred channels of cable. And or the primary motive. Race, sex, drugs, and rock & roll. As the saying goes. Very few rational thinkers. I have played in the midst of all these events and all my friends are from this generation and the past. So I see both sides of it. And it no longer matters to any one any more. Only the average state of mind to sell these products to, happens to be a young mind. And the older mentality is no longer taken seriously. **Selling to children is the key motive**.

Hollywood caters to the young today. As someone said to be on television today you have to be goofy. Be prepared to catch anything from any direction and laugh about it. That is if you want to be back. The young are being conditioned to accommodate this way of doing business very early on in, any way possible. It's for the sake of selling a product. If technology has given rise to anyone to create something musically. Why not interest those that think they can also buy a machine and create ideas to sell. If others have done it, anyone can. We went from a hand full of musical acts to literally millions in one day, at the event of the creation of the computer. Therefore you have a flooded market driven by fame and commerce other than truth. Music is no longer the factor in the media industry. Not to mention how far dumbed down society has gotten. Children are born to this technology today. It does take many years of education to fulfill their minds to the truth. And that more than often happens at a later age. By then they most likely have been used to someone else's advantage, as I have been. And continue to. One becomes a cashed cow for someone else's advantage and not seen on the surface.

We didn't have the technology at first. This is alarming and proves to be even more dangerous, as brain-washing a manchurian candidate would fall in this category. An adult no longer wants to take part or participate in this wild wild west adventure. The media just reads the piece of paper handed to them or teleprompter and asks no questions. Trusting everyone already understands the peculiar and precautious situation of music at hand… And the recording studios have improved tremendously at the same time. It's a double edge sword at hand.

The recordings today are so good, that it is presumed and categorized from that point, before anyone can even say anything about the music. Musical acts are promoted with millions of dollars, and no one had heard their music, but trusted from the amount of money and the technology being poured into it, meaning it sounds better than good. Add a little relaxing substance with the mix and you have an enormous industry that feeds itself by multiple angles. Race, sex, drugs, and rock & roll. Rock & roll is even used for both black and white today. Or country and rock. Country rock. It's all mixed to funnel out money in any way or form possible. This is great for parties, a good time, or unwinding after a hard days work or weekend, maybe for some. But what about the people who get enthralled in this party. Started at a young age. And now grown up to be the world's oldest partier. How is that fair to the performers. (Keith Richards; known as the oldest partier, just said; he fell out of a tree.) This is where this studies have the advantage. By the way, Brett Michaels also just said that sex, violence, fear and greed is the new motive to sell today.

Today you alone can produce any kind of music spontaneous and by yourself at any time place or occasion. This is the truth of seriousness of anyone that wants to learn this language. It is not a party driven state of mind but a seriously profound entity to deal with. It does threaten the other side of the coin though. I have tried it all. And today, I do not veer off too far from my home. Nor go to the same places I once worked. Nor stay too long or talk about something too long at any given place. In-fact there are no were to go anymore. Not even schools were at least someone is seriously trying to understand. Schools are monitored and controlled for the same outcome, unfortunately. After all, schools are were the kids are. And even the professors are being controlled to go along with this fever. Once you're known, then it's all over, as someone said. I treasure my early day's of not understanding my surrounding but experiencing the many facets or sides to this business. Going along with the flow. The unbelievable moments and incidents that when looking back at, would now make me cringe. These things happen and 40 years later you figure them out.

Some incidents can be discussed, as of one I remember walking down a side walk on the day Martin Luther King was shot, when a convertible driven by a white man with a black woman sitting on top of the trunk on the back seat was firing a pistol at anyone walking. She took a shot at me and laughed out very loud with the white man nodding and laughing along with her. I didn't exactly grasp or understand that incident either, or believe it until decades later when I understood what has really happening.

Another incident I remember, I often would skip classes in college and spending the day playing the grand pianos in the music building while having a black man's face look in the little window of the door and smiling with a big happy grin. Decades later I found out that it was Dr. Billy Taylor. The great Jazz artist, composer and educator whom was from the same small town that the university I attended. Incidentally he just passed away. He was one of a few whom had talked and played with Jelly Roll Morton as well as Art Tatum or Thelonious Monk among all the rest of the Jazz Greats. I only found out many years later. Obviously because of the race factor we've endured from the past era.

And incidentally in this same small town I attended college, I found myself downtown in the middle of a riot in which had started by a black man with a wine bottle in his hand. He looked at me and nodded if he should throw it through a store window. I nodded to him not really understanding what was about to take place. But it erupted into a full pledged riot in which the national guard was called in to clear the streets with tear gas and platoon military force. Looking back many decades later I suppose I was in the for-front at the time and not aware of it. People were wearing Nixon masks giving the piece sign in the midst of tear gas etc..

My mother told me to go to the dean of the university and tell him I'm wasting my time in college and to drop out immediately in which I also had my dorm room bashed in by the sheriff department. My roommate at the time was a straight A student in which was arrested, busted for a minute small chunk of cannabis. And soon afterwards I had the first black roommate ever in the dorm whom was a narcotic officer graduate student as they said. This man looked like shaft from the movie. You can imagine what this looked like, I was the youngest in my circle of friends to go to college and this shaft of a character during the civil rights movement was my roommate, in the south, during the civil rights movement. At that time, most of the status quo still used the N word. Everyone lived that way.

Another incident maybe one can talk about, is the day the space shuttle exploded, anticipating the school teacher aboard. And at that time it was a news bulletin for only 3 channels, so the entire country was anticipating it with full coverage. And how hard it was to play at a restaurant that day. One could cut the air with a knife. But I went on to find out at a later date that it is us, that keep the public going from day to day, in incidents as these, not understanding it but at a much later date. Entertainers repeat performances to were if anything occurs, one simply goes into automatic mode and piles right through it. In some gigs I used to watch television while I played cocktail piano.

Another incident I remember is the individual that moved in the basement of the house I was living in showed me his license and it said Simmons. He said he was Gene Simmons's cousin. But no one at that time knew what Gene Simmons looked like because " Kiss " did not reveal their faces at that time. But decades later looking back he did show a close resemblance to Gene Simmons's face and features. And surprisingly at that time, weeks later I was with a new band playing " Kisses " music in clubs up and down the east coast, or playing with bands that were touring with kiss.

I was under age but no one asked. Some days I would have three girl friends lined up spontaneously. The groupies in the rock world are every bit true and very easy pray. I had to go out of my way to stay secluded. Today its quiet different, After all, before I played with bands, all these great artists wrote songs for us. What girl wouldn't want to experience this? As I'm writing this forward I'm rethinking 40 years back and finding out all these incidents in which I've dated almost all the girls not only in my neighborhood growing up but all the neighborhoods it turns out. I thought everyone did this, but now I'm realizing what I didn't at that time. Even one member of " Kiss " wrote a song about my girl friend's name. I just now found that out. Of-course I think we're calling it coincidences at this time. No one will honestly talk about it. And the real issue behind it is hidden while serious people are still alive at this time. Elton John used a lyricist also, so he didn't.

I played with a band that had the same name as Bob Dylan's band, "Topaz" in which one weekend we were playing opposite on the same street. Almost every band I came contact with offered me a position, but hesitantly I refused all because I couldn't take the memorization of four sets immediately from one band to the other. This was immensely draining, hard work and nerve wracking for me. In the seventies there were only analog keyboards, so one had to **memorize a set with the pre programming by hand live only in between or during songs and this required practice to pull off.** Very much hard work, as to the point where one becomes ambidextrous separately with two hands. If you ever see the keyboard player from the Band, with Robbie Robertson, (Garth Hudson) you will see what it does to a keyboard player from the seventies. One has two separate hands playing individually. Horns, clavinet, synthesizer and strings with one and piano and organ with the other. Completely separate parts.

Of-course looking back now, one realizes, moving from one band to the other is the way to go, and that should have been the path to take in moving up the food chain. I even was offered from a Hawaiian band that we played with one date. Female singers used to hook their leg around mine if I refused to play in their band, until I agreed.. And eventually I would give in.

I also had in the back of my mind that I would get to the bottom of classical music eventually. That was foremost more important than anything, obviously. I made more a fool out of myself, than any one else I know because of that issue in the back of my mind constantly luring. Someone said, **if you ever play classical music, you will never want to play anything else**. That is true, and embarrassing to persevere in front of other. Especially the public eye. I lost all sense of reality. People would eventually start attacking.

Which reminds me of my childhood. I will never forget after playing in school at ten years old. I was chased on my bicycle by two boys, cornered and spat on directly in the face while laughing at me. These incidents tends to scar one's emotions growing up. But only later does one recognizes the severity or the explanation.

Or when thwarted to get rest the night before taking the SAT exams at school. Someone shows up at your door step and takes you out and gets you drunk and drugged on purpose. I suppose I'm registered as an idiot on paper somewhere. These incidents happen unexpectantly but with deliberate outcome for the benefit of someone else. As I'm still experiencing today at the very issue at hand. And having to release my notes before being edited for the sake of copyright. No editor wants anything to do with the music business.

Because it's not the music business. Today its people listening on everything you do and putting themselves in between to act like they own everything you worked for, or they uncovered it. Its about them. Ironically falls in line with surrealism. Reminds me of the talent competition in schools, they would train a little girl all year to try to stump me when the talent show was called for. This went on in several schools.

During the birth of the rock era. It paid real money at the time. Almost all other genre's went out of business at that time. And I was just trying to find a peaceful place to sleep. Undawningly at the same house I was living in before I went on the road we experienced the next door neighbor whom was a Vietnam vet that killed himself. As well as one of my roommates staying at this same house who shot himself. I was elated to move to another environment, no questions asked…And the incidents escalated even bigger as time went on, in which one cannot talk about.

I'm thankful that the law enforcement today keep a watchful eye wherever I go. Which is mostly walking everyday. I owe my gratitude and respect and wave to them everyday as they park on the side to keep an eye as I walk my four miles everyday. And have great residue for the many days on call in Nashville or Hollywood and the many incidents experienced together through out across the United States as well as abroad. These are the best people society has to offer hands down. No words said can cover the intensive work they endure. And I owe my life and gratitude to them.. And this kind of talk in the past would have caused me to get fined, paycheck deducted, depending were and with which band I'm playing with at the time..

The many incidents that only can be translated at a later date when all of those that were part of, are long gone. Or weather from experience or knowledge one understands as it uncovers at a much later date. This is what I got out of my experiences and I'm documenting what little information anyone grasps out of it that may strike a truth factor, Is what will be all worth it for someone climbing up in his or her own life to experience and learn from. And this turns out to be my calling. Simply because I was denied the proper path in which should have been the most important element or motive to take. Because of the era or the surrounding group, perhaps? The many factors that were beyond one's control or understanding.

The other day I heard of an artist with an enormous amount of no. 1 hits to his belt on the radio. The truth is, as you can tell, I don't even remember his name. That's because out of his many no. 1 hits. Really only 3 or 4 at the most are really good songs. And he is just lucky to be in the right place at the right time. He is one out of millions of people, who have tried. And most likely didn't write any of the songs that are hits. So he will be remembered by only those good songs. It's like getting a life sentence in court today. What is 5 to 10 years in jail today is 5 to 10 month's with good behavior in reality.

Most good songs are hard to come by, so they're distributed by the record companies, by being in the right place at the right time. By the way the record industry today is not what it used to be. It's primarily kids and accountants working off and on. Unless it's a major music hub. Which have also somewhat dissipated within the computer invention. I say it with respect to all in the record industry of-course. Not that it really matters to any one any more anyway.

In the real world being recognized is considered making it in the Industry standard. For every million artist only a few get there. Today with all the different channels on TV and radio stations. It's nothing to be on. Only in my day growing up, We had one station for radio and television. And all was mono. He who got on, became instant star. I can name you quarter backs and the outstanding receivers of that era. Basketball players, golfers, even roller derby players. They are engraved in my head for-ever. Because it was the only thing we heard day after day. Today it's just another channel. And the ones who get recognized are short lived. And they are still among the few. Also even so politics is playing an even hand in it all. Race and nationality is epic. It's a kids world to say the least. Easy to depict. And also a dangerous one at that.

In my day, you could hitch-hike across the great "America" with nothing but yourself. And people would help you. You could return in one piece eventually. Then we started hearing of someone getting held up in another state, and barely returning with his life. Times have changed. If you add up all the great artist today and study them, I would bet, the ones that are your favorite are from the previous generations when everything made more sense. Or they're artists that have had the music industry behind them for decades. Nurtured and excelled to multi million dollar productions. That is not so today.

As I'm writing this forward, its believed that all the major labels of the past are dissolving. Its said that three to four employees are being laid off on monthly basis. In which have done nothing but work in the music business all their lives. The companies will be ridden to the bottom by the Ceo's until their closing, which is said to be at the end of 2010. There will be one company left called Universal in the west coast housing television outlets and just existing with minimum staff and one Ceo.

I assume Nashville will remain a small town but the biggest music hub in the world. It is being funded by the federal government from time to time after all. And the likes of Johnny Cash would tower over the average talent as John Wayne would tower over the average actor in Hollywood today. It's a much younger business today, housed for the young generation. The economy is being blamed for this. But I can assure you, it's not the economy. It's the many channels of television plus the computer and machine technology invention in which gave access to millions of people the opportunity to make music or create with. And this technology is also very high tech on the other side of the coin. So the past artists that have been fortunate to come at the time of the inception of the media business will rule or be the primary bill headliners until they're gone. And the new will house or support themselves and take a gamble for the next generation, next to nothing. Or just the enjoyment of it. I wonder what's or who are going to take over once these artist are gone. Maybe the seriousness of music will return, if it hasn't already.

Jay Greenberg is a 14 year old composer. Whom has already written 5 symphonies (at the time of this writing). He is considered the first in 300 years. Maybe things are looking up again. Will he take up the classical style seriously as Mozart did? So far it hasn't happened yet. But there are promises due to the machine generated industry present. There is good and bad in all, except in an injustice of-course.

Be aware of the crap shoot industry. It makes more sense to organize and arrange your life and follow your plan to good music consistently. Listen to those that have done it before you. Those with experience. Because that's what you will be remembered by at the end. Even if you don't make any money. It's very easy to be in the music business playing easy. The enjoyment is enormous.

When I was young I could tell a good song on the radio immediately, and I could get confused just as fast in getting fooled by another. The rage of the era at that time would do it over and over again. And you were expected to mimic with everyone else. It's only when time has passed by. You grow up and think about it all, that you can recognize a good song not just by sound, but by its format, or theory for one.

Mozart on the other hand, to speak of one composer, wrote the most beautiful music and all of over hundreds of pieces, were great. And will always be played over and over. And If you walk in a restaurant as a customer, even if you aren't going to dine, you are treated with respect or referred to as sir. Which is common of-course. But if you walk in a restaurant as an employee (pianist) you are treated like the hired help, or servants with dis-respect. That is how it was during Mozart's days, as he documented to his father and that is how it is today, in which I've been treated. In addition, the pun-dents, commentary of this era are very disrespectful. Loud as that of a large family fighting for the limited amount of food on the table.

The music business in my opinion is one of the most dangerous business to get into. It's different than any ordinary business where you finish college and get a job in the market place. It's involved in drugs and all the other elements that are dangerous in real life. The old expression; Sex, Drugs and Rock & Roll has been the expressed phrase of description since the flower revolution. And to be fair and not just blame the sex & drugs, **music is the most powerful art in existence**. That should about says it all. It immediately challenges the bullies who control everything. That does include any ordinary person also. Or the old saying," a man is the king of his castle " type of attitude. Or you have drawn all of my woman's attention towards you, and I'm mad about it. This is the usual attitude that one gets. Sometimes people scream at the top of their lungs in public or interviews. Sometimes the cashiers in the grocery stores open a new line to quickly check me out. Incidents occur uncontrollably on daily basis. One has to keep moving on constant basis. Can you see now, why Beethoven called classical music a woman? **This is not an ordinary job market placement. It involves ego and control recognition on a promotional public exposed scale of outstanding who is who and who is in charge.** It is not run by the music executives. This is something that needs to be pointed out, before everything else! Music is spiritual. The music business may not be, as all other businesses are secular. And it's the media business that any musician or composers go up against. Not the music business.

I do not talk about my mishaps for its best to let water run under the bridge. But if I mentioned my experiences it would not only scare anyone array, which has already done so, but most do not believe or comprehend it. Or it's forcibly suppressed. Real life sometimes is superficially passed by for the best out-come. Mentioning there has been more attempts on my life than one can account for or wish to concur which might turn some heads and get serious quickly to take all the fun out of it. This is the price one pays for defeating all odds and going by their own intuition in achieving serious work. Going against the grain. Refusing offers that cannot be refused. And not really understanding the outcome until later date in life.

It would sound utterly ridiculous if I said pope John Paul once bailed me out of a situation that escalated as they always do. Or having to reluctantly smile back at the Dolly Lama without making contact fearing something would happen as I'm getting ready to board my flight.

Or Richard Nixon used to say I looked thinner than piss on rocks during the Vietnam era when I used to play with bands. In which we actually were told to stop playing in a club one night while he got impeached on television. The good old days, that will never happen again with all the channels today.. Don't take it seriously it's all a mirage with great imagination. Until one faces the music. Then it definitely becomes an imagination in order to face reality and it's everyday events.

Most people in the music world are small people to say the least in reference to physical size and body. You are a target for others to take advantage of. You have to be aware and make situations livable for your-self. You have to understand. You become a target, literally. But once you understand it becomes easier. You will get offers that you can't refuse. But you have to, in order to continue to make your life successful in a subliminal form. Until it pay's off. And you should know when, if you have arranged and planned it.

A drummer for a band once beat one of my friends eye's completely shut until blood burst out of it, in order to get him to play for his band. But he still refused. I won't mention any more serious events, and there are plenty of events of even proportionally larger and more serious historical moments or national events that are best left alone. I'm only trying to share the truth and how ugly it can get in the everyday serious life at hand. But serious music attracts serious situations. And refusal is essential. But I'm not advocating refusing the Corleone family by any means. That is stupid ! Only I'm documenting the experience of any working young pianist getting dealt face to face with reality whipping by at a phenomenal speed uncontrollably and mis-understanding at the same time, passing by with everything in it bigger and greater than life itself, be it what it brings on daily basis or in redundant irony..

Getting offered $400 dollars a week to play piano in the 1980's is a guarantee only if you join the armed forces, the military, by a man sitting at the bar who sang very softly in my ear to reassure he was attuned. That is nothing more than what I would love to do, but I'm in the middle of working on the descending circular fourth and I cannot waist all that time and money spent, practicing while playing publicly. And I eventually paid the arm forces with a song that took me over ten years to complete. I wanted to offer my experience in patriotism the way I know best and can be fully effective and be appreciated in.

No one understands these things. It's a mission. Remembering to look at each project as time consumption. A recording project of other people's music is nothing new. Including the great composers music that is.

Playing with a band is a long term commitment that will stop your own career and what your music is and can be, if you are a pianist that is. Unless you happen to be one that has made it big. **And how would you know ahead of time ?** Remember the age factor. I played cocktail and classical piano in hotels and restaurants in the 1980's for fifty dollars a gig, for ten years. Broadway tunes, the standards, classical, straight and abstract jazz. Trio's, duos, big bands..And I learned from those that came before me, in which they got $5 dollars a night during the great depression. The biggest waste of time in regards to anyone's own career. But a grateful of knowledge and experience to have in regards to theory. I don't recommend it because of its bodily harm and time consumption.

 I learned classical music early from my mother In the 1950's and 60's. She instilled in me early on all the great classical masterpieces, when radio's didn't quite exist yet. We were, the radio. And that is how it should be today again ironically. In our household growing up, if you didn't play Chopin or Beethoven you got laughed at.

 Much less to mention the theatrical rock era of the sixties and seventies in which the disco era slammed right into.

Night after night, weeks of performing. Four sets a night. Ten thousand dollars is the set goal to garner from any one. And spent ahead of time split by a crew. Costumes, make up, busses, trucks, light shows, pa's, stages, expenses…Month's, years, decades. And declining these units eventually just as they begin to return higher investments and a signing of contracts that cannot be broken, for the persument of the truth, studies and variable understanding. Repeatedly over and over. ∞

Ironically as I discuss this with my mentors or older pianists that I have studied from that have come before me, I find out that they have also done the same thing to another extend maybe. And trouble, tension they have also witnessed and gone through for the sake of truth, knowledge and serious profound music and understanding. ∞

 So I took it on myself in order to pass down and document this knowledge for you. Take advantage of it. It will save you decades of work and wasted time. For It just so happens that the cards I was dealt had me take up this task, before I myself will dim down and completely have to stop, in-which I'm there today, and had just enough in me to give examples, video's, what was supposed to be impossible, wrong or false to anyone serious about learning the path to the musical kingdom. And what we went through in real live mode. The doorway to the musical concept, documented in a friendly picture. For I went against all odds and documented it for you. It did end my career and took everything out of me. But I finished my thoughts and confrontation of those that said it is false. And proved them wrong, or found, or uncovered the path that have been long paved over. For experience is priceless in which will eventually turn into our deepest insights and becomes concrete. ∞ " **Follow your heart in playing music but use your head in making decisions.**" You only have one shot at it. Life is short. And the music profession in my opinion is not something to learn and make money or make a living out of. Because it ceases at a certain age as an athlete experiences. Not to mention the luck of being in the right place at the right time scenario. So without a gamble, it's a profession that one can create material that brings joy and recognition as a hobby or for virtuosity, sad to say. Which if followed correctly will be recorded for life for the betterment of mankind. As well as keep someone's name alive forever. That is the irony. Give and take. ∞

Music is as wine. It has to ferment. And you simply cannot know what year will be a good one. Until it passes by. Therefore I have my own perspective and saying that goes something like this:

" Over time, experience not only gives you more information to use, But the exposure to the music that is creating the knowledge that can also spark the imagination in which can lead to a subjective understanding that can inhibit and bring about our deepest insights to come from pure reason altogether, and not experience ".

∞   In plain words; **"One day it will all sink in".**   ∞

The elegant style of the piano at a comfortable pace would be Chopin's elastic and mysterious and subtle method. While Bach's baroquing, short of the grandest instrumental accessibility that has the method with those certain fingering which allows the improvisations to flurry as well with motion and monothematic mysterious tempered restrained and poetic expressiveness. Aside from that approach, Bach's baroquing is also best used for compositioning at a bar to bar very careful attributing of weaving in harmony as recording does in a studio, track on top of a track. Meticulously done one line at a time. Virtuosity at its inception. Bach, the father of music delivering how the physical ability combined with the conscientious element of awareness can create the most structurally emotional divine and metaphysically mathematical composition for interpreters to perform in the highest artistic achievement with a scientific or a mathematical degree. Pure divine intervention. Or in plain words, weaving descends that will stay in your mind wallowing just as a great Beatles song would, but in an indefinite infinite enigmatic restraint.

The Chopin method of piano improvisation is also ideal for the playing of this method with both the science and emotion culminating composition mysteriously in one take. This is also referred to as incidental piano music. It is as of one singing through the piano at will. And free of all other limitations. The elasticity of the beat conforms to the creativity of the thematic element in live mode. Trills and garnishings are part of the composition or playing in one. It has also been described as playing on egg shells...

And the classical style of Mozart is elegance. As well as Beethoven's classical style is perhaps the most powerful to content with, in which I'm gratified to use as a must. The cymbal of power. The geometric patterns compared to a policeman conducting traffic at a multi faceted intersection. Conducting short strokes by definition in order to communicate by geometric patterns or classical directed riddles. Multi faceted to interact with all the keys as all intersections allowed for the harmonious patterns to flow traffic freely with control, taste, power and eloquence. Simplicity and memorability offer maximum opportunity for development and transformation.

Staying in-touch on daily basis is also a must. One must stay concurrent with their own senses and fingering to be able to hear what's asked of or needed to play. As to be able to figure out any piece of music structurally simple and quick. The inner self- being reminded and separated from reality. In practice with both distinctive elements. Science and art. And as for old age. After some time to rest, this book is the reminder.

The Harmonies are infinite. And all the keys are used at any time. At a drop of a hat. Without hardly thinking too much ahead of time. But enjoying the experience within the moment of creation. Be it thunderous tonal classical theories in which I've uncovered by ear, by reason, by science, by math, by accident, by experience, by subconscious, by geometry, by poetical or even abstract motifs. Or for the sake of sweet and happy entertainment. Just sheer enjoyment in the moment. !

" There are two ways to live your life. One is as though nothing is a miracle. The other is as though everything is a miracle " Albert Einstein

∞

This Theoretical Keyboard Method - A playing Technique : Unlocks the directions for the harmonious geometric or the poetical musical conceptual maze or map to follow from any angle properly. By target, sight, patterns and looks of direction, with ease of fingering and with an expressive spontaneous emotional artistic and tonal compositioning methodology. In plain words: Music as it's heard. As it's wished. In a spontaneous scientific emotional moment. And with the ability to create by the God given physical immortal attentive powers you can reach beyond the underlined structures of reality.

<u>The Binary Distinctive Traits and Elements of the Geometric Structural Human Brain and the Poetical, Political Dichotomy in an Artistic Divinity of Subtle Truths within One Conscience working side by side and hand in hand. Persevering the Reassurance and Preservation of the Human Race for all Mankind to follow in the Pursuit of Justice, Happiness with Virtue, Infinite Wisdom, Space and Time, Aware with Eternal Values, and the Freedom of.</u>

∞

∞

Classical - Jazz
Science – Emotion
Government – Religion
Reasonable – Unexplained
Explanation – Magic
Political – Poetical
Pragmatic – Spiritual
Deliberate – Passionate
Structure – Abstract
Hot – Cold
Left Brain – Right Brain
White color – Black color
Energy – Rest
Up – Down
Right – Left
Major - Minor
Legislative – Judicial
East – West
Tonal – Whole-tone
Main dish – Dessert
Dry – Wet
Title – Model
Contextual – Dependant
Mathematical – Metaphysics
Proven rule – Theory
Technological – Intellectual
Render – Poetic
Instrumentalist – Realist
Materialist – Idealist
Lawmakers – Literalist
Action – Talking
Marketing – Computer Prog.
Application – User
Interior Design – Cleric
Economics – Politics
Genes – Environment
Word Production – Emphasis
Banking – Sales
Grammar – Intonation
Factual – Literature
Clinical – Psych
Concrete truth – Abstract Truth
Reason – Reasoning
Constant – Symbolism
Harmonious – Dissident
Form – Anti-Form
Mechanical – Athletic
Build – Resourceful
Empirical - Theoretical

∞

Republican - Democrat
Restraint - Exuberant
Technique - Feeling
Geometrical - A vanguard
Tension - Resolve
Mind - Heart
Serious - Entertaining
Powerful - Vulnerable
Conservative - Liberal
Sharps - Flats
Manual - Automatic
Deliberate - Intuition
Decision making - Talent
Tonal – Modal
Defined - Sincerity
Immediate - Unpredictable
Semantic - Humanity
Sun - Moon
Fire - Ice
Worried - Relaxed
Plain – Sweet
Serious - Mysterious
Concrete – Philosophic
Resonance – Dissidence
Square - Compass
Direct – Subtle
Traditionalist – Modernist
Formal – Romantic
Rationalist – Extravagant
Librarian – Athletical
Coaching – Counseling
Retail – Accounting
Title - Model
Consulting – Human Resource
Self – Society
Subjective - Objective
Psychologist –Computer Technician
Put Together – Making it up as going along
Finance – Hospitality
Analytical – Creative
Engineering – Imaginative
Consonance – Dissonance
Instinctive – Conceptual
Time - Spatial
Symmetry - Asymmetry
Mixing & Engineering – Enterprising
Physics – Resolve
Logic – Experience
Normalcy – Revolution

Robert Kaye

Constitutional – Conceptual		**Design - Experimental**
Organization – Ideal		**Pattern – State**
Shape – Quality		**Configuration – Equality**
Framework – Original		**Construct – Inspire**
Anatomy – Innovative		**Arrangements – Expressive**
Form – Inventive		**Substance - Symbolism**
Knowledge - Intuition		**Events – Visionary**
Technique – by Heart		**Anatomy – Physiology**
Notation – Performance		**Being read – from memory**
Compositional – Improvisations	∞	**Improvisational - Compositions**

xlix

FURTHER STUDIES I

THE MODERN ERA

Pic Flute - Yellow to white
Flutes - Light Blue to thallus blue to yellow
Oboes - Orange to Green to Dark yellow
Clarinets - Blues to Greens to pink to dark yellow
Bass Clarinet - Deep Blue to Greens to light blues
Bassoons - Black to Purple to Lavender to orange to Blue to Green

Trumpets - light Brass or Red to yellow brass
French Horn - Red or Gold Brass
Trombones - Deep Brass Red to Medium Brass Plum
Tuba - Black Brass to plum Brass

Violins - braze to light orange to yellow
Viola - Braze to deep orange to yellow
Cello - dark Braze to gold deep orange to yellow
Bass - Black to Deep brazen to dark orange

Key of C - White
Key of G - Yellow to orange
Key of D - Greens, turquoise and Blues
Key of A - Orange, peach and Greens
Key of E - Gold red and Oranges
Key of B - Brown, lavenders and Deep blues
Key of F# - Purple, dark blues
Key of Db - Deep Blue to blues to Deep lavender
Key of Ab - Blues to Light Blues to thallus rose
Key of Eb - Blues to greens to light Magenta
Key of Bb - Greens to blues to orange
Key of F - Blues to Greens to yellows
Key of C - White

My Feelings towards Sounds, Instruments and their Temperaments.

" *Art however beautiful, is not Art, but Art is natural beauty interpreted to human temperament* "

Art is the Accomplice of love

R. KAYE

ART

Oil & Acrylic

Our own world is mere the shadows
of the eternal ideas of Heaven

plato

I often get confused sometimes because in classical music; The terms harmonic minors are often referred to as minors. Where in jazz one is clear what key or which minor is being referred to. In classical music one is naturally to think of harmonic minors when referring to minors. In this study, I will try to refer accordingly. Whether it's natural minors or harmonic minors or melodic minors. Etc. (Note: true or perfect harmonics lie in the classical minors). I have also included pictures of the examples. If you do not wish to read the notes. Pictures are worth it. It's the picture of the chords that we want to relate to sound. The hand positions, the fingering. The keyboard...I had wished for the publishers to include the different colors of dotting, but that was not possible. The notation can clarify if needed be.

One takes consideration that you already have some knowledge of chords. The basics. The basic scales and their fingering. The classical fingering and the jazz fingering. The difference are only in a couple of keys anyway. And for old people as myself, fingering means taking care of your liver and kidneys, and the fingering will work just fine. The basics meaning the root position. 1-3-5. Basic chord structure and reading notation skills. Which is the standard terminology from any book.

In this study. I will not try to fill the pages with words and musical didactorial complicated terms. For example: There is no need to use such terms or symbols from the figured or thorough-bass figured system of the baroque era.. Or notation descriptive analysis. Because it will merely confuse the targeting method of this book. In fact it cannot be done. I will more less get to the point. And waist no time nor confuse respectively. The terms (1st; 2nd; 3rd.) could mean (root, 2nd. & 3rd.) Or it could mean (root, 1st inversion, & 2nd. inversion.) There is no need for these type of confusements. I, II, III can mean anything. Eliminating notation analysis and symbolism with keyboard fingering positions and target notes creates a path or the pre planned method and the targeting memorization path that leads to a harmonious and a well thought out solution. Conformed, prepared and arranged structure. From the fingers and the keyboard.

Enharmonic notes or keys are the same in regards to target and sight. Which is the true pattern, sought on the keyboard. Therefore there is no need to use notation descriptive analogy when this is a keyboard method. Or a cadential approach. It simply defeats the purpose of understanding or gaining a vision. And when notating your composition, you can use the correct sharps or flats at that point. Note; What I use on most keyboard pictorial examples can be a flat or sharp depending on your compositions. Another words a Db can very well be a C# if used in a composition in that key. Because I do not use other composers captions, or any composition as an example. then the structure can be used from either side depending on what key you are in**. But the target and sight of 12 keys only, is simplification ideal for improvisation**.

I would advise, If you decide to use this method. Do not try to analyze by the standard terminology for it will erase your memory of this methodology. I quote from the standard "Tonal Harmony" text that is used by more than 800 colleges and universities. P. 46 (" You might assume that third position would be the term for a chord with the 3rd as the lowest tone, but musical terminology is fraught with inconsistencies") un-quote. Professor Dr. Robert Greenberg, describes it this way; " Terminology of music is as inexact as the music it purport to describe ". Another words describing music does not tell you what the composers are using.

This method that I've uncovered is the classical cadenza within the sonata and all else. Even the 2-5-1 jazz voicing is described from the cadenza fingering. From that perspective. I do not know of any other book on the cadenza. Which is the primary Improvisational technique that the great composers used. Because the fingering of the keyboard is fluent from the cadenza, then one would assume all analysis is described from the cadential position, but that is not so. All analysis is described from the root position with notated symbolized terminology. Which produces the modern so called western contemporary sound. And not the indigenous classical sounds of the great composers. i.e. Bach, Beethoven, Mozart, Haydn, Chopin. Again I quote from "Tonal Harmony" page 145. The cadential six-four : It is Important at this point to emphasize that the cadential I6/4 does not represent a tonic triad, even though it contains all the notes of a tonic triad...This has led to much debate over the years as to what symbols to use to represent the cadential six-four. Your instructor may use a different method."). Unquote. This book is the other method and the only one I'm aware of that describes the concept of music from the cadential 6/4 and all else from, in which I call 5-1-3.

Also If you happen to spot typing mistakes, please keep in mind this project initially started from my notes for personal use only, and was encouraged by educators to pursue for publication. I am a composer not a book writer. I've done my best to correct the typing errors. In some printings the page numbering referrals are off, but have been corrected. And I started printing and published on the first edition early on because I noticed my work was being echoed by others. This idea or my ideas have always been echoed by others in colleges or media outlets. Therefore I directly started publishing from the first edition just a skeleton being formed till this edition. I'm also notating hundred or thousands of pages on daily basis as well as recording cd's and mixing and engineering all at the same time as I'm writing this book. So my efforts are aimed first and foremost on my music and second hand towards this book. A book award I'm not trying to achieve. But this book is what I use on daily basis. This is why I wrote it. It is impossible to write as much as I do without it. And am constantly finding out the true or real definitions of such in which have been twisted over time, or have not been seriously discussed. As I do, of such issues for example; Romantic is confused with poetic. As impressionism is confused with Improvisations. Or the misprint of a date, to naturally flags up copyright.

One quick note; I use b as the sign for flat. As in Bb or Db. It should be smaller of-course. Also in any notated bar the sharps or flats cancel out just as in any ordinary notation would read…

Once you cover the first three chapters, then you should have the perspective on the "Classical Method". And once you see where you should go, then you will want to continue with the further studies chapters. It's from then on you will build on the twelve key harmonic or symmetrical donut that continues to grow in circumference. And at the end I have stopped at the point where jazz has evolved. You can continue on your own if you wish, exploring the pentatonic, Modes etc.... Ravel did. Although Chopin's method touches the sharpened diminished whol-tone and returns. Chopin was the connecting link to the whole-tone era. Science and Emotion, Geometric and Poetic. All in one. Using the piano.

It's your wish were and how far to get. This journey of evolution from a spiritual enlightenment to the spiritual evolution of today's modern times. We have evolved in harmony. And I thank God for giving me the creativity to go on from day to day, and to continue and evolve another day. Using my knowledge and experience at heart and hand.

Please note: Everything said and done in this book is my, and only my opinion. It's from my experiences and no one else. I respect any other one's opinions and or objectives for the sake of knowledge and truth. My primary goal and concern is to show others that will be following, what and where to point in order to achieve. And what I didn't have available. What we didn't have available. And the mistakes learned from. Therefore, it's primarily and foremost from my experience in going about the right path to foresee ones goal, educational motive and accomplished achievements. I have been driven, possessed and devote my life to this profession.

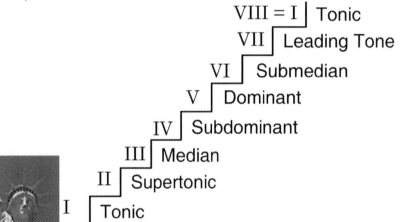

VIII = I | Tonic
VII | Leading Tone
VI | Submedian
V | Dominant
IV | Subdominant
III | Median
II | Supertonic
I | Tonic

The Seven degrees of any key or Musical Scale…. " Everyone has 7 Talents " – Bible Quote
The seven virtues
The seven sins
The seven wonders of the world
The seven sacraments
The seven seas
The seven continents
The seven steps to heaven – Heaven meaning the Diminished seventh – VII Leading Tone
Creating Improvisational composition by using the Seven degrees - **Classical**
Creating Improvisational composition by using the Diminished seventh by itself – **Romantic**
With the exception of Beethoven's style of-course, his Diminished can garner both.

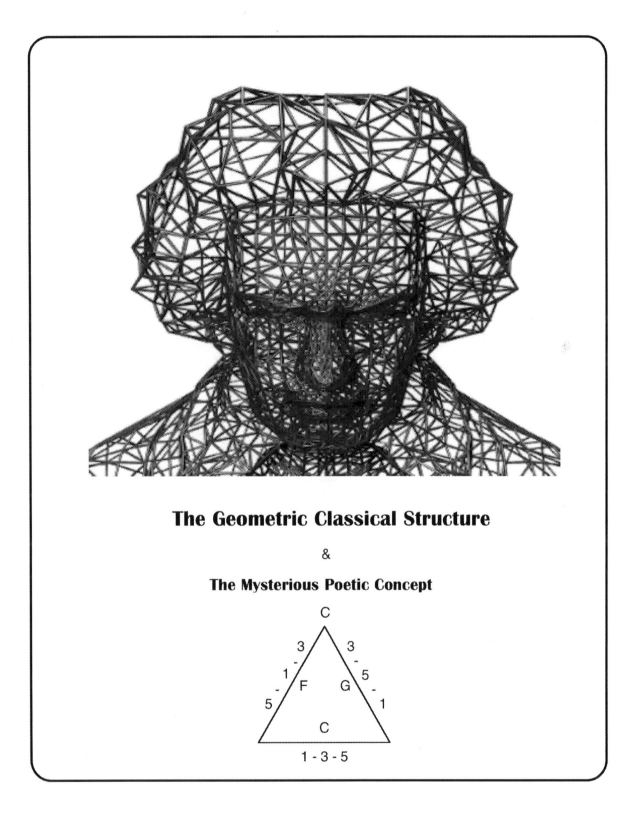

The Geometric Classical Structure

&

The Mysterious Poetic Concept

Chapter 1   5-1-3 Triads
The Classical Third position

These Twelve positions are the Major building blocks of the "Classical Method". They are the essential part of this study. They give in return a technique unlike any other. Mathematically one can explain the product but that's for a mathematician and another day. I can only Theorize what I know from facts. Facts from hearing, playing and facts from the obvious numbers that one can see and explore if desired. Because the 5th is on the bottom or the root, then the door will always be open to play in all the keys with ease. And circle eternally from one key to the other automatically. This 5-1-3 folding technique will enable you to play, not only with out of tune instruments, but instruments that date back to where the dissonance cannot be heard. Or they will not sound like today's pianos. Therefore a blessing if you own a cheap piano. It will give you a whole new perspective in playing modern day synthesizers or string machines. It is the classical element of the orchestra sound of Strings.(Structure). You will be able to technically play symphonies with string machines of today's date. The folding sonata elements of the 5-1-3's are a technique that will be your friend for life. And enrich your playing ability. These are the basic elements for Rag piano, needless to say. Rock piano also, in which no one uses. After you learn this chapter, you can automatically fall into the next chapter. One chapter will automatically throw you into the next. There are three basic steps or chapters. Once completed, then you should see a whole new concept of playing. These triads are one half of the Classical pump. The Tension building pump. The other half is the Dominant. Between the two: The Sonata form is born. Which is the heart of The Classical Method. The Sonata : Structurally and Theoretically it's the heart of the Classical style, Where the fingering is fluent for Improvisational Tension building and release back to the tonic. The Sustain pedal is also born at this time. Originally created with the 3rd. Position Triad. (2nd. Inversion). Anchored with the root note concrete therefore securing fluent fingering amidst Improvisation as the dominant is resolved to the forth up. It could very well be the most defining and Important concept in structural usage in creating music. (Improvisational Composition / A musical Conversation). Straight Jazz, Ragtime, even Bop uses this structure of the Sonata form. Tension building and release using the Dominant and Tonic. 4th from the bottom and 5th. from the top. The Leading pure-tones : 4th & 5th. Harmonize in eternal circles as well as building tension and release. Also used with the Minors thus creating fluent Improvisation that circle eternally. The Musical structure from as early as the baroque and the classical style was formed. Which is Classical Improvisational Compositioning. And all other styles followed using this format; Fugue, Minuet, Prelude, Bagatelle, Ballad, Barcarolle, Bercuase, Etude, Kreisleriana, Nocturne, Polonaise, Scherzo, Fantasie ..etc

1

1-3-5   3-5-1   5-1-3

What do we mean When we use Numbers

Simply the Scale is made up of 1-2-3-4-5-6-7-1-2-3-ect....

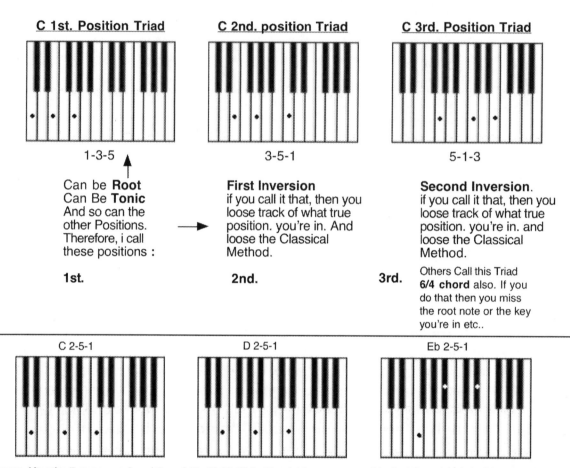

C 1st. Position Triad	**C 2nd. position Triad**	**C 3rd. Position Triad**
1-3-5	3-5-1	5-1-3

Can be **Root**
Can Be **Tonic**
And so can the
other Positions.
Therefore, i call
these positions :

1st.

First Inversion
if you call it that, then you
loose track of what true
position. you're in. And
loose the Classical
Method.

2nd.

Second Inversion.
if you call it that, then you
loose track of what true
position. you're in. and
loose the Classical
Method.

3rd.   Others Call this Triad
6/4 chord also. If you
do that then you miss
the root note or the key
you're in etc..

C 2-5-1	D 2-5-1	Eb 2-5-1

Of-course After the 7 comes an 8 and 9, and 10, 11,12,13 but for right now you must look at these triads in this respect or you will loose the Improvisational picture and the Targetting Method. And its Roots. These others below are just for expansion. We will hardly use any of these in this book. no need to, for what wer'e trying to achieve. But these are for the modern Era which is Discussed in this Book for Reference, Clearity and Improvisation.

Note: I look at the keys in this format for speed in thought and only one sound per key to content with :

1. Am is in the key of **C**
2. Bm is in the key of **D**
3. Em is in the key of **G**
4. Bbm is in the key of **Db**
5. Ebm is in the key of **F#**
6. Abm is in the key of **B**

7. Fm is in the key of **Ab**
8. Gm is in the key of **Bb**
9. Dbm is in the key of **E**
10. Cm is in the key of **Eb**
11. F#m is in the key of **A**
12. Dm is in the key of **F**

This is much better to understand in Improvisations,
Be it en-harmonic keys or notes. The traditional way is
for notation only, which confuses to the point of serialism.
Notation is very simple. But it should be concidered only
after the motif or the fact of the musical content completed.
Not during.

But the Book is en-harmoniced correct for reference and not to be confused by. if you want to play
fluently with any sound called up immediately at will and by the speed of thought, then you
must comply my path only. And only this will give you the proper tone called at heart and mind
spontaneously at will.

How to Achieve these Triads by their Numbers

1-3-5   3-5-1   5-1-3

| 1-3-5 | 3-5-1 | 5-1-3 |

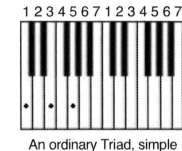

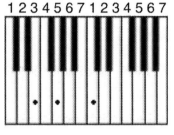

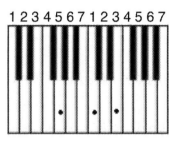

C

An ordinary Triad, simple enough. Everyone knows these 1st. position triads.

Please don't mistake position for Degree. 1st. Degree 2nd Degree ect.. these are positions ! And that's How i look at it.

This is the 2nd. position Triad. Not every one knows these triads. So its an E minor #5. Or a diminished b7th sus 5th. That's how these are found. But not used as much as the next position. But can be Found from the 1st. position. Since Everyone knows the 1st. position minors already. Therefore need not be Memorized.

This is the 3rd. position Triad. This is the Heart of the Improvisational or Classical Technique and Mechanism. **These do have to be Memorized.** They are the only triads that have to be Memorized. If you Memorize these 12 triads. You will Improvise Classical Music. If you were to ask a non Classical pianist what these are. You will get a number of different answers.

If You're wondering why not use the major seventh Chord ? It's because of numerous reasons:

1. If you use the seventh as in a major seventh chord. Then you will lock yourself in that key. Yes you can play fuller. Which is what any jazz teacher tells any student on the first premise. And that sounds wonderful for Voicing. But if you use triads only then you can change from key to key and not even notice, sound wise. Another words you can use all the keys all the time. I wish there were 24 keys. Can you imagine how much more music there would be ? Some call the minors ; keys. I call them a mode. In-fact in notation you can use any key to have the players play a different riff switching keys. I call this modal.

2. You have to understand and keep up of what and where you are going with your Improvisations and compositions. And how to achieve the sound that you're hearing. If you use the seventh then you have invited anything. You will loose your constructions. You want to keep up with your sound structure. As you're hearing or wanting to play as Beethoven heard it in his Head. Because he was the deaf one. Ironic or over use of sound, mind and Body. You can shake the Earth if you want. Major seventh chords are so full, that even the ear gets confused. And one cannot keep up with collages. Floor level.

3. **Triads** Construct Composition. **Major Sevenths Chords** create Voicings, good for already constructed compositions. Or in the case of non-tonal abstract, where anything goes, nice voicings from Maj7th's are welcome. Straight jazz & the blues and classical music are all about dominant 7th's. They're eternal. Tonal music can lie in both of these styles.

4. Major Seventh chords are for songs mainly. You can construct with them, but its going to take up most of the notes with lushness. Or very sweet. Once you use all the notes possible, then there isn't really much left to use. Using triads for the tonic instead of major seventh's secures the composition as infinite. Another words it isn't sweet or too salty or too of any spices. It's neutral. Therefore the tonic will always be a new position to start an idea. That is the constructive basis that allows composition. Furthermore, the 5-1-3 & 3-5-1 both have even a widder split in them for further clearity than the 1-3-5.

5. Triads allow the construction of a building. The architecture. And major seventh's paint the building already constructed. You can construct with major seventh but they only allow so much. Therefore, one can never change moods or style after a while. And if to use major seventh's continuously, then one would be just painting with colors. In which I call abstractism. Or nontonal. The definition of surrealism is also mixed here. Or minimalism is also confused in this aria. You hear Bach's music said to be as abstract. Or mozart's music. By PHD's. These are very far assumptions that might have some merit of distinction. Or an insinuation by abstract definitions itself. Another words, for the same reason Beethoven is still considered contemporary. This is also a fray in definition. Where time has twisted the meaning of the description. So disregard what you hear in words and listen to the style or form of music for proof. After all there is straight and abstract jazz also. So where do you draw the line. Maybe going outside music and to compare art with music, best help describe the true meaning of the definitions used. Draw analogies from outside sources. Sometimes, even that is not correct. But it can help narrow down and simplify for better clearity of definition. A picture is worth a thousand words and called a composition in the art world. This is the method I created, from pictures of the triads and the constructive rendering using geometric poetry .

5-1-3 Triads

Example 1

Majors: 513

These are twelve Triads that have to be memorized by looks !!!!. By sound by familiarity. By feel.

It's only twelve of them so it should be easy. Here they are cromaticaly, not in any particular order.

They are the major Triads in the third position. Or II Inversion. Learn them by Looks !! Thats the trick.

The minors are simply the same with a flattened 3rd.   Picture charts are supplied to explain 513   Example 1
                                                            Scales : for the Right Hand   Example 2

Scales for the 5-1-3 Majors : The 5 is major / The 1 is major / The 3 is Harmonic Minor

Minors : 513   Example 2

Scales for the 5-1-3 Minors : The 5 is Harmonic Minor / The 1 is Harmonic Minor / The 3 is Major

After you get familiar with these Triads. You then practice circulating them in 5th's.

Which is the basis of the classical method. This does not require memorization:

Bacause you now have a target to use just by looking at these chords. The target is the first note from

bottom, which is the 5th. If you use the first note from the bottom, it will throw you into the circular

5th, weather you go up the keyboard or down the keyboard. Example 3 & 4 pages 15,16

Recap Scales : Majors :   Major / Major / H.Minor
              Minors :   H.Minor / H.Minor / Major   Remember them This way !

The Root of The Classical Method

Memorize These as **Symbols** .....As Well as The Minors on the Next Page

Example 1   5-1-3 MAJORS

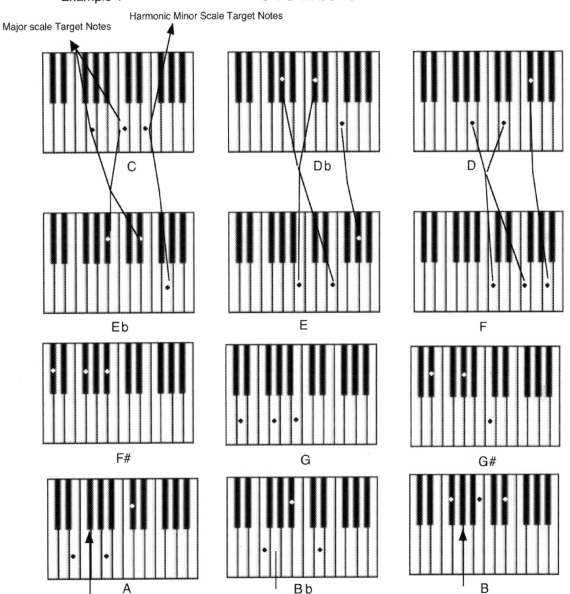

Major scale Target Notes

Harmonic Minor Scale Target Notes

C   Db   D

Eb   E   F

F#   G   G#

A   Bb   B

Also with the Majors you can play the Harmonic Minor Scale of the **Natural** & Dominant Minors, and the Secondary minor as well. The **Natural minors** which are Targeted 1 step above the 5. (Shown above) And the 3 is the third finger. The secondary is 1 step above the root. Ex: C Major 5-1-3 - its **A Harmonic Minor Scale** and the third is E Harmonic minor. And the secondary is D Harmonic minor scale. In all 7 Degrees. The Purpose for all these scales is the Fingering. Certain Keys are difficult to finger so the Variety makes it possible for Fluent Improvisations. As well as a Variety of Harmonies to use. Chopin's and Bach's methods use these religiously. Chopin general folds continously with the natural minors and Bach baroques with continous descends using all the positions for in-depth folding.. But a rule of thumb to use only the harmonic minor scale of the **Natural minors** with the majors, for they are the closest to the major scale. Especially if you have a melody locked in. Or you're using the triangle from page 101.Or geometrically the strict classical style. Only Bach differed, because of the baroque style.

The Root of the Classical Method

Example 2

5-1-3 MINORS

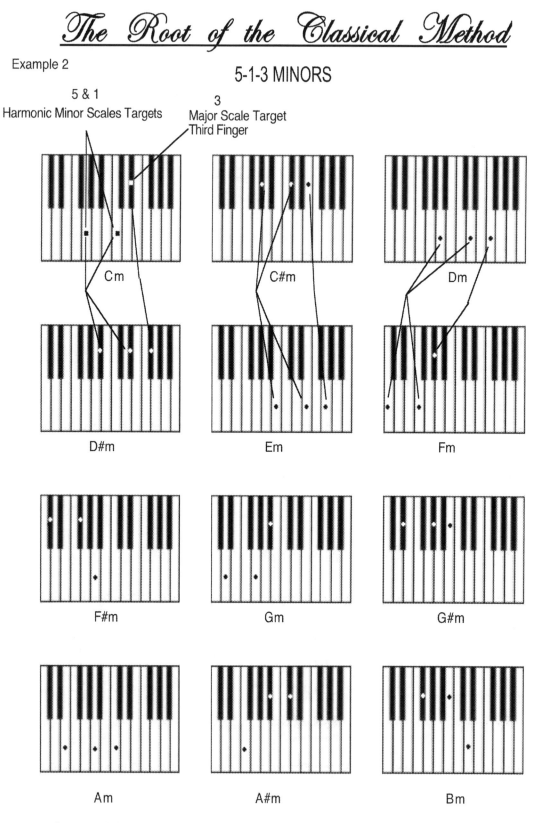

Start practicing with the Major Scales first then gradually implement the H.Minors.

The Sonata Form

The Majors

Basic Folding the 5-1-3 triads

Example 5a

This is the mechanics of the "Classical Method", The motor, The engine, The format. The basic Theory.

The order in which these are written here does not matter nor do they sound like they make sense.

The object is to get familiar with the positions, to see them, to feel them, to have a sense of trust that

the Mechanics or the format will play the harmonics for you automatically. Most importantly see them.

The Majors

Example 5b

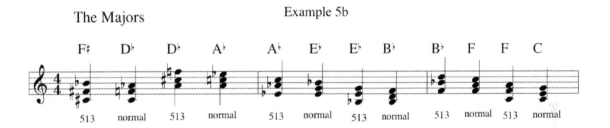

These should fold in your hand naturally. After a while you can add the seventh to the normal

first position and make them into a dominant 7th. If you have played Jazz then you can move

Further along. We're keeping it simple for right now. And mind you simplicity in this form

is very rewarding. It means tastefulness, Motzart stayed in this form. Very Elegantly.

Next: look at the minors before going on to the scales of these positions and then one is

on their way to improvising and composing.

One assumes you have been exposed to the fingering of the scales already. If not; You should.

Purchase a chart on fingering for both hands. Which is necessary for improvisational dexterity.

There are Classical Fingering and Jazz fingering. I use both, mixed sometimes..

Robert Kaye

The Sonata Form

The Majors   Folding

Example #5a

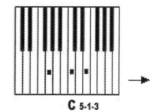

C 5-1-3

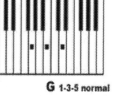

G 1-3-5 normal

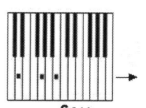

G 5-1-3

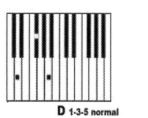

D 1-3-5 normal

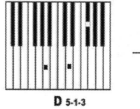

D 5-1-3

A1-3-5 normal

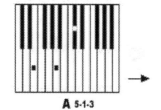

A 5-1-3

E 1-3-5 normal

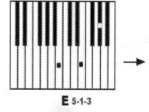

E 5-1-3

B 1-3-5 normal

B 5-1-3

F# 1-3-5 normal

The Sonata Form

Folding

The Majors

Example # 5b

F# 5-1-3

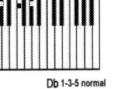

Db 1-3-5 normal

Db 5-1-3

Ab 1-3-5 normal

Ab 5-1-3

Eb 1-3-5 normal

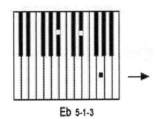

Eb 5-1-3

Bb 1-3-5 normal

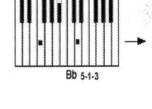

Bb 5-1-3

F 1-3-5 normal

F 5-1-3

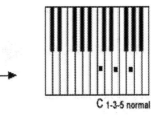

C 1-3-5 normal

The Sonata form
Basic Folding the 5-1-3 minors

The Minors

Example 6a

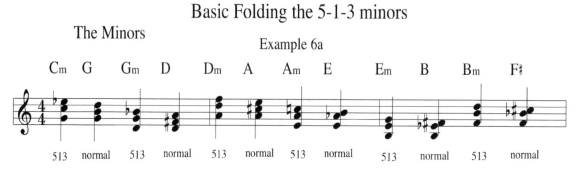

You notice we went from minor 513 to major normal position. There is no rules at this point, you can go from any Minor to

any position. Or first position as its calledLater on you can try what ever you wish, but for right now just follow.

Just Follow !!   Just Follow !!

The Minors

Example 6b

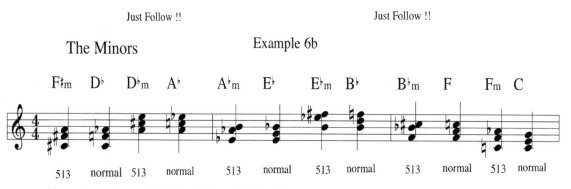

If you have learned all the 513's and folded them.

Then you are almost there. Next are the scales that go with these exercises.

Of-course one assumes you already know the major scales. And one assumes you already know
The Natural Minor scales which are : The third of any 5-1-3 Minor. The last finger. TARGET !

The major scales of 1 and 1/2 steps up from whatever minor you are at.

Example 9 a : | The Natural Minors |

Play scale with right hand for Improvisation

Hence: Am is the key of C Major.
Bm is the key of D Major
Em is the key of G Major
A#m is the key of C# Major
D#m is the Key of F#Major
G#m is the key of B Major

Fm is the key of Ab Major
Gm is the Key of Bb Major
C#m is the Key of E Major

Cm is the key of Eb Major
F#m is the key of A Major
Dm is the key of F Major

same ——— Bbm is in the key of Db Major
same ——— Ebm is in the key of Gb Major
same ——— Abm is in the key of Cb Major

Note: The en-harmonic keys are the same because
this method uses looks ! for Improvisation.
But for notation afterwards, it must coorespond
accordingly as usual notation does for its given key*

The Sonata Form

The Minors

Folding

Example # 6a

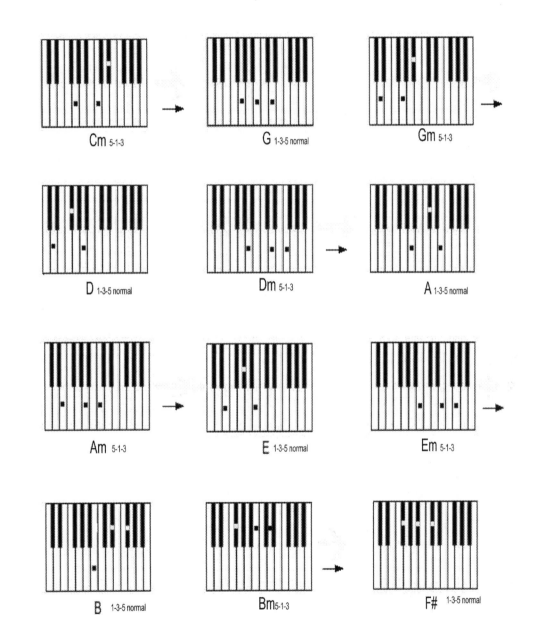

11

The Sonata Form

FOLDING

The Minors - Continued

Example #6B

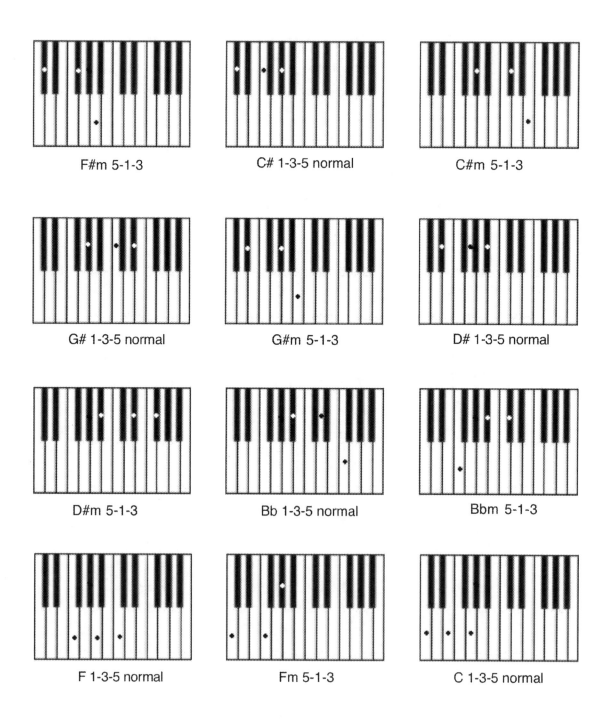

F#m 5-1-3

C# 1-3-5 normal

C#m 5-1-3

G# 1-3-5 normal

G#m 5-1-3

D# 1-3-5 normal

D#m 5-1-3

Bb 1-3-5 normal

Bbm 5-1-3

F 1-3-5 normal

Fm 5-1-3

C 1-3-5 normal

The Harmonic Minor Scales

example 8   Flattened 3rd. & 6th.

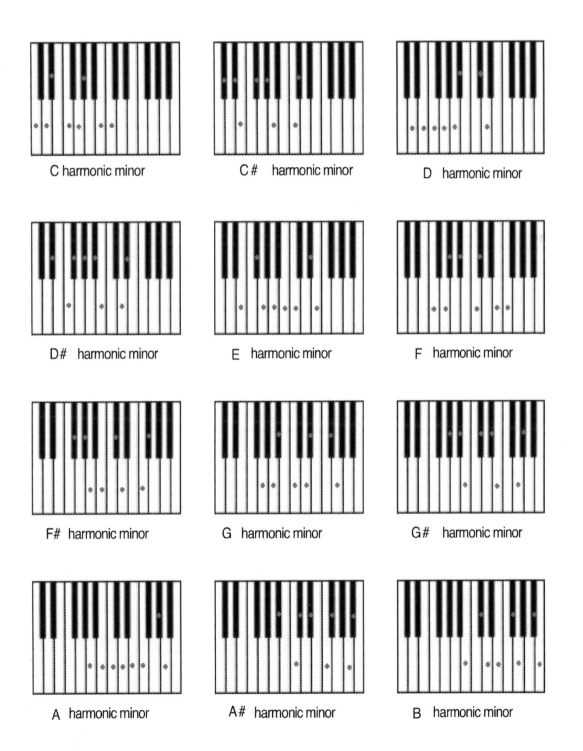

C harmonic minor   C#   harmonic minor   D   harmonic minor

D# harmonic minor   E   harmonic minor   F   harmonic minor

F# harmonic minor   G   harmonic minor   G#   harmonic minor

A   harmonic minor   A# harmonic minor   B   harmonic minor

The Major & Minor Circular 4th & 5th

The Major 5-1-3's in circular 5th's

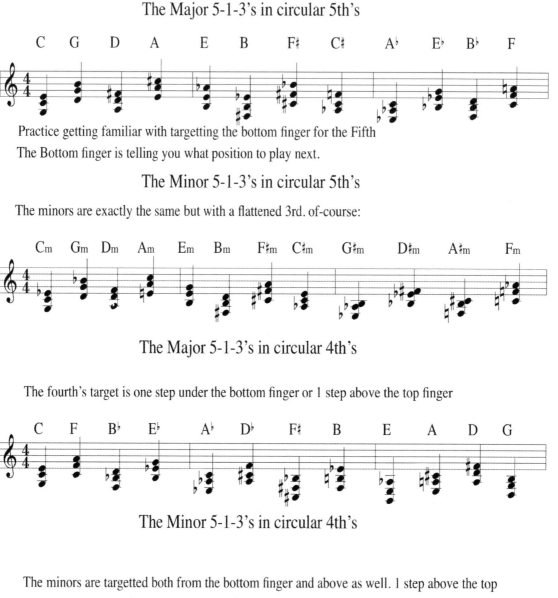

Practice getting familiar with targetting the bottom finger for the Fifth

The Bottom finger is telling you what position to play next.

The Minor 5-1-3's in circular 5th's

The minors are exactly the same but with a flattened 3rd. of-course:

The Major 5-1-3's in circular 4th's

The fourth's target is one step under the bottom finger or 1 step above the top finger

The Minor 5-1-3's in circular 4th's

The minors are targetted both from the bottom finger and above as well. 1 step above the top

Of-course all these positions are to be practiced with their folding families we just covered. Their Dominants

Fold each position for 4 bars while creating a melody with the right hand. Then move to the next position.

example 3

The Major 5-1-3's in Circular 4th & 5th

The Major 5-1-3's in Circular 5th's

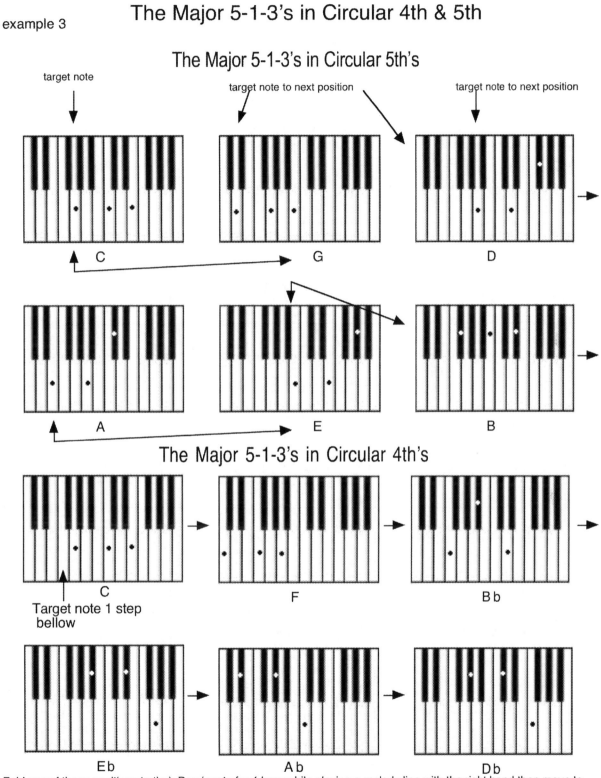

target note

target note to next position

target note to next position

C

G

D

A

E

B

The Major 5-1-3's in Circular 4th's

C

Target note 1 step bellow

F

B b

E b

A b

D b

Fold any of these positions to their Dominants for 4 bars while playing a melody line with the right hand then move to the next position and repeat. Mix alternating between 4'ths, 5th's, going from one position to the other. If you master these positions then move on. By the end of this book you will play these <u>position's fold</u> without even playing these posiions. By-passed just from seeing one step ahead. It adds that much more mystery to the Classical Style.

The Minors in Circular 4th & 5th

example 4

The Minor 5-1-3's in Circular 5th's

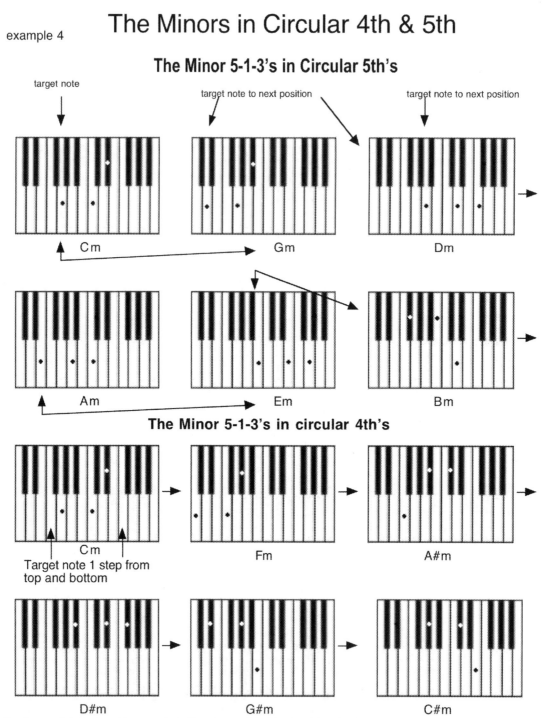

The Minor 5-1-3's in circular 4th's

Fold any of these positions to their Dominants for 4 bars while playing a melody line with the right hand then move to the next position and repeat. Mix alternating between 4'ths, 5th's,Maj & Min. going from one position to the other.. By the end of this book you would even by-pass one key and go straight to another. For ex: above you can by-pass the Fm and go direct to A#m. Or by-pass G#m to C#m. You can see much farther ahead by target and sight. Baroquing in the Harmonic minor scale is enriching.

CHAPTER 2

The Diminished (7th degree)

The Diminished, are the true connecting minors that are designed to inter connect with other positions. First you have to practice them until they sound boring to you, and that's when you really start to appreciate them. If you are new to them then they sound like any other chords when they are not.

The Diminished are the wild cards of the deck. The cards that bail you out when there isn't any other way it seems like. They inter twine with the dominants, which will be next. They intertwine with scales. The different kind of scales you use with the diminished determines what kind of music you are playing be it jazz, Modern jazz, Classical, west-Indy. etc. The set of rules you use determines what kind of music you are playing respectively. They will work between any position. It's the wild card of the deck.

If you want to have a better sound picture of the diminished then think of the girl tied down on the track while the train is coming. The tension is built and climbs upward as you play the diminished up the keyboard. But sometimes that will lock you in thinking that's the only way to use them, when there's many directions and sounds you can create with the diminished without having to lock yourself to one type of sound. Try to avoid that type of rut, if you can.

And of-course they intertwine with 5-1-3's. They are most of the time the next step to the 5-1-3's and one step ahead of the Dominants. Or vice versa. They connect the 5-1-3's major and minors and the Dominants. CMaj 5-1-3 Folds into G7 Dominant. The G7 has a diminished in it. All or any 5-1-3 with its folds will give you an opportunity to take the Diminished wild card, the seventh degree.

The Diminished use different kind of scales, as one is aware of. But in my studies, I find that 3 harmonic scales are simplistically all that is needed to get familiar with at first. And it's the central common denominator for an improvisational dichotomy, if one is to use them in the key of C or its natural minor, which is Am. The 3 scales are "A" harmonic Minor."E" harmonic minor. & "D" harmonic minor. Here we see the root, four and five again surfacing in the minors. The triangle of eternity. And they are from what I can see it's because where this key lies that the improvisational fervor exists. And the fingering. This is where Bach's improvisations started it all. These keys are not overwhelmed with flats or sharps. So they are relatively easy to finger. And they are more or less the common denominator of the middle of the piano. The key of C means you can see it in front of you with clarity. The middle C of the piano. The median between white and black notes. The median between sharps and flats. The orchestrative key to use for concert score or the middle of the staff to read notation from in clarity.. I've charted the 3 diminished families respectively (A,B,C). One is to practice them with all four positions at hand. There are only 3 families and their four positions or 3 inversions. May I suggest listening to

Beethoven's 5th symphony also and practicing these inversions in thirds up and down the keyboard. Beethoven's fury are unleashed from these Diminished families. In-fact the Diminished Dominant is Beethoven's playground.

Chopin's piano tuner once said, what he remembers of Chopin is his arpeggiated-diminished runs up and down the piano. Incidentally it also resonates with art Tatum. He created his own runs to use with the American standards. The famous Improvisational Jazz pianist, whom Chopin's students remember, Chopin playing like Art Tatum. And obviously Chopin came first. So there are al-sorts of correlation involving the Diminished symmetrics or minors as I call them.

To use them with ease is to use them fully and to one's benefit. And that includes the ease of fingering and dexterity. I do not like to use the word symmetric because the way I'm suggesting in using them are in poetic harmony as minors, so it's in realm a true perfect harmonic sense. On the other hand if we used them with their indigenous scales, which is: 1/2 step whole step 1/2 step whole step etc... Then they would be considered symmetric and the sound would take on a more symmetric or machine like inclination. Not to forget that their fingering are not natural and will slow the improvisational conversation down to a sluggish halt.

And so E, A, D harmonic minors gives you the ability to dexterously as well as harmonically improvise eternally at ease using the Diminished with infinity at first, in the key of C or Am. Afterwards you can use all the harmonic minor scales with the diminished, because every diminished can use a different harmonic minor scale. (*Page 23. Diminished in the key you're in*). An exercise that I used to use is; Baroquing with just using the Diminished and their scales, just to get familiar with at first, and it's also fun. At this point you can try out everything covered using Bach's style. The folding of the 5-1-3's especially the minors > circulating the 4th & 5th> and going to the Diminished with using all minors. The minor used will give you the scale to the diminished used with it.

You now should get an even better feel for what and where it all came from. If you play majors then it sounds more of the style of the Sonata, which is Mozart or Bach. You can also use my Diminished and rule of thumb as a starting point all by itself with improvisations, providing you've memorized the rules. Page 191.

And or a major point to remember is: How these Diminished are used depends most of the time on where your melody line and harmonies are going. If you've established a melody line and a distinctive as opposed to geometric then you are going to be in the key established and confined to the keys you're playing. But if you've established a geometric melody i.e. Classical, Mozart or especially Beethoven, then you will be open to any key at a drop of a hat. That's why Beethoven was the master of the Diminished. The transcendent style.

There are different formulas that I beat out of my head using the diminished that should sustain your improvisations as well as compositional theory. Also my diminished golden rule of thumb and targeting. Once these families are learned, then the next chapter "the Dominants" are automatically targeted also. That's when one gets to use a lot of theory just by looks. And it begins to get simple... Incidentally the deeper one goes on, the more the sound changes to the romantic era. It's of-course the piano was modernized to play faster and with more dynamics.

Remember the scales to use here are a basic for now. Later on one will use all the harmonic scales that will harmonize with the diminished depending on your composition or position. From any key or angle.

This method covers all keys in harmonics and pure tones. As well as my " Diminished golden rule of thumb " It's eternal and infinite also as a whole concept. The building of power and harmony as a structure. Page 191 has the chart for the final picture of the Diminished and my golden rule of thumb which can be used as a whole concept all by itself. Especially the romantic style. Strauss or Rachmaninoff. Or scoring for motion pictures. Jazz improvisations, straight or abstract. The Diminished is the wild card that can be used for abstract builds. Romantic ballads. Or emotional concepts. The diminished is essentially a Dominant with one flattened note in it. If you see it that way, it will also open doors for you as well as give you scales to use. And these rules on this page as well as the Dominants rules on page 26 are to be used after one is familiar with this book and then apply these rules to the already learned information or theories documented, practiced and applied harmoniously during the improvisational build. Especially the Dominants on page 26. They are the link or *paradigm* to joint together the already should be memorized theories that I've created, in which should gel or cause the infinite harmonies to sprout eternally between the content of the book to these rules. Theories are : 1.**From any finger of the Diminished up the keyboard 1/2 step ; play a major or minor 1-3-5 or 5-1-3 or (5-b1-3 from the fifth, this is the minor second position.)**

Also practice the diminished in thirds, which is their inversions. **Or a Diminished ½ step under the third finger or under the fifth, which is the third finger counting from the bottom; this is important in fluid Improvisations.** (*Also practice a different diminished exactly one step away up or down. Because you do not want to clash one with the other back to back. Its very rare that you will need to play one back to back with another. But it's done from time to time.*)

Also practice: 2. from any Diminished 1 step up or 1/2 down from any finger : Play a Dominant 7th. Or Octave left hand with 2 root notes, Diminished Ninth's. Etc.Tension Building Harmonies. **Also practice: 3. ½ step down from any finger play a diminished b7th. Move to another Diminished and repeat. 4. Diminished 7th. with one hand and use the bottom finger or root note target to use a Diminished b7th with the other hand.** *And that is Classic Beethoven again. Remember these Geometric harmonies for they might not be mentioned again in this book. And a Diminished b7th Is also the normal minor #5th. Or the 3-5-1 second position. You will be introduced to them later on.*

When they are reduced from the Diminished b7th to the 3-5-1.Chopin

CHAPTER 2

The Diminished

example 7

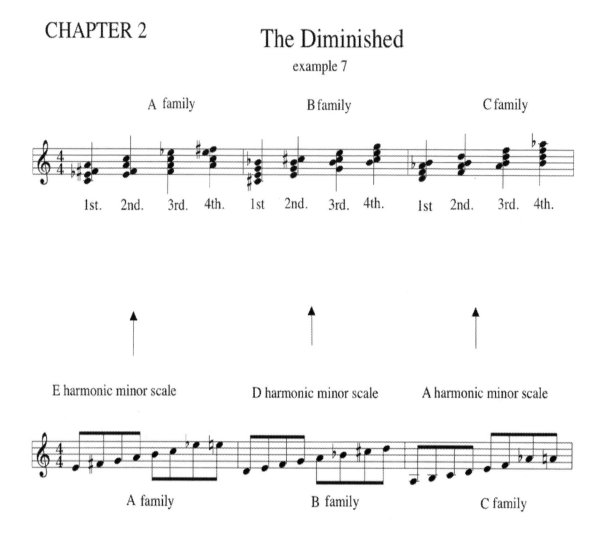

These are the basics of the Diminished cymetry. Onced learned then the next chapter; The dominants are

automatically used. Just by targeting notes. Imagine knowing all the dominants just from the diminished.

It will get deeper as one goes on with the diminished, but for right know just complete the following exer.

This is a good time to also learn the Harmonic minor scales at this point. The Scales consist of minor 3rd.

and a minor 6th.... of any Major scale. (Page 13) Also Check page 101 for using these Diminished in eternal infinity using G, C & f

Here again after you complete all that's been covered so far at this point. Go ahead and try Improvising

Like Motzart, Beethoven or Bach; Using the folding Sonata technique. The simpler it is, the more melodies

you can come up with. Incidently this is the haven for strings. Anything you write here is well suited for

strings, Quartets, early symphonies of Haydn. He wrote 150 symphonies using this basic method.

The Diminished

Example : 7

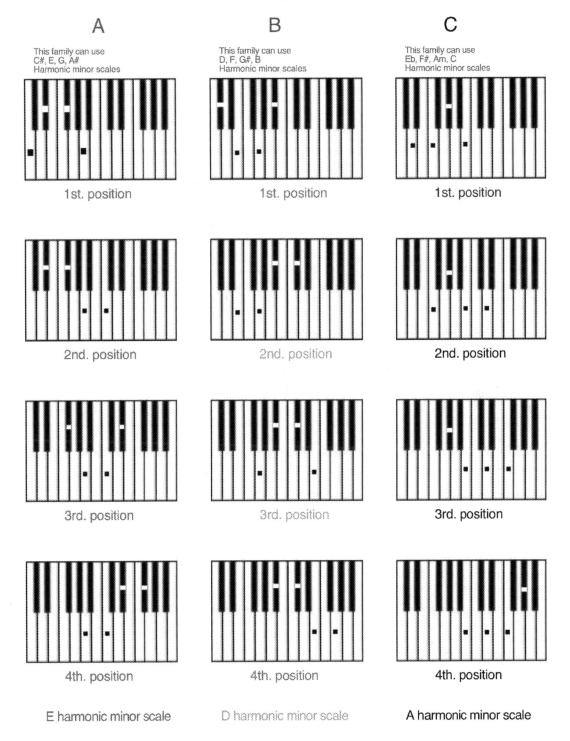

A

This family can use
C#, E, G, A#
Harmonic minor scales

1st. position

2nd. position

3rd. position

4th. position

E harmonic minor scale

B

This family can use
D, F, G#, B
Harmonic minor scales

1st. position

2nd. position

3rd. position

4th. position

D harmonic minor scale

C

This family can use
Eb, F#, Am, C
Harmonic minor scales

1st. position

2nd. position

3rd. position

4th. position

A harmonic minor scale

Further Studies with the diminished
Primary use
&

Example 42

More scales for the diminished

1. Take any Diminished > you can play the harmonic minor scale of the key note ,1/2 step up from any note

C# E G A#

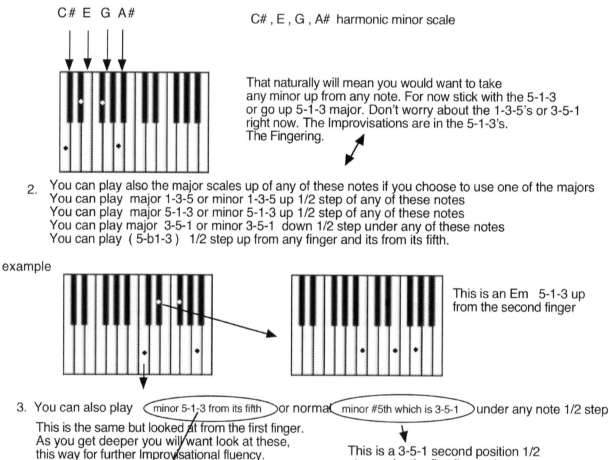

C# , E , G , A# harmonic minor scale

That naturally will mean you would want to take any minor up from any note. For now stick with the 5-1-3 or go up 5-1-3 major. Don't worry about the 1-3-5's or 3-5-1 right now. The Improvisations are in the 5-1-3's. The Fingering.

2. You can play also the major scales up of any of these notes if you choose to use one of the majors
You can play major 1-3-5 or minor 1-3-5 up 1/2 step of any of these notes
You can play major 5-1-3 or minor 5-1-3 up 1/2 step of any of these notes
You can play major 3-5-1 or minor 3-5-1 down 1/2 step under any of these notes
You can play (5-b1-3) 1/2 step up from any finger and its from its fifth.

example

This is an Em   5-1-3 up from the second finger

3. You can also play minor 5-1-3 from its fifth or normal minor #5th which is 3-5-1 under any note 1/2 step
This is the same but looked at from the first finger. As you get deeper you will want look at these, this way for further Improvsational fluency.

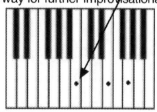

This is a 3-5-1 second position 1/2 step under the first finger also

If you wish to minor it. Then flatten the bottom finger 1/2 step and its a minor 3-5-1

To create the furious Improvisational furver; Beethoven or Chopin. Practice with the Minors. Any Diminished and strike a 5-1-3 minor looked at from both positions. Play their scales and strike another diminished weather it conforms with the harmony at hand or any diminished at random. They will work from any position.

Do not worry about these yet for they will introduce themselves later in this book

Further Studies

ex. 35

<u>Diminished in the key</u>
Concerning the Folding Sonata form or the right Diminished for any Harmonic Minor

1. To find the right Diminished for the key you are in;
   you can find it 1/2 step under the key root note. Shown here below. Or 1/2 step up from the bottom finger.

2. Or just fold any 5-1-3 major or minor or 3-5-1 major only 1/2 step up, you can find the right diminished for that triad that way very quick and kept in the mind if need be. And the scale of that diminished is also the 5-1-3 minor thats used. The three diminished families will work in all the Harmonic minor scales of any minor 5-1-3. Bach, Chopin & Beethoven went up 1/2 step to a diminished on every other fold, rotating between the Dominant and the Diminished. This diminished is used scaresly also, meaning use partial notes instead of the full diminished7. Brake it up for tasteful conotation if desired. Ex: C# minor 5-1-3 folds into an A Diminished 7 ....

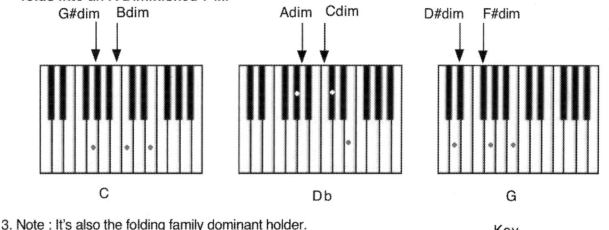

G#dim   Bdim   Adim   Cdim   D#dim   F#dim

C   Db   G

3. Note : It's also the folding family dominant holder.
And the right Diminished to use for the Harmonic
Minor scale of that 5-1-3.

C#m

note: I look at it as a Db minor for quick use

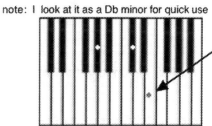

C#m's Fold

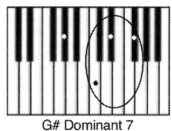

G# Dominant 7
(I always call it an Ab dominant 7th. though)

Key

Target note for any key a Minor 5-1-3 is in, or just what key to notate in.
The Key of E Major

from the beginning understand what key you're in or what key to notate in. And be weary of any chord symbolism or terminology. Although This method will work in just target and sight as well. Understand the key any 5-1-3 minor is in.

With this Diminished you now have a door out to another Key or Folding family. With Triads as the Tonic or tone Dominant you can jump from key to key without that much of a difference in sound but continuos Improv.

Do you see the Diminished of that Key or Folding Family

The scale of C# Harmonic minor will harmonize with C Diminished7

Although this edition of this book is marked correctly for notation, I will always look at any flat or sharp key's as a flat only with the exception of F#. Please note; I do not hardly mention this any further than this page, so keep in mind as you move along or Improvise on the fly.

23

The Improvisational functions of the diminished

in fluent use with the standard classical fingering element

1. To connect to the next step. Or a stepping step. 2. To allow one to jump or connect to another key.
3. To create a dominant which in-turn will be the stepping step or the bridge. which will be discussed on the next chapter. Or to be created from a dominant, which is the opposite. 4. Its the wild card. Used **Geometrically** by Beethoven or **Poetically** by Chopin, in Classical form. It will connect all the keys as one is playing in one key and this is Orchestration or the development of a piece of music. Or Piano music arppegiated all by its own weaving from key to key in use with the 5-1-3 minors at majority, and must be looked at from the 5th of the minor to grasp the key it is in for improvisation use of the scales quickly or fluently, another words; one knows what key to be in at all times while switching on the fly without hesitation. And finally,It will meet at the serious point and switch in binary form. Which will be modal or Romantic, or Jazz as the cyclical cycle rotates. And the sharpened Diminished is Ravel & Debussy.

<u>Primary standard sonata technique form among others</u>

For now start using it in this manner until the fingering becomes standard

Take any Diminished major or seventh, you then can play any 5-1-3 major or minor following any note , 1/2 step up.Within the melody line and key used. But lets take the 5-1-3 from the 5th. Which is the same but looked at from another point of view or angle for fluent Improvisations especially on the modern pianos and not weary of staying in one key . But Chopin refused to call his technique Romantic. He maintained its Classical. You are in control of where to take it. Classical will keep you in a normal, tonal state of mind, perhaps avoiding a sweet tooth. Later on jump to the Modern if desired for a change. But the classical below will harmonize despite which diminished used. Hit as many Diminished as you like any where while playing a melody line with the right hand from the scales of the 5-1-3 minor and all will harmonize despite.

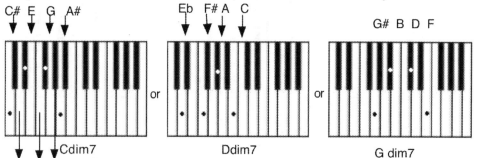

C# E G A#   Cdim7   Eb F# A C   Ddim7   G# B D F   G dim7

1/2 step under any key will give you the 5-1-3 from the 5th. Which is the same but looked at from this angle.

Here a G minor 5-1-3 looked at from the bottom of Eb. 1/2 step under. Right away you will hit the G minor 5-1-3 without thinking its name, but seeing the geometric figure of the 5-1-3 minor from the fifth.If you have memorized the 5-1-3's as cymbals by looks that is.

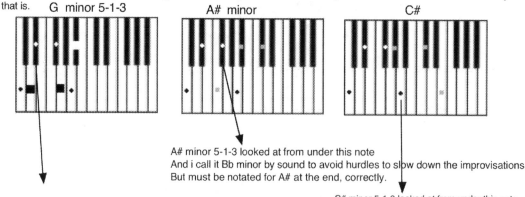

G minor 5-1-3   A# minor   C#

A# minor 5-1-3 looked at from under this note
And i call it Bb minor by sound to avoid hurdles to slow down the improvisations
But must be notated for A# at the end, correctly.

G minor 5-1-3 looked at from under this note

C# minor 5-1-3 looked at from under this note
And i call it Db minor to avoid extential hurdles slowing down the fluency of Improvisations, but must be notated correctly at the end as C#. (just a reminder)

CHAPTER 3

THE DOMINANTS

The Dominants are actually the automaticall elements of one chapter throwing into another. They are automatically achieved by both chapter one and chapter two. Infact if you have done all of one asked for so far, in this study, then believe it or not, but you already know all of the Dominants. They are automatically in front of you. And they will show themselves to you as one is getting familiar.

The Dominants are one of the primary tools to use among the tension builders. They are the sound that will automatically go into another for resolve. One can think of music building up volume or tension and at the height of the build-ups are the dominants that will go to the soft relieving part. And thus the process starts all over again. Or continue to escalate up in scale. As in the use of scoring for motion pictures for example.

The Dominants most commonly and more than often resolve to a 4th. up from the key you are in. Or descend in the descending circular 4th's which will be covered in more ways than one. The parallel ascending and descending 4th's. Any one who have played jazz can verify it's the fourth's that are the sweet harmony's that create the sweetness. 5-1-3 & 3-5-1 triads have an even fourth split in them.

Most often all the songs are driven over a bridge to the other side which is the fourth's. But one need not worry where is the fourth. Because there is a target note that will tell you, and that just makes life and playing a whole lot more tolerable. If you have a target note that tells you where to go then you can improvise and play and think way ahead of time with hardly much of any effort. That's when you can switch from key to key and not have to worry where you are. Because targeting is not complex thinking but simplification. So lets begin with the obvious. The first position Dominants.

The first position dominants are the second basic folding position that's been covered in the first chapter. All you have to do is add the seventh note on to it. Another words; Where "C" 5-1-3 folded into "G" the G now becomes a G7. So here we see the basic concept of the Classical Method is already figured out with the dominants at hand. They fold right into your hand. They are harmonious for orchestration of the even plit in them. No dissidence. And in this G7 one should mention there is a diminished that also lies in it, so you also are given a way out of the key if desired or further Improvisations. Important harmonies to conquer is playing a **1. Dominant 7th from the first position and exactly one step up or down from any finger play a normal minor7th and repeat from the normal minor7 this time. After any finger exactly one step up or down**

play a Dominant 7th. (Also from any finger use a normal minor7th or dominant7th without going up or down, this is ordinary harmonies). Also practice playing a Dominant 7th one step away from another dominant 7th from any finger exactly one step away up or down**. 2. The Diminished is also at play here..and theoretically a golden rule is - The Dominant 7th lies ½ step under any finger of any Diminished7th, And a diminished 7th lies ½ step up of any finger of any Dominant 7th . 3. Also play a Diminished b7th or 3-5-1 ½ step down from the last finger of the Dominant (can be minored also by flattening the bottom finger, the 3 of the 3-5-1). 4. Another Harmony is play any Dominant 7th. from the first position and exactly ½ step up from the first finger play a Diminished octaved. (with or without the 7th) (this is a flattened 9th.) 5. Any Dominant7th can play a diminished from any finger but the first.** And That is Classic Beethoven Geometric tension building Harmonies. His fury, Loud and Domineering. Remember these rules for they will come handy in any part of this book. ! Another

Standard exercise is the Dominant ninth. Which is of-course the two octaved ninth notes with the left hand and the dominant with the right hand. This is Tension building.

   These rules are the paradigm to the material or theories, patterns and formulas that should be learned already then used with these rules on this page afterwards to complete the cycle or concept that should gel into infinite eternal harmonies and or Improvisational compositions. The methodological concept.

   After that, will uncover how the Dominants are achieved from the Diminished. All the Dominants are on a staff and with pictures, but don't let them scare you, because there is a trick on playing them from target without even having to memorize or worry about them. Which will be covered in this chapter. If you know all the Diminished which are only 3 positions. (and their inversions). Then you already know all the dominants already. It's much easier to learn 3 diminished chords. Than a slew of 48 Dominants. The dominants will introduce themselves to you systematically Or Geometrically

You need not have to memorize them !

CHAPTER 3

The Dominants

example : 9

example : 10

example : 11

example : 12

Chapter 3
The Dominants

You need not worry about all these Dominants for they will introduce themselves to you without having to memorize them at all

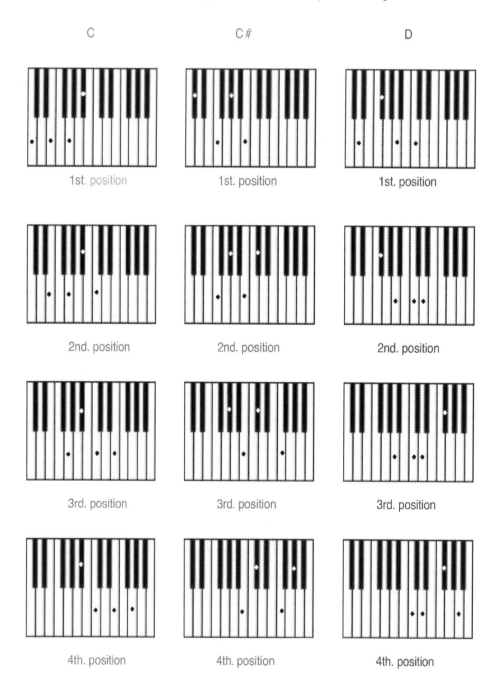

The Dominants

You need not worry about all these Dominants for they will introduce themselves to you without having to memorize them at all

Eb	E	F
1st. position	1st. position	1st. position
2nd. position	2nd. position	2nd. position
3rd. position	3rd. position	3rd. position
4th. position	4th. position	4th. position

Chapter 3

The Dominants

You need not worry about all these Dominants for they will introduce themselves to you without having to memorize them at all

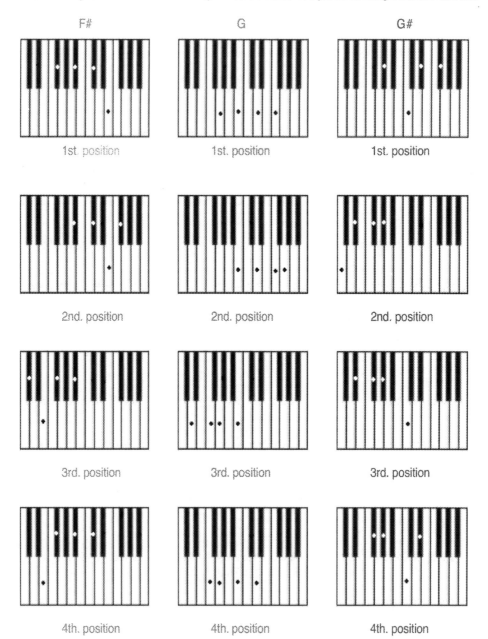

Chapter 3

The Dominants

You need not worry about all these Dominants for they will introduce themselves to you without having to memorize them at all

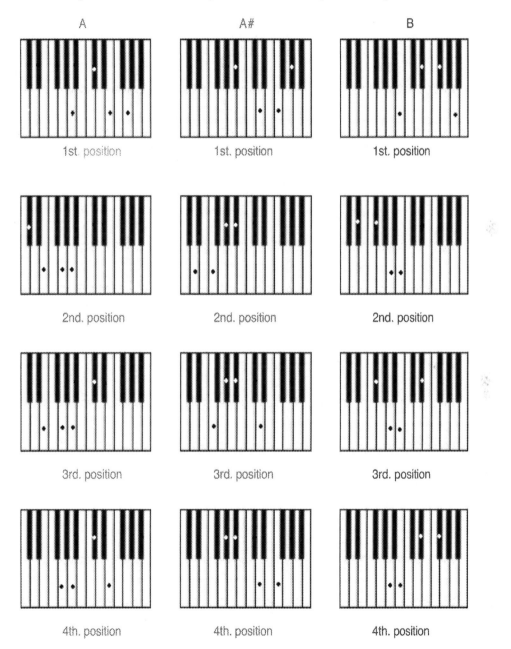

Basic Folding 5-1-3's with the dominant 7th.

example 13

you already know you'r 5-1-3's folding from chapter 1.Then you should very easily know these.Which is just one note added on to make a dominant 7th.

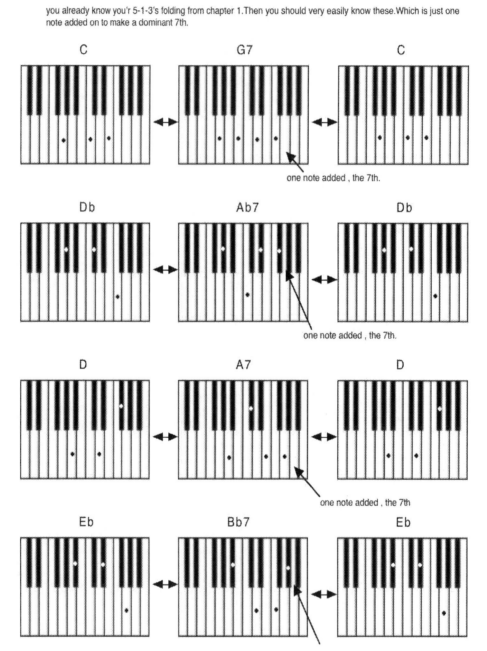

Basic Folding 5-1-3's with the dominant 7th.

example 14   continued

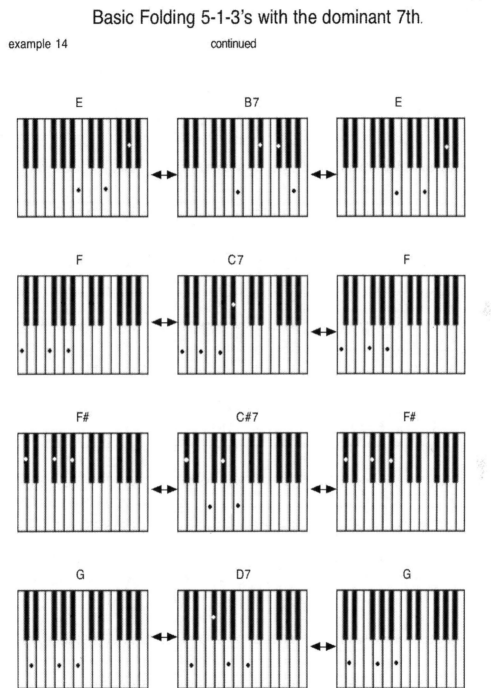

Basic Folding 5-1-3's with the dominant 7th.

example 15   continued

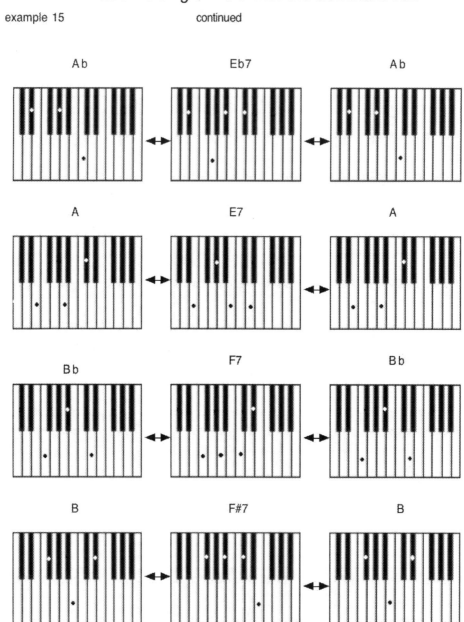

Folding 5-1-3's with the dominant 7th.

example : 13

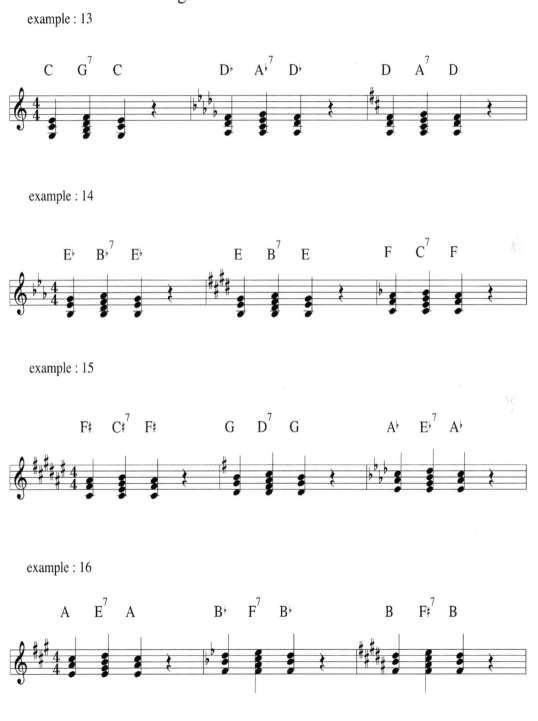

example : 14

example : 15

example : 16

Further Studies
Basic Folding Extended

example 52   5-1-3's

1. Go a little deeper into basic folding and push the 1 and the 3.in majors and minors
   and know the scales you are in.This even gives you more to use with the folding
   sonata technique.

2. The key note is of course the 1. or the second finger.Take the scale of it.

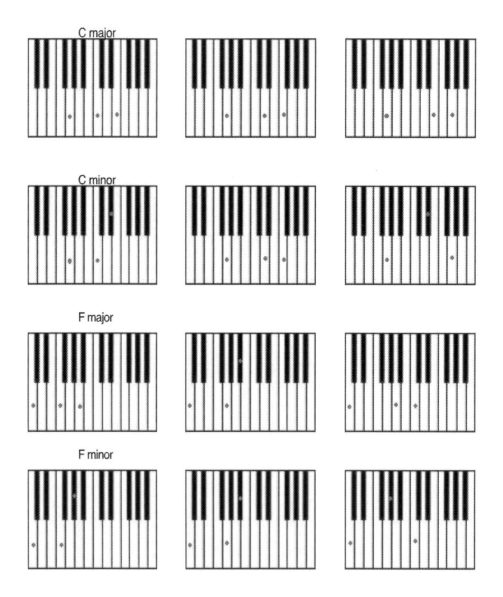

Further Studies

using the 5-1-3 and basic folding in speed

the sonata form

example 34a

A m

1. Take any multiple of 5-1-3 minors. And fold to their dominants back and forth with speed with (right Hand). Rolll the notes not just chord them.Roll them.

2. With left hand play the harmonic minor scale but with one note at a time with each 5-1-3 triad. so with every right hand rolling three note , the left hand plays one note in the harmonic minor scale of that triad.Play the left hand note first.So now it has become 4 notes all together rolling.In speed and technique.

3. This is were the common denominator we talked about earlier comes in handy.If you concintrate around the A minor, D minor, E minor.You not only can play the harmonic minor scale but the diminished positions as well.So now this speed rolling sonata form has become more to create with.Beethoven's fury emerges with this technique.

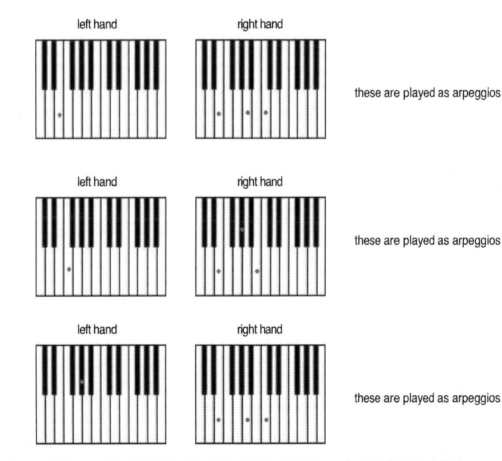

left hand   right hand   these are played as arpeggios

left hand   right hand   these are played as arpeggios

left hand   right hand   these are played as arpeggios

A harmonic minor scale with F diminished, G# diminished, B diminished, D minor diminished Mode.

Further Studies
using the 5-1-3 and basic folding in speed
the sonata form

example 34 b

Dm

1. Take any multiple of 5-1-3 minors. And fold to their dominants back and forth with speed with (right Hand). Rolll the notes not just chord them.Roll them.

2. With left hand play the harmonic minor scale but with one note at a time with each 5-1-3 triad. so with every right hand rolling three note , the left hand plays one note in the harmonic minor scale of that triad.Play the left hand note first.So now it has become 4 notes all together rolling.In speed and technique.

3. This is were the common denominator we talked about earlier comes in handy.If you concintrate around the A minor, D minor, E minor.You not only can play the harmonic minor scale but the diminished positions as well.So now this speed rolling sonata form has become more to create with.Beethoven's fury emerges with this technique.

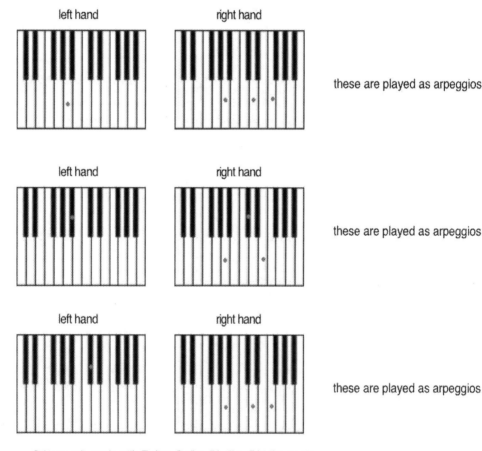

left hand	right hand

these are played as arpeggios

these are played as arpeggios

these are played as arpeggios

D harmonic scale with E dim, G dim, Bb dim, Db dim mode

Further Studies

using the 5-1-3 and basic folding in speed

the sonata form

example 34c

EM

1. Take any multiple of 5-1-3 minors. And fold to their dominants back and forth with speed with (right Hand). Rolll the notes not just chord them.Roll them.

2. With left hand play the harmonic minor scale but with one note at a time with each 5-1-3 triad. so with every right hand rolling three note , the left hand plays one note in the harmonic minor scale of that triad.Play the left hand note first.So now it has become 4 notes all together rolling.In speed and technique.

3. This is were the common denominator we talked about earlier comes in handy.If you concintrate around the A minor, D minor, E minor.You not only can play the harmonic minor scale but the diminished positions as well.So now this speed rolling sonata form has become more to create with.Beethoven's fury emerges with this technique.

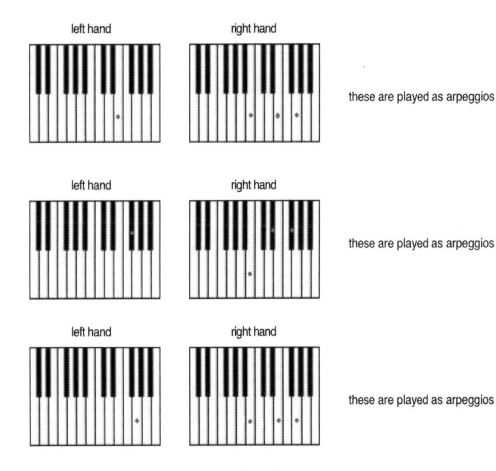

left hand	right hand	
		these are played as arpeggios
left hand	right hand	these are played as arpeggios
left hand	right hand	these are played as arpeggios

E harmonic scale with C dim, D# dim, F#dim, Adim. Mode

Basic Folding 5-1-3's with the dominant 7th.
and developing melodies from octaved notes

example 15

continued with the Minors
Arpeggiations / Mordents / Garnishings

The Minors

Remember ! With the minors you can arpeggiate . Using the normal minor with the right hand one on top another in the same octave. Or try a different variation switching hands. Or rolling notes backwards, or leaving distinct notes out but following the Fingering pattern etc.. using Improvisations in the Harmonic minors. Try all the keys to see what key feels natural to your fingering. You can also see the octaved mordents for baroquing.

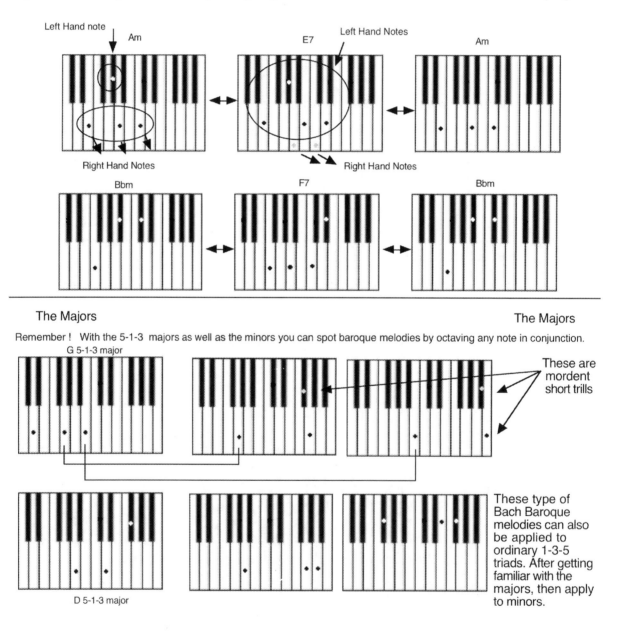

The Majors

Remember ! With the 5-1-3 majors as well as the minors you can spot baroque melodies by octaving any note in conjunction.

These are mordent short trills

These type of Bach Baroque melodies can also be applied to ordinary 1-3-5 triads. After getting familiar with the majors, then apply to minors.

ex 16   **The Diminished Golden rule of thumb**

Achieving the Dominants and their resolve from the Diminished

1. take any Diminished from any position

2. flatten any note 1/2 step   (the note you flattened landed on its name)

3. It now is a Dominant

Now you are automaticaly using all the Dominants without hardly thinking about them.

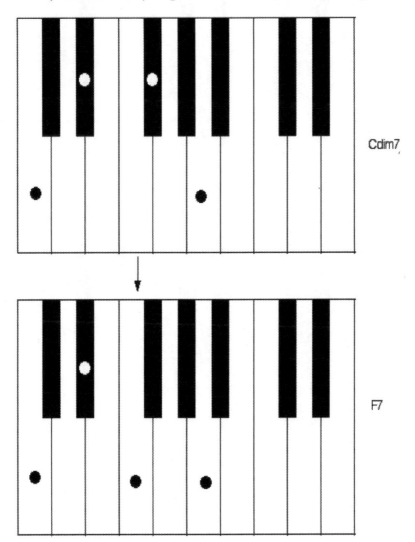

Cdim7

F7

Robert Kaye

4. Now we'll take the dominant 7th. and resolve it.
5. You find its resolve by targeting the next note up from the flattened note.
6 The next note up is the "A", so we go up 1/2 step to Bb.
7. Play 5-1-3 major or minor Bb

continued

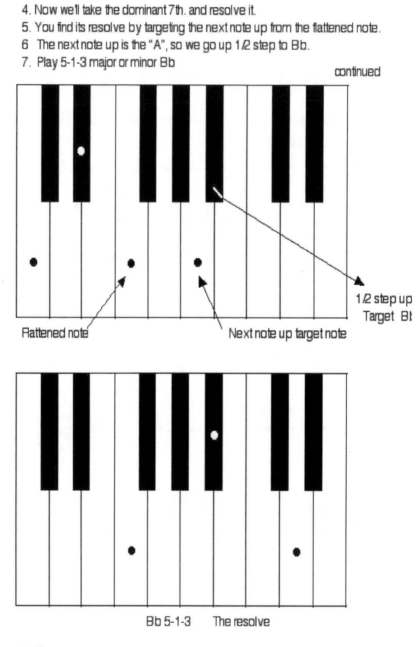

1/2 step up
Target Bb

Flattened note   Next note up target note

Bb 5-1-3   The resolve

ex 17

Achieving the Dominants and their resolve from the Diminished

If its the last note of the Diminished; then you go back to the beginning note and take its 1/2 step up.

example 18   continued

The Diminished golden rule of thumb

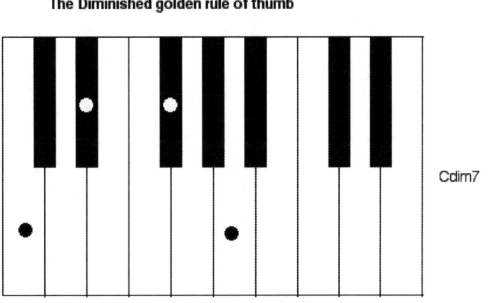

Cdim7

If its the last note then target the beginning note

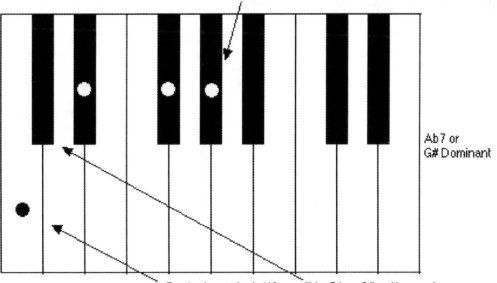

Ab7 or
G# Dominant

Beginning note & 1/2 up will be Db or C# as the resolve

Resolving the Dominants

example 19   more examples

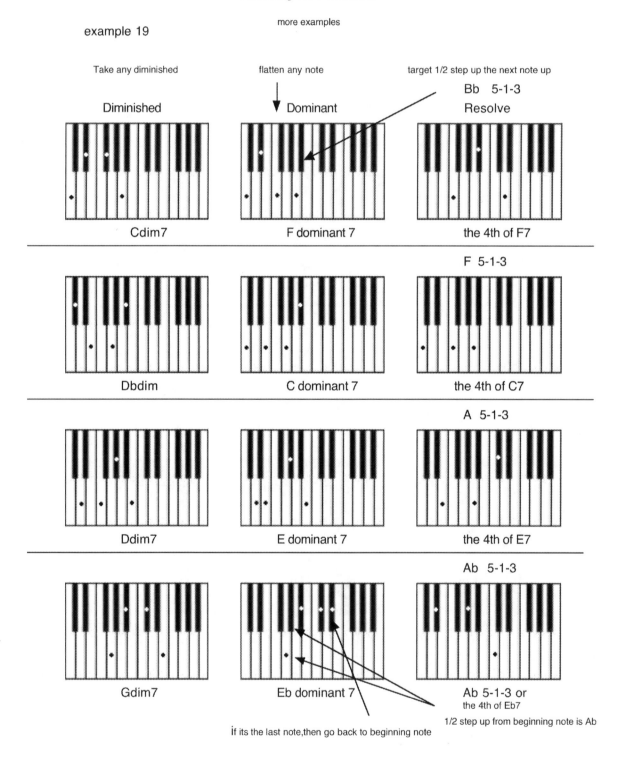

Take any diminished   flatten any note   target 1/2 step up the next note up

Diminished   Dominant   Bb   5-1-3 Resolve

Cdim7   F dominant 7   the 4th of F7

F   5-1-3

Dbdim   C dominant 7   the 4th of C7

A   5-1-3

Ddim7   E dominant 7   the 4th of E7

Ab   5-1-3

Gdim7   Eb dominant 7   Ab 5-1-3 or
the 4th of Eb7

if its the last note,then go back to beginning note   1/2 step up from beginning note is Ab

44

Resolving the Dominants into Minors

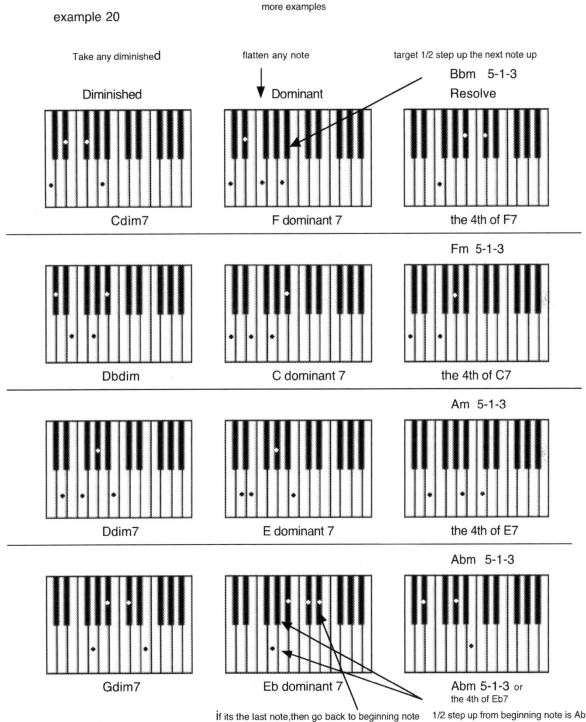

more examples

example 20

Take any diminished — flatten any note — target 1/2 step up the next note up

Diminished — Dominant — Bbm 5-1-3 Resolve

Cdim7 — F dominant 7 — the 4th of F7

Fm 5-1-3

Dbdim — C dominant 7 — the 4th of C7

Am 5-1-3

Ddim7 — E dominant 7 — the 4th of E7

Abm 5-1-3

Gdim7 — Eb dominant 7 — Abm 5-1-3 or the 4th of Eb7

if its the last note,then go back to beginning note — 1/2 step up from beginning note is Ab

Try all the keys of-course. Explore and play at the same time.

The Mozart Method

1. Start with the Sonata form. Establish a melody line most usually in the majors. Maintained by improvisations.
2. Once the idea is established and written down then parallel the sonata form. If Orchestrating for Chamber.
3. Your left hand will automatically find the right position in harmony. It could land on
   a normal minor octave in parallel. Or it could land on a 5-1-3 major or minor in parallel.
4. When it lands on a diminished. Its a diminished octave in parallel also. (usually with no 7th).
5. The harmonic minor scales are used exclusively as well as the major scales.
6. The Neapolitans are targeted as well as the second position in folding as a predominants in the Sonata Form.
   As well as Expositioning in all three Triadactal Forms. Interweaving in and out of another. As the Development
   throughout the 7 degrees of the scale. The 5-1-3 in Cadential Sonata form with forward developmental
   in flexed rhythmic Improvisations.

    Having said the format; And all of the above. For Just piano Improvisation; use the following pages only to grasp
Mozart's style. Its very spread in structure and most harmonious with full allowance and forward motion delivery. The left
hand is in constant motion with the sonata form; Be it the 1, 2nd or 3rd. position. 3rd. is the tonic of the course and the
Improvisational from and all else follow. Harmonic chromatics is used quiet often in pre recapitulation.
These are the pages to follow after you've learned everything up to here: 101, 89, 98, 90, 92, 94, 95, 96, 97, 100,104,
133 - The Descending Circular fourth - 52 - 98

Folding the sonata form in parallel

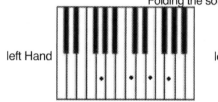
left Hand

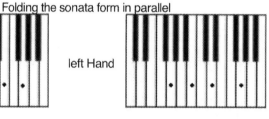
left Hand

Walk the outside fingers 1 step up or down   Walk the inside fingers 1 step up or down

left Hand

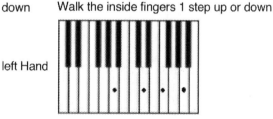
left Hand

This is a diminished octaved with no seventh notice !   These are right hand trill notes

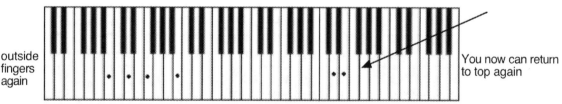

outside
fingers
again

You now can return
to top again

Remember it all can be finger targeting. For example the descending fourths are merely outside fingers moving and inside fingers.. etc. You
then can brake the rules by crunching fingers if you wish. Meaning moving the inside fingers twice before the outside fingers or vice versa.
And jumping. But its all targeting, which is writing for you automatically along with the melody line. Creating the melody line for you al-along.
Hence reminder : The Parallels are an orchestrative tools; Its recommended that one use them only after learning the Improvisational
fluency of the keyboard. They are a Compositional tools at large and could restrict your Improvisation as a pianist. After all Mozart was the
master of the Sonata. Unparalleled. Mozart Also used the rotating Finger technique as did Beethoven. Except Mozart on the whole stayed in
the Majors. Melodic and Facile. Mastered the Neapolitans as a predominant. In the Sonata Form. Brahms was the master of the parallel
Improvisations. To stay in an influential piano improvisations in the mozart method. Use all the Minors in any key,(The Dominant & Natural
Minors that is) And that's including the Subtonic Diminished and the secondary Minor. Turn all 4 into a Minor #5 or 3-5-1 Second position and
fold in the Sonata Form again. That will keep you in the key you're in, and Improvising in an eternal circles of Harmony. Having the picture and
the tools of the Sonata form with target notes at hand; One can then write directly to conductor's score, if need be !

The "Mozart Method" continued: This is all about feeling good with humanistic quality with rhythmic flexibility. Just as long as you stay in the key and eventually capitulate to the dominant, everything will harmonize. Try this as an experiment; The right hand can do anything and the left hand can move anywhere just as long as it's in the key. So for ex; In the key of C: The right hand can play anything in the C scale and the left can parallel an octaved 5-1-3 and move the outside fingers and inside fingers anywhere just as long as its in the scale of C. The outside fingers will always be on the white keys. And everything will harmonize automatically. While you just think of moving inside & outside fingers in parallel. But the sonata is not paralleled. So you don't have to worry about what position you are in, then you just target fingers and listen to pick what notes you want to sound good. It's the finger targeting that's the key here. And you begin to see how he composed mentally without using a keyboard. Listen to Mozart's music and then attempt it. It is very much heard in the mind. Of-course Haydn was the one who gave him his confidence. And JC Bach showed him his lesson at the first written symphony at a very young age. And his father exposed him to all of Europe's classical masters at the time. As an educator once said: Mozart is the great assimilator. Mozart was also the master of the sonata. Unparalleled. He was the heart of the classical method and style. His style usually moved anywhere from 4, 8, sixteen bars or so at a time before he capitulated and trilled back to the tonic. He new all the tridactal inversions by target and sight. This is what I'm insinuating of-course. He relied on happy jumping and vivacious bounces of tridactal shifting, of melodies that were riddles of the sonata form and occasionally threw a diminished. **Melodic simplicity was his complexity**. Because of his age and knowledge of the violin. He was the youngest of any composer to become a master at his craft. His compositions are full of trills, garnishings, accents, forward movements in momentum, rhythmic flexibility and perfection. His music is quality and content, and is timeless. He brought more technique and imagination, melodic and harmonic taste to the compositional table than anyone before or after him. He single handily created the happy and conductive bounce in classical music. Thus opening the style into its celebrated epic. And in my opinion, secured classical music as the most enjoyable style to create with. Just as Chopin was with the Piano, or Bach in poetic arranging, or Beethoven for power and strength. These are the greatest pianists that have played live at a very young age also.

Beethoven also learned from Haydn but at an a little older age. And the keyboard transformed during Beethoven's age so he broke the first sonata form, and Haydn advised him to stop. But of-course he didn't. Beethoven claimed that Haydn didn't teach him anything. Of-course the piano at this point was improved also. Take the number of symphonies written by Haydn & Mozart; Are in the hundreds. Beethoven wrote 9. They were of-course of more complex form. But taste has an issue also here to some extent as well as the pure" Classical Method ". And it's the finger targeting that's the key here. Improvisational speed. One does go on to cover the rest of the modern romantic era with targeting also, to a certain extend. But first recap the sonata form, which is pure Mozart style:

1. Basic folding in " **the Sonata form "** / **Cadential -** (Tonic).

2. Use the circular 4th. & 5th. (Subdominant & Dominant) – (5-1-3 & 3-5-1 Orchestrative in all keys). Alternating between majors and minors. If you use continuous harmonic minor scales then it would sound like Beethoven and Chopin. If you use major scales with occasional harmonic minors then it would sound like Mozart, JC Bach, Haydn, Schubert. But obviously this theory pertains to all the composers. Its all literary the same. When you're completely familiar with the triads then parallel. What Beethoven used with his left and right hand, The quick successive notes climbing up in the harmonic minor scale. Mozart used in the major scale using both hands. Alternating. Facile improvisation. (Indicative of their knowledge of the violin).

3. Resolve to the dominant diminished and trill back to the Root. (Tonic) .

4. The use of all the triads in Harmonies with their folds i.e; Neapolitans, the seven degrees, descends as a Predominant, is the enrichness of the complexity or the simplicity of a method. That is the root of the "Classical Method" from fingering. And If you Parallel. Then you have automatic string voicings spread

for orchestration, normally with no sevenths. And when used with all of what's been covered then it's endless composition or improvisation in harmony, as well as piano music with geometric poetry. And there is a target note for everything.

You have 12 keys and how to go about around very easily in harmony by a targeting system. And you will find an enormous relief by being able to create anything musical, eternally. Meaning mathematically it circles eternally into a free state of creativity. Proof by sound and sound by hearing. I think, this is undoubtedly the very geometric system that we as human beings strive to accomplish for the freedom of man. This is the very system that was intended from the beginning of time by Jesus's birthday. This is the very system that is in charge of our existence; our well-being. Our freedom. Thomas Jefferson, Frances Bacon and Isaac Newton. *" Freedom of the mind "*. **With mathematical proof from a musical or sound perspective**. Einstein said*; " A free mind from expression or thought is necessary for creativity ".*

When I used to gig from night to night. I became very frustrated that playing material already written was like denying one the freedom to speak out at Free will. I had no problem improvising on the standards, my own tunes, or creating improvisational methods that one can use, by the many vast material that is in existence already. But I couldn't rest until I figured out the secret to this mathematical free state of mind. And only had a faint vision of the founding fathers view by written documentation. The founding fathers I refer to can be Johann Sebastian Bach. Or George Washington or Joseph Haydn, the creator of the classical style and the creator of the Constitution. (Both born on the same year, 1732). They looked alike. And were in the midst of this same time. How coincidental the peak of the classical era was 1776. It became clear that my deprivation, frustration and lack of education not only was overwhelmed with too much information. But it was only going to become real and rewarding by sheer experience of playing the piano and with quick results. Often, someone would whisper in my ear: It sounds like two people playing.

The other day I saw Winton Marsalis whom is a trumpeter playing these magnificent notes on the piano. If I could reach out and ask him what were those voicings at hand, I would have made a note of it. Voicings today are still defined from an old term and an era. As the voice of a person and not voicings of a piano of this modern era. In-fact the spelling of it is not even in the computer. The misspelling window as I'm writing this keeps telling me, there's no such thing as voicings with an s. As in plural. So it's not how long you have played but what and how you are playing and at what age, and how hard you work. The mastery of the instrument and the most relevant and important; how far accomplished ?

Mozart's strength was his age also, as well as how accomplished, and indeed the mastery of his instrument. In-fact the youngest accomplished composer ever. Which made him the best in terms of improvisation and composition. And with a fluent piano left hand much the same as Winton Marsalis's strength was indeed his age and accomplishments as a master of his instrument also. Marsalis's tapes of his improvisations in his teens are the proof. The word for that in this modern age is, he cooked. And pretty much the only one popular from my generation. As opposed to classical from Mozart's. Both accomplished at a young age. Both had fathers whom have experienced it professionally in the business coaching them.

As the piano matured, an argumentative point would arise such as; Has the music become more complex or deeper? So Mozart might have been the best composer ever, It's argumentative that his music might be simpler than Mendelssohn's for example, whom is also a child prodigy and as accomplished composer. There are subjective differences that can be argumentative at that indeed…

And as with this method and using your mind and body in conjunction with math and the very freedom that the founding fathers intended for us to have, i think I found the many secrets to it, especially by targeting. And it has given me an enormous relief. I am now enriched with more music than one lifetime can accomplish. I live in contentedness by the proof of the freedom of the mind. Can understand and accept it spiritually as well as scientifically and have an array of pages accumulating everyday in composition. Never frustrated what to play, improvise, compose, display or demonstrate **" The Classical Method "** .

The Three Building Blocks of the Classical Method

Consists of :

Exposition - Development - Capitulation

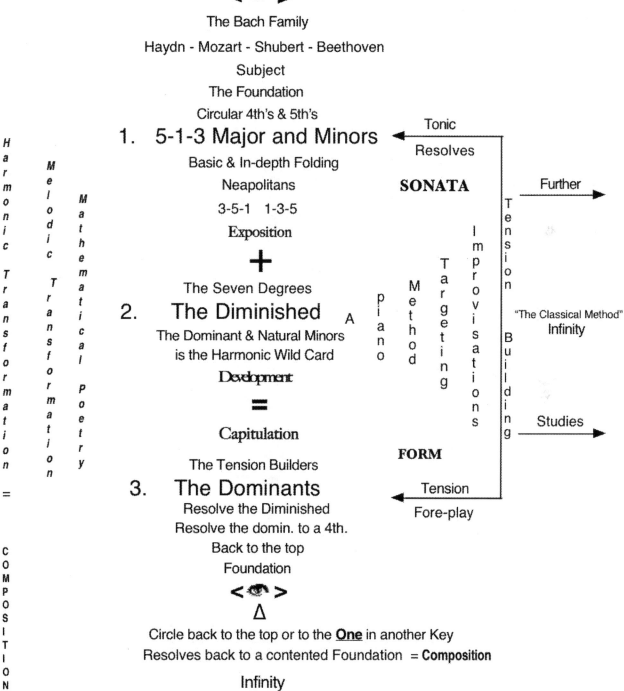

The Bach Family

Haydn - Mozart - Shubert - Beethoven

Subject

The Foundation

Circular 4th's & 5th's

1. **5-1-3 Major and Minors**

Basic & In-depth Folding

Neapolitans

3-5-1   1-3-5

Exposition

+

The Seven Degrees

2. **The Diminished**

The Dominant & Natural Minors

is the Harmonic Wild Card

Development

=

Capitulation

The Tension Builders

3. **The Dominants**

Resolve the Diminished

Resolve the domin. to a 4th.

Back to the top

Foundation

Δ

Circle back to the top or to the **One** in another Key

Resolves back to a contented Foundation = **Composition**

Infinity

Tonic

Resolves

SONATA

Further

Tension Building

Improvisations

Targeting

Method

piano

FORM

Tension

Fore-play

"The Classical Method"

Infinity

Studies

Harmonic Transformation =

Melodic Transformation

Mathematical Poetry

COMPOSITION

* Rated PG 14

"The mind always seem to be reaching looking for patterns that go beyond and captures
underlined structures of reality".
" Every discovery contains an irrational element or a creative intuition."
" Inductives agrees with the inspirits view that " All knowledge must come from experience".
" Karl Popper's position by contrast parallels the rationalist view that " Our deepest insights come
from pure reason, not experience".
- *Science is a series in exercises in imitation - which is normalcy .*
  punctuated by changes in fashion - which is revolutionary.
- *Einstein speaks of the search of those mighty universal laws from which the picture of the world*
  can be obtained by pure deduction. There is no logical paths leading to these laws. They can be
  reached by intuition based upon something like an intellectual love of the object of experience.
- *Popper crystalized another conception of science essentially theoretical. That theory transforms*
  in the head.
  - *Theories - " Imaginative posits invented in one piece for application to nature ".*

George Washington And Joseph Haydn - Remarkable resemblance between the two.

Both born in 1732

Both witnessed the inception of a method or a system declaring the preservation and
independence of the human mind in 1776. The Freedom of the mind from a musical and Political
Poetical parallel. The Classical Construct. The assurance and preservation of the human species
for all mankind to follow.

Have a good one !

The Dollar is monitored on daily basis
and is currently very low set against crude oil, gold,
silver and other commodities. *And for the 21 century*
you can add Google, Amazon, Paypal, Wickipedia, Apple
etc......

Doesn't that make the dollar
a medical condition for the human race?

The currency that houses the entire world
through a systematic geometrical binary
structure that is set to in-trust at one
conscience reassuring everyone is in
harmony and all monetary funds are sound...

The DESCENDING CIRCULAR

FOURTH

Chapter FOUR

A work of Art is:

The result for the search of deeper values

CLASSICAL TECHNIQUE

R.K. art

In-Depth Folding

The Descending Circular Fourth's are the resolves of the dominants. When the build up has reached its epic, then its time to descend for relief. Or its the complete Baroque technique all by itself. Here you can take any resolves that has been covered, and fold them in any key. These in Depth Foldings are the other side of the bridge that opens doors. They are to be practiced and memorized. The fingering most of the time will throw you into the next position. They will indulge you in patience. They are the link to other methods of playing. ie Jazz, Ravel, Debussy etc... They are used almost exclusively during the baroque era. Probably 90 percent of Bach's music consists of the descending fourth's. Palestrina, Vivaldi, Scarlatti, Handel.. p. 88, 101, 102

They are appropriately entered from any positions. I have developed Entrances from the 5-1-3 Major and Minors. These entrances seem to be most common to use. Also check out brainstorming, there are Many different entrances that will work from any 5-1-3. They should be essential tools to memorize for fluent Improvisations. Page 102 is the identical but in triad form. Also page 87.

The **Two Bass notes** that most likely get used from the bass that descends in fourth's can be altered to be used from any degree of the key just as long as they will harmonize for you. This is not pictured but its commonly used that way. You may go up the scale while the folding goes down. But first learn what's pictured. Bach went directly to the **two Bass notes** and built his Baroque compositions by weaving the two notes in lines using the scales that they belong to. Which is pictured here in all the keys. I've prepared them in octaves which suites the Partimenti practical applications for baroquing applications in infinity all by themselves. If you know what scale you are in, meaning what key or position or page you're on, then you can create by grabbing the bass notes first, and building by improvising on that key first. Notate, and then add other lines by ear. Here the practical comes in by using the ear to find the suitable lines for your composition. Bach's lines are sacred, because he prepared them for church congregations. If you've played live venues in high class restaurants, then you will understand what audiences can take and cannot take at any given point. Sometimes forks go flying out of ladies hands, or an older gentleman will choke on his food if not careful. Anyone who have played live understands how andwhere to use these creative descends. In Jazz its melancholic descends with belling piano overtones. Striking bells as you're creating the progressions. But for strict compositions, there are nothing like the weaving lines or point-counterpoint, or punctual counter-punctual weaving that Bach used. He was the master of arranging. This is not an Improvisational approach, but a compositional approach but first improvised with both hands. I like to use both thumbs inside walking up and down in thirds or fourth's like a latter stepping up or down in the midle of the improvisations to create many different harmonies on the fly for composition. Perhaps using page 101 for example and score afterwards.Then add the multiple counters for other instruments afterwards by ear. This is also useful in songwriting. Where the bass can harmonize from a different root against any chord. The major seventh's are pictured on the first page in the key of C only. And can very well be used in songwriting. As well as the positions themselves if not memorized. All the keys are pictured . One can take any position from any key and use for whatever music is in that regard. Songwriting can be complex or simple. It all depends on the song. If they come to you by surprise, then you have a choice of making it a masterpiece. And if you want to make a song a masterpiece. Then it takes beaten out. You have to beat them out of you. They write themselves eventually. But you have to beat them out by playing them over and over until they write themselves correctly, as a sculpture does with a statue. And these tools can help. Also check p. 160-173 in using the major 7th for song writing.

You must indulge yourself in learning all the positions from every key. You must have the correct fingering to execute the folds. Without the correct fingering its a recipe for disaster. They must be fingered correctly for improvisations. For it will sometimes find the positions for you. By feel. If you practice them on regular basis. These foldings are actually fifty percent of this books material. After you master the other essential theories in this book and their targets then these will be the other half of the majority half of this book. That's how important and vastly essential and lengthy as well as a must these foldings are. And Both hands should know both positions. Sometimes you need to use them with the right hand and sometimes with the left hand. It may take a while but it will make all the difference later on. I used to use these In-depth foldings in public 2 to 3 keys at a time. With the proper grand pianos they can sparkle any gig with any style of music. Learning them in public in a gig is much more comprehensible than learning them at home. And much more rewarding and enjoyable for the player. They will keep one amused. And can be learned at lightening speed that way.

preparation for descending circular fourth's
A Clear Picture before in depth folding Starts

example: 28

1. Take any Key and walk its scale in triads. Any of the positions can be entrances for foldings. Immediately you are confronted with which positions to use. The 1-3-5 standard, or the classical 5-1-3 fingering improvisational positions. Bach used both after simplification, and a clever way to spot them at the speed of thought. Folding in descends. The next few pages will be the 5-1-3 and 1-3-5 infinite patterns in octaved or simplified forms for improvisations. You will see how easy it is going from 1-3-5 majors and minors to 5-1-3 folds. These are the first to spot and learn and are the standard descends. From page 87 will be the other approach that will combine a duel approach to descends that Bach used on daily basis. First learn these from pages 50-80. After you can spot and implement at any point during improvisations which will give you descends from the baroque or bach method under your fingers instantaneously and a pattern to follow directly and indirectly for composition as well.

Mnemonic - 2. *The pattern is going to be* **MAJ**-*min*-*min*-**MAJ**-**MAJ**-*min*-*dim* ; Here we see a pattern : The first position is always a major and then 2 minors and 2 majors and 2 miners . This pattern will be true for any key or positions. We're only concerned with the 1-3-5's and 5-1-3's primarily for fluent improvisational technique and methodology. Now, the last position in-wich i call a minor also which is the subtonic of-course is going to be a diminished b7th for the 1-3-5's. Or diminished 5-1-3 for the 5-1-3's. The seven degrees are comprehended in this mnemonic pattern as standard knowledge of-course. But it is not necessarily found in this manner. To find them on the fly while improvisational fingering is at epic and influential from key to key in simplification format is as follows: First of all, if you deduct the subtonic momentarily for clarity. Then one is left with three majors and three minors period. Ok to find these three majors and minors on the fly; take any key you are working with first of all, take the 5-1-3 of the key, sharpen the 3rd. finger 1/2 step, look at the notes left, they are the three major positions of that key. For the minors; You take the natural minor of the key you're on, again take this 5-1-3 minor and sharpen the 3rd. finger 1 step this time, again look at the three notes left of the 5-1-3 and this is the three minors of that key this time . That is the proper way to find the 7 degrees of any key on the fly. Mind you this is simplification and un-octaved for fluent sub-conscience improvisations. As Bach used every day. Knowing how to use descends on a pattern in any key, or after the fact that you have established a melody, motif or already committed to a key. Knowing how to use the descends of any key. You can clearly see the simplificant folds from any ordinary 1-3-5 major or minor to 5-1-3's in-which is the descends used scientifically or mathematically on the fly. Please refer to **pages 101 and 88** for further descriptive analysis. **And page 87 for the other pattern and approach in combination with these in-depth foldings**. Bach knew both and used both of them on the fly at any point .... One small final item to remember is the subtonic of any 5-1-3 descends will be the fourth major position folded to diminished 5-1-3. Example: In the key of C : F is the fourth and will fold to 5-1-3 diminished. That is the subtonic of C.

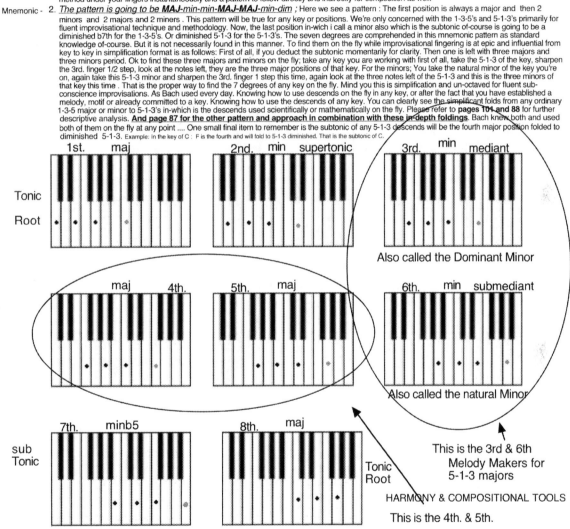

1st. maj   2nd. min supertonic   3rd. min mediant

Tonic

Root

Also called the Dominant Minor

maj 4th.   5th. maj   6th. min submediant

Also called the natural Minor

7th. minb5   8th. maj

sub Tonic

Tonic Root

This is the 3rd & 6th Melody Makers for 5-1-3 majors

HARMONY & COMPOSITIONAL TOOLS

This is the 4th. & 5th.

3. The Dominant Minor (the 3rd.) & Natural Minor (the 6th.) are always going to harmonize with the Root. **Target notes**: **The 3 of any 5-1-3 major** and **the 6th. of any 5-1-3 major** which is 1 step up from any 5. These are also entrances for in-Depth Folding. Know how to spot these target notes immediately for harmony or entrances as well.

You notice the 4th. & 5th. are majors. Always harmonizing with the root. The 4th. is the subdominant and the 5th. is the dominant. They are the pure tones of the scale. If you follow the target method in this book. Everything will work itself out automatically for you.

Theoretically any of these 7 steps are entrances for in-depth folding of the key you're in. The target notes should correspond to just about all the positions of any key. And if you simplify and spot these 7 degrees from any angle or understand which and where they are from any angle, you would then can improvise any sound or tone you wish instantaneously and at the speed of thought, as Bach did with or without any piece of music. 5-1-3 triads are the key to simplification and in-depth improvisations with ease of fingering...

Robert Kaye

example: 29a BACH Folding the Descending Circular Fourth's The Key of C
Simplified in triads for fluent Improvisations *practice all the keys*

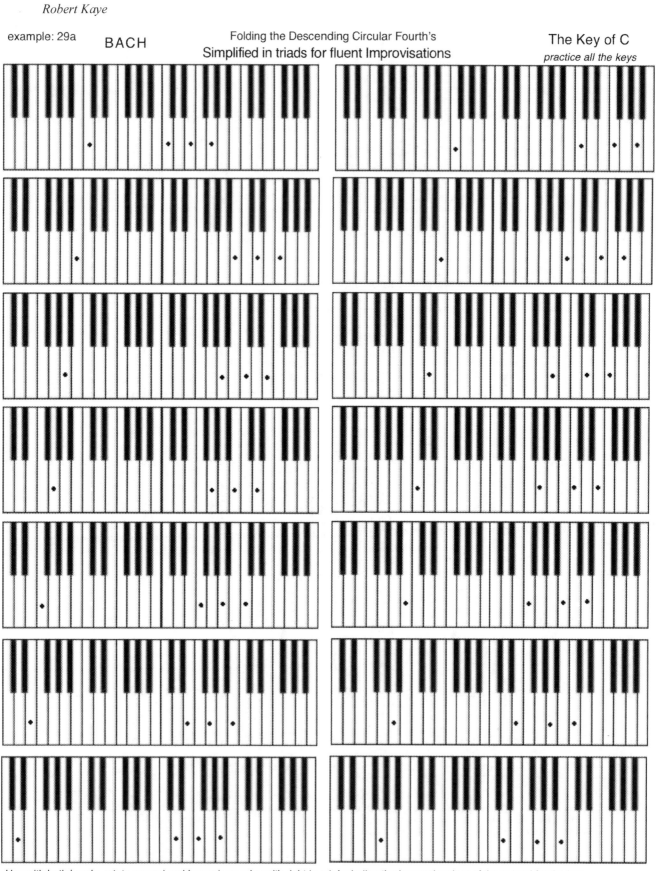

Use with both hands, rotate around and Improvise scales with right hand. Including the harmonic minor of the natural for the key. Here A harmonic minor

54

Descending 4th. in the key of C

example 29 b 1

The seventh is not added right now but later on you can add the
7th in all the keys. The minor7th and the major 7th that is. Right now we're just
octaving in diatonics. For Classical ∞ its Eternal, as opposed to Songwriting.

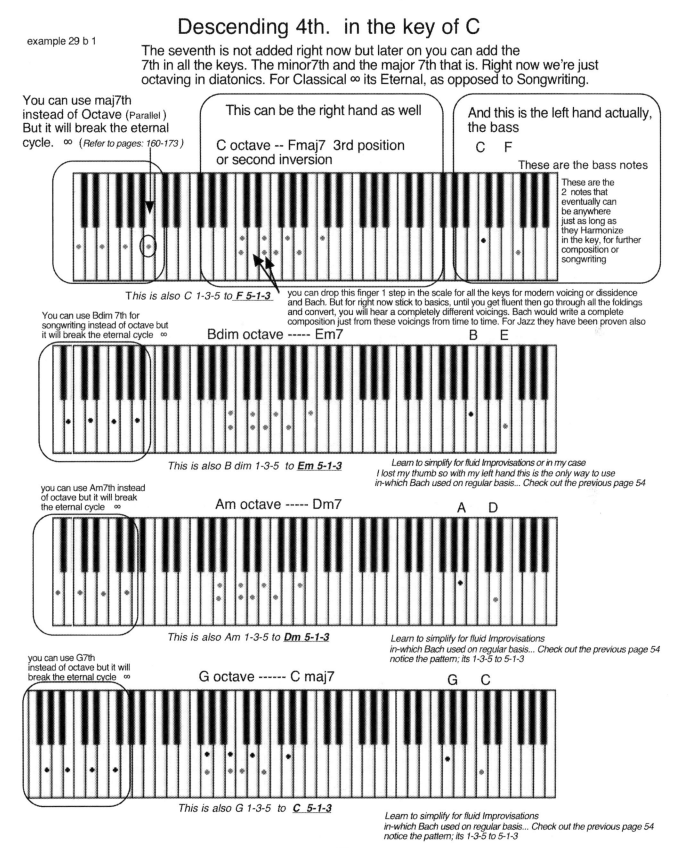

You can use maj7th
instead of Octave (Parallel)
But it will break the eternal
cycle. ∞ (*Refer to pages: 160-173*)

This can be the right hand as well

C octave -- Fmaj7 3rd position
or second inversion

And this is the left hand actually,
the bass

C F

These are the bass notes

These are the
2 notes that
eventually can
be anywhere
just as long as
they Harmonize
in the key, for further
composition or
songwriting

This is also C 1-3-5 to **F 5-1-3**

you can drop this finger 1 step in the scale for all the keys for modern voicing or dissidence
and Bach. But for right now stick to basics, until you get fluent then go through all the foldings
and convert, you will hear a completely different voicings. Bach would write a complete
composition just from these voicings from time to time. For Jazz they have been proven also

You can use Bdim 7th for
songwriting instead of octave but
it will break the eternal cycle ∞

Bdim octave ----- Em7

B E

This is also B dim 1-3-5 to **Em 5-1-3**

*Learn to simplify for fluid Improvisations or in my case
I lost my thumb so with my left hand this is the only way to use
in-which Bach used on regular basis... Check out the previous page 54*

you can use Am7th instead
of octave but it will break
the eternal cycle ∞

Am octave ----- Dm7

A D

This is also Am 1-3-5 to **Dm 5-1-3**

*Learn to simplify for fluid Improvisations
in-which Bach used on regular basis... Check out the previous page 54
notice the pattern; its 1-3-5 to 5-1-3*

you can use G7th
instead of octave but it will
break the eternal cycle ∞

G octave ------ C maj7

G C

This is also G 1-3-5 to **C 5-1-3**

*Learn to simplify for fluid Improvisations
in-which Bach used on regular basis... Check out the previous page 54
notice the pattern; its 1-3-5 to 5-1-3*

Descending 4th. in the key of C

∞ Classical ∞

example 29 b2

continued

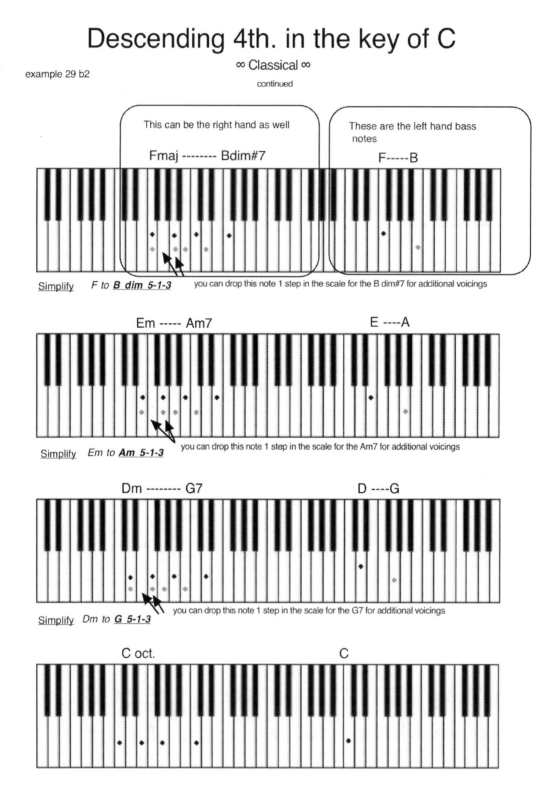

This can be the right hand as well

Fmaj -------- Bdim#7

These are the left hand bass notes

F-----B

<u>Simplify</u>   *F to **B dim 5-1-3***   you can drop this note 1 step in the scale for the B dim#7 for additional voicings

Em ----- Am7   **E ----A**

<u>Simplify</u>   *Em to **Am 5-1-3***   you can drop this note 1 step in the scale for the Am7 for additional voicings

Dm -------- G7   **D ----G**

<u>Simplify</u>   *Dm to **G 5-1-3***   you can drop this note 1 step in the scale for the G7 for additional voicings

C oct.   **C**

The Folding Descending 4th's
∞ Classical ∞
Key Db

example : 29 b3

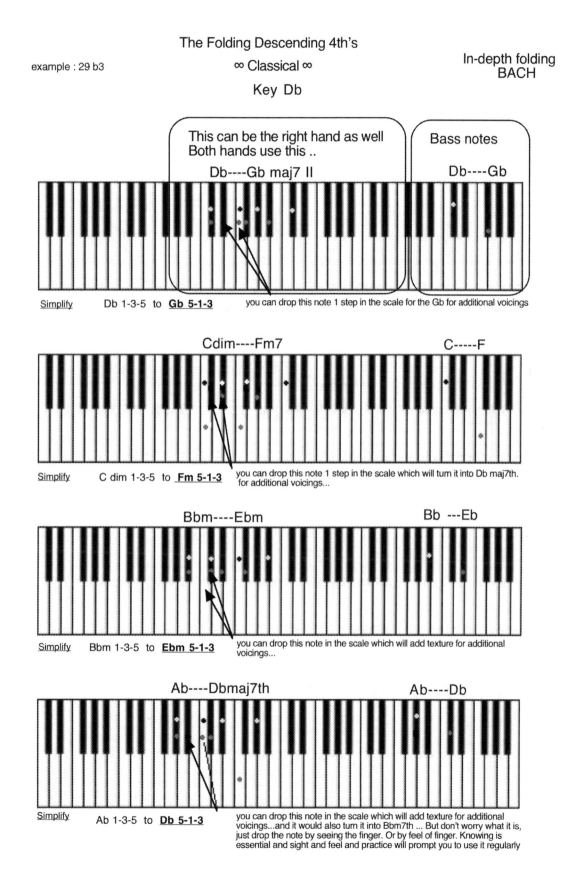

This can be the right hand as well
Both hands use this ..

Db----Gb maj7 II

Bass notes

Db----Gb

Simplify   Db 1-3-5 to **Gb 5-1-3**   you can drop this note 1 step in the scale for the Gb for additional voicings

Cdim----Fm7

C-----F

Simplify   C dim 1-3-5 to **Fm 5-1-3**   you can drop this note 1 step in the scale which will turn it into Db maj7th. for additional voicings...

Bbm----Ebm

Bb ---Eb

Simplify   Bbm 1-3-5 to **Ebm 5-1-3**   you can drop this note in the scale which will add texture for additional voicings...

Ab----Dbmaj7th

Ab----Db

Simplify   Ab 1-3-5 to **Db 5-1-3**   you can drop this note in the scale which will add texture for additional voicings...and it would also turn it into Bbm7th ... But don't worry what it is, just drop the note by seeing the finger. Or by feel of finger. Knowing is essential and sight and feel and practice will prompt you to use it regularly

57

The folding Descending 4th's

∞ Classical ∞

example: 29 b4

In-depth folding
BACH

Key Db

continued

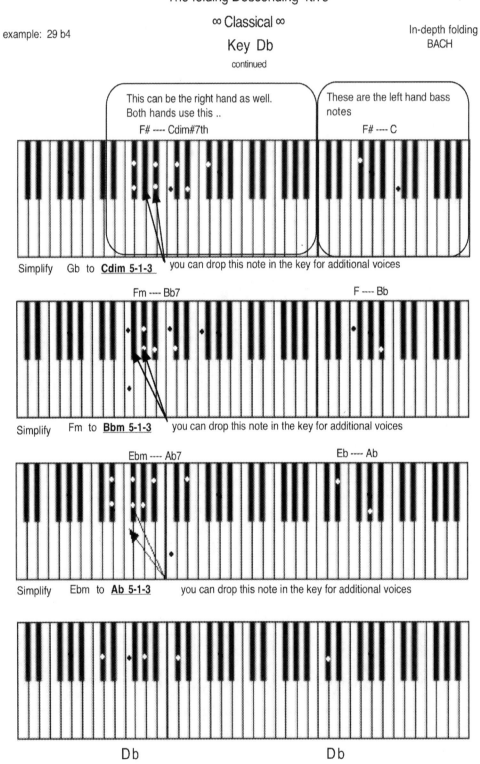

This can be the right hand as well.
Both hands use this ..

F# ---- Cdim#7th

These are the left hand bass notes

F# ---- C

Simplify   Gb to **Cdim 5-1-3**   you can drop this note in the key for additional voices

Fm ---- Bb7

F ---- Bb

Simplify   Fm to **Bbm 5-1-3**   you can drop this note in the key for additional voices

Ebm ---- Ab7

Eb ---- Ab

Simplify   Ebm to **Ab 5-1-3**   you can drop this note in the key for additional voices

Db

Db

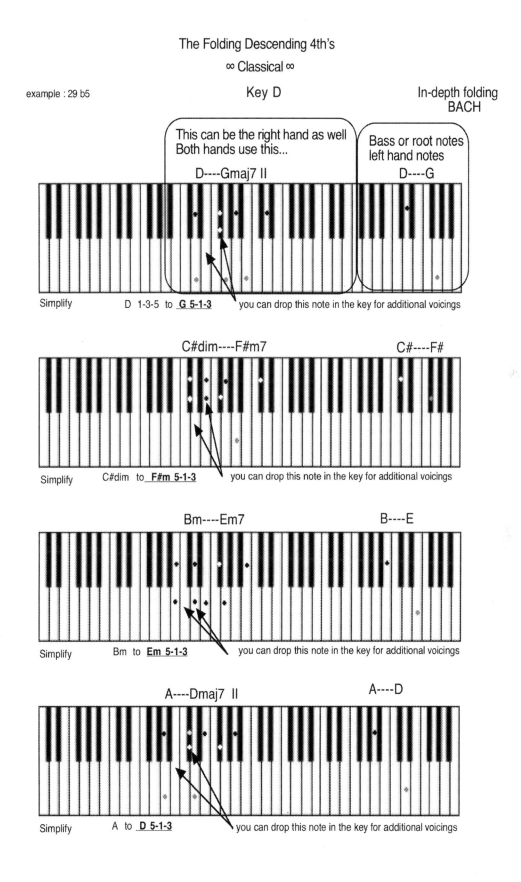

The Folding Descending 4th's

∞ Classical ∞

example : 29 b5   **Key D**   In-depth folding
BACH

This can be the right hand as well
Both hands use this...

D----Gmaj7 II   Bass or root notes
left hand notes

D----G

Simplify   D 1-3-5 to **G 5-1-3**   you can drop this note in the key for additional voicings

C#dim----F#m7   C#----F#

Simplify   C#dim to **F#m 5-1-3**   you can drop this note in the key for additional voicings

Bm----Em7   B----E

Simplify   Bm to **Em 5-1-3**   you can drop this note in the key for additional voicings

A----Dmaj7 II   A----D

Simplify   A to **D 5-1-3**   you can drop this note in the key for additional voicings

The Folding Descending 4th's

example 29 b6

∞ Classical ∞

In-depth folding
BACH

Key D

continued

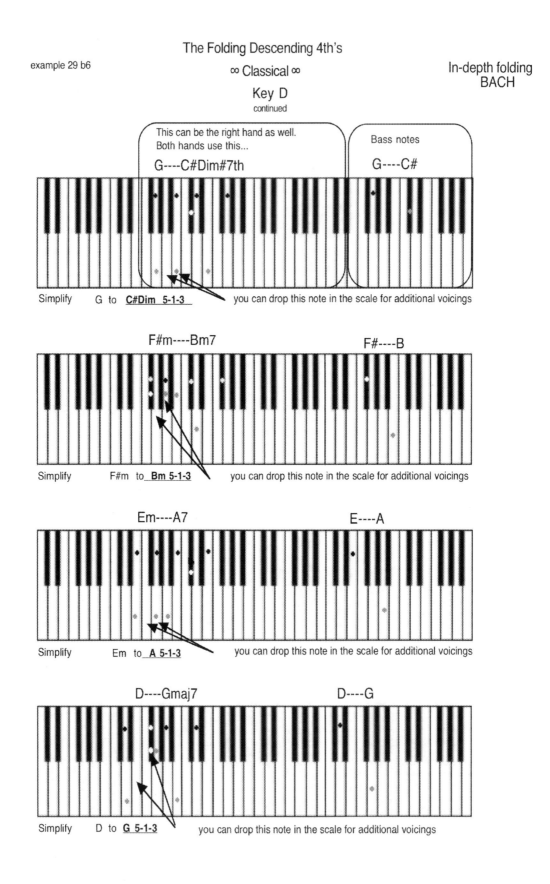

This can be the right hand as well.
Both hands use this...

G----C#Dim#7th

Bass notes

G----C#

Simplify   G to   **C#Dim 5-1-3**   you can drop this note in the scale for additional voicings

F#m----Bm7

F#----B

Simplify   F#m to **Bm 5-1-3**   you can drop this note in the scale for additional voicings

Em----A7

E----A

Simplify   Em to **A 5-1-3**   you can drop this note in the scale for additional voicings

D----Gmaj7

D----G

Simplify   D to **G 5-1-3**   you can drop this note in the scale for additional voicings

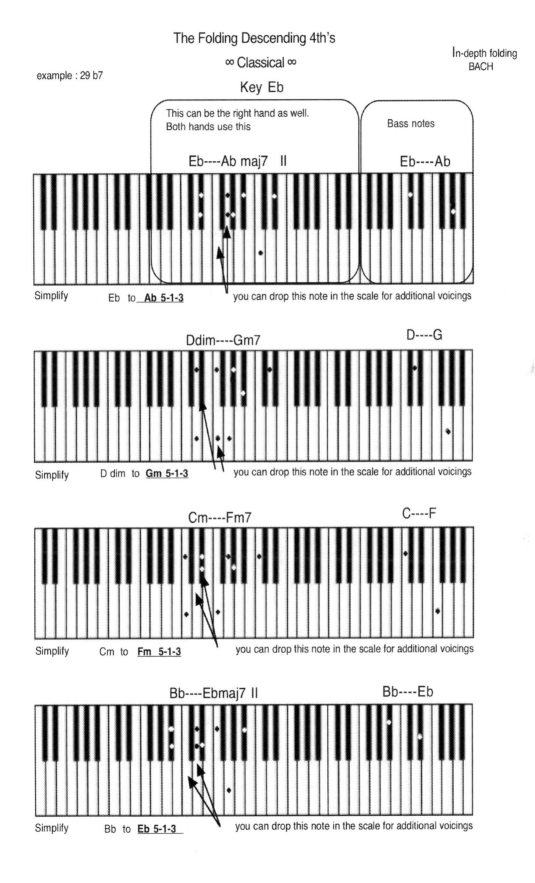

The Folding Descending 4th's

∞ Classical ∞

In-depth folding
BACH

example : 29 b7

Key Eb

This can be the right hand as well.
Both hands use this

Bass notes

Eb----Ab maj7 II

Eb----Ab

Simplify   Eb to **Ab 5-1-3**   you can drop this note in the scale for additional voicings

Ddim----Gm7

D----G

Simplify   D dim to **Gm 5-1-3**   you can drop this note in the scale for additional voicings

Cm----Fm7

C---F

Simplify   Cm to **Fm 5-1-3**   you can drop this note in the scale for additional voicings

Bb----Ebmaj7 II

Bb----Eb

Simplify   Bb to **Eb 5-1-3**   you can drop this note in the scale for additional voicings

The folding descending fourth's
∞ Classical ∞
Key Eb
continued

example : 29 b8

In-depth folding
BACH

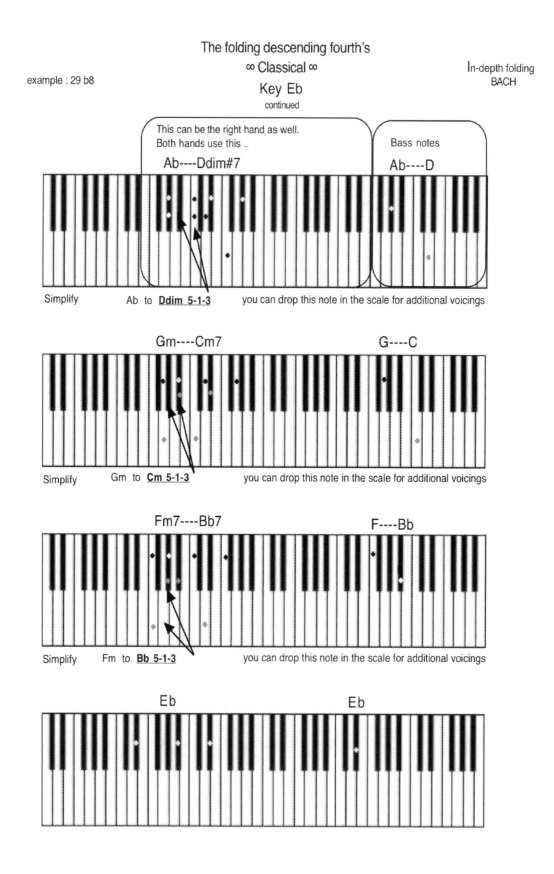

This can be the right hand as well.
Both hands use this ..

Ab----Ddim#7

Bass notes

Ab----D

Simplify   Ab to **Ddim 5-1-3**   you can drop this note in the scale for additional voicings

Gm----Cm7   G----C

Simplify   Gm to **Cm 5-1-3**   you can drop this note in the scale for additional voicings

Fm7----Bb7   F----Bb

Simplify   Fm to **Bb 5-1-3**   you can drop this note in the scale for additional voicings

Eb   Eb

The Folding Descending 4th's

example : 29 b9

∞ Classical ∞

Key E

In-depth folding
BACH

continued

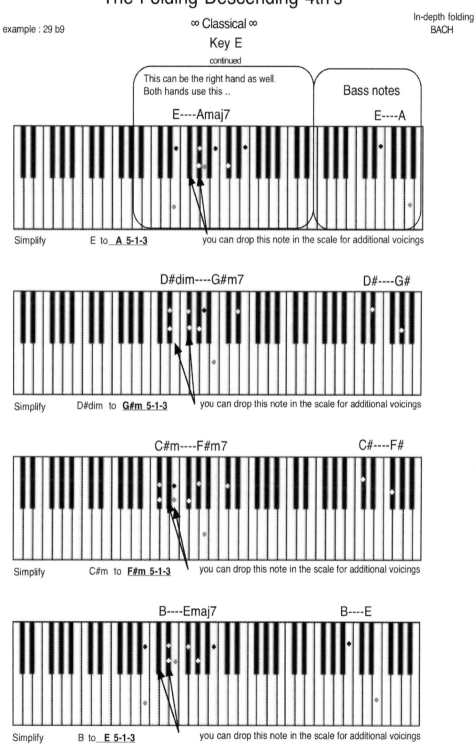

This can be the right hand as well.
Both hands use this ..

Bass notes

E----Amaj7

E----A

Simplify   E to __A 5-1-3__   you can drop this note in the scale for additional voicings

D#dim----G#m7

D#----G#

Simplify   D#dim to __G#m 5-1-3__   you can drop this note in the scale for additional voicings

C#m----F#m7

C#----F#

Simplify   C#m to __F#m 5-1-3__   you can drop this note in the scale for additional voicings

B----Emaj7

B----E

Simplify   B to __E 5-1-3__   you can drop this note in the scale for additional voicings

The Folding Descending 4th's
∞ Classical ∞

example : 29 b10

Key E
continued

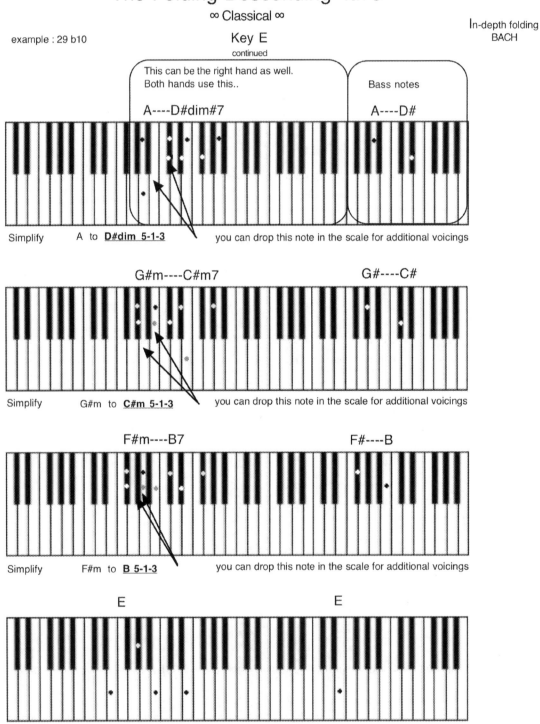

This can be the right hand as well.
Both hands use this..

A----D#dim#7

Bass notes

A----D#

Simplify   A to **D#dim 5-1-3**   you can drop this note in the scale for additional voicings

G#m----C#m7   G#----C#

Simplify   G#m to **C#m 5-1-3**   you can drop this note in the scale for additional voicings

F#m----B7   F#----B

Simplify   F#m to **B 5-1-3**   you can drop this note in the scale for additional voicings

E   E

The Folding Descending 4th's

∞ Classical ∞

Key F

continued

example : 29 b11

In-depth folding
BACH

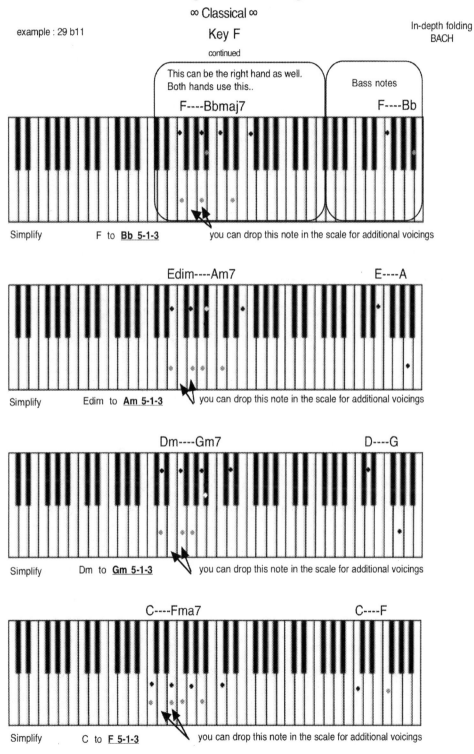

This can be the right hand as well.
Both hands use this..

F----Bbmaj7

Bass notes

F----Bb

Simplify   F to **Bb 5-1-3**   you can drop this note in the scale for additional voicings

Edim----Am7   E----A

Simplify   Edim to **Am 5-1-3**   you can drop this note in the scale for additional voicings

Dm----Gm7   D----G

Simplify   Dm to **Gm 5-1-3**   you can drop this note in the scale for additional voicings

C----Fma7   C----F

Simplify   C to **F 5-1-3**   you can drop this note in the scale for additional voicings

The Folding Descending 4th's

∞ Classical ∞

example 29 : b12

Key F

continued

In-depth folding
BACH

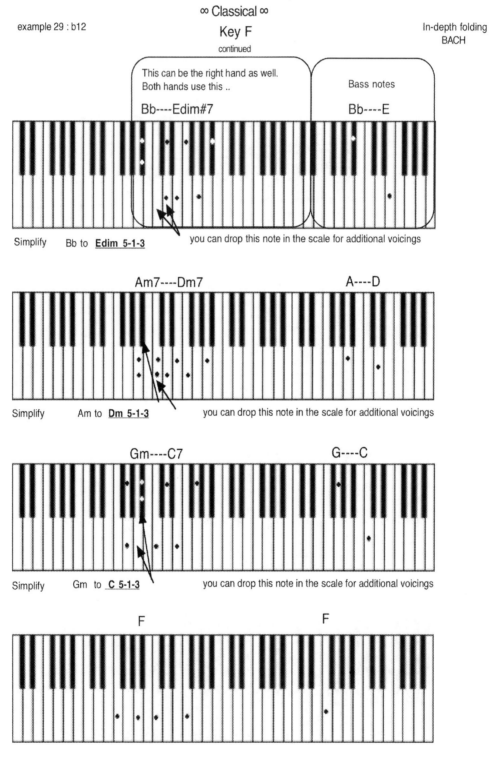

This can be the right hand as well.
Both hands use this ..

Bb----Edim#7

Bass notes

Bb----E

Simplify   Bb to **Edim 5-1-3**   you can drop this note in the scale for additional voicings

Am7----Dm7   A----D

Simplify   Am to **Dm 5-1-3**   you can drop this note in the scale for additional voicings

Gm----C7   G----C

Simplify   Gm to **C 5-1-3**   you can drop this note in the scale for additional voicings

F   F

The Folding Descending 4th's

∞ Classical ∞

example : 29 b13

Key F#

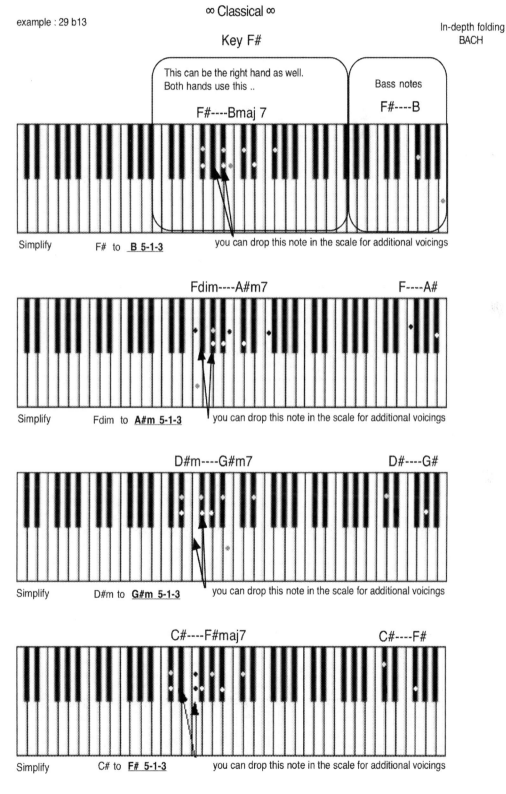

This can be the right hand as well.
Both hands use this ..

F#----Bmaj 7

Bass notes

F#----B

Simplify   F# to **B 5-1-3**   you can drop this note in the scale for additional voicings

Fdim----A#m7   F----A#

Simplify   Fdim to **A#m 5-1-3**   you can drop this note in the scale for additional voicings

D#m----G#m7   D#----G#

Simplify   D#m to **G#m 5-1-3**   you can drop this note in the scale for additional voicings

C#----F#maj7   C#----F#

Simplify   C# to **F# 5-1-3**   you can drop this note in the scale for additional voicings

The Folding Descending 4th's

∞ Classical ∞

example : 29 b14

Key F#

continued

In-depth folding
BACH

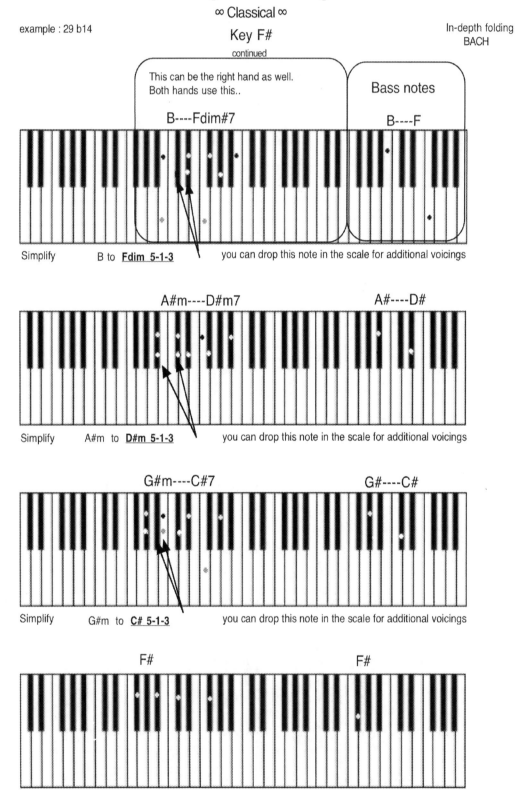

This can be the right hand as well.
Both hands use this..

B----Fdim#7

Bass notes

B----F

Simplify   B to **Fdim 5-1-3**   you can drop this note in the scale for additional voicings

A#m----D#m7   A#----D#

Simplify   A#m to **D#m 5-1-3**   you can drop this note in the scale for additional voicings

G#m----C#7   G#----C#

Simplify   G#m to **C# 5-1-3**   you can drop this note in the scale for additional voicings

F#   F#

The Folding Descending 4th's

example : 29 b15   ∞ Classical ∞   In-depth folding
                                                 BACH

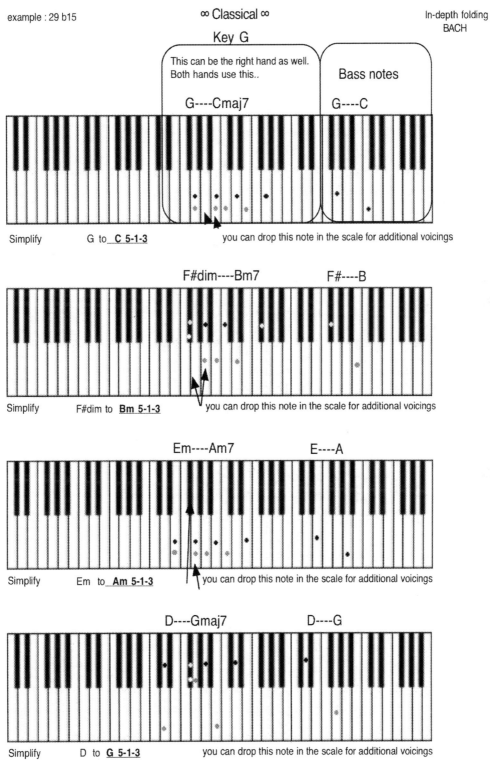

Key G

This can be the right hand as well.
Both hands use this..

Bass notes

G----Cmaj7   G----C

Simplify   G to **C 5-1-3**   you can drop this note in the scale for additional voicings

F#dim----Bm7   F#----B

Simplify   F#dim to **Bm 5-1-3**   you can drop this note in the scale for additional voicings

Em----Am7   E----A

Simplify   Em to **Am 5-1-3**   you can drop this note in the scale for additional voicings

D----Gmaj7   D----G

Simplify   D to **G 5-1-3**   you can drop this note in the scale for additional voicings

69

The Folding Descending 4th's
∞ Classical ∞
Key G

example : 29 b16

In-depth folding
BACH

continued

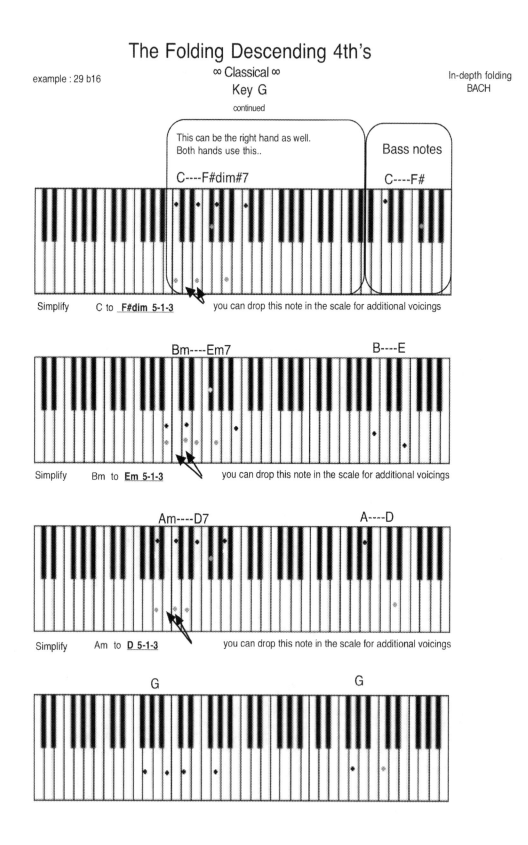

This can be the right hand as well.
Both hands use this..

C----F#dim#7

Bass notes

C----F#

Simplify   C to **F#dim 5-1-3**   you can drop this note in the scale for additional voicings

Bm----Em7   B----E

Simplify   Bm to **Em 5-1-3**   you can drop this note in the scale for additional voicings

Am----D7   A----D

Simplify   Am to **D 5-1-3**   you can drop this note in the scale for additional voicings

G   G

The Folding Descending 4th's

example : 29 b17   ∞ Classical ∞   In-depth folding
                                        BACH
                                    Key Ab

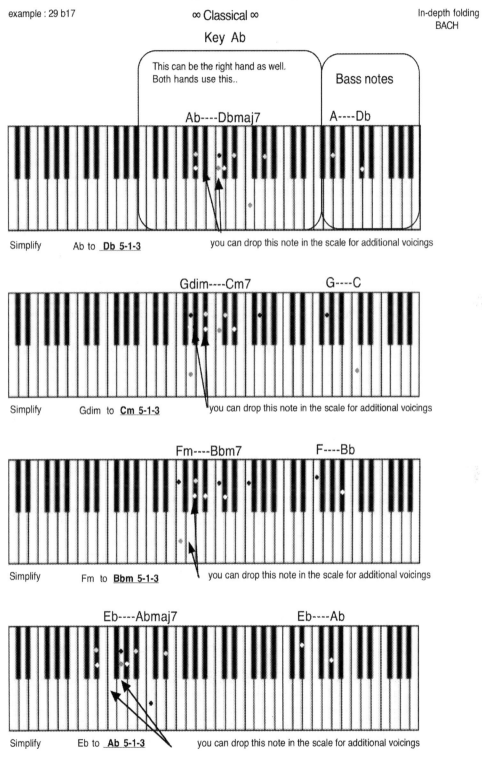

This can be the right hand as well.
Both hands use this..   Bass notes

Ab----Dbmaj7   A----Db

Simplify   Ab to **Db 5-1-3**   you can drop this note in the scale for additional voicings

Gdim----Cm7   G----C

Simplify   Gdim to **Cm 5-1-3**   you can drop this note in the scale for additional voicings

Fm----Bbm7   F----Bb

Simplify   Fm to **Bbm 5-1-3**   you can drop this note in the scale for additional voicings

Eb----Abmaj7   Eb----Ab

Simplify   Eb to **Ab 5-1-3**   you can drop this note in the scale for additional voicings

71

The Folding Descending 4th's

∞ Classical ∞

example : 29 b18

Key Ab

continued

In-depth folding
BACH

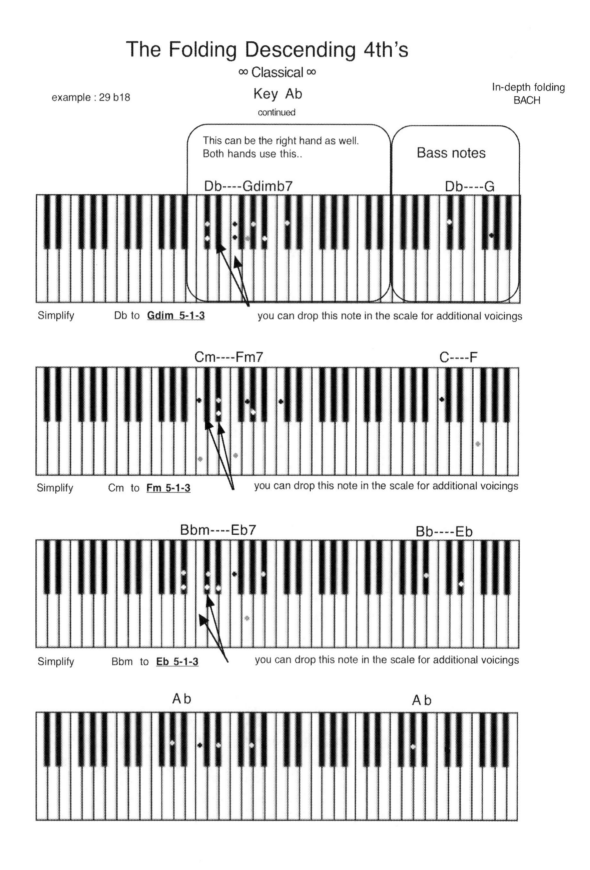

This can be the right hand as well.
Both hands use this..

Db----Gdimb7

Bass notes

Db----G

Simplify Db to **Gdim 5-1-3**   you can drop this note in the scale for additional voicings

Cm----Fm7

C----F

Simplify Cm to **Fm 5-1-3**   you can drop this note in the scale for additional voicings

Bbm----Eb7

Bb----Eb

Simplify Bbm to **Eb 5-1-3**   you can drop this note in the scale for additional voicings

A b

A b

The Folding Descending 4th's

example : 29 b19

∞ Classical ∞

Key A

In-depth folding
BACH

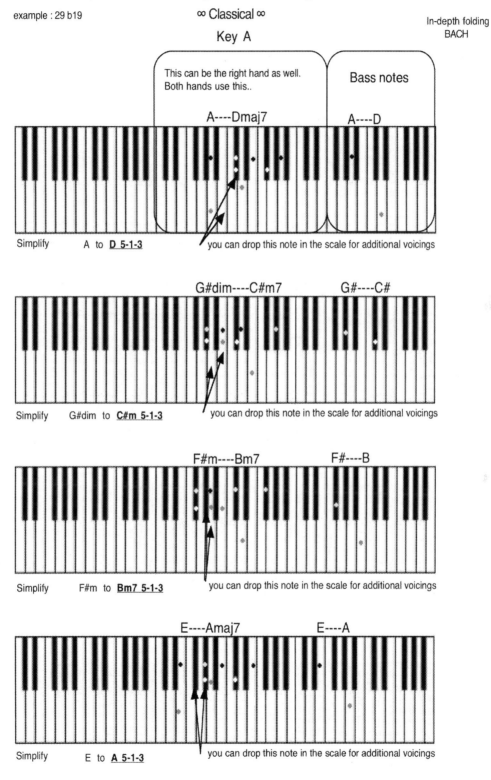

This can be the right hand as well.
Both hands use this..

Bass notes

A----Dmaj7

A----D

Simplify   A to **D 5-1-3**   you can drop this note in the scale for additional voicings

G#dim----C#m7   G#----C#

Simplify   G#dim to **C#m 5-1-3**   you can drop this note in the scale for additional voicings

F#m----Bm7   F#----B

Simplify   F#m to **Bm7 5-1-3**   you can drop this note in the scale for additional voicings

E----Amaj7   E---A

Simplify   E to **A 5-1-3**   you can drop this note in the scale for additional voicings

73

The Folding Descending 4th's

∞ Classical ∞

example : 29 b20

Key A

continued

In-depth folding
BACH

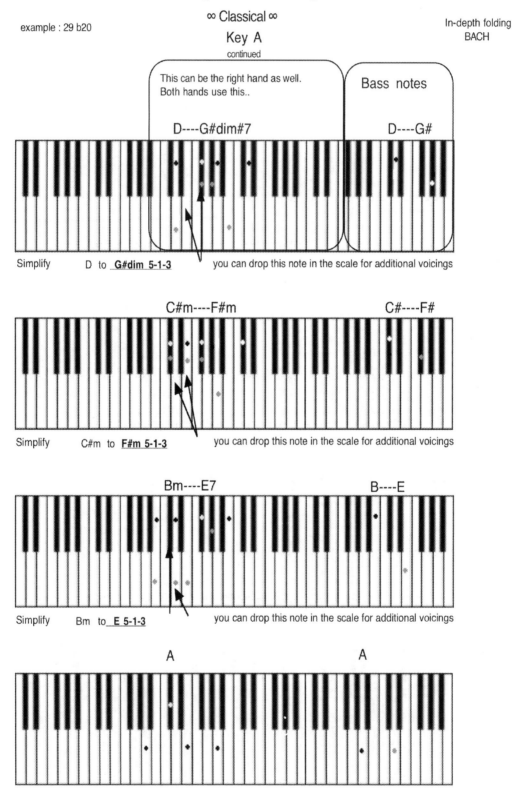

This can be the right hand as well.
Both hands use this..

D----G#dim#7

Bass notes

D----G#

Simplify   D to **G#dim 5-1-3**   you can drop this note in the scale for additional voicings

C#m----F#m

C#----F#

Simplify   C#m to **F#m 5-1-3**   you can drop this note in the scale for additional voicings

Bm----E7

B----E

Simplify   Bm to **E 5-1-3**   you can drop this note in the scale for additional voicings

A

A

74

The Folding Descending 4th's

∞ Classical ∞

example : 29 b21

Key Bb

In-depth folding
BACH

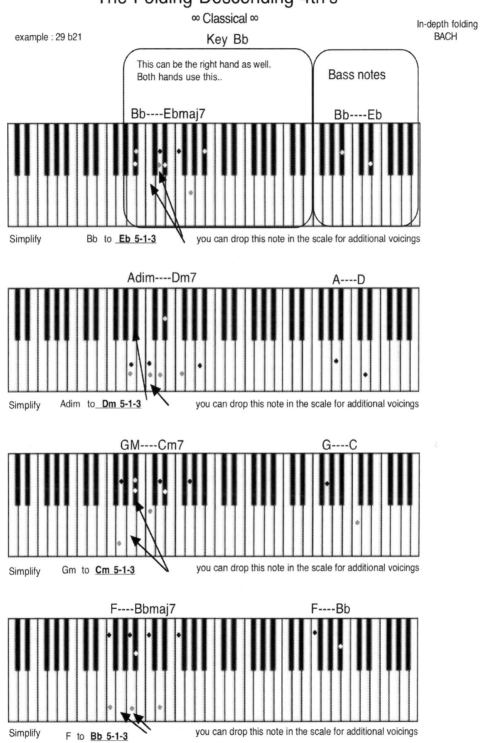

This can be the right hand as well.
Both hands use this..

Bass notes

Bb----Ebmaj7

Bb----Eb

Simplify   Bb to **Eb 5-1-3**   you can drop this note in the scale for additional voicings

Adim----Dm7   A----D

Simplify   Adim to **Dm 5-1-3**   you can drop this note in the scale for additional voicings

GM----Cm7   G----C

Simplify   Gm to **Cm 5-1-3**   you can drop this note in the scale for additional voicings

F----Bbmaj7   F----Bb

Simplify   F to **Bb 5-1-3**   you can drop this note in the scale for additional voicings

The Folding Descending 4th's

∞ Classical ∞

example : 29 b22

Key Bb

In-depth folding
BACH

continued

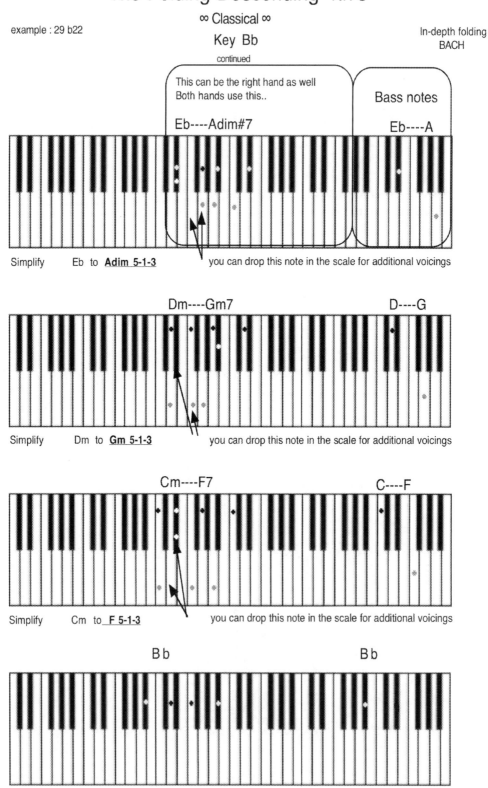

This can be the right hand as well
Both hands use this..

Eb----Adim#7

Bass notes

Eb----A

Simplify   Eb to **Adim 5-1-3**   you can drop this note in the scale for additional voicings

Dm----Gm7   D----G

Simplify   Dm to **Gm 5-1-3**   you can drop this note in the scale for additional voicings

Cm----F7   C----F

Simplify   Cm to **F 5-1-3**   you can drop this note in the scale for additional voicings

B b   B b

The Folding Descending 4th's

∞ Classical ∞
Key B

In-depth folding
BACH

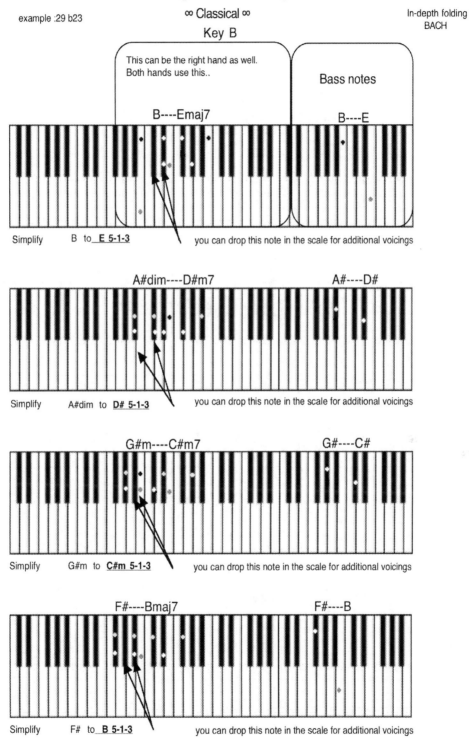

This can be the right hand as well.
Both hands use this..

Bass notes

B----Emaj7

B----E

Simplify   B to **E 5-1-3**   you can drop this note in the scale for additional voicings

A#dim----D#m7   A#----D#

Simplify   A#dim to **D# 5-1-3**   you can drop this note in the scale for additional voicings

G#m----C#m7   G#----C#

Simplify   G#m to **C#m 5-1-3**   you can drop this note in the scale for additional voicings

F#----Bmaj7   F#----B

Simplify   F# to **B 5-1-3**   you can drop this note in the scale for additional voicings

77

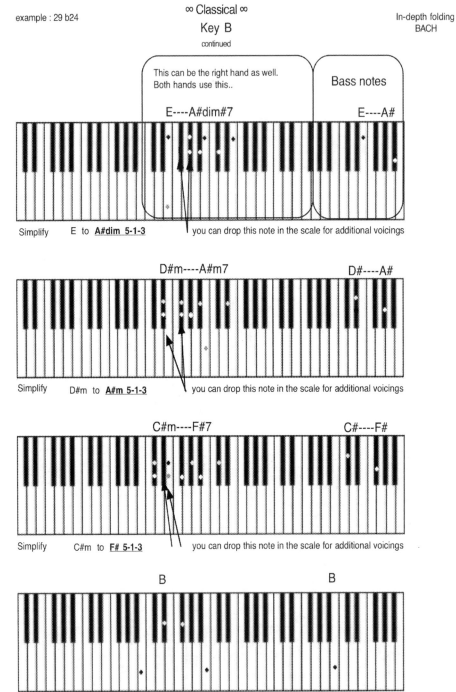

Robert Kaye

The Folding Descending 4th's

∞ Classical ∞

example : 29 b24

Key B

In-depth folding
BACH

continued

This can be the right hand as well.
Both hands use this..

E----A#dim#7

Bass notes

E----A#

Simplify   E to **A#dim 5-1-3**   you can drop this note in the scale for additional voicings

D#m----A#m7

D#----A#

Simplify   D#m to **A#m 5-1-3**   you can drop this note in the scale for additional voicings

C#m----F#7

C#----F#

Simplify   C#m to **F# 5-1-3**   you can drop this note in the scale for additional voicings

B

B

78

NOTATED
The Folding Descending 4th's

example : 29

In- depth Folding

The Classical Technique

79

Robert Kaye

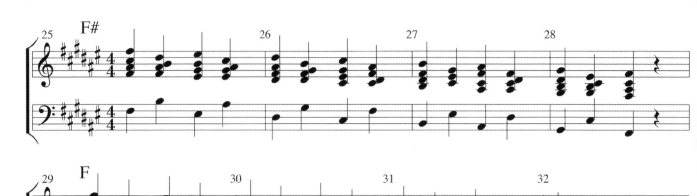

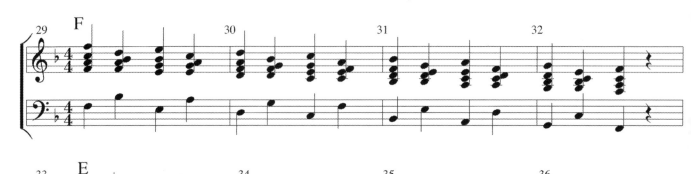

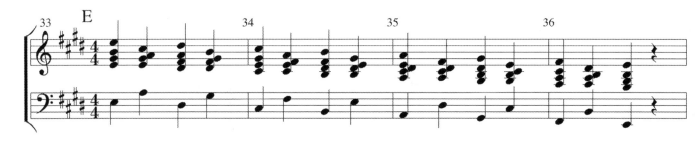

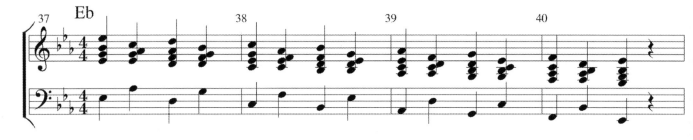

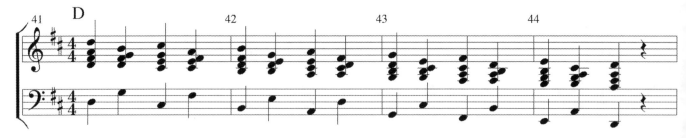

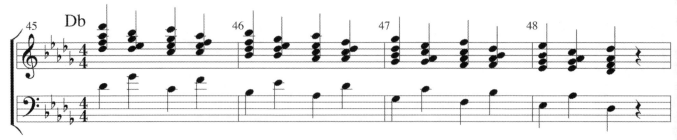

Further Studies

Building Composition

IMPROVISATION
The Ninth Tension builders

The Classical Style
as a predominant

The rules and first step in building your compositional Improvisation. Or building a conversation or building your foundation. Or creating a dish of meal to eat. Or going to town to create a business. Whatever the analogy you want to use. This should be your first steps in creating your musical conversation. We now are aware of the basic folding principles. In-fact lets go ahead and say. That whenever we are talking about any 5-1-3 triad. We are most likely 99 percent of the time sure that we are talking about its fold also. Any 5-1-3 that is mentioned will assume that it's being folded with it's family. Ex. A C Maj. 5-1-3 will fold to its G7. This is what I call pumping. Classical Music is continuos pumping with the left hand. It's a prime water pump. We prime for tension and resolve. Non stop. Among the first conversation tools to use are the Dominant minors and the Natural minors. They are also referred to from time to time as : The Mediant & the Submediant. Right ? respectively. The Mediant or the Dominant Minor happens to also be the subject of conversation that we are addressing here now. It also happens to be the Ninth. The ninth's are found from the third of any root. From the Mediant. Now we use a target note just the same as we use for the circulating 4ths & 5ths. Except this target note will be the 3rd. or the third finger if we are talking about 5-1-3 triads. And we most certainly are. The Ninth's can be a Maj. Ninth, or a Minor Ninth, or a Dominant Ninth, or a Flattened or Sharpened Ninth. The Dominant, flattened & sharpened Ninth's are to be discussed later on and they are of a more Later stage of Harmonies. The maj. and Minor Ninth's are the subject of detail of any ones first few words of conversation. An easy way to remember their description is: One is a Maj. from a Minor and the other is a Minor from a Major. An opposite way of remembering their characteristic. So the description is for a clearer picture :
Whenever you want to use a Major Ninth you play a Minor from the third of the Root. And Whenever you want to play a Minor Ninth you play a Maj. from the minor third of the root. So If We are using C Maj. 5-1-3. Then its third would be the E Minor 7 chord. that would be the Maj. Ninth. If we are using a C Minor 5-1-3 then its third would be Eb Maj. 7 chord. you see how they are opposite to each other from that regard. These Ninth's are Tension builders. So we now have the Pumping action of the 5-1-3 basic folding building tension and we are building more tension from using the Ninth's as a Melody line construction to spark more Imagination of sound. I usually use the right hand to build a Major or Minor 7th. Chord which is of 4 notes, thus more richness and more variety of notes to use. Adding a richer Harmony to the sound. Not to forget the main ninth note is the D note of the Maj. or minor 7th chord, as the right hand is building the melody Line. And sometimes a simple 5-1-3 triad of the Ninth is used instead of a 7th chord. If you do use a 5-1-3 instead of an ordinary 7th chord then you now can fold with the right hand at the same time as the left hand and they will harmonize together. And now even more Harmony is even being built for spark and imagination. I most likely use the harmonic minor scale in conjunction of a major scale. continuos pumping from both directions in harmony and creative conversation to build on. The Diminished comes in for other resolves and thus circling in all the key's eternally for Composition.

C Maj. 5-1-3

folds to

G7 or
G#Dim7

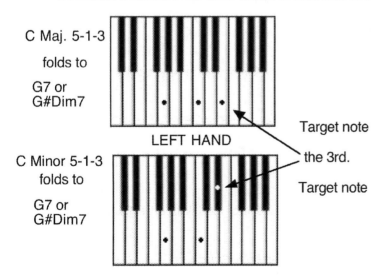

LEFT HAND

C Minor 5-1-3
folds to

G7 or
G#Dim7

Target note

the 3rd.

Target note

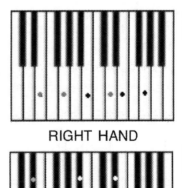

RIGHT HAND

E Minor 7th
is the original 9th.

or

E m 5-1-3
folds to
B7 or Cdim7

Eb Maj. 7th
is the original 9th.

or

Eb Maj 5-1-3
folds to
Bb7 or Bdim7

Further Studies
The Dominant & Natural Minors
or
The Mediant & Submediant

Example 32   The most used target notes

These minors are a harmony to the root, which is usually a Major 5-1-3. When first trying to find a melody line. These should be a walking first step to building your melody line. They are just as important as the Circular Fourth and fifth. Keep your target notes in mind just as the others. Again they usually follow any 5-1-3 Major. These Natural & Dominant Minors are the most important step in any building of any Composition. They should be in front of this Book. They should be regarded the first step in exploration of a Composition, everytime, and kept in memory extensively at reach and on call at any time. At the drop of a hat. In all styles. 5-1-3 Harmonies

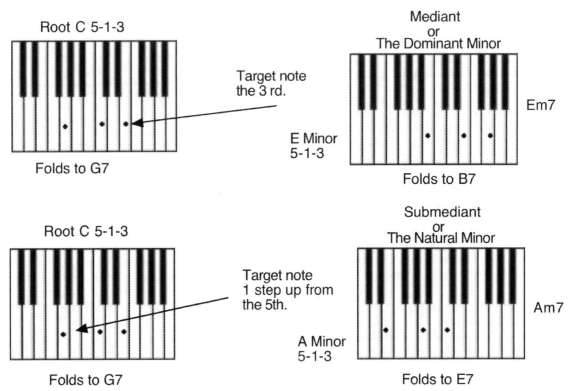

Root C 5-1-3

Target note the 3 rd.

E Minor 5-1-3

Folds to G7

Mediant
or
The Dominant Minor

Em7

Folds to B7

Root C 5-1-3

Target note 1 step up from the 5th.

A Minor 5-1-3

Folds to G7

Submediant
or
The Natural Minor

Am7

Folds to E7

You would of-course fold any of these 5-1-3's during the Improvisational Composition especially in strict Classical style. Mozart ,Haydn, Beethoven .....

Practice all the keys first to get a handle on what are these Harmonies. And which is its target notes. Since these are in Congruent with Majors, then one assumes HAYDN, MOZART, BEETHOVEN used these targets during the Classical style..

And if you wish to Harmonize in eternal circles. Then bypass the majors altogether from after resolving from the dominants to directly to " The Dominant Minor " and " The Natural Minor ". **ex**: Diminished / Flatten any note / its a Dominant now / Target next finger up & 1/2 step up is its resolve to a major 5-1-3 except this time take the resolve to any of these " Dominant Minor " or " Natural Minor " Of the 5-1-3 Major And repeat. **Eternal harmonies. (providing you know your target notes memorized from the major Roots. Important !)**

Recapping : In the Key of F : The Mediant would be Am7 & Submediant would be Dm7 Try figuring out the flower waltz by Tchaikovsky in the key of F. Fold F to C7 back and forth and then use the submedian or natural minor first and fold. (Dm - A7) and then the median and fold (Am - E7) and take the bridge to F - C7 - Dm-A7 / and Bb - Am - Gm- C7. Use 5-1-3 's Exclusively. The most beautiful waltz ever written. And simply quiet effective. Uses the dominant and natural minors exclusively. Good practice.

Entering the Descending 4th's
the way they are used

example # 41

1. Enter to the Descending 4th's. Take any 5-1-3 **minor** triad.

Minors 5-1-3

2. Start folding 1/2 step up from the 5th. or first finger target.

3. Remember you are in the key of the 5-1-3 minor. So its the 3rd. of the minor that will tell you what key to fold in. And most important for the Baroque sound. Octave the 5-1-3 Minor and simply go up 1/2 step with both outside fingers to start the in-depth folding.

target note to start folding from

Recapping the Minors

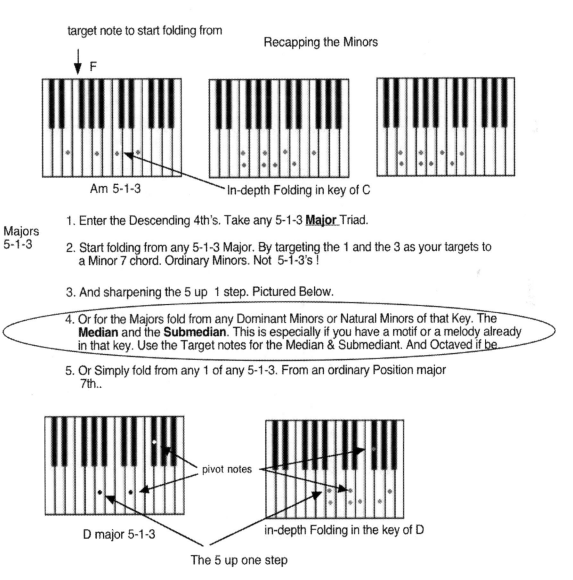

Am 5-1-3

In-depth Folding in key of C

Majors 5-1-3

1. Enter the Descending 4th's. Take any 5-1-3 **Major** Triad.

2. Start folding from any 5-1-3 Major. By targeting the 1 and the 3 as your targets to a Minor 7 chord. Ordinary Minors. Not 5-1-3's !

3. And sharpening the 5 up 1 step. Pictured Below.

4. Or for the Majors fold from any Dominant Minors or Natural Minors of that Key. The **Median** and the **Submedian**. This is especially if you have a motif or a melody already in that key. Use the Target notes for the Median & Submediant. And Octaved if be.

5. Or Simply fold from any 1 of any 5-1-3. From an ordinary Position major 7th..

pivot notes

D major 5-1-3

in-depth Folding in the key of D

The 5 up one step

Additional Studies
Baroque Folding
Brainstorming from key to key
Vivaldi
Scarlatti-Handel-Bach
Chopin & Mozart

example 1a

1. Take any 5-1-3 minor.

2. The 5 and the 1st. or the first and second fingers have the same pattern of target note.

3. The 3rd or the third finger has its own rule of target notes. slightly different.

The target notes for the 5th. and the 1st. are 1/2 up to a major seventh and 1 whole step down to a minor seventh or a dominant 7th.. Then fold in depth. Even if its not in the key.

The target notes for the 3rd. are 1 whole step up to minor seventh or dominant 7 and 1 whole step down to a major seventh. Then fold in depth. Even if its not in the key.

F major 7th. target for 5th.

start folding from f maj. 7th in the key of C.

start folding from f maj. 7th in the key of F.

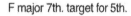
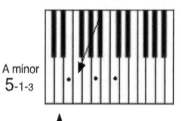

A minor
5-1-3

D minor 7th. or D7 target for 5th.

start folding from D minor 7th. in the key of C

start folding from Dminor 7th. in the key of F

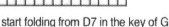

start folding from D7 in the key of G

84

Additional Studies

Baroque Folding

Brainstorming from key to key

Vivaldi
Scarlatti-Handel-Bach
Chopin & Mozart   example 1b

1. Take any 5-1-3 minor.

2. The 5 and the 1st. or the first and second fingers have the same pattern of target note.

3. The 3rd or the third finger has its own rule of target notes. slightly different.

The target notes for the 5th. and the 1st. are <u>1/2 up to a major seventh and 1 whole step down to a minor seventh</u>. Then fold in depth. Even if its not in the key.

The target notes for the 3rd. are <u>1 whole step up to minor seventh or dominant 7 and 1 whole step down to a major seventh.</u> Then fold in depth. Even if its not in the key.

Bb is target for 1st.

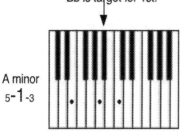

A minor
5-**1**-3

G minor7 or G7 target for 1st.

start folding from Bb maj.7th in the key of F.

start folding from Bb maj.7th in the key of Bb.

start folding from Gm7 in the key of F or

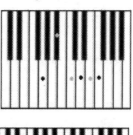

start folding from G7 in the key of C.

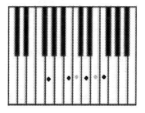

start folding from Gm7 in the key of Bb

Additional Studies
Baroque Folding
Brainstorming from key to key
Vivaldi
Scarlatti-Handel-Bach
Chopin & Mozart

1. Take any 5-1-3 minor.   example 1c

2. The 5 and the 1st. or the first and second fingers have the same pattern of target note.

3. The 3rd or the third finger has its own rule of target notes. slightly different.

The target notes for the 5th. and the 1st. are <u>1/2 up to a major seventh and 1 whole step down to a minor seventh or a dominant 7th.</u>. Then fold in depth. Even if its not in the key.

The target notes for the 3rd. are <u>1 whole step up to minor seventh or dominant 7 and 1 whole step down to a major seventh</u>. Then fold in depth. Even if its not in the key.

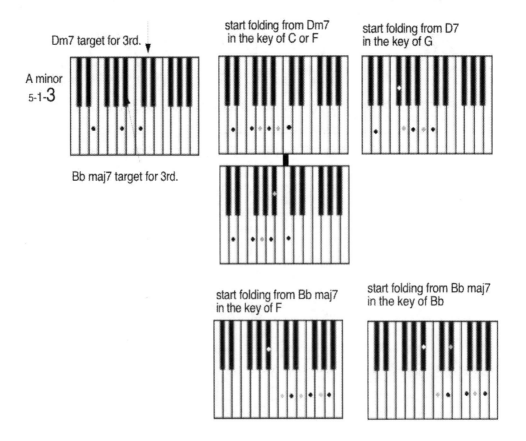

Dm7 target for 3rd.

A minor
5-1-**3**

Bb maj7 target for 3rd.

start folding from Dm7
in the key of C or F

start folding from D7
in the key of G

start folding from Bb maj7
in the key of F

start folding from Bb maj7
in the key of Bb

BACH ## The descending and ascending parallel 4th's *High Baroque*

This is an easy way to use the descending circular fourth's .....

1. Octave any triad in normal position. **2**. Walk the inside 2 fingers on its scale. **3**. Walk the outside 2 fingers also. And repeat. in the minor scale, or major or others. This pattern works for the minor scales as well as jumping from one scale or any position to the other. **4**. Or start with a 5-1-3 octaved and drop the outside fingers crunched first. ! Then the inside. Or you can **Reverse the process** by moving the outside fingers up and dropping Down. But start on a 5-1-3 octaved ; Hence this is also found in other theory material, but proves to be non improvisational approach. But yet still a very nice progression that is widely heard in the Baroque compositional style. .. For Fluent Improvisations un-octave this step and learn the pattern for all keys. This step will be familiar within the next few pages. Getting familiar in going from 5-1-3 to 3-5-1. During this pattern and process.

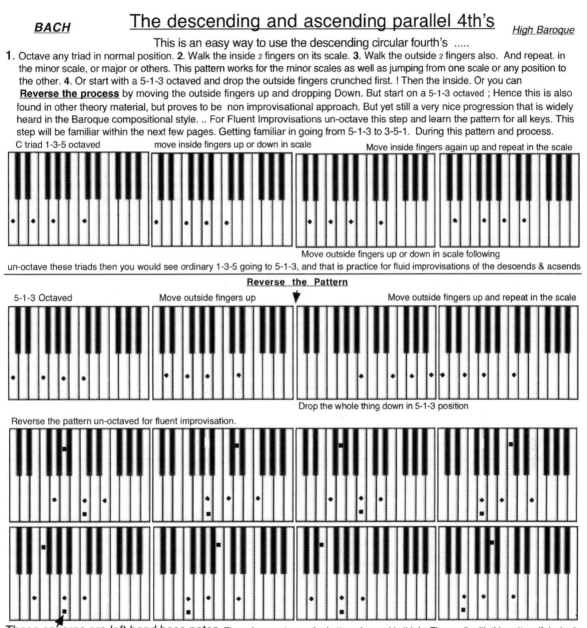

C triad 1-3-5 octaved   move inside fingers up or down in scale   Move inside fingers again up and repeat in the scale

Move outside fingers up or down in scale following

un-octave these triads then you would see ordinary 1-3-5 going to 5-1-3, and that is practice for fluid improvisations of the descends & acsends

Reverse the Pattern

5-1-3 Octaved   Move outside fingers up   Move outside fingers up and repeat in the scale

Drop the whole thing down in 5-1-3 position

Reverse the pattern un-octaved for fluent improvisation.

These squares are left hand bass notes. These bass notes on the bottom descend in thirds. They walk with this pattern if desired, although without the bass notes this pattern is very influential and a must to master as a filler during classical Improvisations. Much of these positions will be fixated and focused on in the next few pages. As a non Improvisational tools, these positions can be octaved with these bass notes or other harmony bass notes (on top bass notes in 4th's , Beatles - "you never give me your money ") and with the proper notes altered maybe, Voicings come alive at play. (check p.147 for same but octaved for voicings) As with the in-depth foldings of chapter 4. Compositional voicings are not only songwriting but they can be the revised step by step from improvisations to composition, slowly applied afterwards. .. To descend these important triads for Improvisation use the middle finger as target. The middle finger will walk the key you're in to guide you through the key. And the subtonic will be a Diminished sus 3rd. Key Items ! & finally , also Ascend in the key. Use with the left hand also for fluent Improvisations.

Robert Kaye

∞ **Baroquing**
Toccata

The BACH METHOD
Toccata

The art of the Fugue
Toccata ∞

For any 5-1-3 minor, sharpen the 3rd 1 step. Now look at the notes you have and play the harmonic minor scales of those notes with both hands.
Improvise ,weave and general fold,one scale at a time.. And from that scale originates a new 5-1-3 minor in which the 3rd. is sharpened in the mind and the process
is repeated infinite. Folding here is permitted. Am into E7 etc.. Both hands weave one scale at a time from the notes of the 5-1-3 minor. Fluid Improvisations.

1. Take any 5-1-3 minor. The 5'th is used to target the circular minor fourth. **2.** use the 1st. for scale. Its the harmonic minor
scale of that note. And also use the 1st. to start folding in depth by starting with a normal minor seventh. **3.** Use the 3rd. for
targeting the major key of that note. And its the key for the folding circular fourth above. Starting the in depth folding of
chapter four (pages 50-80) by using a normal minor seventh of the 1st. (Example below:)

Use the harmonic minor scales and circle the fourth's as much as possible going from key to key. And when you want to pop out of it, start
folding in major scale. And repeat. The right hand melody improvisation will carry you forever. In baroquing try to bypass general folds. As in Am
to E7. Baroquing is much more appealing and creative from that aspect because of the difference from pure classical. This is the other
classical music to go to when the mind is spent from the other contour. Creativity and surprises are also epic with a different refreshing
approach... (Example bottom of page: with page numbers also).

   And on the other side of the coin (Not pictured below) also dont forget to use the three diminished families, which are the 1 and 4th and 5th.
with three harmonic scales only . Am, Dm, Em. And use an ordinary Minor seventh every once in a while with its rules from pages: 139, 129, 25-
26 and that should keep you in the vicinity of in-depth folding in the major keys of C, F and G. Here you can general and in-depth fold with
these three keys and 3 Diminished... Pages 50-80, 193, 82, 126,127, 133, 149. Stay in the major keys of C, F, and G. Or Am, Dm and E minor.
They will circle in Episode. Start with pages (50-80) 101,133 & 90 they will automatically sound like Bach, use first to grasp the baroque style and
how bach established his improvisations, they will fold for you automatically.

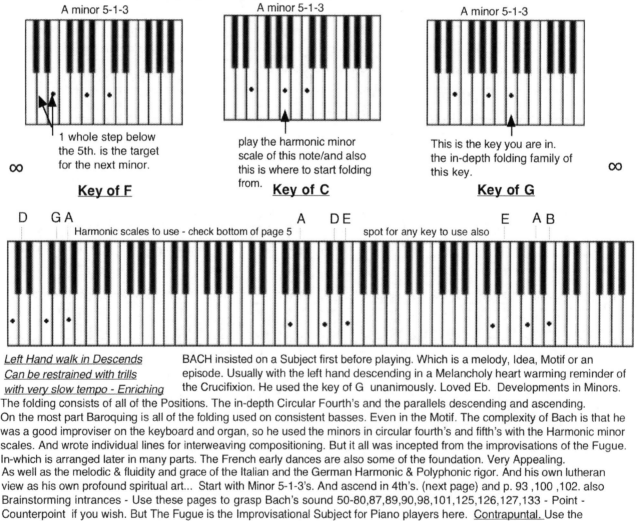

A minor 5-1-3

A minor 5-1-3

A minor 5-1-3

1 whole step below
the 5th. is the target
for the next minor.

play the harmonic minor
scale of this note/and also
this is where to start folding
from.

This is the key you are in.
the in-depth folding family of
this key.

∞ **Key of F**

Key of C

Key of G ∞

D G A   A   D E   E   A B
Harmonic scales to use - check bottom of page 5   spot for any key to use also

Left Hand walk in Descends
Can be restrained with trills
with very slow tempo - Enriching

BACH insisted on a Subject first before playing. Which is a melody, Idea, Motif or an
episode. Usually with the left hand descending in a Melancholy heart warming reminder of
the Crucifixion. He used the key of G unanimously. Loved Eb. Developments in Minors.

The folding consists of all of the Positions. The in-depth Circular Fourth's and the parallels descending and ascending.
On the most part Baroquing is all of the folding used on consistent basses. Even in the Motif. The complexity of Bach is that he
was a good improviser on the keyboard and organ, so he used the minors in circular fourth's and fifth's with the Harmonic minor
scales. And wrote individual lines for interweaving compositioning. But it all was incepted from the improvisations of the Fugue.
In-which is arranged later in many parts. The French early dances are also some of the foundation. Very Appealing.
As well as the melodic & fluidity and grace of the Italian and the German Harmonic & Polyphonic rigor. And his own lutheran
view as his own profound spiritual art... Start with Minor 5-1-3's. And ascend in 4th's. (next page) and p. 93 ,100 ,102. also
Brainstorming intrances - Use these pages to grasp Bach's sound 50-80,87,89,90,98,101,125,126,127,133 - Point -
Counterpoint if you wish. But The Fugue is the Improvisational Subject for Piano players here. Contrapuntal. Use the
Diminished b7th in circular 4'th and 5th.. That's were chopin got his method. Almost all of the theories used in this book will
work in baroquing. Bach also used the black notes as a landmark targets to keep up with his weaving melodies as he's
playing. He is the greatest arranger of Composition. That's because he is fluent in Improvisations. And one name will always
be a reference to research on Bach. That's Glen Gould. Search out his humanism of Bach's Gospel. All the great Composers
came from Bach. ∞

Using the Minor Triads in an Ascending Circular fourth
but this time not in octaved parallel
BAROQUING

1. Take any 5-1-3 Minor and use the second position folding technique by
2. Sharpening the outside fingers. The first finger 1/2 step and the last 1 step.
3. The same as the second position. Pivoting the middle finger firmly.
4. And now sharpen the outside fingers and inside finger. And repeat in the key.
5. Although not all notes will pattern in the exact 1/2 step and 1 whole step pattern. The ascend is in the Key
   and does allow Improvisations to render build ups and descends. Lock fingers and don't loose the
   pattern. Its the circular fourths. Or the equivalent to in-depth folding. Outside / inside / outside / inside / etc.....

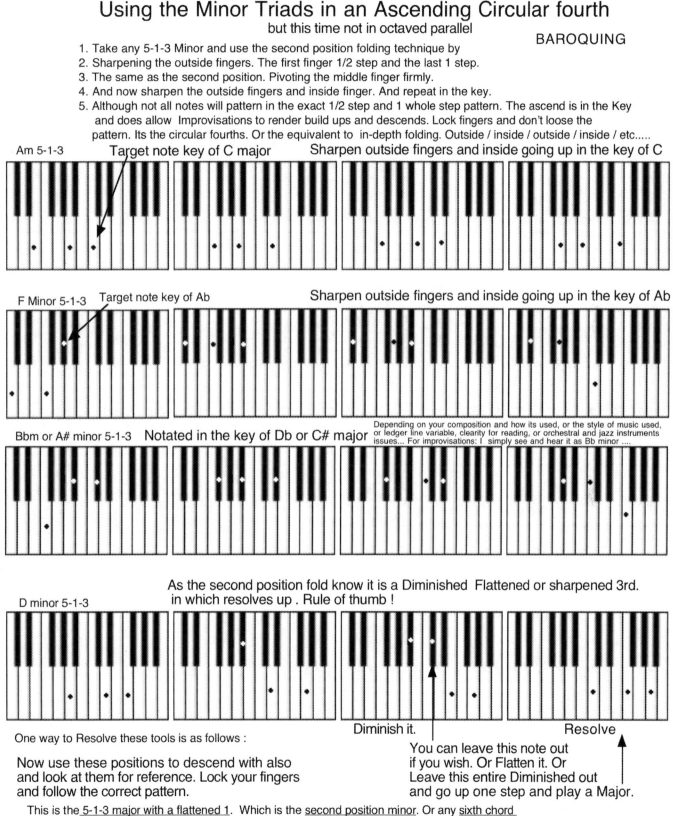

Am 5-1-3 — Target note key of C major — Sharpen outside fingers and inside going up in the key of C

F Minor 5-1-3 — Target note key of Ab — Sharpen outside fingers and inside going up in the key of Ab

Bbm or A# minor 5-1-3 — Notated in the key of Db or C# major — Depending on your composition and how its used, or the style of music used, or ledger line variable, clearity for reading, or orchestral and jazz instruments issues... For improvisations: I simply see and hear it as Bb minor ....

As the second position fold know it is a Diminished Flattened or sharpened 3rd. in which resolves up . Rule of thumb !

D minor 5-1-3

Diminish it. | Resolve

One way to Resolve these tools is as follows :

Now use these positions to descend with also
and look at them for reference. Lock your fingers
and follow the correct pattern.

You can leave this note out
if you wish. Or Flatten it. Or
Leave this entire Diminished out
and go up one step and play a Major.

This is the 5-1-3 major with a flattened 1. Which is the second position minor. Or any sixth chord
suspended fifth. All of these positions with the fingers alternating; Outside / inside / outside / inside etc....thats all it is.

THE Major SECOND POSITIONS
Entering the Classical major second position from the third positions
Ascending the circular fourth in the Key

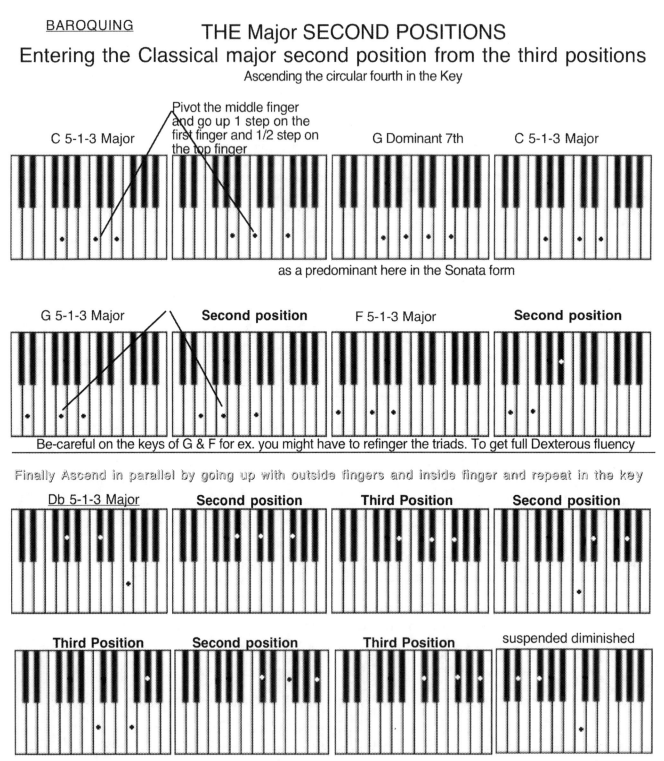

Pivot the middle finger and go up 1 step on the first finger and 1/2 step on the top finger

C 5-1-3 Major   G Dominant 7th   C 5-1-3 Major

as a predominant here in the Sonata form

G 5-1-3 Major   **Second position**   F 5-1-3 Major   **Second position**

Be-careful on the keys of G & F for ex. you might have to refinger the triads. To get full Dexterous fluency

Finally Ascend in parallel by going up with outside fingers and inside finger and repeat in the key

Db 5-1-3 Major   **Second position**   **Third Position**   **Second position**

Third Position   **Second position**   **Third Position**   suspended diminished

Practice all the keys to get the fluency of the fingering and familiarity going from the third position (5-1-3). And then after the next few pages, you will get familiar with the second position 3-5-1 major and minors And then reverse the pattern going from ascend to descend. You will look at the second position going to the third position. These are folds that are used in Arias when the keyboard during the Baroque era would only sound clear in triad form.

The Classical Second position
3-5-1 Triads

The Second position is not as influential or important as the 5-1-3 third position with regard to the whole Classical Method at hand. But it's the other triad that's involved with the third position. These triads are not as fluent for Improvisation if not looked at by the way that I'm presenting them. The only way to use them is by the proper fingering or dexterous flexibility and contrived implementation. As well as by certain characteristic importance of thought. While the 5-1-3 Third position is the mainstream of the classical method, The 3-5-1 Second position is the inheritance of a more complex and beautiful way to use and create, all within a targeted method that is mathematically sound, harmonic, Poetically feasible by the fingering and the knowledge of how to go about in a cordial method intertwined by the keyboard and its allowable rules of fingering. I've chosen these elements only by a vast long understanding of what is needed from the keyboard in order to provide an instinctive path in which one needs to follow by. These 3-5-1 Triads can be used as a passing tone for fill. Or they can be used as a theoretical sound all by themselves as well. Baroque or Romantically. Or they can intertwine with the other positions especially the 5-1-3 Triads in a surprising turn and twist of events that culminate an instinctive compositioning that is not only rare but the true path that the great composers of a virtuous skill used long ago. This is why I use the main four composers, as I do. Bach, Mozart, Beethoven & Chopin. It's because they were the virtuous keyboardists and pianist of the highest skills. The 3-5-1 and the 5-1-3 Triads have been considered the Neapolitans of-course. And the reason why is because the fourth semi tone split in them. Tchaikovsky obviously loved the 5-1-3 triads. His most tasteful Romeo and Juliet overture is based on these triads exclusively.. And he used them in the romantic sense as apposed to Mozart And Beethoven whom used them in a classical sense. As apposed to Chopin in which he declared them part of the keyboard along with their indigenous positions. Chopin saw the 3-5-1 as an ordinary Minor #5th. As one gets deeper in these positions ; as in using the minors then other significant landmarks or memorable traits will arise in-which I've documented. Like they can also be considered a diminished b7th. Or any 5-1-3 with flattened 1. (5-b1-3). As I find them on daily basis. For the sake of Poetic jurisdiction and significant methodological Harmonies.

Classical

Haydn
Mozart
Schubert
Beethoven

The Second Position Major
and its fold
3-5-1

1. The Second position major is easily found and used by using an ordinary Minor with a # 5th.

2. And its fold is easily found by Moving the outside fingers up. The top finger up 1 step and the bottom finger up 1/2 step.

3. Its scales and target notes are
The bottom finger is Harmonic Minor and the Middle and top finger are Major scales.
Better Know all the positions before trying to use them

Major Scale Target note

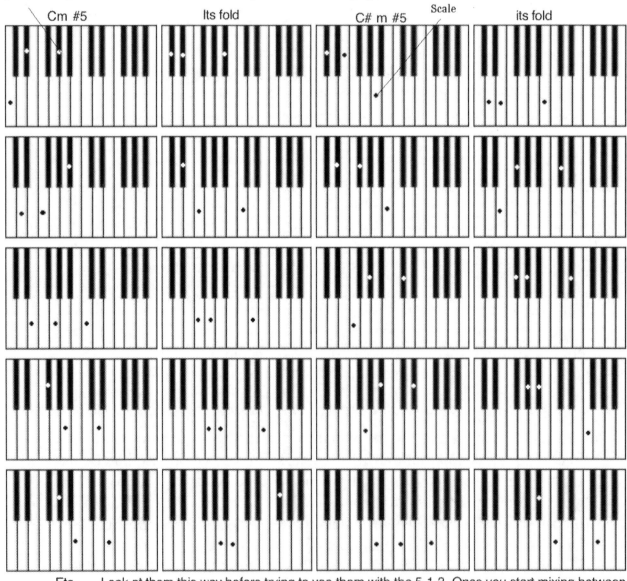

Etc........Look at them this way before trying to use them with the 5-1-3. Once you start mixing between both. then music starts to happen unexpectedly and with surprises.

Harmonies using the second position

BACH Beethoven Mendelssohn Chopin

Entrances, patterns and formulas

1. If you take any 5-1-3 minor and flatten the 1st. a whole step.   or
2. If you take any diminished flattened 7th. sus 5th. or
3. **If you take any normal minor and sharpen the 5th. 1/2 step.**
4. If you octave any normal major triad and drop the bottom finger it will leave you a major 3-5-1. **Or wrap around the 3 of any 5-1-3.**
all of the above lead to the Second position **Majors 3-5-1.** But what's important to remember is that you want to go to the second position from preferably a 5-1-3 format, that way you are working with the sonata Cadenzal and folding mechanism format. At whole. One rule to remember with the 3-5-1 second position majors is they will fall under any tonic or Diminished. Because they are also a Diminished b7th. So You can play a 3-5-1 under any major or minor 5-1-3. 1/2 step under the 1 especially. That's one way to use the major 3-5-1.. ... . And the pattern on the bottom below can be reversed going down also.. Use the pattern below in conjunction with page 98. Now entrances to the **Minors 3-5-1** are as follows :

1. **If you take any 5-1-3 major and flatten the middle finger 1/2 step then its a second position 3-5-1 minor.**
2. **If you take any 5-1-3 minor and use the same folding technique as the previous page. which is moving the outside fingers up. The top finger up 1 step and the bottom finger 1/2 step. This is the correct way in using the 3-5-1 second position minors entrances in harmony. In 4th's, (Classic Bach).**
3. If you take any 5-1-3 minors and wrap the 3 to the front. This will give you also the minor 3-5-1 .

The first is flattened 1 step

C minor 5-1-3

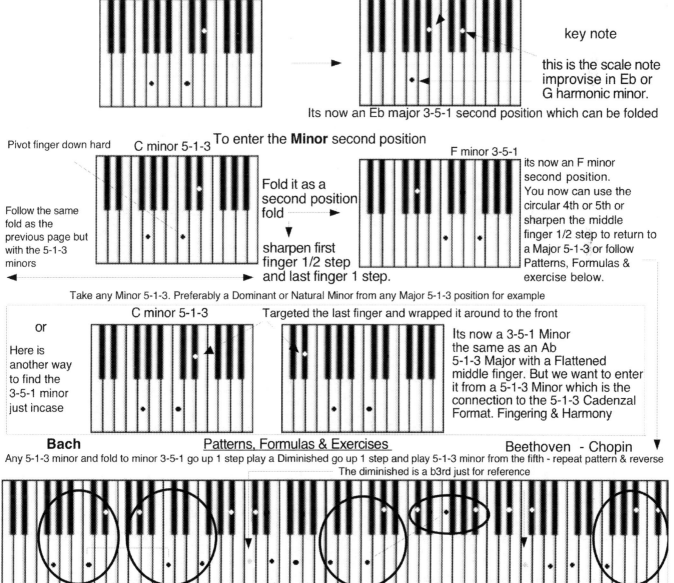

key note

this is the scale note improvise in Eb or G harmonic minor.

Its now an Eb major 3-5-1 second position which can be folded

Pivot finger down hard   C minor 5-1-3 **To enter the Minor second position**   F minor 3-5-1

Follow the same fold as the previous page but with the 5-1-3 minors

Fold it as a second position fold

▼

sharpen first finger 1/2 step and last finger 1 step.

its now an F minor second position. You now can use the circular 4th or 5th or sharpen the middle finger 1/2 step to return to a Major 5-1-3 or follow Patterns, Formulas & exercise below.

Take any Minor 5-1-3. Preferably a Dominant or Natural Minor from any Major 5-1-3 position for example

or

Here is another way to find the 3-5-1 minor just incase

C minor 5-1-3   Targeted the last finger and wrapped it around to the front

Its now a 3-5-1 Minor the same as an Ab 5-1-3 Major with a Flattened middle finger. But we want to enter it from a 5-1-3 Minor which is the connection to the 5-1-3 Cadenzal Format. Fingering & Harmony

Bach   Patterns, Formulas & Exercises   Beethoven - Chopin ▼

Any 5-1-3 minor and fold to minor 3-5-1 go up 1 step play a Diminished go up 1 step and play 5-1-3 minor from the fifth - repeat pattern & reverse
The diminished is a b3rd just for reference

Haydn's
Sonata form

The Basic Folding of the 2nd. Position Major

A different angle and look at the second position. Used with the Sonata Form

1. If you take any Octaved Triad and drop the bottom note then you're left with a 2nd. (3-5-1)

2. Now if you target the 5 as a root note which is the middle finger and triad it and add the note 1 step under it then it is its folding dominant.

3. If its easier for you to take a Minor seventh from the bottom note and sharpen the bottom note 1/2 step then find it that way by all means. Which ever way is easier for you to find.

4. **Diminished b3 1/2 step up. Is what I use.**

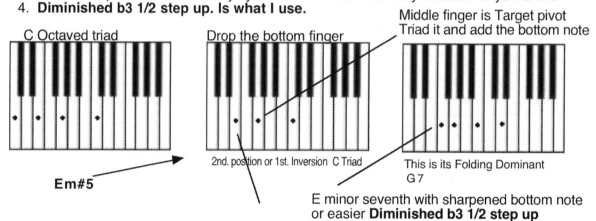

C Octaved triad

Em#5

Drop the bottom finger

2nd. position or 1st. Inversion C Triad

Middle finger is Target pivot
Triad it and add the bottom note

This is its Folding Dominant
G 7

E minor seventh with sharpened bottom note
or easier **Diminished b3 1/2 step up**

You can also Play a minor seventh from bottom note and sharpen the bottom note 1/2 step

3. Another Dominant that can be used is Target one step under the C Triad and use a Diminished flattened third finger.

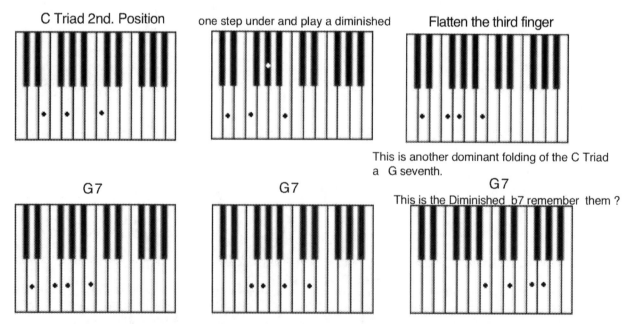

C Triad 2nd. Position

one step under and play a diminished

Flatten the third finger

This is another dominant folding of the C Triad
a G seventh.

G 7

G 7

G 7

This is the Diminished b7 remember them ?

Now You have All G7 Dominant Positions for the C Triad. Practice all the Keys and then go back to add the Original 5-1-3 foldings to them. You now have the Tension and resolve from all directions.

The Second Position Major & Minor Triads

Their Scales, Dominant & Natural Minors, Circular 4th & 5th and more

The **Second** position is best remembered by the **Second** finger. The **Second** finger is the Pivot. So you have some improvisations unlimited here. Both in the Major and Minor Triad. The scales are remembered by the reverse analogy from the root note as well as the 5-1-3's Also the scales will open new doors for you going into other theories that have been covered. You will see new positions to take from the different scale possibilities. Have trust in yourself. While Improvising you will see and hear other possibilities to go to.

The Majors : Remembered by the # sign and its fold is sharpened outside fingers The Majors .Up

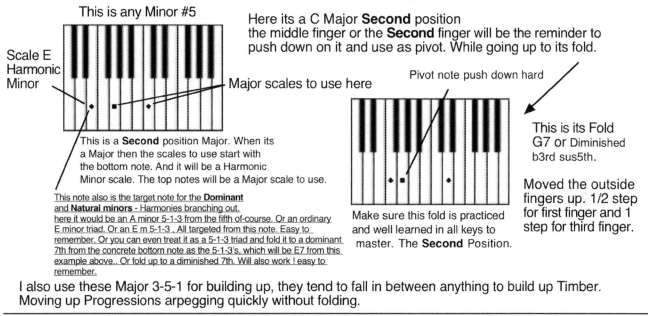

This is any Minor #5

Scale E Harmonic Minor

Major scales to use here

This is a **Second** position Major. When its a Major then the scales to use start with the bottom note. And it will be a Harmonic Minor scale. The top notes will be a Major scale to use.

This note also is the target note for the **Dominant** and **Natural minors** - Harmonies branching out. here it would be an A minor 5-1-3 from the fifth of-course. Or an ordinary E minor triad. Or an E m 5-1-3 , All targeted from this note. Easy to remember. Or you can even treat it as a 5-1-3 triad and fold it to a dominant 7th from the concrete bottom note as the 5-1-3's, which will be E7 from this example above.. Or fold up to a diminished 7th. Will also work ! easy to remember.

Here its a C Major **Second** position the middle finger or the **Second** finger will be the reminder to push down on it and use as pivot. While going up to its fold.

Pivot note push down hard

Make sure this fold is practiced and well learned in all keys to master. The **Second** Position.

This is its Fold G7 or Diminished b3rd sus5th.

Moved the outside fingers up. 1/2 step for first finger and 1 step for third finger.

I also use these Major 3-5-1 for building up, they tend to fall in between anything to build up Timber. Moving up Progressions arpegging quickly without folding.

The Minors : Remembered by its flattened middle finger and its fold is flattened outside fingers. Down

This is any 5-1-3 with flattened **Second** finger ... or the triad above with flattened first finger.. 1/2 step.

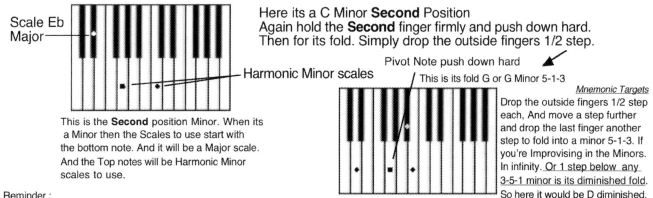

Scale Eb Major

Harmonic Minor scales

This is the **Second** position Minor. When its a Minor then the Scales to use start with the bottom note. And it will be a Major scale. And the Top notes will be Harmonic Minor scales to use.

Here its a C Minor **Second** Position Again hold the **Second** finger firmly and push down hard. Then for its fold. Simply drop the outside fingers 1/2 step.

Pivot Note push down hard

This is its fold G or G Minor 5-1-3

Mnemonic Targets
Drop the outside fingers 1/2 step each, And move a step further and drop the last finger another step to fold into a minor 5-1-3. If you're Improvising in the Minors. In infinity. Or 1 step below any 3-5-1 minor is its diminished fold. So here it would be D diminished.

Reminder :

From Either the Major or Minor 3-5-1 - You can drop 1/2 step from **second finger** and play a Diminished b7th. Or Minor #5 And resolve it up 1/2 step. To ordinary or 5-1-3 major or minor. This is the true circular 5th. The **second position** and the middle finger. Remembrance again ! From Either the Major or Minor 3-5-1 - You can use the similar target notes for the circular 4th or 5th. as the 5-1-3 already covered. from the Majors they will branch out to Minors 5-1-3. And from the Minor 3-5-1 they will branch out to Major 5-1-3 flattened middle finger. Which is a 3-5-1 minor. Reverse analogy again to remember by. The majors may not correspond exactly as the 5-1-3. But they will give you the circular 5th and the secondary degree. The Minor 3-5-1 will correspond exactly a circular 4th. and 5th. by using the 5-1-3 majors with a flattened middle finger. Also : Any Major 3-5-1 can fall under any Minor 3-5-1 1/2 step under the top finger of the 3-5-1 minor. The 1 finger. They Harmonise !

Further Studies
The Second position Minor Triad
Beethoven-Chopin

Using the minor second position or 1st. inversion circulating in harmony
1. if you take a 5-1-3 with flattened 1st. 1/2 step. Which is the Natural Minor. This is the proper
   way to use this position. A begining of a Conversation. Most likely to be used on the second verse.
   ----- If you take any normal triad and sharpen the fifth 1step or a Dominant b7th sus 5th. then its a minor
   second position of the last finger..Or any diminished sus 5th & # 3rd. The diminished is a wild card.
2. You then can flaten the outside notes 1/2 step to its fold and inside note and repeat. Easy !
3. drop the first finger & second finger down 1/2 step to its dominant seventh. And go through all keys.

Eb 5-1-3 with flattened 1 or Normal Eb triad with # fifth or Diminished sus 5th & # 3rd.

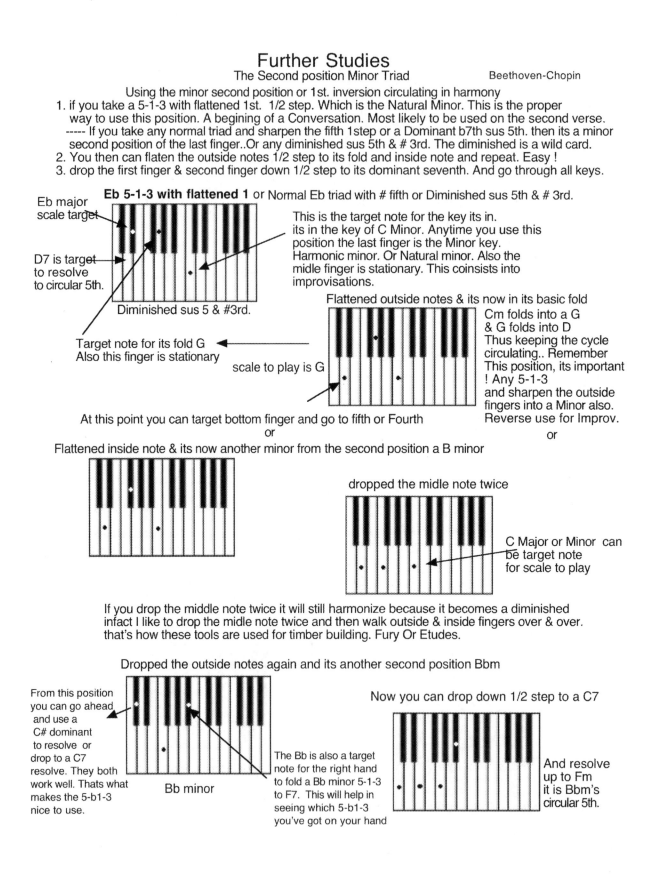

Eb major
scale target

D7 is target
to resolve
to circular 5th.

Diminished sus 5 & #3rd.

This is the target note for the key its in.
its in the key of C Minor. Anytime you use this
position the last finger is the Minor key.
Harmonic minor. Or Natural minor. Also the
midle finger is stationary. This coinsists into
improvisations.

Flattened outside notes & its now in its basic fold

Target note for its fold G
Also this finger is stationary

scale to play is G

Cm folds into a G
& G folds into D
Thus keeping the cycle
circulating.. Remember
This position, its important
! Any 5-1-3
and sharpen the outside
fingers into a Minor also.
Reverse use for Improv.

At this point you can target bottom finger and go to fifth or Fourth

or   or

Flattened inside note & its now another minor from the second position a B minor

dropped the midle note twice

C Major or Minor can
be target note
for scale to play

If you drop the middle note twice it will still harmonize because it becomes a diminished
infact I like to drop the middle note twice and then walk outside & inside fingers over & over.
that's how these tools are used for timber building. Fury Or Etudes.

Dropped the outside notes again and its another second position Bbm

From this position
you can go ahead
and use a
C# dominant
to resolve or
drop to a C7
resolve. They both
work well. Thats what
makes the 5-b1-3
nice to use.

Bb minor

The Bb is also a target
note for the right hand
to fold a Bb minor 5-1-3
to F7. This will help in
seeing which 5-b1-3
you've got on your hand

Now you can drop down 1/2 step to a C7

And resolve
up to Fm
it is Bbm's
circular 5th.

The Second Position Triads

My Neapolitans in Fluid Improvisations

In Circular 4th's & 5th's

You can treet the Second position Triads just as the third position 5-1-3 Major and Minors in regard to circulating in 4th. and 5th. The Second position Majors and Minors. (3-5-1) and the Third Position Majors and Minors (5-1-3) all have a four note semitone split in them. Therefore they will harmonize if used in circular 4th. & 5th. Targets are the same as the 5-1-3 thats been covered in this book. The scales and folds for these positions have been covered in this book already. So try using all the triads with the circular patterns.

C minor 5-1-3

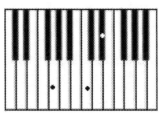

Flattened the Middle Finger

Its now a second position Triad

This is the fifth of the triad

A g minor 5-1-3 with flattened 1 or Dm #5

This is its fifth again

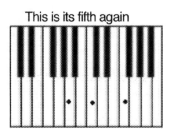

This is its fifth again

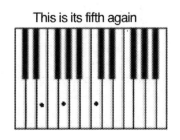

If you wish to fold it at this point

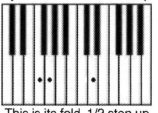

This is its fold. 1/2 step up a Diminished b3rd.

C minor 5-1-3

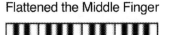

Here Lets start again

This is its Forth this time

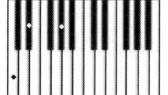

And you can keep going or pop in a 5-1-3 again

Add this note to make it a Diminished b7th.

resolve it as a Diminished b7th. And go 1/2 step up to Major or Minor or 5-1-3 b1

went up to a Db 5-1-3 b1

F minor 3-5-1

Cm 3-5-1

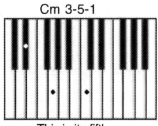

This is its fifth

This is its fifth

My Patterns, Formulas & Exercises using the 2nd. position

The sus 3rd. is silent for now, but know it is a flattened 3rd. so the Key you're in for the Diminished is 1/2 step up on top of next finger. (the Diminished golden rule of thumb).. And you can play the third. After all. Hence: This is also the folds of the Minor #5 (3-5-1). Therefore the pattern is easy to spot. I also do use it as a diminished 7th without suspending the 3rd. or flattening it. just the same for its quick change of directions going Down. Below.

Pattern ----- 1. **Min#5** - up 1/2 step - **Dim7 sus 3rd.** - up 1 step - **5-1-3 Major** - up 1 step

or

clearer ------ **Min#5** - Fold - up 1 step to a **major 5-1-3** up 1 step to **Minor#5** - Fold - up 1 step to **major 5-1-3**

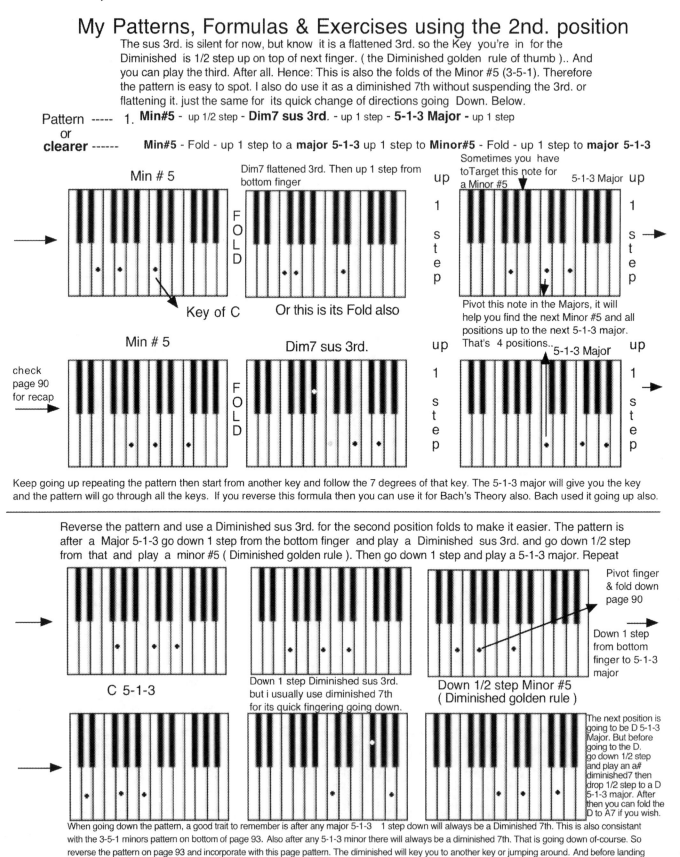

Min # 5

Dim7 flattened 3rd. Then up 1 step from bottom finger

Sometimes you have to Target this note for a Minor #5   5-1-3 Major   up 1 step

Key of C   Or this is its Fold also

Pivot this note in the Majors, it will help you find the next Minor #5 and all positions up to the next 5-1-3 major. That's 4 positions..

Min # 5   Dim7 sus 3rd.   5-1-3 Major

check page 90 for recap

Keep going up repeating the pattern then start from another key and follow the 7 degrees of that key. The 5-1-3 major will give you the key and the pattern will go through all the keys. If you reverse this formula then you can use it for Bach's Theory also. Bach used it going up also.

Reverse the pattern and use a Diminished sus 3rd. for the second position folds to make it easier. The pattern is after a Major 5-1-3 go down 1 step from the bottom finger and play a Diminished sus 3rd. and go down 1/2 step from that and play a minor #5 (Diminished golden rule). Then go down 1 step and play a 5-1-3 major. Repeat

Pivot finger & fold down page 90

Down 1 step from bottom finger to 5-1-3 major

C 5-1-3

Down 1 step Diminished sus 3rd. but i usually use diminished 7th for its quick fingering going down.

Down 1/2 step Minor #5 (Diminished golden rule)

The next position is going to be D 5-1-3 Major. But before going to the D. go down 1/2 step and play an a# diminished7 then drop 1/2 step to a D 5-1-3 major. After then you can fold the D to A7 if you wish.

When going down the pattern, a good trait to remember is after any major 5-1-3 1 step down will always be a Diminished 7th. This is also consistant with the 3-5-1 minors pattern on bottom of page 93. Also after any 5-1-3 minor there will always be a diminished 7th. That is going down of-course. So reverse the pattern on page 93 and incorporate with this page pattern. The diminished will key you to another key or jumping around. And before landing on the major 5-1-3 you can always hit its dominant fold first. But instead of hitting its dominant turn it into a diminished and drop 1/2 step to the major 5-1-3. page 23. use a diminished instead of the dominant fold. And after all else you can use the dominant afterwards. Its up to your improvisations.

Entering the Second position minor and fluent Improvisational Progressions

Beethoven

pictured below

1. If you take any 5-1-3 Major with left hand and sharpen the outside fingers. Then the top finger is target minor key to fold back and forth. With right hand target that same finger for the note to play the basic folding in the Minors but from a 5-1-3 position with the right hand. While the left hand is folding the outside fingers back and forth.

not pictured below - Classic Beethoven

2. If you take the same 5-1-3 Major and this time flatten the middle finger then its the second position Minor again right ? . And again target the outside finger by using it on the right hand and folding with its 5-1-3 minor while the left hand is folding with the second position minor and outside fingers flattening 1/2 step again. Back and forth.

For both excercises above. you can turn the bottom finger into a Dominant 7 at any time and resolve it to another 5-1-3 fold and repeat the process. In another key up or down. Or apply the circiular fourth on the dominant to another 5-1-3 with a flattened middle finger which is a Minor second position. And repeat the process.

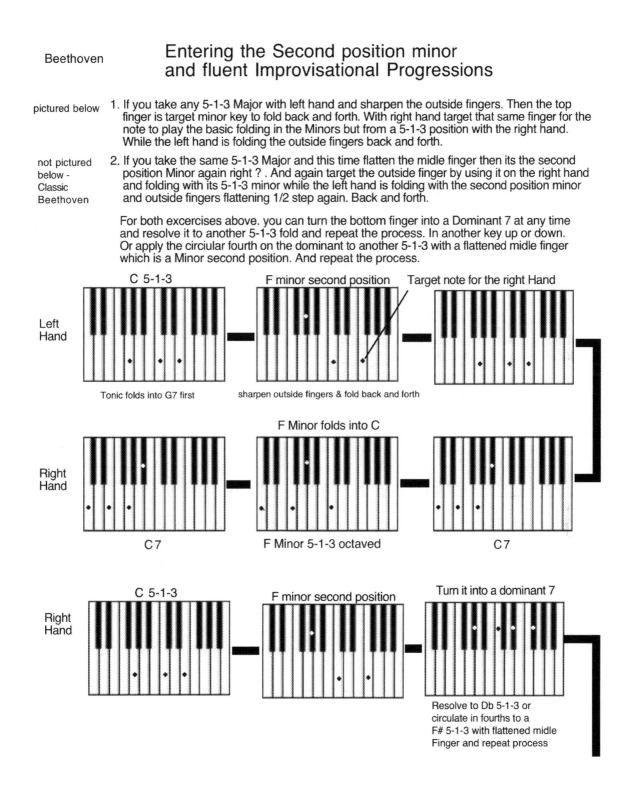

99

Baroque - sacred
songs & Dances

Pattern

Practice and Exercises for the Second positions
The Improvisatory fluency of the Second

Poetically Romantic
Beethoven's string
quartet - op. 127- Eb
Richard Strauss - Poems

1. Remember the pattern for the 7 degrees on page 53. It's as follows:

Mnemonic - **Maj**-*min*-*min*-**Maj**-**Maj**-*min*-*min*. (The last minor is a Diminished flattened 5th. to be exact.). Nevertheless a Minor in Harmonics. Or in this positions it can also be 5-1-3 major. But a diminished will do just fine.

2. Take any 5-1-3 minor - The subdominant of any key. And flatten the middle finger 1 step. Its now the major of that key from the second position(3-5-1). Here follow the pattern above. By using only the Second positions majors and minors only. The 3-5-1 majors and minors. Spot them in the key going up the scale one note at a time.

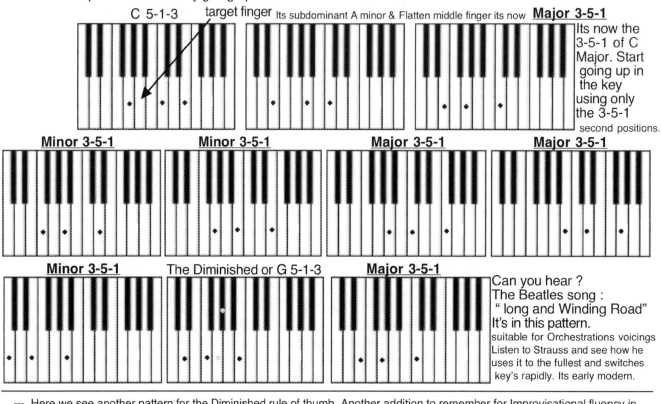

C 5-1-3   target finger Its subdominant A minor & Flatten middle finger its now **Major 3-5-1**

Its now the 3-5-1 of C Major. Start going up in the key using only the 3-5-1 second positions.

Minor 3-5-1   **Minor 3-5-1**   **Major 3-5-1**   **Major 3-5-1**

Minor 3-5-1   The Diminished or G 5-1-3   **Major 3-5-1**

Can you hear ?
The Beatles song :
" long and Winding Road"
It's in this pattern.
suitable for Orchestrations voicings Listen to Strauss and see how he uses it to the fullest and switches key's rapidly. Its early modern.

--- Here we see another pattern for the Diminished rule of thumb. Another addition to remember for Improvisational fluency in the poetically Romantic style. A reverse analogy from the 5-1-3 rule. This time its targeting downwards.

1. If you take any Diminished and flatten any finger 1/2 step. Target the lower finger for a 3-5-1 major or the minor #5th.

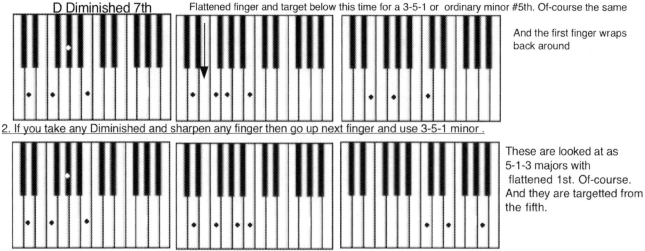

D Diminished 7th   Flattened finger and target below this time for a 3-5-1 or ordinary minor #5th. Of-course the same

And the first finger wraps back around

2. If you take any Diminished and sharpen any finger then go up next finger and use 3-5-1 minor .

These are looked at as 5-1-3 majors with flattened 1st. Of-course. And they are targetted from the fifth.

Further Studies

Bach ∞ Mozart
© minors ∞ majors

G△F

40% of our brains is involved in the seeing part
The Minds Eye build of the Triangle

The minors are Ideal for Baroquing or hand to hand combat poetry as well as Beethoven's trancidental Geometric & Chopin's Incidental poetic style.

Finding the "Central Intelligence Agent" Keys for the majors & minors on the fly

A quick way to find the Keys that are closest in harmony to each other is by using (5-1-#3 in-sight), which is almost similar to the 2-5-1 on page 157. But easier to spot. **They pair in three's.** 33.3. And the middle key is the central intelligent key to keep track of. Thus always working in three triangular pairs.

1. Take any **5-1-3 major** and (sharpen the 3) 1/2 step. Or take any **5-1-3 Minor** and (sharpen the 3) 1 step this time. Sharpen them in your mind. (You can convert switch them also. meaning turn the 5-1-3 notes into majors and turn the majors into minors. Know where you're at and what you are doing. also at any time take any note in these triads and turn into a minor or major 5-1-3, they will harmonize .) Practice

2. Look at the notes left. They are the harmonious keys closest to each other. For the Minors: the 3rd. is the common denominator relative major scale to use to connect to the other keys with.. For the Majors the natural minor of the root key is the common denominator between the other keys. Ther's always **three keys** to play with as the closest. And always **three diminished to use**, different one for each key. Each diminished has its own harmonic minor scale. When you sharpen the 5-1-3 minor in your mind, you now have **3 harmonic minor scales** to use. Or branch out to. Always using 5-1-3's. Always in 3's. The triangle will branch out to 3 other 5-1-3's, in your mind sharpen the 3rd of any to branch.

3. Next find the **natural** minors for the major keys. Page 82. And the secondary minor will be found from the natural minor as the top finger gets sharpened 1/2 step. **That's 3 minors again.** Another words all three minors of the seven degrees can be used. Once you have these **3 minors** then you can use the descends from the bottom of page 87. Or branch out to other minor or major keys. And **The three diminished families** are also used with for ex; Cmaj, Gmaj and Fmaj for the majors. And Am, Dm and Em and their harmonic minor scales for the minors (page 23). G & F are the neighboring keys of C. And from these keys one can expand to the rest of the keys. If you know where you are to return. Or not return but expand in development. Try the key of C first, and then expand to the other keys. All the other keys follow the same routine or pattern. And will always use all **three Diminished** and their **3 harmonic minor scales** are available for infinite Improvisations on page 23. Staying in the majors is Mozart. or Chopin. **Reminder** :of what key you're in weather in the minors or majors or notating, or the scales of the diminished or how they are found quickly are on page: 23 . Remember the majors can have a minor scale also. page 5. ex: the key of C can play A harmonic minor scale. Further modal branching ... Its infinite !

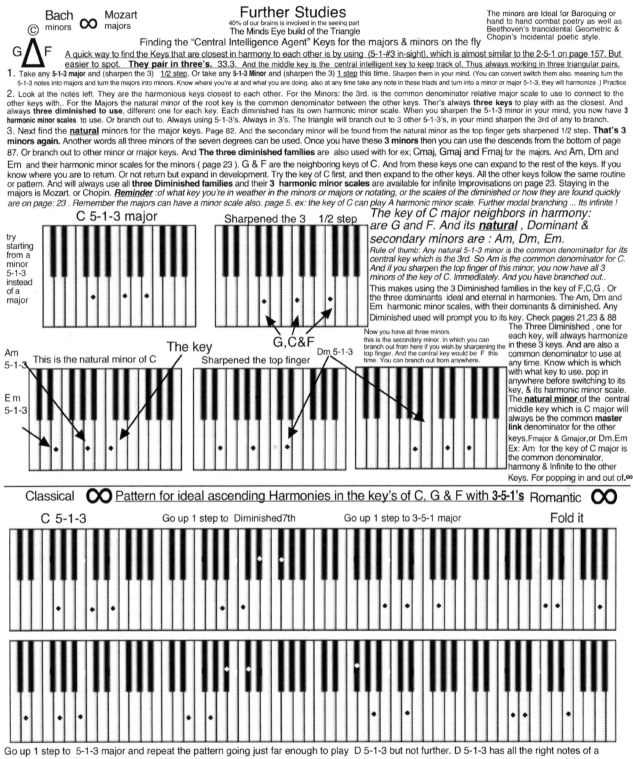

C 5-1-3 major

try starting from a minor 5-1-3 instead of a major

Sharpened the 3   1/2 step

G,C&F

Am 5-1-3

Em 5-1-3

This is the natural minor of C

The key
Sharpened the top finger

Dm 5-1-3

*The key of C major neighbors in harmony: are G and F. And its **natural** , Dominant & secondary minors are : Am, Dm, Em.*

Rule of thumb: Any natural 5-1-3 minor is the common denominator for its central key which is the 3rd. So Am is the common denominator for C. And if you sharpen the top finger of this minor, you now have all 3 minors of the key of C. Immediately. And you have branched out..

This makes using the 3 Diminished families in the key of F,C,G . Or the three dominants ideal and eternal in harmonies. The Am, Dm and Em harmonic minor scales, with their dominants & diminished. Any Diminished used will prompt you to its key. Check pages 21,23 & 88

Now you have all three minors. this is the secondary minor, in which you can branch out from here if you wish,by sharpening the top finger. And the central key would be F this time. You can branch out from anywhere.

The Three Diminished , one for each key, will always harmonize in these 3 keys. And are also a common denominator to use at any time. Know which is which with what key to use. pop in anywhere before switching to its key, & its harmonic minor scale. The **natural minor** of the central middle key which is C major will always be the common **master link** denominator for the other keys.Fmajor & Gmajor,or Dm,Em Ex: Am for the key of C major is the common denominator, harmony & Infinite to the other Keys. For popping in and out of.∞

Classical ∞ Pattern for ideal ascending Harmonies in the key's of C, G & F with **3-5-1's** Romantic ∞

C 5-1-3   Go up 1 step to Diminished7th   Go up 1 step to 3-5-1 major   Fold it

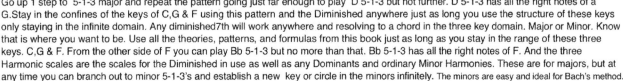

Go up 1 step to 5-1-3 major and repeat the pattern going just far enough to play D 5-1-3 but not further. D 5-1-3 has all the right notes of a G.Stay in the confines of the keys of C,G & F using this pattern and the Diminished anywhere just as long you use the structure of these keys only staying in the infinite domain. Any diminished7th will work anywhere and resolving to a chord in the three key domain. Major or Minor. Know that is where you want to be. Use all the theories, patterns, and formulas from this book just as long as you stay in the range of these three keys. C,G & F. From the other side of F you can play Bb 5-1-3 but no more than that. Bb 5-1-3 has all the right notes of F. And the three Harmonic scales are the scales for the Diminished in use as well as any Dominants and ordinary Minor Harmonies. These are for majors, but at any time you can branch out to minor 5-1-3's and establish a new key or circle in the minors infinitely. The minors are easy and ideal for Bach's method.

Baroqing Aria's

Further Studies

Symphonic poems

Descends using all the positions

To use all positions with and without a distinct pattern but sheer gut or what is allowed by experience or what sounds good and fresh. Or by the different fingering of a certain key. The second position 3-5-1 are in between the 5-1-3 and 1-3-5. They are used most of the time as the key positions for descends in the circular fourth or fifth. Or any pattern that is grasped by ear even. This is what makes baroquing with these positions a vast area to draw from. The aria. The dances.. The fugue ... This is also the expansion of the modern symphonic poems..

The pattern below is the same as the descending circular fourth's but simplified for the triads. Which means more.

1. Strart with any 5-1-3 major. And fold if desired. Then return as usual. Now although the pattern from page 100 is the basis or pattern to follow, start improvising on what other alternatives or choices to use .
2. Start looking for 3-5-1 positions with perhaps followed by 5-1-3 minors.
3. So take the pattern fold position from page 98. From a 5-1-3 major to a 3-5-1 major. Going up. Middle finger pivoted.
4. Now go up on the pivoted middle finger 1 more step. It should be now a minor 5-1-3.
5. Go down 1 step in the key, and find another 3-5-1 its going to be a minor this time. But better yet you have a choice of using the dominant or the original fold of the key also. For better or fuller sound. Then
6. Drop again and find other alternatives but merely staying close to the patterns. Adding what sounds better to use. An ordinary minor seventh sometimes is fuller to use. Or a suspended diminished..... We'll use the key of Db for example below : You do have some-what many different alternatives. Perhaps the right hand melody is what finds the structure. Or vise versa. This is the same pattern as the in-depth folding of page 51 - 82. Chapter 4

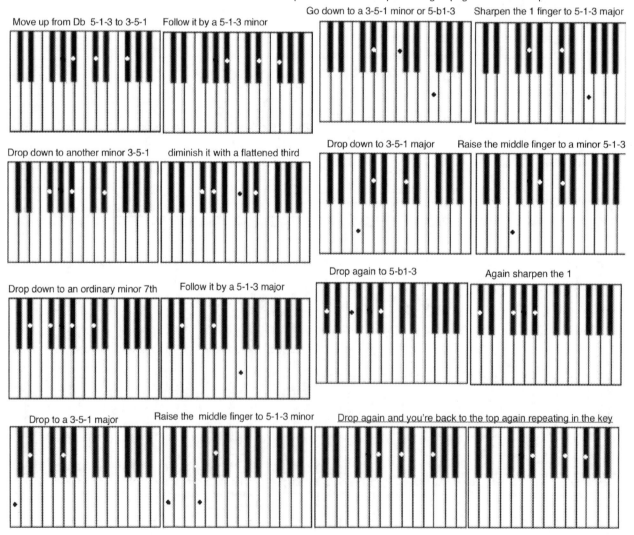

102

The Neapolitan Harmonies
How to locate them Fluently for Improvisations

3 possibilities

The Neapolitan Chords are another harmonies to use, there are three from this direction. and you enter them from the Dominant & Natural Minors from any Major 5-1-3's, That is if you're using them as a Predominant. In the Sonata Form. But this is the opportunity in using the second position. Or also called the first inversion. The best way for me to understand the Neapolitan 6th. is to call it the Minor Circular fourth with a sharpened fifth. A minor sharpened 5th. from any fourth position. And the #5th. will be the Major scale note. You can fold any position you land on. Or not. You can use these targets for any minor. Branch your Harmonies out. Its endless.

1. First and formost. Take the 5-1-3 Minor and from 1st. position Sharpen the 5th. So Am#5. **That's one**. Its pictured the last keyboard box in the corner on the bottom. Am#5 Which is an F. Next
2. Take the 5-1-3 Minor. Target notes are 1/2 steps above the 5 and 1. Play : Maj. 7th. Chord. Scales will be the same as target notes. To play the Neapolitan Triads Positions for both Targets.
3. First use the Circular fourth formula we covered already with any 5-1-3. Which is 1 step under the first finger and 1 step above the top finger and play a normal minor with a sharpened fifth. **That's two**. Next Take the F and look at it as 5-1-3 and drop the middle finger 1/2 step. **Thats three.**
This becomes the second position minor we covered earlier. In which you fold the outside fingers inside finger, outside, inside. How wonderful to have so many different Harmonies with different folds to play with.

Target Notes for playing Maj 7th. Chords that Harmonizes with A Minor

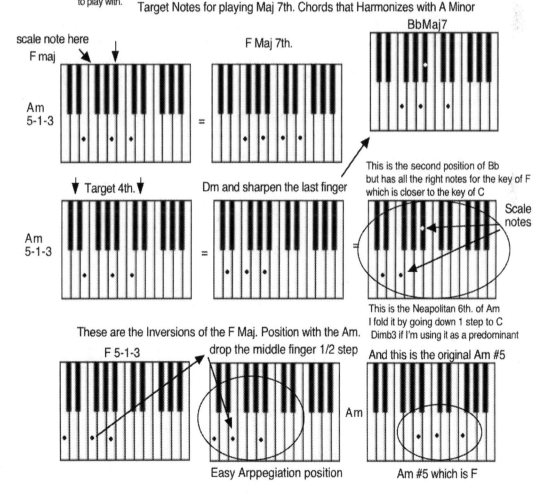

scale note here
F maj

F Maj 7th.

BbMaj7

Am
5-1-3

Target 4th.

Dm and sharpen the last finger

This is the second position of Bb
but has all the right notes for the key of F
which is closer to the key of C

Scale notes

Am
5-1-3

This is the Neapolitan 6th. of Am
I fold it by going down 1 step to C
Dimb3 if I'm using it as a predominant

These are the Inversions of the F Maj. Position with the Am.
drop the middle finger 1/2 step

F 5-1-3

And this is the original Am #5

Am

Easy Arppegiation position

Am #5 which is F

Subtracting Flatts or
Adding Sharps

The Neapolitans
Neighboring Harmonies

2 Possibilities
and more

The Neapolitans are best described as the Harmonies to the key you're in. They are the window of opportunities to new harmonies in other keys or remaining in the subtle key you're in but voiced from a second position Triad. The Circular key pattern in harmony is the Circular 4th and 5th. Meaning if you're to look at the keys from C. then the closest keys in harmony would be F or G. Because F has but one flat in it and G has but one sharp in it. therefore both keys are close to C. you can add more flats on to the key you're closest to, subtract flats. Or you can add more sharps to the key your in or subtract sharps going the other way. these are the keys closest to the key you're in thus called the neapolitans. Used with the second position. In this Targeted positions. We will be subtracting flats or adding sharps. The wheel will go in this direction as opposed to the other page of Neapolitans we covered.. From this direction there are only two Neapolitan possibilities.

1. First and formost.Take any Minor 5-1-3 and target the 1. Middle finger and drop it 1 step. Its now the ordinary Minor #5th. **Thats one**. Next

2. Take any Minor 5-1-3 and target the Last finger. The 3. go down 1/2 step and play an ordinary minor #5th. **Thats two.**

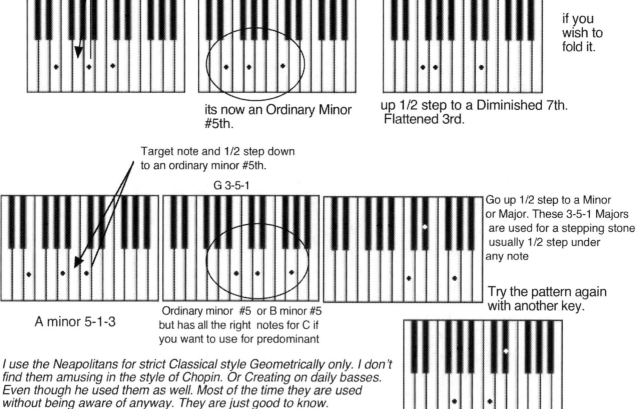

Target Notes

Drop Middle finger 1 Step

This is its fold

if you
wish to
fold it.

its now an Ordinary Minor #5th.

up 1/2 step to a Diminished 7th. Flattened 3rd.

Target note and 1/2 step down to an ordinary minor #5th.

G 3-5-1

Go up 1/2 step to a Minor or Major. These 3-5-1 Majors are used for a stepping stone usually 1/2 step under any note

A minor 5-1-3

Ordinary minor #5 or B minor #5 but has all the right notes for C if you want to use for predominant

Try the pattern again with another key.

I use the Neapolitans for strict Classical style Geometrically only. I don't find them amusing in the style of Chopin. Or Creating on daily basses. Even though he used them as well. Most of the time they are used without being aware of anyway. They are just good to know.

The Neapolitans for Am from this page would be : <u>C 3-5-1</u> & <u>G 3-5-1</u>.

And the Neapolitans for Am from the other page is : <u>Am 3-5-1</u> & <u>Bb 3-5-1</u> & <u>F 3-5-1</u>

5 Possibilities al-together. 4 are Ordinary Minor #5. (underlined). Which are all major Triads from the second position. Something Mozart used. Obviously because they're all majors. Major scale positions. Melodic and as a predominant. And something Beethoven circulated in Minors. Geometrically and was the master of like no other.

Further Studies

with the 5-1-3's Alternatives in theory

The Leading pure tones

Targeting Harmonies in a pattern

Pure Classical- Haydn, Motzart, Shubert, Beethoven

Take any 5-1-3 in circular 5th but this time alternate between major and minor, folding in Sonata form. Targeting Harmonies in a Pattern for Composition.

example 23

I've included the folding families-- And you can also include the seventh's if you wish

By alternating this way: Its the fourth thats being icluded in harmonies.

The fourth (subdominant) & Fifth (dominant) are the leading pure tone harmonies to the tonic.

The fourth is always targeted from 1 step from below the 5. And is always more harmonious with the minors. But Mozart & Haydn on the whole remained in the majors. Using the seven degrees mostly.

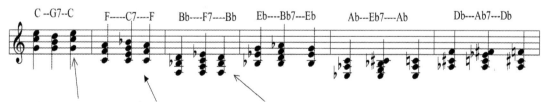

This is the target note. One step below is an F and one step below F is Bb and etc....

Now Alternate these also between Majors and Minors.

C - G7 - C ----- Fm - C7 - Fm ------ Bb - F7 - Bb ------- Ebm - Bb - Ebm   ect....

Using all positions in Poetry and motion
Chopin's delicate piano Method is ideal

1. Take the 5-1-3 minors and use the pattern from the bottom page of 93 to convert to 3-5-1 minor. Memorize it going up and down. As well as the pattern from page 98.
2. Use the pattern and progress up to ordinary minors. Know your scales.
3. Also use the rules from page 127 and progress to another key. And repeat in all keys or to what ever the poetic harmony takes you. The patterns from any page will poetically harmonize at any place in this manner. Check the scale pages for each position - pages 5, 22, 41 - 43, 88, 95, 128, 129. <u>To simplify the 3-5-1 majors folds I sometimes use a diminished, especially when going in different directions on the fly.</u>

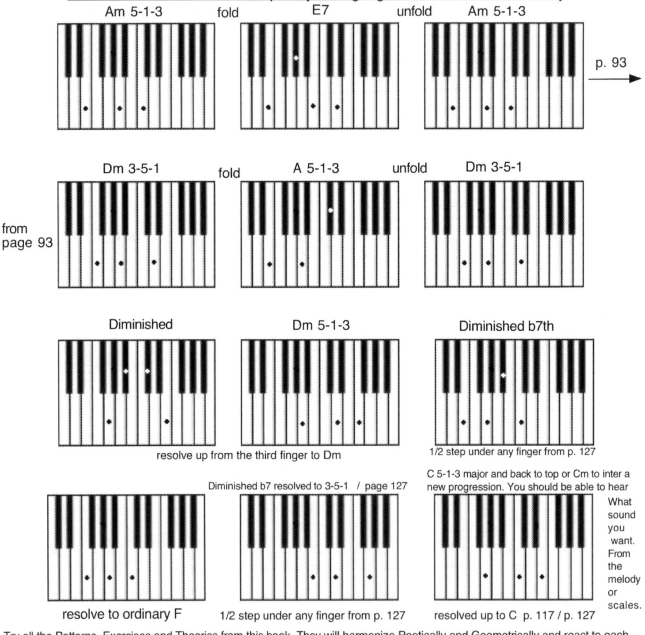

Try all the Patterns, Exercises and Theories from this book. They will harmonize Poetically and Geometrically and react to each other creatively, spontaneously and different from day to day. When one has control over structure instantly. One can crescendo in a furious powerful and explosive manner at any time or be as delicate as one wishes. This is the only type of music this can happen to. While the structure is being formed humanistically. I almost always stay in 5-1-3 and 3-5-1 format exclusively.

Timber Improvisational Arpeggiation
Bach-Beethoven-Schumann-Chopin-Tchaikovsky
Delicate Piano Magic

1. With left hand take the extended folding families covered earlier. On (p.36) start in the minors. With right hand start picking a melody line with the harmonic minor scale of that minor triad. (melody) Use quarter notes at first on the one.

2. Basic fold al-along in arpeggiation and go up 1/2 step to a diminished 7th. and back down, back and forth. In triplets and throw the extra note of the diminished 7th. in between.

3. Since they are triads on the whole. then the arpeggiation is going to be in the triplets form. Can be in 2/4 or 4/4 time if you wish also.

4. Then take the diminished of the bottom note, which is the target note. and play a diminished 7th. With right hand picking a melody al-along with the harmonic minor scale. Usually 1/2 step on top of the last finger is target for scale.

5. Now from that diminished play the Minor 5-1-3 of the same target note. 1/2 step above the last finger. this is of-course the circulat minor 4th's.

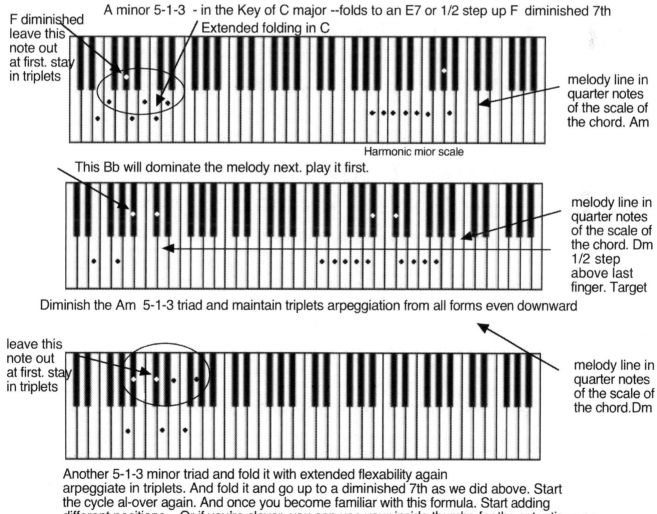

F diminished leave this note out at first. stay in triplets

A minor 5-1-3 - in the Key of C major --folds to an E7 or 1/2 step up F diminished 7th Extended folding in C

melody line in quarter notes of the scale of the chord. Am

Harmonic mior scale

This Bb will dominate the melody next. play it first.

melody line in quarter notes of the scale of the chord. Dm 1/2 step above last finger. Target

Diminish the Am 5-1-3 triad and maintain triplets arpeggiation from all forms even downward

leave this note out at first. stay in triplets

melody line in quarter notes of the scale of the chord.Dm

Another 5-1-3 minor triad and fold it with extended flexability again arpeggiate in triplets. And fold it and go up to a diminished 7th as we did above. Start the cycle al-over again. And once you become familiar with this formula. Start adding different positions.. Or if you're clever, you can use your inside thumbs for the extentions as Bach does and in the romantic style arpeggiating quickly in harmony as Schumann did.

Additional Studies

Beethoven's fury

Chopin's bombs

1. Take any Dominant 7. With the right hand first.
2. With left hand, play the 1st. & 3rd. notes back and forth
3. With right hand resolve the dominant 7th. from its root note to a 5-1-3 minor
4. What ever the key of the 5-1-3 minor is, its the harmonic minor scale of it.
5. Walk the two notes of the left hand in that harmonic minor scale.
6. With right hand, walk up in the key of the harmonic minor.. then switch hands

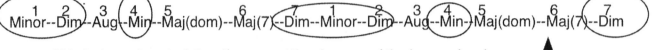

Minor--Dim--Aug--Min--Maj(dom)--Maj(7)--Dim--Minor--Dim--Aug--Min--Maj(dom)--Maj(7)--Dim

This is the pattern to follow if you want the degrees of the harmonic minors
it will also fit in sync with the folding rotation of the Gm 5-1-3 to D7 and that will also
harmonize with Gm 5-1-3 and target up from the (5th) 1/2 step up and down 1 step to
dim 7. Thats the Harmonic fury that allows Furious, Quick or Bombish Improvisation to
built timber.

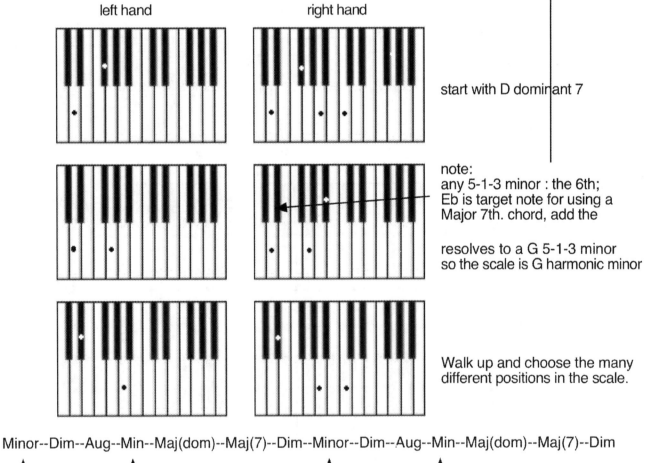

left hand

right hand

start with D dominant 7

note:
any 5-1-3 minor : the 6th;
Eb is target note for using a
Major 7th. chord, add the

resolves to a G 5-1-3 minor
so the scale is G harmonic minor

Walk up and choose the many
different positions in the scale.

Minor--Dim--Aug--Min--Maj(dom)--Maj(7)--Dim--Minor--Dim--Aug--Min--Maj(dom)--Maj(7)--Dim

Here Do you see the Circular fourth in the minors. Recapping the circular fourth is found 1 step below
the 5. Or 1 step above the 3. If its a minor of-course. The minors like to circulate by fourth's.

example 31

Further Studies
Beethoven's geometric Patterns, Scales and rule of thumb

1. Any Diminished flattened 7th. You can play as we covered earlier the Ab scale or you can play the Ab harmonic minor scale because we flattened the last note and the target note is the first now so we take 1/2 step up from 1st. note.

recapping

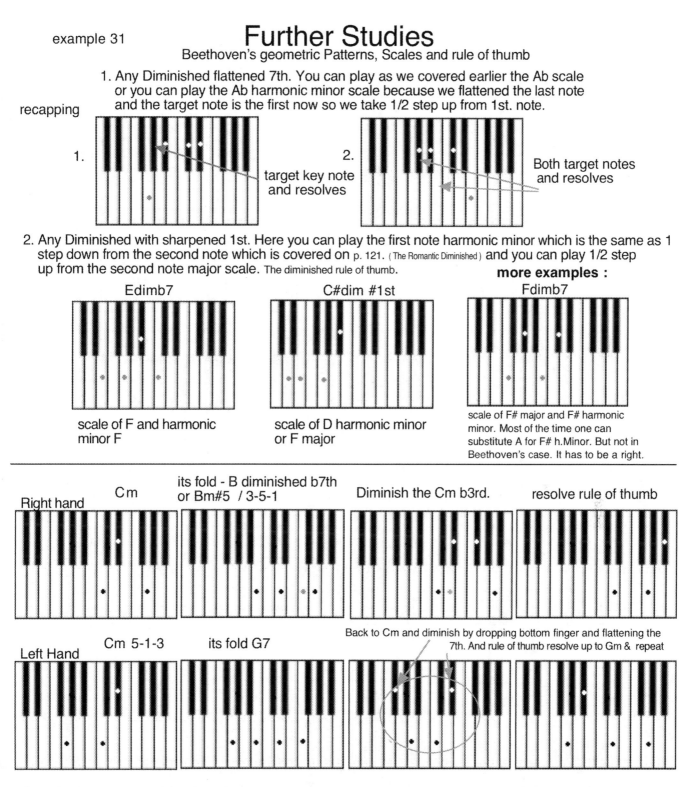

1.

2.

target key note
and resolves

Both target notes
and resolves

2. Any Diminished with sharpened 1st. Here you can play the first note harmonic minor which is the same as 1 step down from the second note which is covered on p. 121. (The Romantic Diminished) and you can play 1/2 step up from the second note major scale. The diminished rule of thumb.

more examples :

Edimb7

C#dim #1st

Fdimb7

scale of F and harmonic
minor F

scale of D harmonic minor
or F major

scale of F# major and F# harmonic minor. Most of the time one can substitute A for F# h.Minor. But not in Beethoven's case. It has to be a right.

Right hand

Cm

its fold - B diminished b7th
or Bm#5 / 3-5-1

Diminish the Cm b3rd.

resolve rule of thumb

Left Hand

Cm 5-1-3

its fold G7

Back to Cm and diminish by dropping bottom finger and flattening the 7th. And rule of thumb resolve up to Gm & repeat

Now the hands are switched in another key. These are of-course the circular fifth's. But practice playing a Diminished b7th. under any finger 1/2 step of any triad. 1-3-5 / 5-1-3 / 3-5-1 and resolve weather going up to a major or minor of another triad. Any triad. And repeat. Then start adding other theories and repeat the process. Its endless Improvisations. !

Further Studies

example 39

The Sharpened diminished

1. Take any Diminished and if you sharpen any note 1/2 step. Then the next note up
   1/2 step up above it is your scale or resolve. Much the same as if you ar flattening
   any note to achieve a dominant. Except this time we are just achieving scales and resolves.
   Also the note you sharpen will take Harmonic minor scale. This is the Circular fourth's in Harmony..
2. Or you can play a Major or Minor of the note you sharpen.. Practice in all the keys. Please note:
   The sharpened Diminished is a 13th. or a Wholetone.. Minor 6th. or Minor7b5. Be-careful, and
   Know how to use them for a Strict Classical style Sound. This pattern on bottom is one way I
   figured out to use.

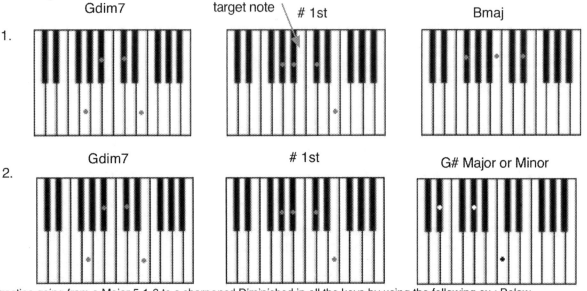

Gdim7   target note   # 1st   Bmaj

Gdim7   # 1st   G# Major or Minor

Practice going from a Major 5-1-3 to a sharpened Diminished in all the keys by using the following ex.: Below -
This is the Circular fifth. Then - (Not pictured below). You may also use the sharpened Diminished under the second
finger of the 5-1-3 major.. See if you recognize the sound. It is the hook of Chopin's Polonaise in Ab op.53 which is
considered the national anthem of the piano. And also Tchaikovsky's Romeo & Juliet's Overture. They are used with the
folding Dominant of the 5-1-3 major. And altering the last finger from the sharpened 7th. to the 6th. back and forth
against the dominant. These two pieces of music are regarded as among the highest of any music. They're also the
beginning of the romantic sharpened diminished era. Both Chopin and Tchaikovsky touch the modern and return
quickly. They emphasized it as the hook in both of their most popular and important masterpieces ever written by
anyone.

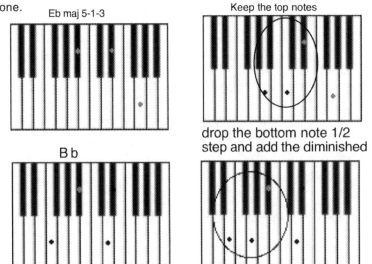

Eb maj 5-1-3

Keep the top notes

Bb

drop the bottom note 1/2
step and add the diminished

This is a Sharpened diminished

or a Minor 7th. b5 - the same

Which can resolve to a Bb
Major or Minor.

And this Sharpened diminished
resolves to an F. Thus circulating in
fifth's. The circular fifth.

Further Studies

example: 22a

Beethoven & Orchestration
Chopin   (turnarounds)

1. If you take any Diminished flattened 7th.
2. go up 1/2 step from the 1st. to minor 5-1-3 octaved.
3. Flatten the last finger 1 step and sharpen the 1st. 1 step.
4. You are now at step #1 again, back to the top again. It's your call from here on. There are many places to go to.

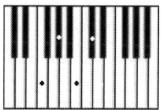

Gdim7

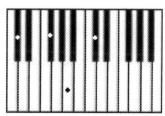

Flatten the 7th

Here you can fold this parallel

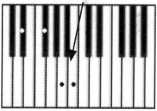

1/2 step up from 1st. note to Abm 5-1-3 octaved

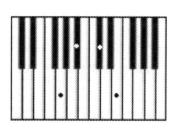

then sharpen 1st. note 1 step and flatten last note 1 step,you're back to top at another diminished b7 position

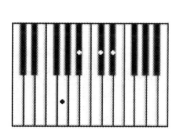

1/2 step up from 1st. now you're at another octave 5-1-3 minor, repeat.

note: for orchestration using an ordinary B7 would fit the sound better than notes that are very close together

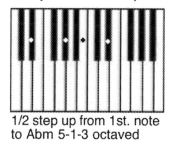

then sharpen 1st. note 1 step and flatten last note 1 step,you're back to top at another diminished b7 position

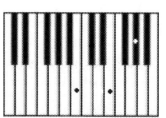

you can go to a major 5-1-3 to break the minor monotony

preparing for a parallel

Flatten the first finger. A diminished here is acceptable.

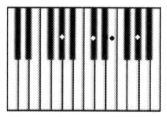

Drop the first finger again and now you're back to a Minor parallel. And repeat the process.

111

Further Studies

example 22 b   Beethoven & Orchestration
Chopin Turnarounds

1. If you take any Diminished flattened 7th.
2. go up 1/2 step from the 1st. to minor 5-1-3 octaved.
3. Flatten the last note 1 step and sharpen the 1st. 1/2 step.
4. then sharpen the 1st. 1/2 step.You are now back to top again. Repeat

Its your call from here on. There are many places to go to. The right hand is deciding the melody line so it can decide for you.

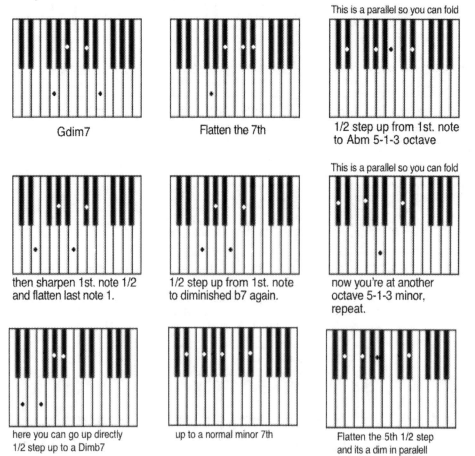

Gdim7

Flatten the 7th

This is a parallel so you can fold

1/2 step up from 1st. note to Abm 5-1-3 octave

then sharpen 1st. note 1/2 and flatten last note 1.

1/2 step up from 1st. note to diminished b7 again.

This is a parallel so you can fold

now you're at another octave 5-1-3 minor, repeat.

here you can go up directly 1/2 step up to a Dimb7

up to a normal minor 7th

Flatten the 5th 1/2 step and its a dim in paralell

Further Studies

ex. 22c

My Harmonic Ascends

Classical - Romantic

1. Take any Major 5-1-3 and scale is the 1.
2. Now go up 1 step and play minor 5-1-3 from the 5 and scale is still the 1 of the previous 5-1-3 above. And now you can switch to Harmonic Minor scale of the 5 of this new Minor 5-1-3.
3. And Go up again 1 step and play major 5-1-3 and the scale of the previous will work and the new one is the major scale of 1 of the present Major 5-1-3.
4. Now go up 1 step again and play a Minor 5-1-3 from the 5 and use the scale of the previous and the Harmonic Minor scale of the 5. Repeat .... See the pattern.! It works for all styles.

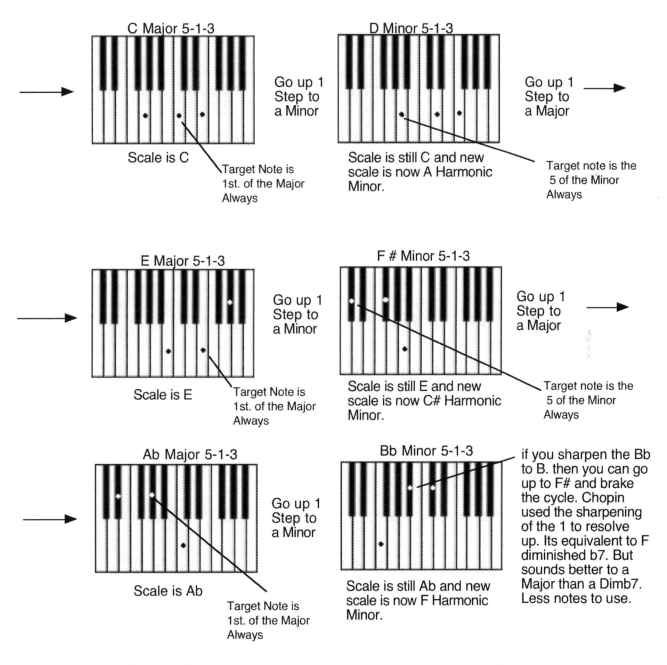

These will also work in ordinary positions. Not just 5-1-3's.

Further Studies

The Diminished Dominant
The Dominant Diminished

Beethoven, Brahms, Schumann,
Chopin's Geometric playground

Reminder

1. Any Diminished and 1/2 step down from any finger play a Dominant..... Poetic
2. Any Diminished and 1/2 step down from any finger play a 3-5-1 major or minor.. To minor drop the 3 1/2 step... Poetic
3. Any Dominant and 1/2 step up from any finger play a Dim7. Play the Dim with the right hand & Dom with Left Hand...Geometric
4. Any Diminished and 1 step up or down play a Dominant 7th. .... Geometric and imperfect. .. I don't use this one....
5. Any Check the Dominant and the Diminished - pages 19, 26, 191, and 158 on bottom for more Patterns to use.

Use the root Dominant position. To help open doors for Harmonies.
Also octave double notes with left hand. As in the Diminished ninth.
There are numerous ways to use these Geometric Harmonies.
Especially with speed or Arpeggiations ...... The fingering allows a scherzo
The Diminished is the Wild card, It can be anything.....

Poetic - follow the rule of thumb. Bach, Chopin, Mozart
Geometric - Trancidental, jump around at random. Beethoven
Symmetric - Western Modern, Abstract, Jazz

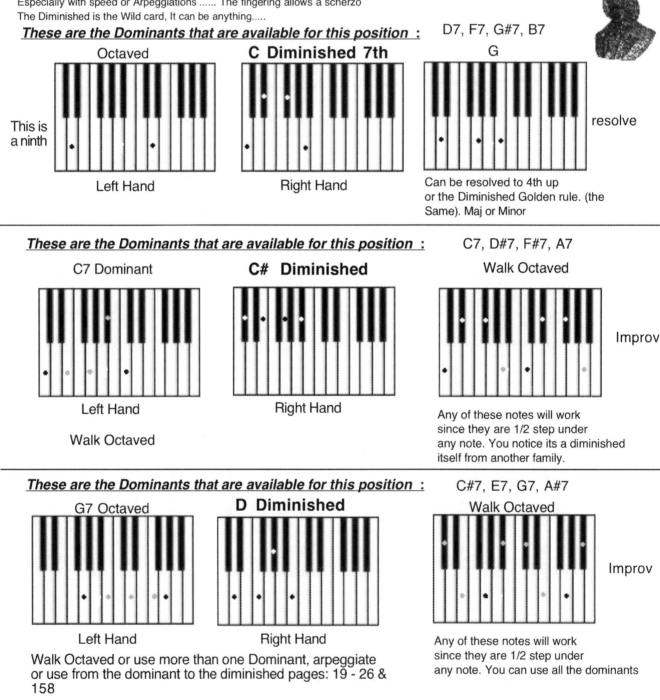

These are the Dominants that are available for this position :

D7, F7, G#7, B7

Octaved

C Diminished 7th

G

This is a ninth

resolve

Left Hand

Right Hand

Can be resolved to 4th up
or the Diminished Golden rule. (the
Same). Maj or Minor

These are the Dominants that are available for this position :

C7, D#7, F#7, A7

C7 Dominant

C# Diminished

Walk Octaved

Improv

Left Hand

Right Hand

Walk Octaved

Any of these notes will work
since they are 1/2 step under
any note. You notice its a diminished
itself from another family.

These are the Dominants that are available for this position :

C#7, E7, G7, A#7

G7 Octaved

D Diminished

Walk Octaved

Improv

Left Hand

Right Hand

Walk Octaved or use more than one Dominant, arpeggiate
or use from the dominant to the diminished pages: 19 - 26 &
158

Any of these notes will work
since they are 1/2 step under
any note. You can use all the dominants

Further Studies
Using the Parallels for fluid Improvisations

Beethoven

Parallel Folding with Minors and majors

Schumann

Chopin

1. Take any 5-1-3 minor paralleled.
2. Fold it which is dropping the middle fingers 1/2 step.
3. Go back to minor parallel.
4. Go up on outside fingers 1 step. Its now a Diminished parallel.
5. You now can go up 1/2 step to a Major or Minor parallel. We will go to minor for Exercises.
   If you take a Major then you can target a Dominant or Natural minor. p. 101

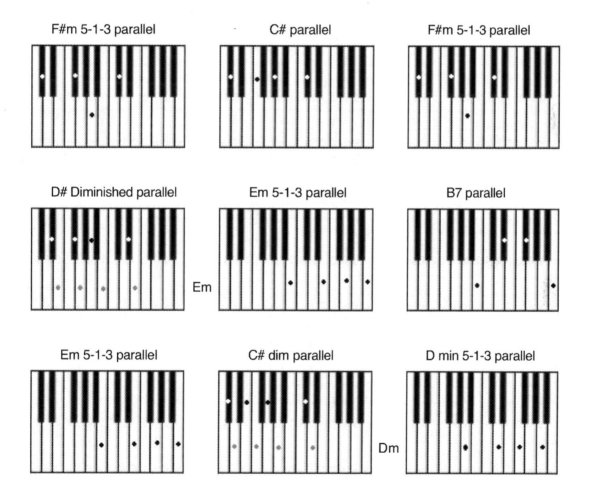

F#m 5-1-3 parallel   C# parallel   F#m 5-1-3 parallel

D# Diminished parallel   Em 5-1-3 parallel   B7 parallel

Em 5-1-3 parallel   C# dim parallel   D min 5-1-3 parallel

Delicate Piano Magic in Triplets or forceful Domination of Beethoven. With the parallels the improvisation tends to slow down a bit. So tender delicacy is introduced here for the finer grand pianos. And the selection of more notes to substitute is applicable for enjoyable accations. Or the poetic style.

Building a Composition from Improvisation

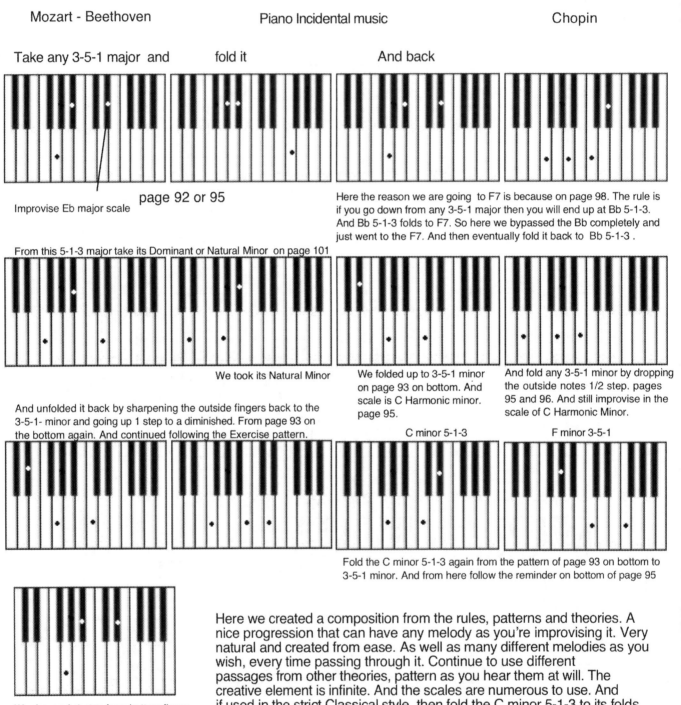

Mozart - Beethoven   Piano Incidental music   Chopin

Take any 3-5-1 major and   fold it   And back

Improvise Eb major scale   page 92 or 95

Here the reason we are going to F7 is because on page 98. The rule is if you go down from any 3-5-1 major then you will end up at Bb 5-1-3. And Bb 5-1-3 folds to F7. So here we bypassed the Bb completely and just went to the F7. And then eventually fold it back to Bb 5-1-3 .

From this 5-1-3 major take its Dominant or Natural Minor on page 101

We took its Natural Minor

We folded up to 3-5-1 minor on page 93 on bottom. And scale is C Harmonic minor. page 95.

And fold any 3-5-1 minor by dropping the outside notes 1/2 step. pages 95 and 96. And still improvise in the scale of C Harmonic Minor.

And unfolded it back by sharpening the outside fingers back to the 3-5-1- minor and going up 1 step to a diminished. From page 93 on the bottom again. And continued following the Exercise pattern.

C minor 5-1-3

F minor 3-5-1

Fold the C minor 5-1-3 again from the pattern of page 93 on bottom to 3-5-1 minor. And from here follow the reminder on bottom of page 95

We dropped 1 step from bottom finger from the F 3-5-1 minor to 3-5-1 major on page 95 on the bottom reminder:

Here we created a composition from the rules, patterns and theories. A nice progression that can have any melody as you're improvising it. Very natural and created from ease. As well as many different melodies as you wish, every time passing through it. Continue to use different passages from other theories, pattern as you hear them at will. The creative element is infinite. And the scales are numerous to use. And if used in the strict Classical style, then fold the C minor 5-1-3 to its folds also. G7. And any other position that can be folded. Geometrically

example 26 a

The Diminished b7

Chopin

The most used diminished because its also the second position triad. 3-5-1

--- This diminished b7 position is very simple to achieve and is a must in learning in all the keys
you must have a picture of each one or get familiar with each one by feel or fingering.
of-course these are dominants 7th. of the last note; But we wont look at them that way this time and that's
how simplicity comes in from the piano. This is how you can jump from key to key easily.

--- The Diminished b7 are also the General fold dominant family of any ordinary triad. Practice all the keys to
get familiar with. Simply drop down 1/2 step from any normal triad to Dimb7. (pictured on bottom)
Use a Diminished b7th with one hand and a 3-5-1 major with the other hand of the root note of the diminished, and rotate both with the
left hand in arpeggiating runs.(not pictured below) (As Chopin used as the idea that gave him the hook in his Etude no.12)

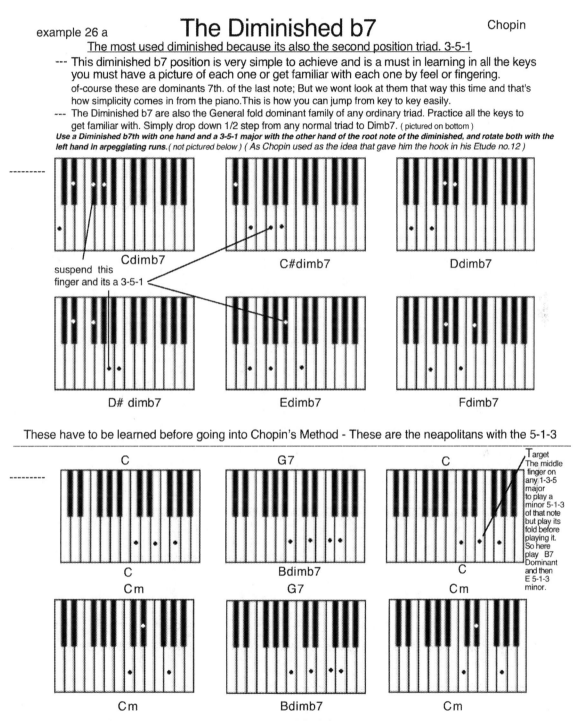

Cdimb7

suspend this
finger and its a 3-5-1

C#dimb7

Ddimb7

D# dimb7

Edimb7

Fdimb7

These have to be learned before going into Chopin's Method - These are the neapolitans with the 5-1-3

C

G7

C

Target
The middle
finger on
any 1-3-5
major
to play a
minor 5-1-3
of that note
but play its
fold before
playing it.
So here
play B7
Dominant
and then
E 5-1-3
minor.

C
Cm

Bdimb7
G7

C
Cm

Cm

Bdimb7

Cm

Using the Diminished b7 with ordinary Major & Minor Triads. The Classical Sonata Folds
with the ordinary Triads. " The Classical Method " Practice all the Keys.

example 26

My Ascending Harmonics
chromatic and harmonic progressions

Chopin builds - fluent and subtle arppegiation

Piano & Orchestration Tools
Bach & Beethoven

ALL OF THESE THEORIES WILL WORK AND HARMONIZE WITH EACH OTHER. This top part is simple but effective. Its when you can apply the theories on the bottom with one another, that will give you the power of Improvisational composition at will !

1. Take any Dimb7 and play the harmonic minor scale of the 1/2 step up from the first note
2. Then go 1/2 step up from 1st. note and play normal minor octaved
3. Then again go 1/2 step up from 1st. note and play dimb7. and repeat...through all keys
   If you catch yourself using minor 5-1-3's and folding them to dominants, then you're on the right track.
   And if you start using the diminished up and down the piano and then flattening the 7th.
   then you've poetically and mysteriously now have chopin's method. And you will see and hear chopin's mysterious Improvisations.

You can also play major scale from 1/2 step above the second finger of dim

play harmonic minor scale of
Db

or   you can play major scale of
            F#

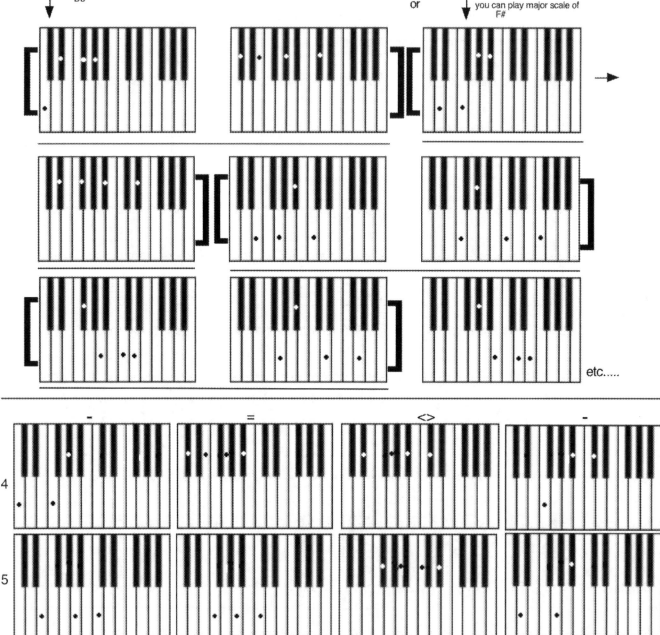

etc.....

4. **Try this progression :** Major or minor 5-1-3, 3-5-1, 1-3-5 / up 1/2 step to Diminished 7th / up 1 step to Dominant 7th and resolve to major or minor 5-1-3, 3-5-1,1-3-5 or go up 1 step again to a new 5-1-3 minor for example from the 5th. This will work if baroque since it goes to the 4th. And any of these positions can be gotten from the 5th. Harmonies are inevitable. Resolving the 5-b1-3 which is a 3-5-1 minor from the 5th. Or resolving to the 5-1-3 major or minor from the 5th as well.

5. **Try this chromatic combination :** 5-1-3 minor up 1/2 step to 1-3-5 Major up 1/2 step to diminished7 up 1/2 step to 5-1-3 minor of that note and you can fold the minor before you hit it.

6. **Try this harmonic progression :** Take any minor 5-1-3 go up 1/2 step to diminished7 up 1 step to diminished7 again and up 1 step to minor 5-1-3. Now at any time you can substitute or switch any of the minor 5-1-3's to major 3-5-1's or rotate between the two. (not pictured above) . Although this is not a chromatic. But apply in between ...

7. The simplest creep-ups; Is take any minor 1-3-5 / 3-5-1 / 5-1-3 then go up1/2 step to diminished7 and repeat chromatically up or down. They always give room to breath. and the 5-1-3's can be gotten from the fifth which will regress the progression down to pick up more momentum climbing back up gradually. As well as the 5-b1-3, minor 3-5-1 can be used both ways to pick up momentum. (not pictured above). Practice using any minor go up 1/2 step to diminished7 go up 1/2 step to minor 3-5-1 up diminished7 etc..

Ascending Progressions
Creep ups

example 26

* This part is from previous page *

1. Take any Dim b7 and play the harmonic scale of the 1/2 step up from the first note
2. Then go 1/2 step up from 1st. note and play normal minor octived
3. Then again go 1/2 step up from 1st. note and play Dim b7 and repeat through all keys

you can also play major scale from 1/2 step above the second finger of Dim b7

* This part is not on previous page.*

The Ordinary folding of the Classical Method. (1-3-5 to Dominant)
is achieved by using the diminished b7 with ordinary Triads. 1-3-5

These can also be used for Creep ups for Improvisation. The idea that your root finger does not remain rooted as with the

5-1-3's folding families make them not the ideal position to use for fluent Improvisation. but they are worth using here and

The Minors are ideal for creep ups.

Try This Harmony Breather : Universal Harmonies

Play any minor or major and go up 1/2 step and play minor #5th or 3-5-1 and go up 1/2 step and play minor or major and repeat

* not on previous page.*

Further Studies

example 27

other Dominant resolves and arpeggiation runs

1. If you land on a dominant from the first position, then sharpen the 1st. 1 step

2. Flatten the 1st. and the last note 1/2 step and you are at a Dimb7

3. Then up 1/2 step from first to major.Or minor 5-1-3 whatever you whant .

or just simply go up 1/2 step from any dominant to a diminished b7th

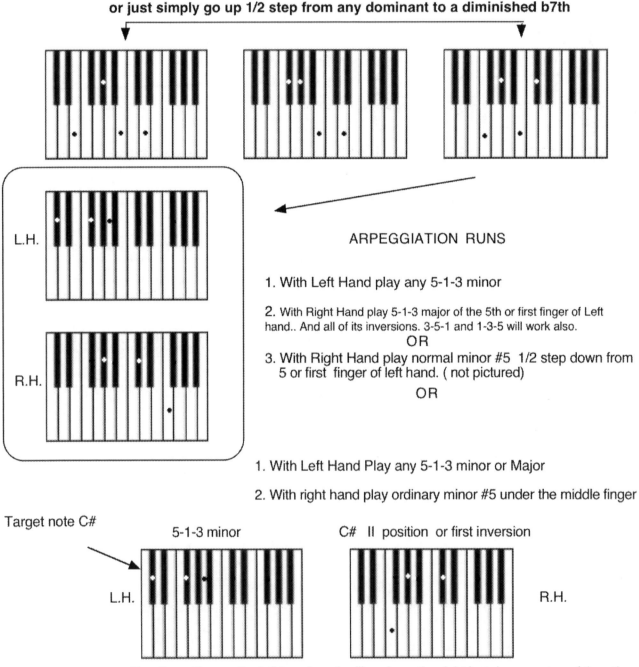

ARPEGGIATION RUNS

1. With Left Hand play any 5-1-3 minor

2. With Right Hand play 5-1-3 major of the 5th or first finger of Left hand.. And all of its inversions. 3-5-1 and 1-3-5 will work also.

OR

3. With Right Hand play normal minor #5 1/2 step down from 5 or first finger of left hand. (not pictured)

OR

1. With Left Hand Play any 5-1-3 minor or Major

2. With right hand play ordinary minor #5 under the middle finger

Target note C#

5-1-3 minor

C# II position or first inversion

L.H.

R.H.

Practice rolling up the left hand and rolling down the right hand one on top of the other

Further Studies
My Romantic and Tensioned Diminished

example : 30

1. Take any diminished 7th. and flatten its 7th. Now lock your position.

2. Next flatten the 3rd. & the 5th. 1/2 step. Which are the inside fingers.

3. We now go to the outside fingers which are the 1st & the 7th and flatten them 1/2 step

4. and back to the inside fingers 1/2 step down

5. And back to the out side fingers 1/2 step down. repeat..... Walk through all the keys.

These are used for loud crescendos as well. If you stay in one position and move the outside fingers back and forth, then you're in the same scale which can be useful for build ups. But practice all the positions so that the one type of position is in harmony. And because the Diminished is the trigger, then its open for any position.

The way to find the scale to use is very simple, target the second finger or the 3rd. and its always going to be the 1 whole step down from the second finger. You play the harmonic minor scale of that note.

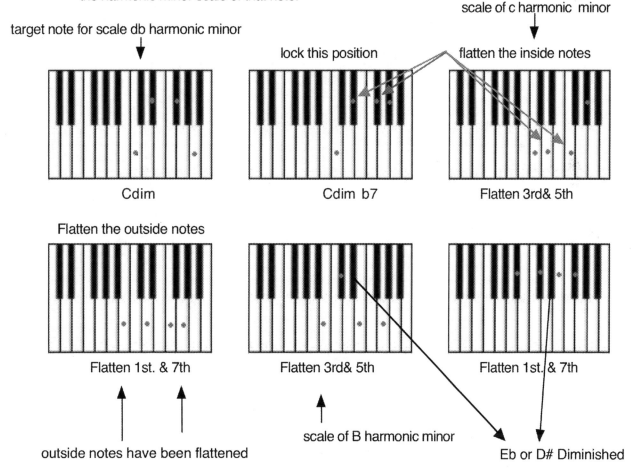

At any time you can take another diminished 1/2 step under the third finger to a fourth. Circle the Minor fourth's and then take another one under the next third finger. Thats the harmonies with these positions.

Further Studies

example : 30

The Romantic Diminished

example : 30a

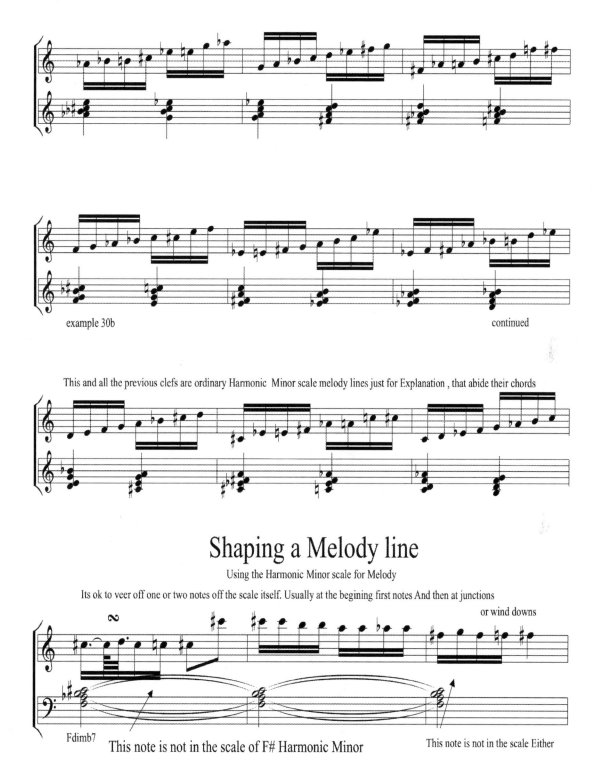

example 30b   continued

This and all the previous clefs are ordinary Harmonic Minor scale melody lines just for Explanation , that abide their chords

Shaping a Melody line

Using the Harmonic Minor scale for Melody

Its ok to veer off one or two notes off the scale itself. Usually at the begining first notes And then at junctions

or wind downs

Fdimb7   This note is not in the scale of F# Harmonic Minor   This note is not in the scale Either

Practice Veering off with all the different key's by using the Romantic Diminished as an Exercise.

Once the Veered notes start finding themselves then its sheer poetry.

The Improvisational Arppegiated Diminished b7 ease of fingering

These two Diminished b7 positions make ideal for arppegiation runs up and down

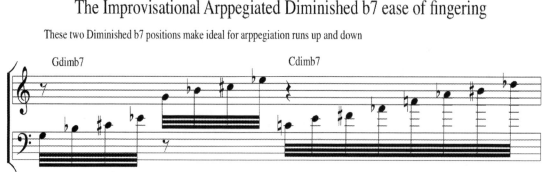

Additional Exercises for Practice

Suggestive Idea

The Harmonic Minor Scales are Ideal

Try this Formula / and circulate in Chopin Style : Create a Melody or let it create a melody for you

Bm7   5-1-3 ------------------------- Melody in the Key of B & F# Harmonic minor or D Major

F#7 ---------------------------------- Melody in the Key of B Harmonic Minor or B & D Major

Bm7   5-1-3 ------------------------- Melody in the Key of B & F# Harmonic minor or D Major

F dim7 -------Fdimb7----------------------- Melody in the Key of F# & A Harmonic Minor

F# min   5-1-3 -------------------------- Melody in the Key of F# & C# Harmonic Minor or A & E Major

C#7 ---------------------------------- Melody in the Kay of F# Harmonic Minor or F# Major

F# min   5-1-3 ----------------------- Melody in the Key of F# & C# Harmonic Minor or A & E Major

C dim7 --- Cdimb7 ----------------- Melody in the Key of F# & C# Harmonic Minor or E Major

C#m7 5-1-3 -------- and Fold to G#7 Melody in the Key of C# & G# Harmonic Minor or E Major

C#m7 5-1-3 -------- and Fold to G#7 Melody in the Key of C# & G# Harmonic Minor or E Major

F# min   5-1-3 -------------------------- Melody in the Key of F# & C# Harmonic Minor or A & E Major

C#7 ---------------------------------- Melody in the Kay of F# Harmonic Minor or F# Major

F# min   5-1-3 -------------------------- Melody in the Key of F# & C# Harmonic Minor or A & E Major

A#dim7 ---- A#dimb7 --------------------Melody in the Key of B or F# Harmonic Minor or D Major

Back to Begining - This time swap the Majors to Minors and Minors to Majors. Chords and Scales. (Diminished & Dominants excluded).

Circling between 4th's & 5th's Major & Minor, Alternating with a Spontaneous Ear Melodically making the right choices at hand

example 25
The Chopin Method

1. Take any 5-1-3 minor triad *using the diminished flattened 7 in Circular Fourth & Fifth's*
2. Drop from the 1st. note 1/2 step and play a diminished b7 from that target note
3. Go up from the 1st. note 1/2 step to play a 5-1-3 minor of that target note.
4. keep repeating the process through all the keys using harmonic minor scales.
5. Use the 3 or 4 of the 5-1-3 minor for the target Dominant 7th. to take for resolve.

dont forget to fold as you are going through the changes , you should already have a memorable picture of the diminished b7 in all the keys.

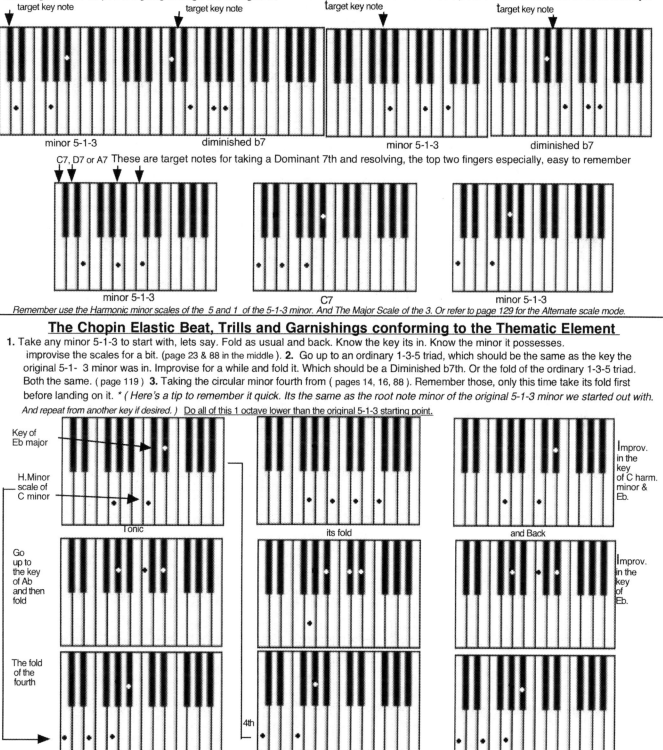

C7, D7 or A7 These are target notes for taking a Dominant 7th and resolving, the top two fingers especially, easy to remember

Remember use the Harmonic minor scales of the 5 and 1 of the 5-1-3 minor. And The Major Scale of the 3. Or refer to page 129 for the Alternate scale mode.

The Chopin Elastic Beat, Trills and Garnishings conforming to the Thematic Element

1. Take any minor 5-1-3 to start with, lets say. Fold as usual and back. Know the key its in. Know the minor it possesses.
improvise the scales for a bit. (page 23 & 88 in the middle). **2.** Go up to an ordinary 1-3-5 triad, which should be the same as the key the
original 5-1- 3 minor was in. Improvise for a while and fold it. Which should be a Diminished b7th. Or the fold of the ordinary 1-3-5 triad.
Both the same. (page 119) **3.** Taking the circular minor fourth from (pages 14, 16, 88). Remember those, only this time take its fold first
before landing on it. * (Here's a tip to remember it quick. Its the same as the root note minor of the original 5-1-3 minor we started out with.
And repeat from another key if desired.) Do all of this 1 octave lower than the original 5-1-3 starting point.

Beethoven   Chopin

Using the Diminished b7 in a Circular 4ths

1. Take any 5-1-3 Minor Triad and of-course fold it and back if you wish.   **2.** Target the 1/2 step above the 3

3. Play either a minor #5 or a Diminished b7   **4.** Go up 1/2 step to an ordinary Minor

5. Play this minor from a 5-1-3 position and repeat the process from a new key

6. For Beethoven's run below; Use the same format above, but sharpen the middle finger of the Eminor #5, and go directly to 5-1-3 minors. You will see the structure a little more plainly that way. Use only minor #5 and sharpen the middle finger every time you get to it.

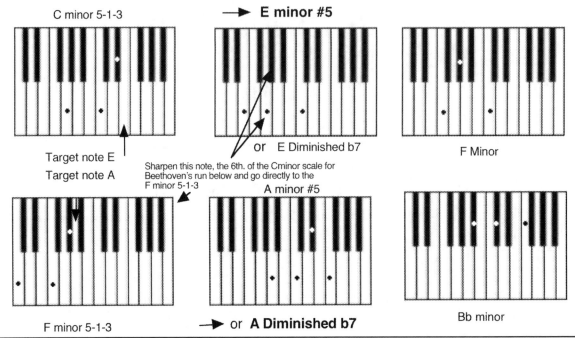

C minor 5-1-3

➝ **E minor #5**

F Minor

Target note E
Target note A

or   E Diminished b7

Sharpen this note, the 6th. of the Cminor scale for
Beethoven's run below and go directly to the
F minor 5-1-3

A minor #5

F minor 5-1-3   ➝ or **A Diminished b7**

Bb minor

Beethoven used structure to create scales or runs. Here's an example : He has in mind a target note for the fourth from any 5-1-3 minor. Which is one step from the bottom finger or 1 step from the top finger. Right ? we know that correct ? Now use just one note from the Diminished b7 before going up 1/2 step to another minor 5-1-3. And before all else use 2 notes from the 6th which is the tonic triad 1/2 step up from the 5 of the 5-1-3. Remember that from page 108 ? Ok. Now start circulating the minor 5-1-3's in fourth's, use only one note of the diminished b7 under the 1 of the 5-1-3 before going up to another 5-1-3 minor and use the structure for a run marked allegro assai. That's Beethoven's geometric runs. You can vary from any degree or jump around as he does to good taste. Its almost pentatonic but geometrically structured. He brakes the pattern on purpose because he doesn't want to sound poetic or monotonous. But powerful. See if you can spot this minor run with the Dimb7th, 6th added in circular. 4th.. This is Beethoven's signature. And most likely did get the run from the thorough-bass baroque method. Which delves in the fourth's as have been said on page 88. The Bach method. And now Chopin takes this from Beethoven and adds his touch.

Further Studies

Bach - Mozart
Beethoven

CHOPIN

Schumann - Brahms
Tchaikovsky

Using the Dimb7 with Majors & Minors with Tonic & Inversions in circular 4th. & 5th.

Every 5-1-3 or 1-3-5 Triad has 3 Dimb7 that Harmonizes - 1/2 step under, (and can be above any note also.)
This is the quickest way to improvise fast and forward in a motionly poetic manner. Stay in minor triad form which will automatically
circle in 5th and 3rd. Folding and poetically in technique. If used 1/2 under. You will eventually use the majors as well within time,
after you begin to hear yourself ahead of time, and begin to amuse yourself as well. The creation of a poetic composition is heard
and lured by a mysterious force.   <u>These are all 1/2 step under but they can be 1/2 step above also. The 4th.</u>

MAJORS - 5-1-3 or 1-3-5
1. Target 1/2 step under the 1st. play Dimb7 then go up 1/2 step to 5-1-3 or 1-3-5. Major or Minor
2. Target 1/2 step under the 3rd play Dimb7 then go up 1/2 step to 5-1-3 or 1-3-5. Major or Minor
3. Target 1/2 step under the 5rd play Dimb7 then go up 1/2 step to 5-1-3 or 1-3-5. Major or Minor

MINORS - 5-1-3 or 1-3-5
1. Target 1/2 step under the 1st. of a Minor play Dimb7 and go up 1/2 step to 1-3-5 or 5-1-3
2. Target 1/2 step under the 3rd. of a Minor play Dimb7 and go up 1/2 step to 1-3-5 or 5-1-3
3. Target 1/2 step under the 5th. of a Minor play Dimb7 and go up 1/2 step to 1-3-5 or 5-1-3

<u>The diminished flattened 7th. is a 3-5-1 with one extra note. Try suspending it and use only the 3-5-1</u>

And thats how one uses all 3 triads fluently without much thinking & with fluent Improvisations

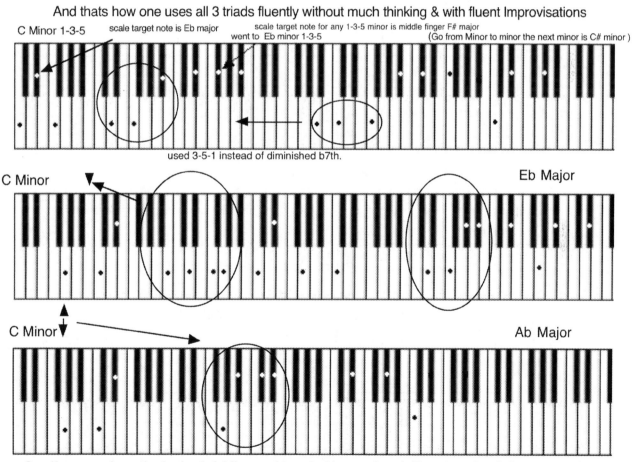

C Minor 1-3-5   scale target note is Eb major   scale target note for any 1-3-5 minor is middle finger F# major
                                              went to Eb minor 1-3-5   (Go from Minor to minor the next minor is C# minor)

used 3-5-1 instead of diminished b7th.

C Minor   Eb Major

C Minor   Ab Major

See if you can hear the in-depth folding as they wind in your hand. First start slow in baroque style
then afterwards try faster in classical & romantic style. And incorporate all of the Diminished flattened 7th's.
The other exercises. In circular 4th. & 5th. With constant folding its Chopin's poetic piano method.

Again the general rule with the Diminished b7th. is it can fall under any finger of the 5-1-3 or 1-3-5 1/2
step, even all the ordinary minor .. But first improvise with the major and minor triads and let the melody
line tell you what position to use. When you have complete control of what to play and can hear it then
Experiment with the others.

Using the Second & Third Positions

Bach   Beethoven

chopin

1. If you take any 5-1-3 Minor, and wrap the top finger around to the bottom and convert it into a minor second position. (Left Hand)
2. Then target the top note and with the right hand play a minor 5-1-3 and fold it. At the same time fold the minor second of the left hand also by dropping the outside fingers. And if you go up with the left hand. That is sharpen the middle finger to a Major 5-1-3. You can start in-depth folding. and start descending. The target key to descend is the bottom finger.
3. From the 5-1-3 major drop 1/2 step to a minor #5. Or Second position major. The same and start the in-depth folding. The descending circular fourth. And repeat the process with another Minor. Most likely a Dominant or Natural Minor of a **Major key**. Or maybe a Minor from a Circular fifth. Etc..Or Start
4. If you are Baroquing with this theory. You can also play the folds against each other. Meaning while the left hand is folding. The right hand is using the opposite position. Alternate in positions !

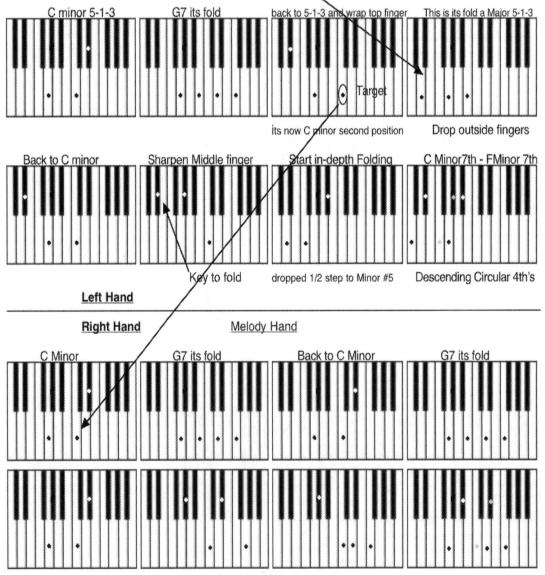

128

Further studies with the 5-1-3's minor

example : 21

Alternate scale Mode

used for **Chopin's** style

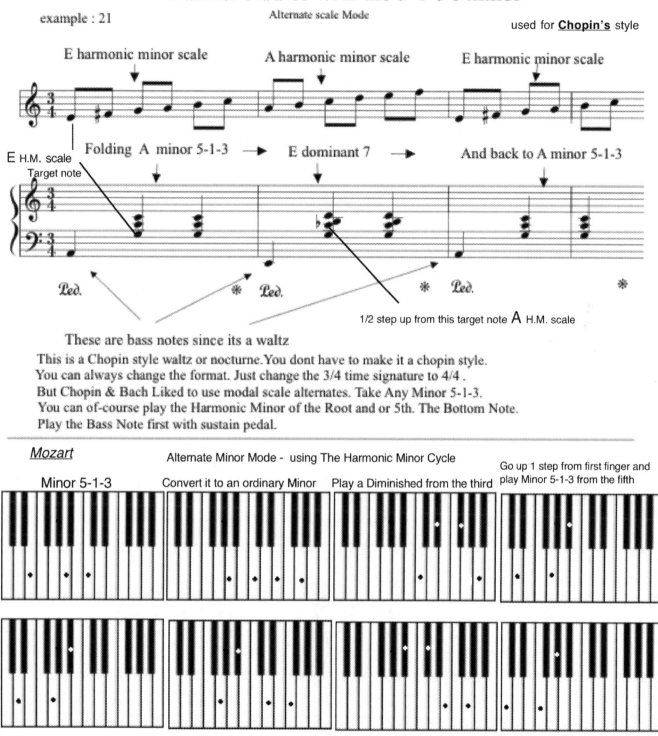

E harmonic minor scale

A harmonic minor scale

E harmonic minor scale

E H.M. scale
Target note

Folding A minor 5-1-3 →

E dominant 7 →

And back to A minor 5-1-3

1/2 step up from this target note **A** H.M. scale

These are bass notes since its a waltz

This is a Chopin style waltz or nocturne. You dont have to make it a chopin style.
You can always change the format. Just change the 3/4 time signature to 4/4 .
But Chopin & Bach Liked to use modal scale alternates. Take Any Minor 5-1-3.
You can of-course play the Harmonic Minor of the Root and or 5th. The Bottom Note.
Play the Bass Note first with sustain pedal.

Mozart

Alternate Minor Mode - using The Harmonic Minor Cycle

Go up 1 step from first finger and
play Minor 5-1-3 from the fifth

Minor 5-1-3

Convert it to an ordinary Minor

Play a Diminished from the third

1. Take any Minor 5-1-3. After folding. Convert it to an ordinary minor 7th.
2. Take its third and diminish it.
3. Go up 1 step and play a Minor 5-1-3.. Or a Major if you wish to brake the cycle. Repeat from
   another Minor or Major.

The Chopin Tenth's

for Ballads and Timber build ups

Left hand

1. Take any position Tonic Octaved and arpeggiate up to the tenth note and back.

2. Take any Minor octaved and play the tenth note in arpeggiation up and back.

3. Take any Diminished octaved and play its tenth in Arpeggiation up and back.

4. Take any Dominant 7th octaved and hit the tenth in arpeggiation up and back.

The Tenth is of-course always going to be the third of any position

Notice the Circled 5-1-3 Major & Minors. Spot them this way !

C 10th   Db 10th   D minor 10th

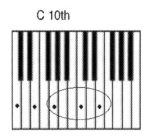 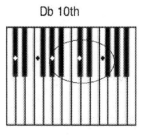 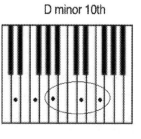

Ab 5-1-3 10th which is Ab maj 7th
but don't look at it as an Ab maj 7th Or
you will loose your construct hearing.

E 10th   F minor 10th

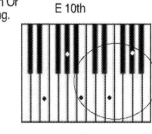 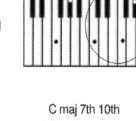

F # Dim 10th   G Dominant 10th   C maj 7th 10th

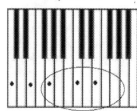

The left hand can roll and construct composition until you use a Maj7th not from a 5-1-3.
So be careful on how you use the maj 7th.

The Diminished 6th Sharpened 7th

1. Take any Diminished and sharpen its seventh.

2. And add the sixth.

3. Arpeggiate and resolve up to a Tonic Triad to return to the Classical style. Or

4. The fact ther's consecutive arpeggiation. The right hand can also arpeggiate with inversions of the same notes for multi colored whole-tones Arped runs.

Although it may not be the Ideal Improvisational fingering of this Diminished it doesn't hurt to use as a prerequisite into the whole tone stage. Or a turnaround back to the Classical format.

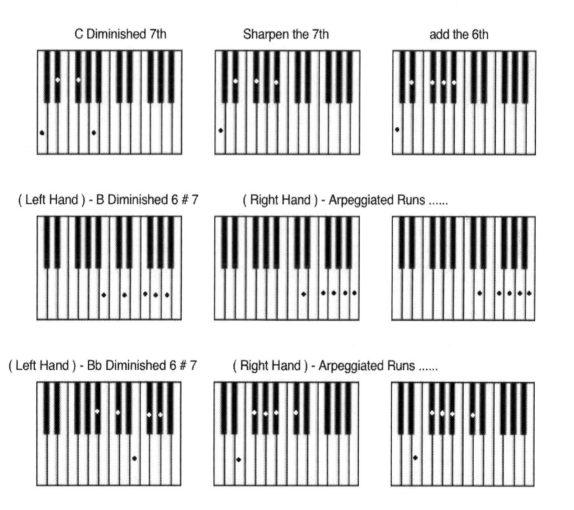

C Diminished 7th   Sharpen the 7th   add the 6th

(Left Hand) - B Diminished 6 # 7   (Right Hand) - Arpeggiated Runs ......

(Left Hand) - Bb Diminished 6 # 7   (Right Hand) - Arpeggiated Runs ......

Further Studies

a Progression example

example 37 a   chopin style

1. Take any 5-1-3 major go up 1/2 step from 1st. to diminished 7th.Then flatten the 7th.
2. Then up 1/2 step from 1st. to normal minor.
3. Then up 1 whole step from 1st. to diminished b7

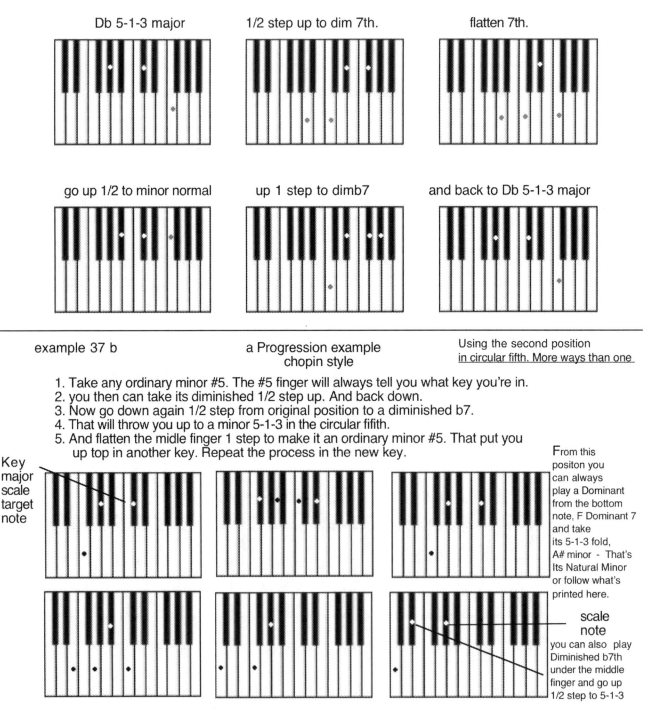

Db 5-1-3 major   1/2 step up to dim 7th.   flatten 7th.

go up 1/2 to minor normal   up 1 step to dimb7   and back to Db 5-1-3 major

example 37 b   a Progression example   Using the second position
                                   chopin style   in circular fifth. More ways than one

1. Take any ordinary minor #5. The #5 finger will always tell you what key you're in.
2. you then can take its diminished 1/2 step up. And back down.
3. Now go down again 1/2 step from original position to a diminished b7.
4. That will throw you up to a minor 5-1-3 in the circular fifith.
5. And flatten the middle finger 1 step to make it an ordinary minor #5. That put you
   up top in another key. Repeat the process in the new key.

Key major scale target note

From this positon you can always play a Dominant from the bottom note, F Dominant 7 and take its 5-1-3 fold, A# minor - That's Its Natural Minor or follow what's printed here.

scale note

you can also play Diminished b7th under the middle finger and go up 1/2 step to 5-1-3

Final Full Classical Harmonic Minor Progression

Beethoven loved the F Minor Key. For its fingering and sight of Positions. This progression
will orchestrate any piece of Music. Or give you the Improvisational Fluency on the piano.

The pattern is: 1/2 - 1 - 1/2 - 1/2 - 1/2 - 1 - 1 - 1 -   Half / Whole / Half / Half / Half / Whole / Whole / Whole

Mnemonic: I keep the Fm key in my mind because its easiest to remember, and I use it to remember the other keys by picturing it.
On the fourth position you hit the daily double in harmonies. Don't be confused I went up and back down and up again.

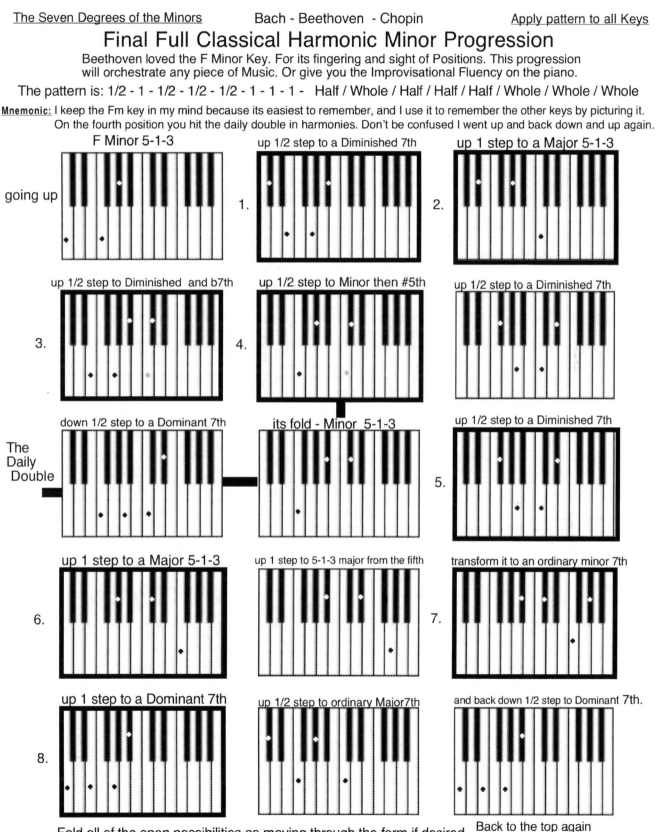

Fold all of the open possibilities as moving through the form if desired. Back to the top again
And best of all - Arpeggiate these formula's fast. The piano is played like schumann and chopin.
Instinct speed of thought ! This is what Beethoven played when he improvised for Mozart. He loved the Cm key also.

Robert Kaye

POP # Further Studies II JAZZ

Whole Tone series

Suspense, Thrill & Romance — Scoring for Motion Pictures

A-Tonal — Debussy - Shoenberg - Stravinski - Wagner - J.Williams - Q.Jones - George Martin — **Emotional**

Note : The 5-1-3 Minors are also Whole Tone Tools. Paralleled rich and full used in the style of Brahms. He was the begining of it. Or Bach and baroquing in counterpoint is very much in use here also.

Therefore everything from previous studies also applies

Although over-whole the harmonic minor scales tend to dissipate into major and melodic minor scale. That doesn't mean you cannot use them.

From Streight Jazz to Abstractionism --- From Rag and Stride to Miles - Hancock, Monk & Coltrane

To BACH'S : point-counterpoint, punctual-counterpunctual harmonious Improvisational miracles

Abstractism

Song-writing

Impressionism

Modal

Entertainment

Broadway

Show business

Take any Diminished

Sharpen the first note 1/2 step

Lavender

Indigo

Purple

Mauve

Rose

Blue

Violet

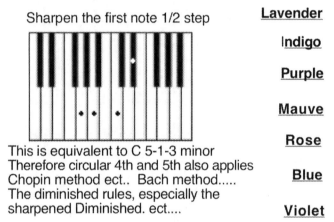

This is equivalent to C 5-1-3 minor
Therefore circular 4th and 5th also applies
Chopin method ect.. Bach method.....
The diminished rules, especially the
sharpened Diminished. ect....

Sharpen the A to add the Bb for a rich full sound from a new era of clearer instruments or louder entertaining voices. The Jazz era is born. Playing rich and full against rythm and steady bass.

This is the 5-1-3 minor
and 3-5-1 major together.

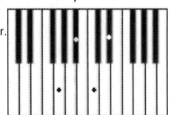

Bb can be target scale or C melodic minor can be scale or Eb is the scale

G Harmonic minor is of-course scale but stay in Major & Melodic minor scales for now

NOTE : A Dominant 7th. Chord 1 step on top of another Dominant 7th. Chord creates a whole tone. scale note is the third finger or the fifth of the Left Hand and will use a Melodic Minor scale. So also any Flattened Diminished studied earlier will now also come in play. Since its a Dominant 7th.

Flattened and Sharpened Ninth's - Pure **Abstractionism**. The new "**American Impressionistic art Form**" used against rythm and bass. Or Orchestrated alone.

THE MODERN

MODAL

ERA

As The Century turned (1800 - 1900) modern elements began to surface. The piano of one, we begin to hear, even clearer. Thanks to modern industrialization. We begin to experiment with harmonies and dissonance as opposed to theory and technique. Thus fresh jazz elements were born. If you were to pick a composer who was in the thick of this transformation. You would first have to look at Chopin's 3 "Ecossaise" in which he wrote in his teens, and derived them from the scottish dances. They are undoubtedly the first in my experience in stride piano. Scott Joplin, the American composer who clearly was one of those who joined the classical to jazz element with the syncopated style of ragtime is in the midst of this era. Next came among the popular, Ravel and Debussy who inscribed the harmonious modal and modern orchestrative elements of the modern grand pianos. Where now we hear abstract dissonance and harmonious theoretical elements inscribed. George Gershwin was one who was in the midst of this movement. As well as Jelly Roll Morton. And Louis Armstrong who taught everyone how to sing jazz correctly, like he played the trumpet. Within the early Shout. The Duke, the King, the Count, the Earl, and the Barons Followed. And finally Herbie Hancock inscribed the American Quartet and Quintet's as truly an American virtuous ingenious improvisational art form. He himself played Mozart with the chicago symphony orchestra at the age of 14. The binary element of a milestone juncture again by an educated composer surfaces the innovative ingenious element in music.

The Statue of Liberty - Built by the French in 1876 to celebrate the centennial of the Declaration of Independence of 1776. The first to use electricity. Symbolizes the enlightenment age. The french wanted to reassure the electoral system as opposed to the monarchy in which they were struggling with at the time. Gustave Eiffel builder of the Eiffel tower was the designer. The funds were raised from operas, dances, theaters, prize fights, exhibitions supplemented by the US. Music from composer Charles Gounod was used for the accation. General James Tucumsa Sherman selected the site. The keystone held in her hand represents the knowledge and shows the date of the US Declaration of Independence in Roman numeral. July 4th. 1776. The facial or Classical appearance is of an ancient Rome's Goddess of Freedom from slavery, repression and tyranny. The seven spikes in crown opitomizes the 7 seas and the 7 continents.. The Torch symbolizes Enlightenment.

" This woman called classical music " -- Ludwig Van Beethoven

The Greek Goddess - Genius of Liberty

Adolphe Yvon - Genius of America

135

Further Studies II

Wholtone Harpish Elements
Ravel, Debussy

1. Take any Dimnished 7th.

2. If you sharpen any note 1/2 step and arpeggiate. It sounds like Ravel & Debussy.

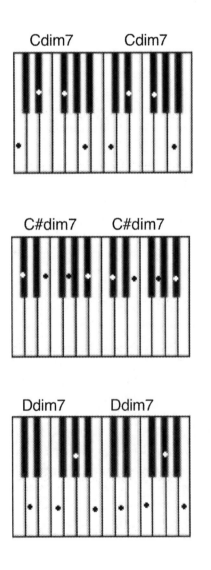

Cdim7   Cdim7

C#dim7   C#dim7

Ddim7   Ddim7

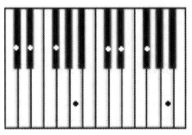

Cdim7 #1st.-Cdim7 #1st.

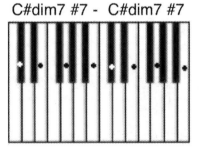

C#dim7 #7 - C#dim7 #7

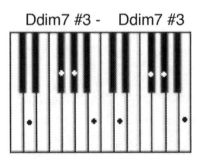

Ddim7 #3 - Ddim7 #3

Further Studies II

Wholtone Harpish Elements
Ravel , Debussy

example 36

1. If you take any normal minor 7th. With the left hand

2. Then take with the right hand 1 whole step up from root or first note and play dimb7.

   arpeggiate up and down the keyboard. with sustain pedal

3. If you take any dimb7 with one hand and exactly one whole step above with the other hand play another dimb7. Roll and arpeggiate with sustain pedal.

   Experiment with dim7 and create your own, there are many ways using these elements
   For example sustain certain notes for further clearity. Suspend the 3rd of the left hand
   and the 5th. of the right hand. Thus opening up voicings.

4. The basics are dim7 one with one hand and 1 whole step above or below with the other hand

Split these into 2 octaves using both hands not just necessarily one as shown here.

Gm7--Adimb7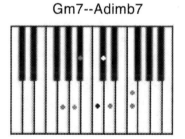

Edimb7----Fdimb7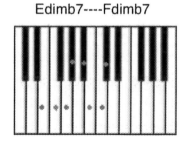

Cdim7----Ddim7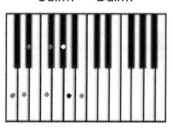

left hand   Adimb7---------Gm7   right hand

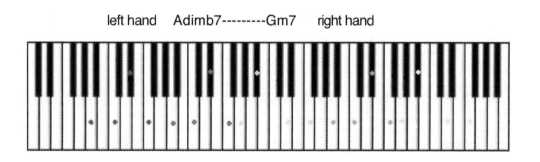

Further Studies II

example 38   Basic Minor Harmonies

1. When using any 5-1-3 minor, add the second position note along to create a jazz full voicing appropriate for the diminished improvisations.
2. When using any diminished drop the las two fingers 1/2 step. Or raise the first two fingers 1/2 step. The same !
3. Exercise in circular fifth to get the sound of it. And stick with major scales first. Then start using the Diminished rule and targets to Improvise and create continously new ideas.
4. The second position (3-5-1 or Minor #5th) gets all the target scale notes.

C minor 5-1-3

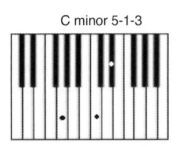

C minor 5-1-3 & Eb major 3-5-1

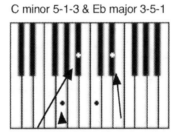

Improvise in the key of Eb major
or Bb major , Bb melodic minor
or G harmonic minor

Droped down 1/2 step to

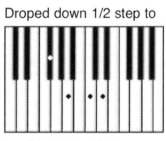

Diminished b7th

resolve to G minor 5-1-3
& Bb maj or 3-5-1

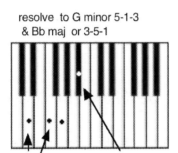

Droped down 1/2 step to

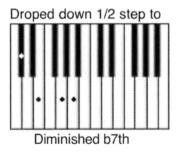

Diminished b7th

resolve up to D minor 5-1-3
& F major 3-5-1

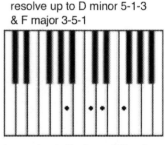

Improvise in the key of Bb major
or   F major , F melodic minor
or D harmonic minor

Improvise in the key of F major
or C major , C melodic minor
or A harmonic minor

The object here is to use all the Diminished and its golden rule of thumb to create and play with all its rythm & glory
with a distinct melody line continously being created as one Improvises against the rythm or steady beat. Always something new.
And not necessarily Abstract. But can be.

---

1. If you take with left hand 1st. & 5th
2. And with right hand play the minor of the fifth

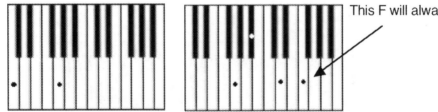

This F will always be the scale note

Debussy used this formula

138

Further Studies II

Cocktail Piano or
The original Hollywood sound

Songwriting
Baroquing

Modal Harmonies

example 43

Ravel, Debussy, Herbie Hancock, Burt Bacharack, Bach

1. With left Hand take any normal first position Minor 7th.
2. With right hand play a normal Major 7th from its third. Or the second finger.
3. The scale of any normal minor 1-3-5 and 7th is the third or the second finger.

<u>key note for major scale is always the third of any normal Minor - this is a key target note</u>

From Jump Around key to key

Scale is Eb major

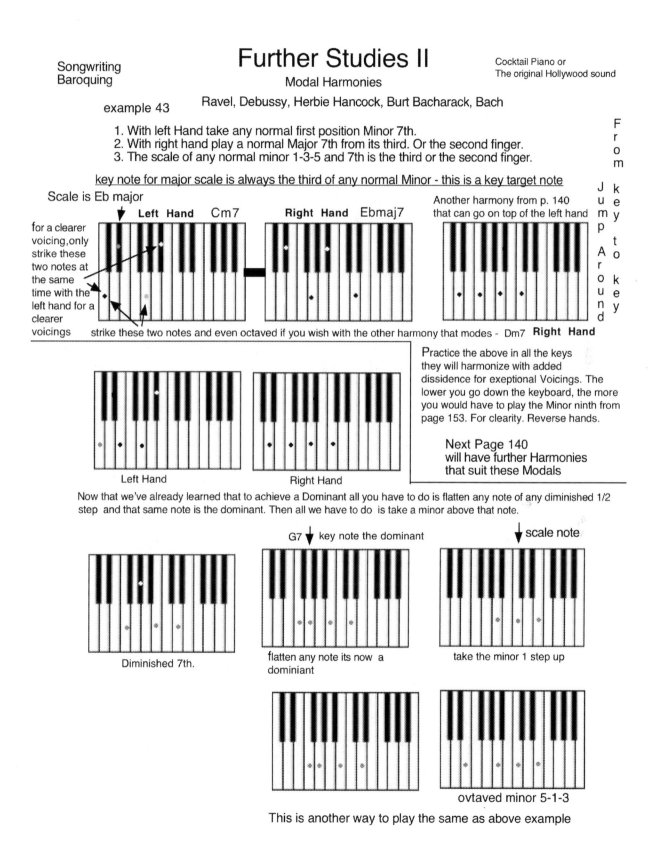

for a clearer voicing,only strike these two notes at the same time with the left hand for a clearer voicings

Left Hand Cm7   **Right Hand** Ebmaj7

Another harmony from p. 140 that can go on top of the left hand

strike these two notes and even octaved if you wish with the other harmony that modes - Dm7 **Right Hand**

Left Hand   Right Hand

Practice the above in all the keys they will harmonize with added dissidence for exeptional Voicings. The lower you go down the keyboard, the more you would have to play the Minor ninth from page 153. For clearity. Reverse hands.

Next Page 140 will have further Harmonies that suit these Modals

Now that we've already learned that to achieve a Dominant all you have to do is flatten any note of any diminished 1/2 step and that same note is the dominant. Then all we have to do is take a minor above that note.

G7 key note the dominant

scale note

Diminished 7th.

flatten any note its now a dominiant

take the minor 1 step up

ovtaved minor 5-1-3

This is another way to play the same as above example

Further Studies II
Chordal Layering
Recapping

These Layerings are merely breathing tools to use during Improvisational conversations.
They are played at the same time for voicing coloration's. Or modern modal Piano.
All 1 step on top of another in all the keys. The 5-1-3's will work as well. Try layering 5-1-3's
minors on top another popping in and out of both, ordinary 1-3-5-7's and 5-1-3's. The target
note major scale for the 5-1-3's will be 1 step under the left hand middle finger.

mnemonic- *A Minor chord will take the scale target note most of the time. One way to remember.*

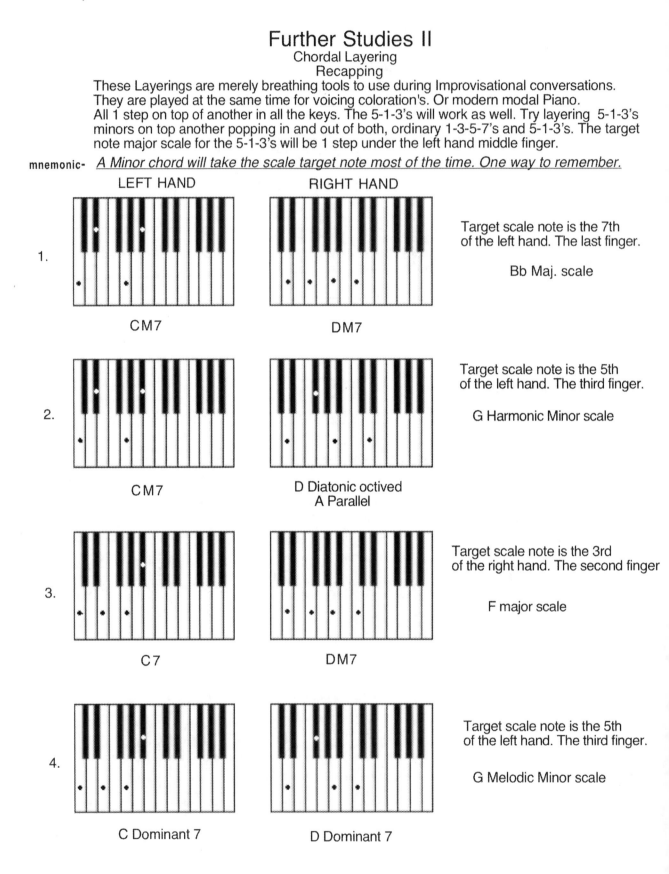

LEFT HAND   RIGHT HAND

1.

CM7   DM7

Target scale note is the 7th
of the left hand. The last finger.

Bb Maj. scale

2.

CM7   D Diatonic octived
A Parallel

Target scale note is the 5th
of the left hand. The third finger.

G Harmonic Minor scale

3.

C7   DM7

Target scale note is the 3rd
of the right hand. The second finger

F major scale

4.

C Dominant 7   D Dominant 7

Target scale note is the 5th
of the left hand. The third finger.

G Melodic Minor scale

Further Studies II

Modal Harmonies

example 45   Ravel, Debussy, Herbie Hancock

1. Take any major 7th. with left hand
2. Take octaved major diotonic normal.with right hand.1 step up from left hand 1st.
3. Convert left hand to 5-7-1-3. And right hand to 5-1-3.

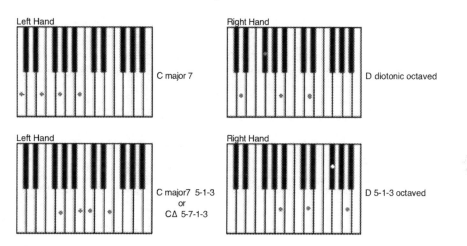

Modal Harmonies

1. With left hand, use any 5-1-3 triad. Major or Minor.
2. With right hand take its 5. The low finger, and play a 5-1-#3 Triad with the right hand.

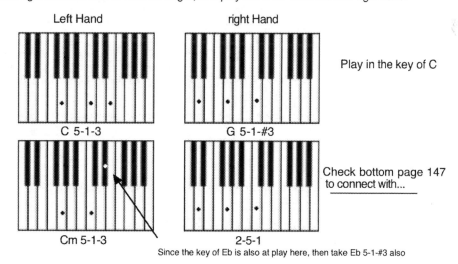

Play in the key of C

Check bottom page 147
to connect with...

Since the key of Eb is also at play here, then take Eb 5-1-#3 also

Robert Kaye

Further Studies II

example 33

Other Diminished resolve alternatives
And a Bach theory to apply it with.

BACH

1. Take any Diminished 7th. Flatten the 3rd. & 5th. or the middle notes. 1/2 step, it is now
   in the key of the root note. --3rd finger which is C in this case is also scale note. The last finger
   which is E takes the Harmonic minor scale.
2. Take the same as above and this time sharpen the middle notes 1/2 step and its in the same
   key as the root note. The third finger which is D takes scale note and second finger which is B
   takes Harmonic minor scale.

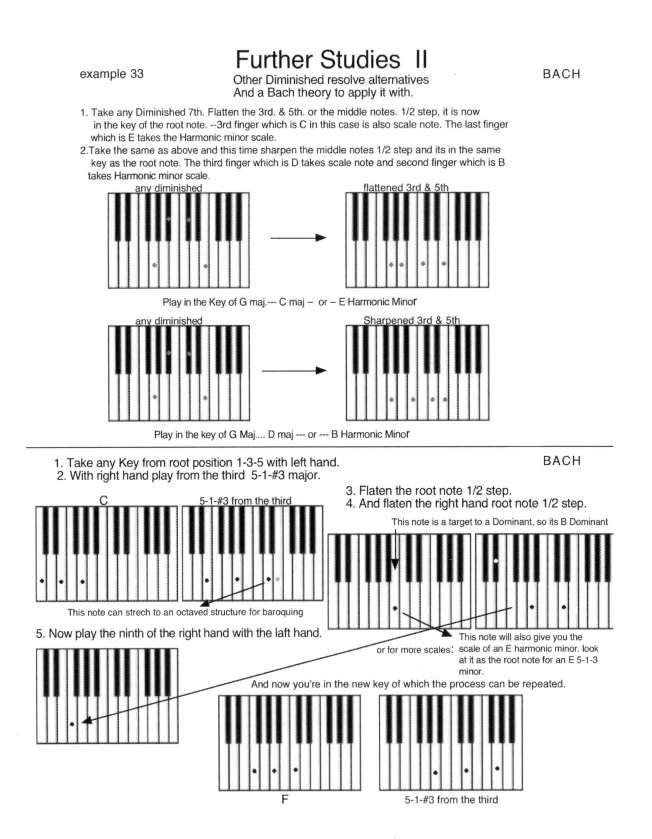

any diminished

flattened 3rd & 5th

Play in the Key of G maj.--- C maj -- or -- E Harmonic Minor

any diminished

Sharpened 3rd & 5th

Play in the key of G Maj.... D maj --- or --- B Harmonic Minor

BACH

1. Take any Key from root position 1-3-5 with left hand.
2. With right hand play from the third 5-1-#3 major.

3. Flaten the root note 1/2 step.
4. And flaten the right hand root note 1/2 step.

C

5-1-#3 from the third

This note is a target to a Dominant, so its B Dominant

This note can strech to an octaved structure for baroquing

5. Now play the ninth of the right hand with the laft hand.

This note will also give you the
or for more scales: scale of an E harmonic minor. look
at it as the root note for an E 5-1-3
minor.

And now you're in the new key of which the process can be repeated.

F

5-1-#3 from the third

142

Further Studies II

example 47

<u>Modal Harmonies & The basic folds</u>
Ravel, Debussy, Herbie Hancock

1. Take any 5-1-3 minor with left hand

2 With right hand take 5-1-3 minor 1 whole step under the 5th. or the first note
or the same note is 1 whole step above the 3rd. normal minor.Another words
the outside notes are the target for the minor. The Fourth.

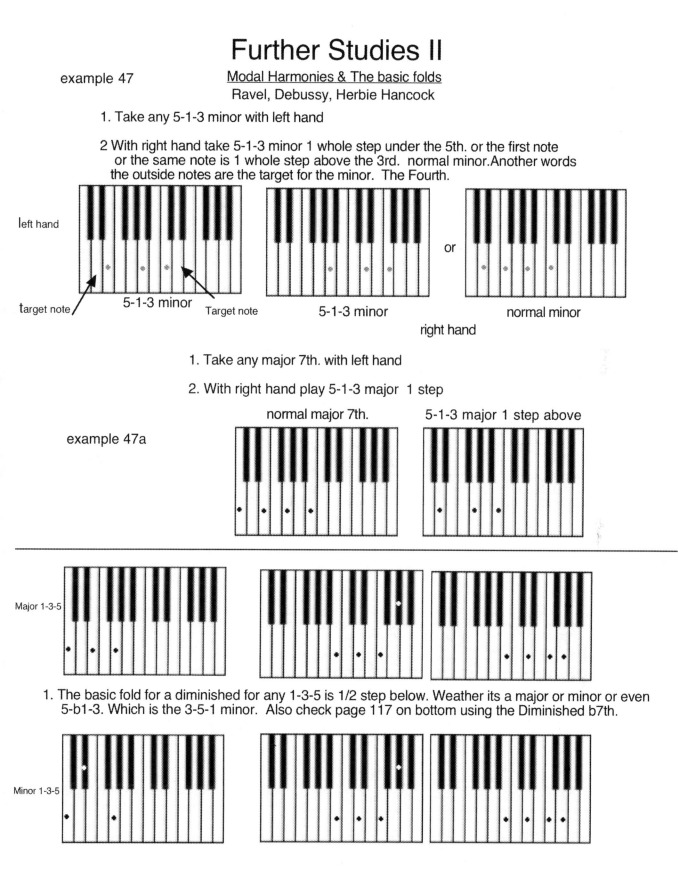

left hand

target note 5-1-3 minor Target note

5-1-3 minor

or

normal minor

right hand

1. Take any major 7th. with left hand

2. With right hand play 5-1-3 major 1 step

normal major 7th.

5-1-3 major 1 step above

example 47a

Major 1-3-5

1. The basic fold for a diminished for any 1-3-5 is 1/2 step below. Weather its a major or minor or even
5-b1-3. Which is the 3-5-1 minor. Also check page 117 on bottom using the Diminished b7th.

Minor 1-3-5

Further Studies II
Modal Harmonies
Ravel, Debussy, Herbie Hancock

example 48

1. With left hand any 5-1-3 minor

2. With right hand play 5-1-3 minor or normal minor 1/2 step under the 3rd. of the right hand. or the fifth 5-1-3 of the Minor. Or Convert to Minor 7th. of root note.

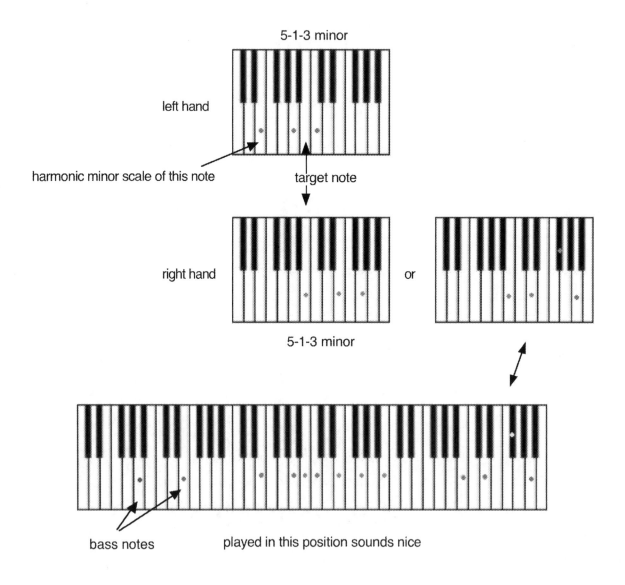

5-1-3 minor

left hand

harmonic minor scale of this note

target note

right hand   or

5-1-3 minor

bass notes   played in this position sounds nice

This formula can be reversed from one hand to the other many ways

Targeting The Dominant Blues

for playing
The walking Tenth's

1. With left hand play any normal triad but without the third.
2. With right hand play the third anywhere on the piano.
3. Walk these voicings all over the piano. And also skip around
   These voicings enables you to play the piano al the way to the
   bottom. And to give yourself a chance to breath from a complex
   progression

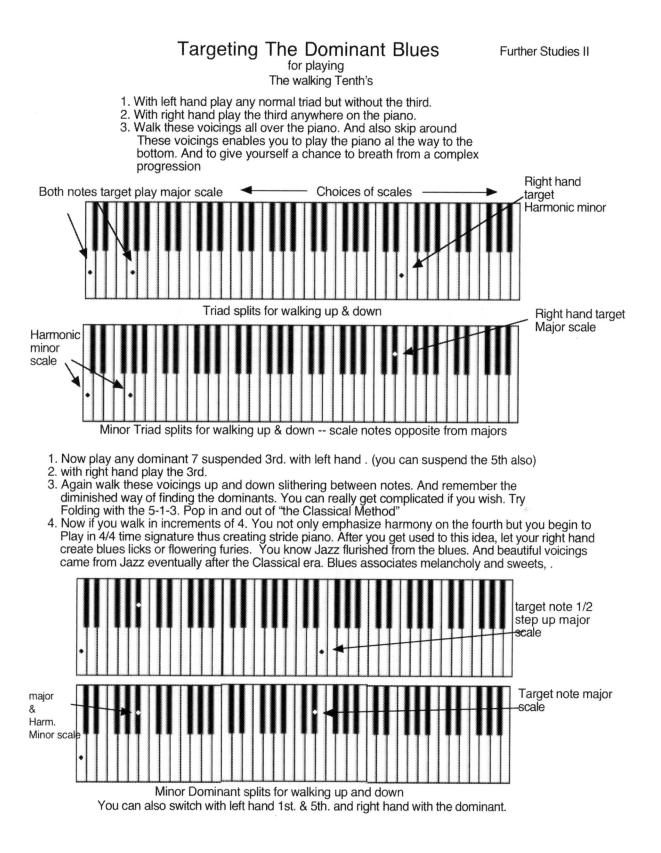

Both notes target play major scale ◄——— Choices of scales ———►

Right hand target Harmonic minor

Triad splits for walking up & down

Right hand target Major scale

Harmonic minor scale

Minor Triad splits for walking up & down -- scale notes opposite from majors

1. Now play any dominant 7 suspended 3rd. with left hand . (you can suspend the 5th also)
2. with right hand play the 3rd.
3. Again walk these voicings up and down slithering between notes. And remember the
   diminished way of finding the dominants. You can really get complicated if you wish. Try
   Folding with the 5-1-3. Pop in and out of "the Classical Method"
4. Now if you walk in increments of 4. You not only emphasize harmony on the fourth but you begin to
   Play in 4/4 time signature thus creating stride piano. After you get used to this idea, let your right hand
   create blues licks or flowering furies. You know Jazz flurished from the blues. And beautiful voicings
   came from Jazz eventually after the Classical era. Blues associates melancholy and sweets, .

target note 1/2 step up major scale

major & Harm. Minor scale

Target note major scale

Minor Dominant splits for walking up and down
You can also switch with left hand 1st. & 5th. and right hand with the dominant.

Further Studies II
Modal Harmonies
Ravel, Debussy, Herbie Hancock

example 51

1. With left hand take any dim#7

2. With right hand play diminished 1/2 step up from 1st. of left hand

3. Or with right hand play diminished b7 1 whole step up.

HARPISH ARPEGGIOS & MODAL ELEMENTS

left hand 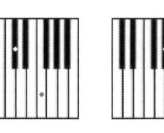 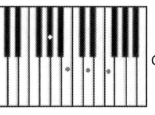 OR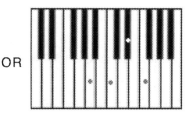

right hand   right hand

This is a reminder to practice all the II inversions of the 7th's series degrees in all the keys. This takes a while but have to be practiced from time to time. These positions open the melody line by ear in all its possibilities while Improvising. Spontaneously !

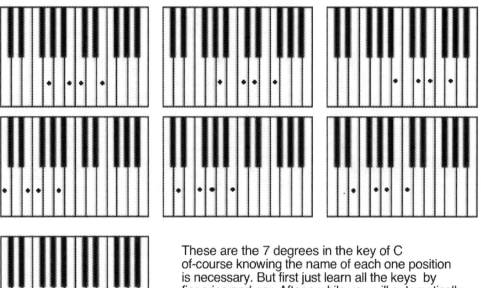

These are the 7 degrees in the key of C of-course knowing the name of each one position is necessary. But first just learn all the keys by fingering and ear. After a while you will automatically walk any key at will. The in-depth folding we covered earlier go in-conjunction as songwriting does also with these important voicings.

Additional studies II.

Modal Voicings   **Chromatics**

Harmonic Descends

These Descends are the same as on page 87 on bottom. They descend in 3rd's. Octaved for voicings

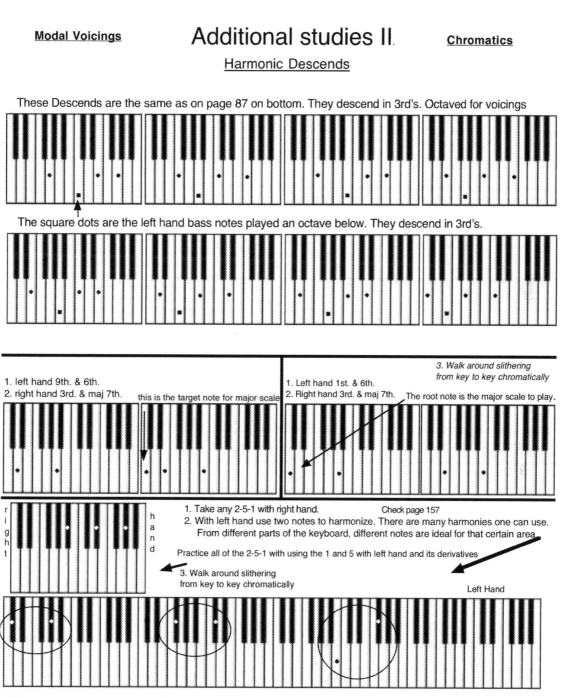

The square dots are the left hand bass notes played an octave below. They descend in 3rd's.

1. left hand 9th. & 6th.
2. right hand 3rd. & maj 7th.   this is the target note for major scale

1. Left hand 1st. & 6th.
2. Right hand 3rd. & maj 7th.   The root note is the major scale to play.

3. Walk around slithering from key to key chromatically

1. Take any 2-5-1 with right hand.   Check page 157
2. With left hand use two notes to harmonize. There are many harmonies one can use.
   From different parts of the keyboard, different notes are ideal for that certain area.

Practice all of the 2-5-1 with using the 1 and 5 with left hand and its derivatives

3. Walk around slithering from key to key chromatically

Left Hand

right hand

The **Pentatonics** are ideal for these chromatics. You will learn them if you are interested in these voicings

Additional studies II

Classical & Modal

1. Take any 5-1-3 major or minor. with left hand.

2. Take any 5-1-3 major or minor with right hand.

3. Sharpen the 1st. of the left hand 1/2 step

4. Flatten the first of the right hand 1/2 step.

5. You can use any combination and walk through keyboard.

left hand A 5-1-3   right hand A 5-1-3

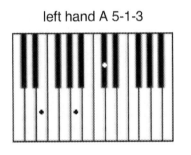

Sharpen the first of the left hand   flatten the first of the right hand   Scale is Ab Harmonic Minor

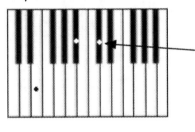

if you stay in majors then the top note is always the target scale note and its a melodic minor scale.. Here its a Db melodic minor.

OR

A major 5-1-3 with flattened 1st.   A minor 5-1-3 with sharpened 1st.

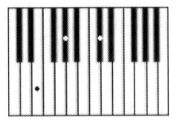
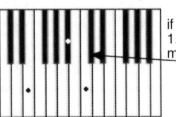

if you use a minor, then target note 1.2 step up.always.. the same melodic minor scale.

The Seven Degrees of the Harmonic Minors from the First position

Further Studies II

<u>The Classical Composers</u>   Arpeggiation & Composition   <u>The Jazz Composers</u>

The pattern is not really a pattern here. Only its foreseen with symbolism for exact harmony. The fingering is extremely easy and willing. And its good to know the Progression for further composition. Remember to use the Natural Minors of this pattern for the 1-3-5. For all music. for example the pattern below is for E flat major. Especially strict classical. Haydn - Mozart / and without the seventh. Chopin and Schumann used the seventh. Then came Tchaikovsky & Richard Strauss. In which they mixed together the Minor Harmonics from p. 133 and below.

Tonic Minor - up 1 step - Diminished 7 - up 1/2 step Major7th - up 1 step Diminished 7 - up 1 step Dominant up 1/2 step Diminished 7 - up 1 1/2 steps Diminished flattened 7th

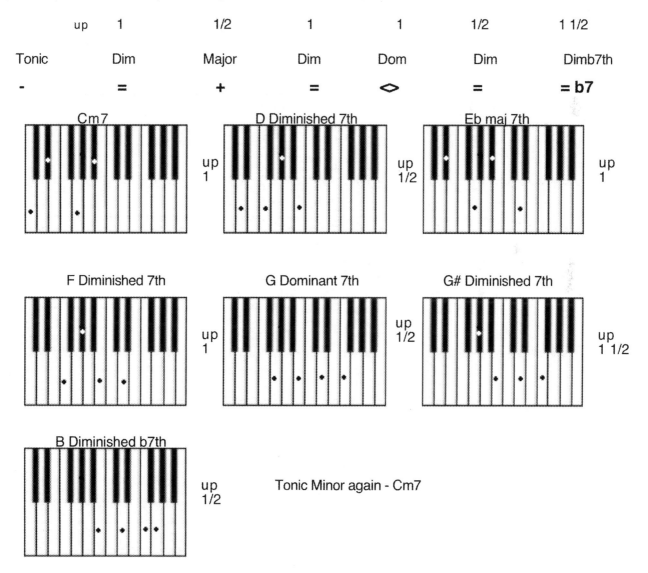

	up	1	1/2	1	1	1/2	1 1/2
Tonic		Dim	Major	Dim	Dom	Dim	Dimb7th
-		=	+	=	◇	=	= **b7**

B Diminished b7th

up
1/2

Tonic Minor again - Cm7

Further Studies II
the Thirteenth's

1. The thirteenth's are the fullest sound allows
2. They are easily captured by taking the minor 7th chord of any root note from the third.
   and add the sixth with it. They fall in your hands. but there arn't but so much one
   could do with a full sound. So further on we'll get deeper. and explore a vast labyrinth

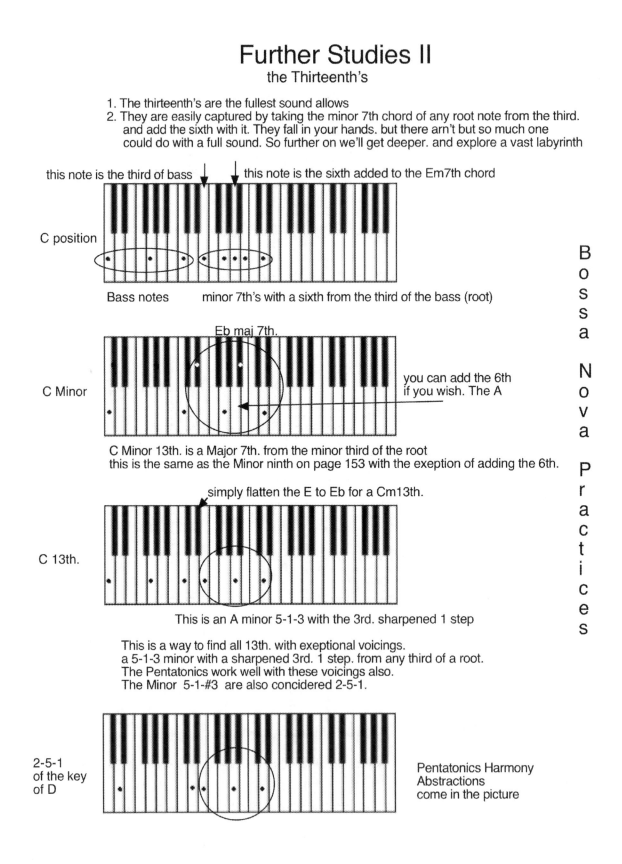

this note is the third of bass   this note is the sixth added to the Em7th chord

C position

Bass notes   minor 7th's with a sixth from the third of the bass (root)

Eb maj 7th.

C Minor

you can add the 6th
if you wish. The A

C Minor 13th. is a Major 7th. from the minor third of the root
this is the same as the Minor ninth on page 153 with the exeption of adding the 6th.

simply flatten the E to Eb for a Cm13th.

C 13th.

This is an A minor 5-1-3 with the 3rd. sharpened 1 step

This is a way to find all 13th. with exeptional voicings.
a 5-1-3 minor with a sharpened 3rd. 1 step. from any third of a root.
The Pentatonics work well with these voicings also.
The Minor 5-1-#3 are also concidered 2-5-1.

2-5-1
of the key
of D

Pentatonics Harmony
Abstractions
come in the picture

B
o
s
s
a

N
o
v
a

P
r
a
c
t
i
c
e
s

Further Studies II

Using the thirteenth's

1. Take any thirteenth's with right hand
2. Root note with left hand
3. Flatten the root note and the first of the right hand.
4. then play the ninth of the right hand which will
5. go to a forth up or down.

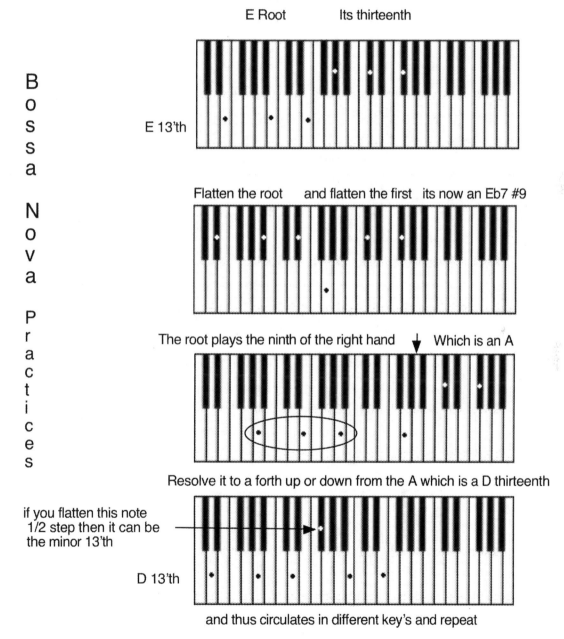

B
o
s
s
a

N
o
v
a

P
r
a
c
t
i
c
e
s

E Root   Its thirteenth

E 13'th

Flatten the root   and flatten the first   its now an Eb7 #9

The root plays the ninth of the right hand   Which is an A

Resolve it to a forth up or down from the A which is a D thirteenth

if you flatten this note 1/2 step then it can be the minor 13'th

D 13'th

and thus circulates in different key's and repeat

The thirteenth can be an orchestrative tragic sound as well. It is the fullest or pushed against the wall sound. If you get a chance, check out Lili Boulanger's orchestrations and voices, the sister of Nadia Boulanger. You will get another complete different type or feel of sound created with these thirteenth's.

Further Studies II

Tenth's, Six'th, Seventh's, Thirteenth's ....
Overtones and Breathing Improvisational Harmonies
Standard Chromaticism Voicings

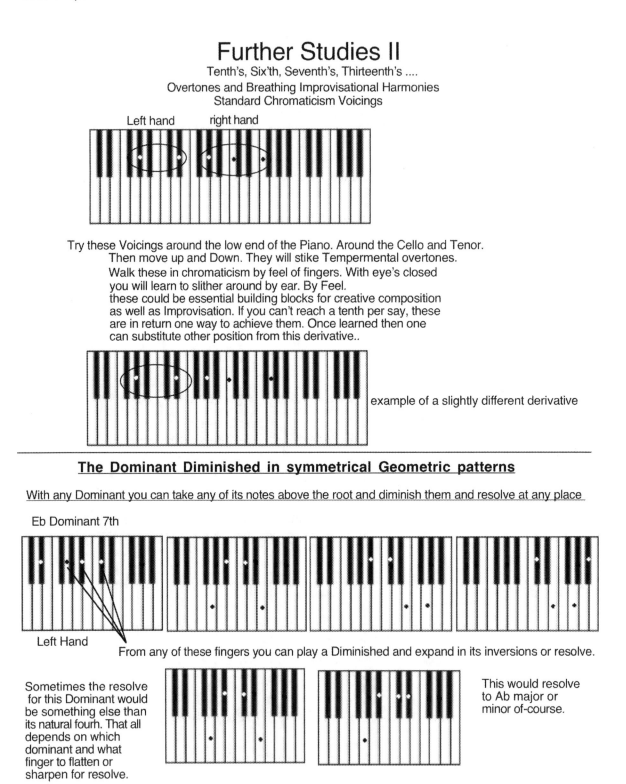

Left hand   right hand

Try these Voicings around the low end of the Piano. Around the Cello and Tenor.
Then move up and Down. They will stike Tempermental overtones.
Walk these in chromaticism by feel of fingers. With eye's closed
you will learn to slither around by ear. By Feel.
these could be essential building blocks for creative composition
as well as Improvisation. If you can't reach a tenth per say, these
are in return one way to achieve them. Once learned then one
can substitute other position from this derivative..

example of a slightly different derivative

The Dominant Diminished in symmetrical Geometric patterns

With any Dominant you can take any of its notes above the root and diminish them and resolve at any place

Eb Dominant 7th

Left Hand

From any of these fingers you can play a Diminished and expand in its inversions or resolve.

Sometimes the resolve
for this Dominant would
be something else than
its natural fourh. That all
depends on which
dominant and what
finger to flatten or
sharpen for resolve.

This would resolve
to Ab major or
minor of-course.

Further Studies II

Flattened 9th & The Minor 9th & The Dominant 9th

The 9th's are also Tension builders. Therefore they are essential to music making of-course. And so it is important to explore and use all aspects of the ninth series.
An easy way to find them is root note with the **third** a diminished, Sharpened diminished, and Maj. 7th. The Sharpened 9th's are on the next few pages. But the dominant ninth is the Exceptional Voicing in which Debussy used with the sharpened diminished. It's a tension builder that Harmonizes with exceptional voicing all the way down the keyboard with clarity. Paralleling for (Composition). The flattened 9ths. seems to take the role of a turn around. The Sharpened 9ths. tends to be used for playing Jazz. (Voicings). The Minor 9ths. Seems to take the role of Melodic Improvisational Compositions. (Jazz) Hollywood pop sounds ect..

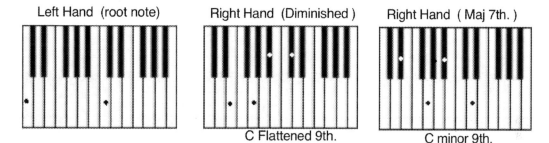

Left Hand (root note) Right Hand (Diminished) Right Hand (Maj 7th.)

C Flattened 9th. C minor 9th.

The 9ths. is found from the third of any root by using a diminished or for Minors use Major sevenths.

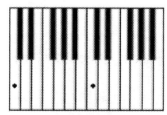
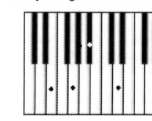

Sharpened Diminished

Whole tone voicing

The Dominant ninth is found the same with the exception of the sharpened 7th of the diminished

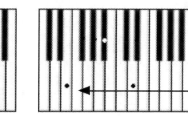

An easier way to find the dominant 9ths.
is look for a minor 7th. flattened 5th. suspended 3rd.

This F is always target note for major scale. (Modal)

Walk this resolved voicing all the way down the keyboard. Left hand 1 & 5th. And right hand Diminished sharpened seventh suspended third. Since its used with the left hand already. Debussy's most popular orchestration came from this. "Prelude a lapres-midi d'un Faune"

D dominant 9th C# dominant 9th C dominant 9th

Improvise in G Improvise in F# Improvise in F

Additional studies II

using the 7#9 or
purple/ blue/ lavender/ Rose/
indigo/ Low register Voicings
modal

part 1

1. Take any root note with left hand.

2. With right hand , play the 5-1-#3 major of the 3rd. of the left hand, then sharpen the 1st. 1/2 step, and sharpen the 3rd. 1/2 step.its now the 7#9. A Jazz Harmony.

3. Drop everything 1/2 step and go up a 4th.

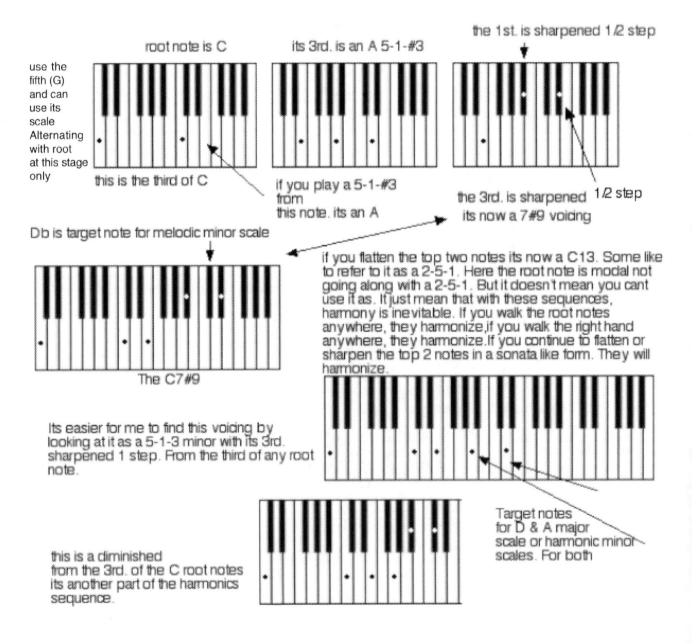

root note is C

use the fifth (G) and can use its scale Alternating with root at this stage only

this is the third of C

its 3rd. is an A 5-1-#3

if you play a 5-1-#3 from this note. its an A

the 1st. is sharpened 1/2 step

the 3rd. is sharpened 1/2 step
its now a 7#9 voicing

Db is target note for melodic minor scale

The C7#9

if you flatten the top two notes its now a C13. Some like to refer to it as a 2-5-1. Here the root note is modal not going along with a 2-5-1. But it doesn't mean you cant use it as. It just mean that with these sequences, harmony is inevitable. If you walk the root notes anywhere, they harmonize,if you walk the right hand anywhere, they harmonize.If you continue to flatten or sharpen the top 2 notes in a sonata like form. They will harmonize.

Its easier for me to find this voicing by looking at it as a 5-1-3 minor with its 3rd. sharpened 1 step. From the third of any root note.

Target notes for D & A major scale or harmonic minor scales. For both

this is a diminished from the 3rd. of the C root notes its another part of the harmonics sequence.

Additional studies II

using the 7#9 or purple/ blue/
lavender/ Rose/ indigo/ Low register
Voicings

part 2

modal

1. Take any root note with left hand.

2. With right hand , play the 5-1-#3 major of the 3rd. of the left hand, then sharpen
   the 1st. 1/2 step, and sharpen the 3rd. 1/2 step.Its now the 7#9. A Jazz Harmony.

3. There is more than one direction the root note can go here. Which will open many
   doors.

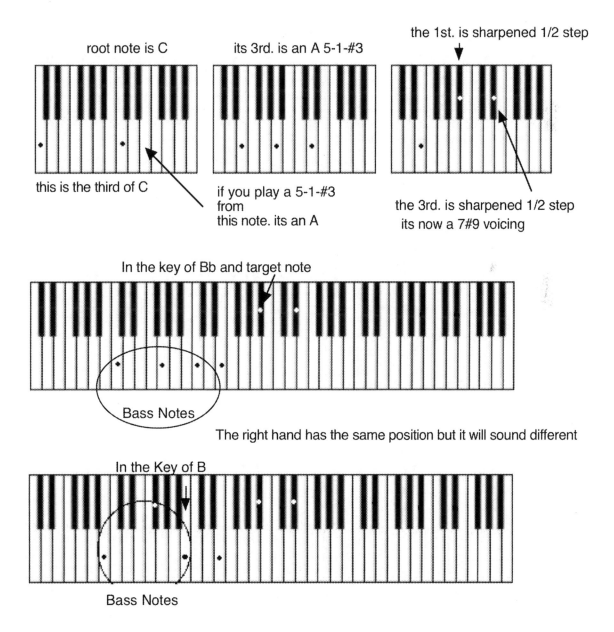

root note is C

this is the third of C

its 3rd. is an A 5-1-#3

if you play a 5-1-#3
from
this note. its an A

the 1st. is sharpened 1/2 step

the 3rd. is sharpened 1/2 step

its now a 7#9 voicing

In the key of Bb and target note

Bass Notes

The right hand has the same position but it will sound different

In the Key of B

Bass Notes

Additional studies II
using the 7#9 or purple/ blue/ lavender/ Rose/ indigo/ Low register Voicings
modal

part 3

1. Take any root note with left hand.

2. With right hand , play the 5-1-#3 major of the 3rd. of the left hand, then sharpen the 1st. 1/2 step, and sharpen the 3rd. 1/2 step.Its now the 7#9. A Jazz Harmony.

3. There is more than one direction the root note can go here. Which will open many doors.

.

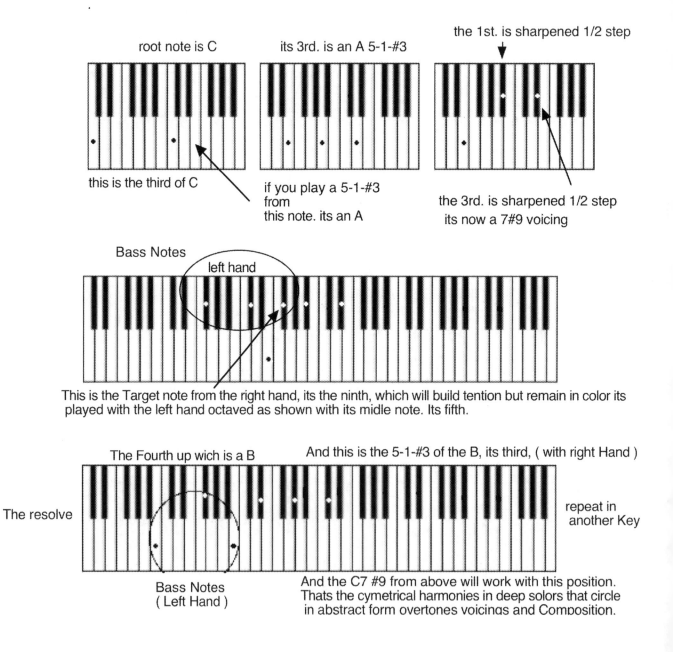

root note is C

its 3rd. is an A 5-1-#3

the 1st. is sharpened 1/2 step

this is the third of C

if you play a 5-1-#3 from
this note. its an A

the 3rd. is sharpened 1/2 step
its now a 7#9 voicing

Bass Notes

left hand

This is the Target note from the right hand, its the ninth, which will build tention but remain in color its played with the left hand octaved as shown with its midle note. Its fifth.

The Fourth up wich is a B

And this is the 5-1-#3 of the B, its third, (with right Hand)

The resolve

repeat in another Key

Bass Notes
(Left Hand)

And the C7 #9 from above will work with this position. Thats the cymetrical harmonies in deep solors that circle in abstract form overtones voicings and Composition.

The 2-5-1

Finding it in any key and using it in its seven degree scale

When transfering chords of a chart for jazz voicings. One tends to go directly to the 2-5-1
The 2-5-1 which some call nice sounds or voicings. If you want to replace the chords of a
tune or chart. And need a target to follow in any key. This is what I use.

Determine what key you are in first. Then from the second degree play a 5-1- #3. Sharpen
the third 1/2 step only. Unless the third winds up on a note not of the scale, then in that case
sharpen again for the next note. It will always land on that odd position on the fourth degree.
then sharpen both notes. The 1 and the 3.

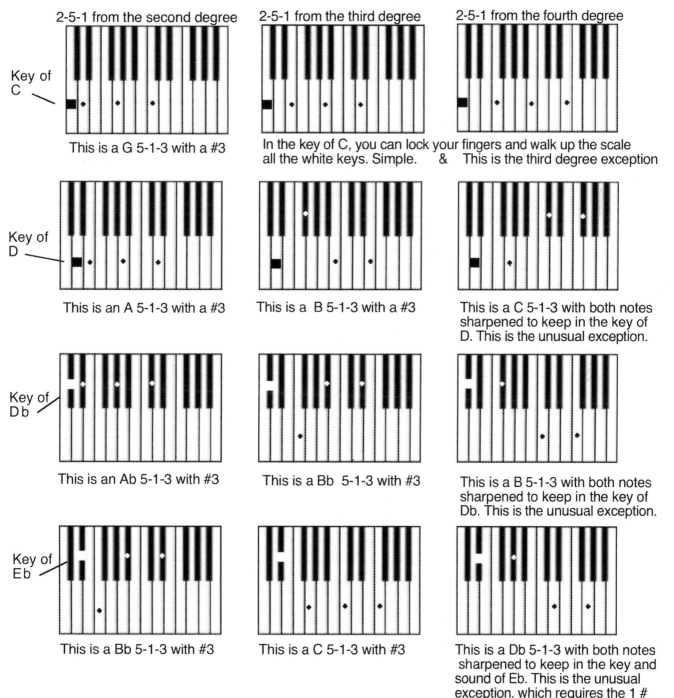

2-5-1 from the second degree

2-5-1 from the third degree

2-5-1 from the fourth degree

Key of C

This is a G 5-1-3 with a #3

In the key of C, you can lock your fingers and walk up the scale all the white keys. Simple.   &   This is the third degree exception

Key of D

This is an A 5-1-3 with a #3

This is a B 5-1-3 with a #3

This is a C 5-1-3 with both notes sharpened to keep in the key of D. This is the unusual exception.

Key of Db

This is an Ab 5-1-3 with #3

This is a Bb 5-1-3 with #3

This is a B 5-1-3 with both notes sharpened to keep in the key of Db. This is the unusual exception.

Key of Eb

This is a Bb 5-1-3 with #3

This is a C 5-1-3 with #3

This is a Db 5-1-3 with both notes sharpened to keep in the key and sound of Eb. This is the unusual exception. which requires the 1 # 1/2 step and the 3 # 1 whole step

Additional Studies

Supplements for Improvisation
The Modern Fourth's for Arpeggiation
In Congruent with the 9's & The Dominants or
use with pentatonics

HARPISH

These Fourth's are sought after from patterns
Do you see the 1- 2 note patterns, These are made to arpeggiate. and
use with pentatonics for example. And the modern sounds covered.

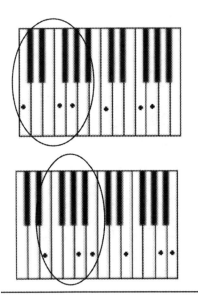
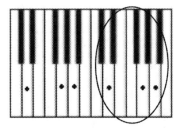
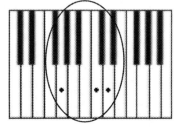

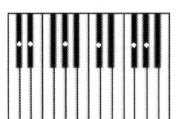
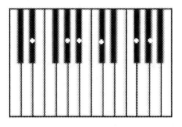

---

1. Octave any ordinary Triad and strike an ordinary Minor 7th 1 step above the root

C octaved

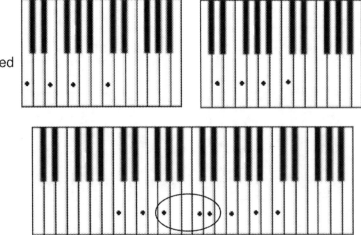

Minor 7th. 1 step above

This is what it looks like together.
Notice the fourth in the middle.
Scales and arpeggios to
Improvise with.

Further Studies II

Modal Harmonies

Ravel, Debussy, Herbie Hancock

example 50

1. Take any 5-1-3 minor with left hand. Sharpen the 3rd. 1 whole step
   its now a 2-5-1 Jazz voicing of the note you sharpened..

2. With right hand you can play the scale of the 1st. which is the last note.or the note you
   sharpened Major or harmonic minor

3. Now take the 2-5-1 and flatten the 2 or the first note 1/2 step.Its now a sharpen 9th.
   and you can play the 1/2 step up from the middle finger.This is another Jazz voicing.

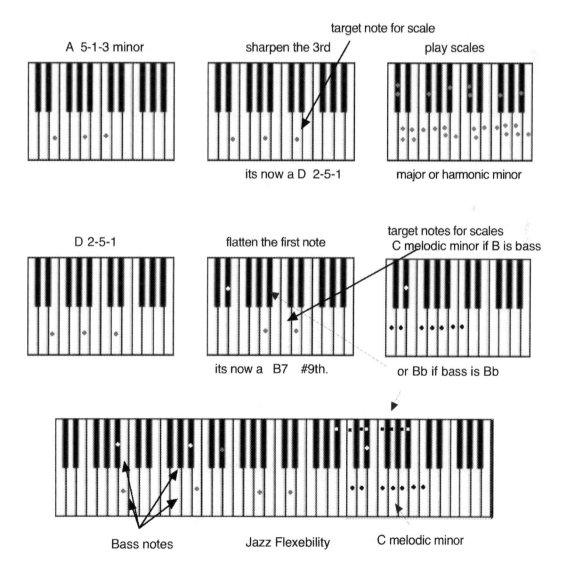

A 5-1-3 minor

sharpen the 3rd   target note for scale

play scales

its now a D 2-5-1   major or harmonic minor

D 2-5-1

flatten the first note

target notes for scales
C melodic minor if B is bass

its now a B7 #9th.   or Bb if bass is Bb

Bass notes   Jazz Flexebility   C melodic minor

Major 7'th Circular 4th's in Harmony with 5-1-3 's
Basic and in depth folding pattern: Classical & General
In all 12 Keys
Can be applied to Clasical and Jazz / Bach to BeBop / Chopin to Latin

R.Kaye

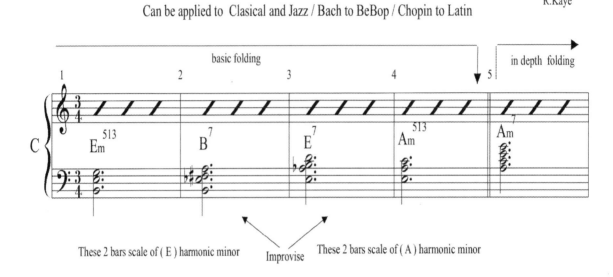

basic folding — in depth folding

These 2 bars scale of (E) harmonic minor   Improvise   These 2 bars scale of (A) harmonic minor

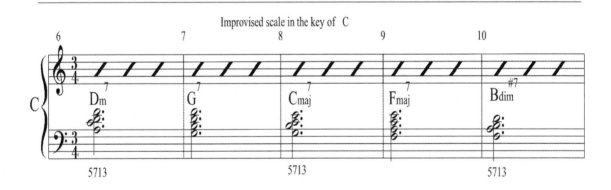

Improvised scale in the key of C

5713   5713   5713

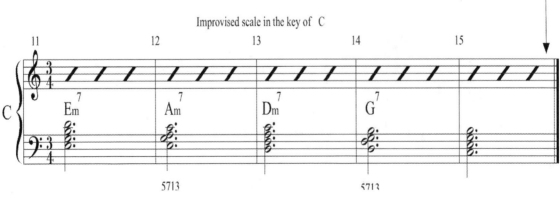

Improvised scale in the key of C

5713   5713

Key of F

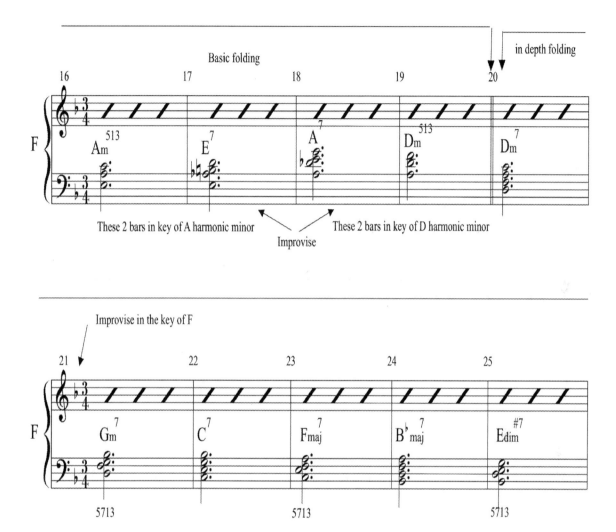

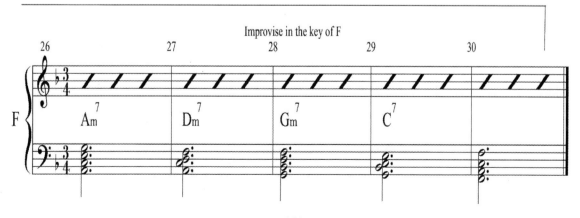

Key of Bb

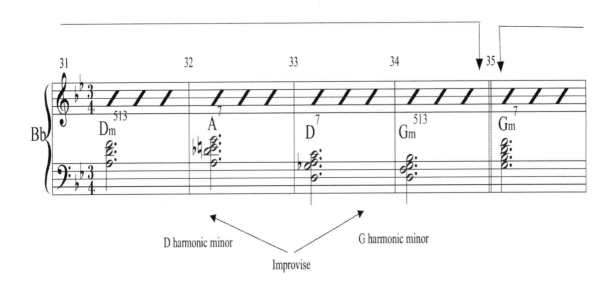

D harmonic minor   G harmonic minor

Improvise

scale of Bb

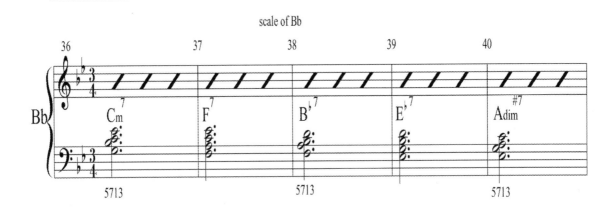

scale of Bb

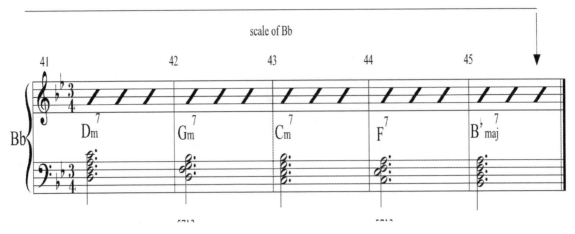

Key of Eb

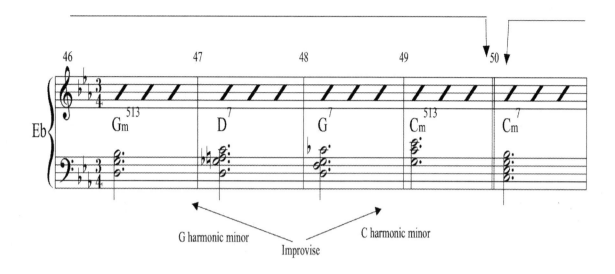

G harmonic minor   Improvise   C harmonic minor

Improvise scale of Eb

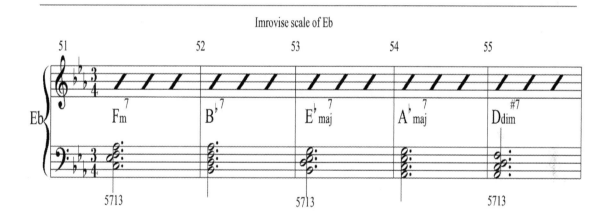

Improvise scale of Eb

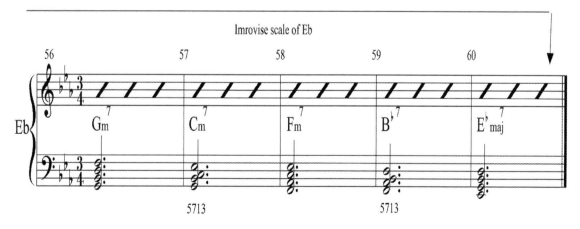

Key of Ab

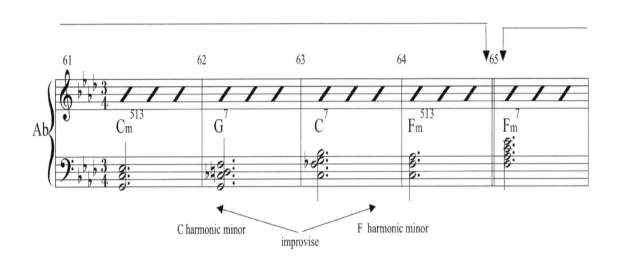

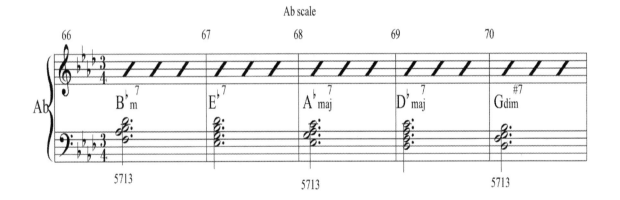

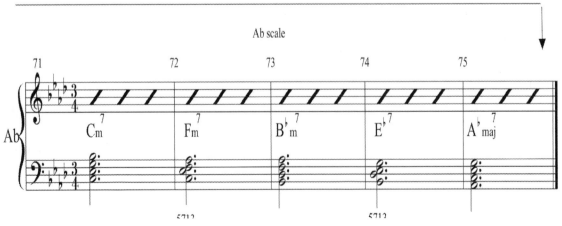

Key of Db

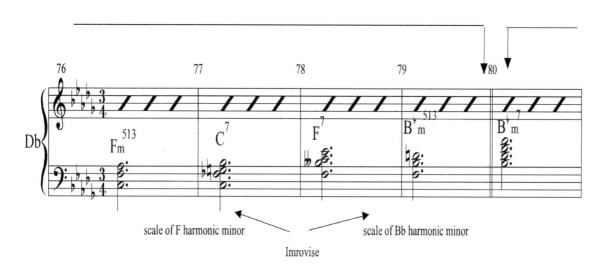

scale of F harmonic minor — Imrovise — scale of Bb harmonic minor

scale of Db

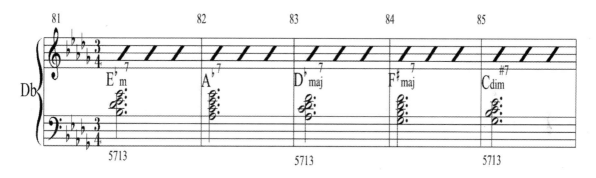

scale of Db

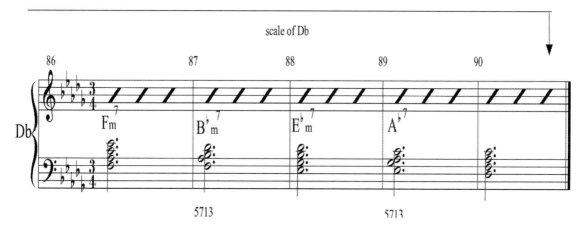

Key of F#

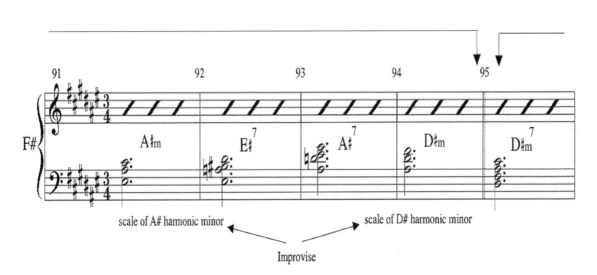

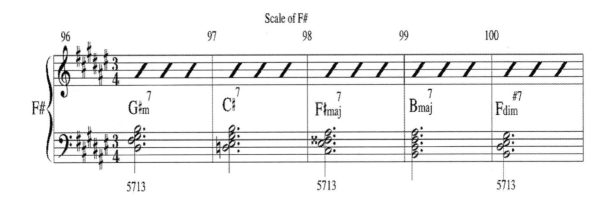

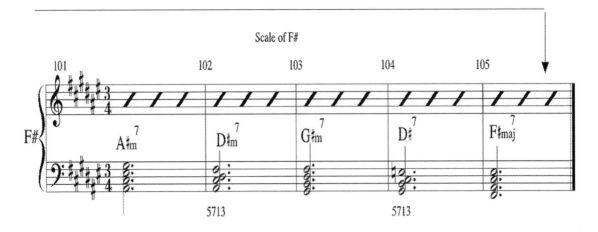

Key of B

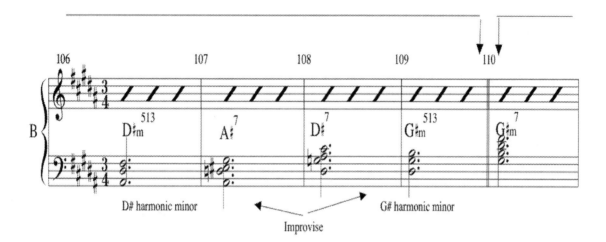

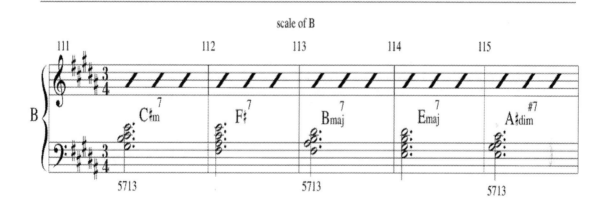

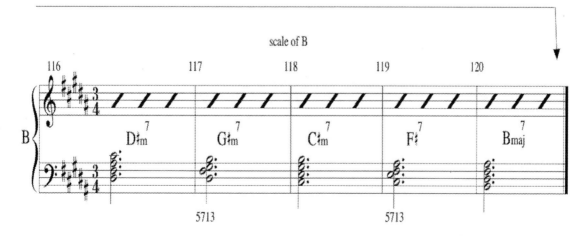

Key of E

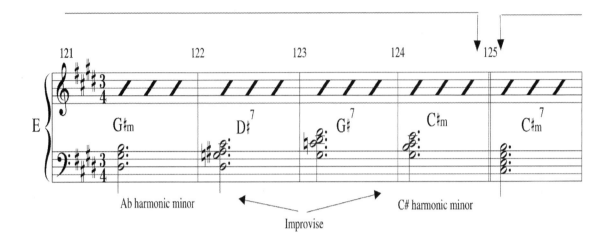

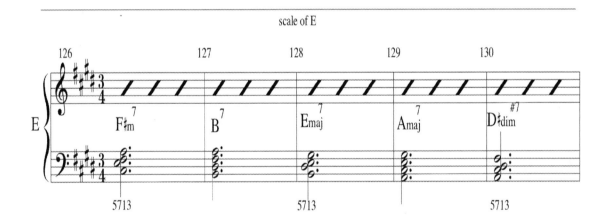

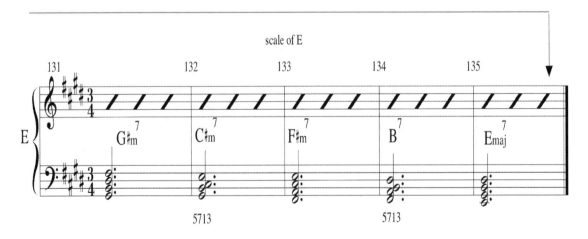

Key of A

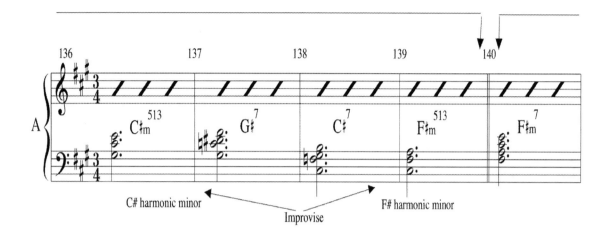

C# harmonic minor   Improvise   F# harmonic minor

scale of A

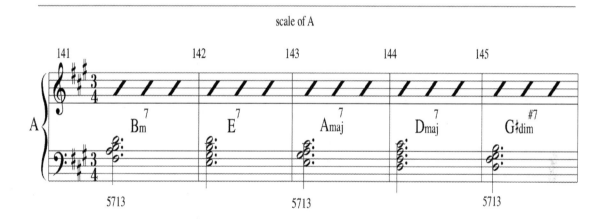

scale of A

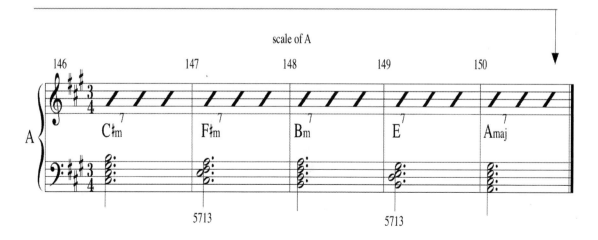

Key of D

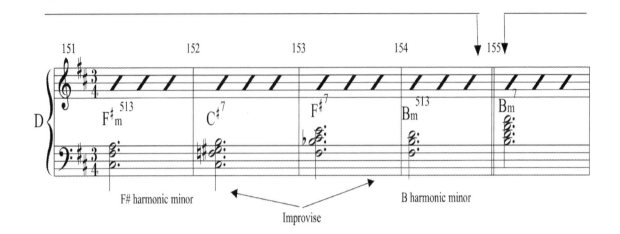

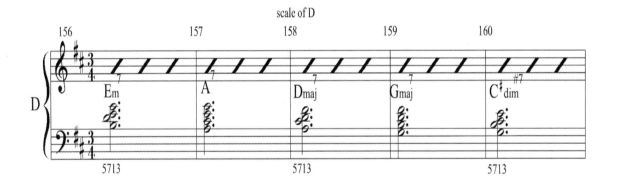

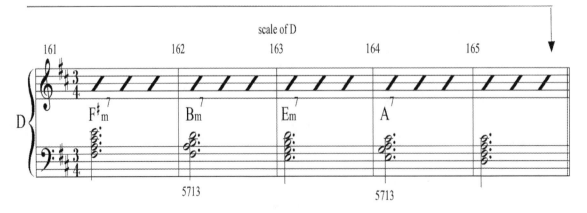

Key of G

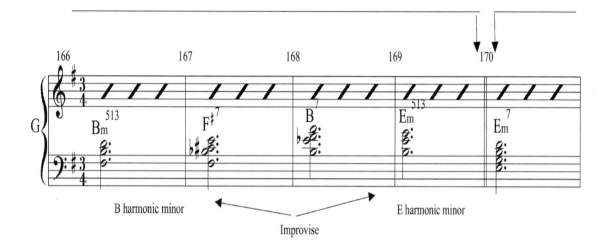

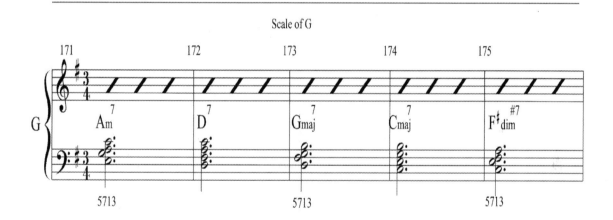

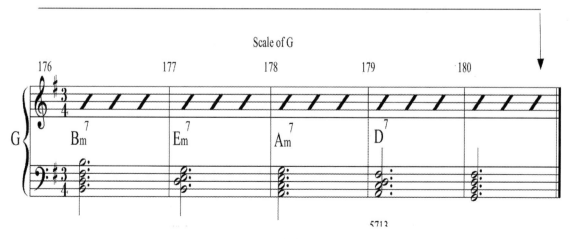

Maj 7 Circular 4th's " Folding in Harmony "

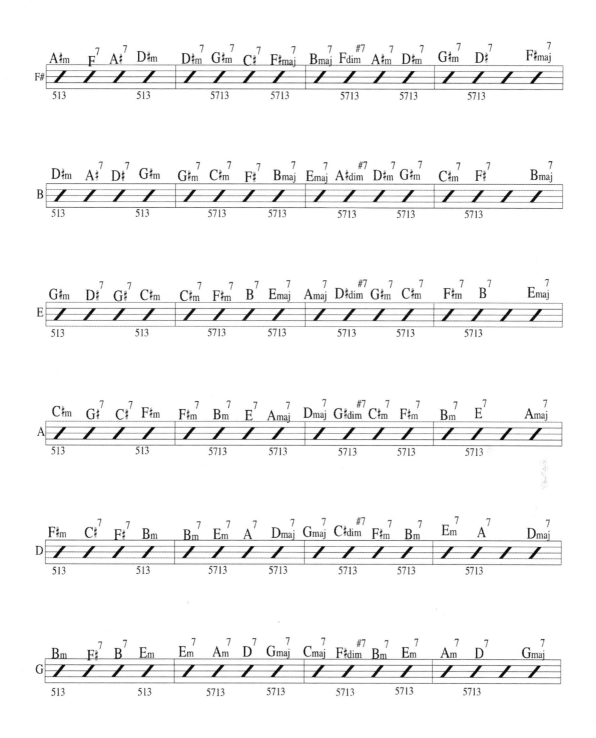

Robert Kaye

The present musical Analogy

"For a better picture "

Lets say music is what food is to us, for a quick diagnostic analogical understanding in parallel.

In the centuries past the great classical composers gave us the classical method which is meat and potatoes. Or the essential main course ingredient in a meal. And classical had a variety of forms as it is, in its own style. Boroque, sonata, romantic, ect.. As is fish, chicken, broccoli and beef. This is the necessity of our well-being.

Then came another form of classical music which is the modern romanticism. Which can be compared to cool or soft or sweet. Lavender, blue, magenta. So here is the dessert and the other part of the colors or taste. Or the complete buffet. Or is it gourmet ? The taste is of one's choice. How much money is relevant to how much to spend. How much education is relevant to how much experience and understanding.

Is Jazz the dessert ? There are many forms of jazz. rag, stride, modern ect.. Are the pentatonics, the gin and tonic ? They evidently relate to colors or temperature, or the mood or atmosphere. You face understanding a heat and cool repair man. There have always been a fire to heat with. But its just recent that the air conditioner has been invented. Thus Vegas is born. The swinging big bands. Show business. The Entertainment capital of the world. In the middle of the desert. So why is desert and dessert at parallels here ? There is obviously something here in analogy. As the Sharps and flats on the staff or the keyboard are, hot and cold, black and white. Even the creation of slavery throughout the world was originally from the sugar plantations by Napoleon in which eventually New Orleans was the breeding grounds for, thus harboring jazz as an outburst. Irony, Coincidence, the dichotomy in parallel. You be the judge.

So to deny an earlier study of theory is to deny your self a balanced meal to say. And to deny yourself sweets is also a missing part of a diet. Thus the mind of today will shut down understanding that there are two forms of music to use when prompted tired or spent from one to the other. Where centuries ago, only one form of music would render the mind spent, but not today. The mind understands there is the dichotomy of balance and nature as food nurtures energy with replenishments from both sides of the taste venue, or both sides of the structural architectured mechanism of science and art. This is the honest poetical binary conscience at present, thus taking centuries to fulfill. The plight of the human spirit in revelation.

One must first have the proper essential material to put up a structure, and add as the building is taking shape. These analogies have proven to be the essential parallel in today's present world of understanding. The proper and recognizable facts or elements from all angles that one must consider or reproof, if to be a serious genuine composer,

player, chef, builder, writer, a judge or a president......

History as the Keyboard Matured

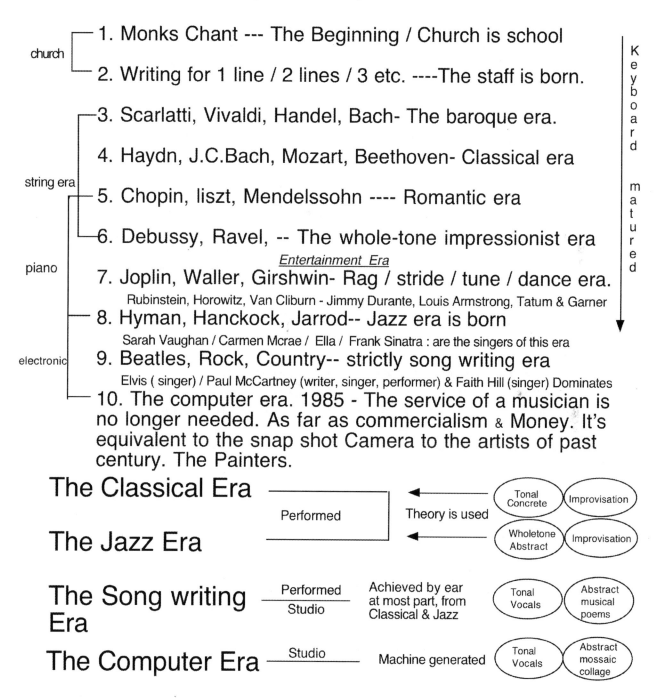

church

1. Monks Chant --- The Beginning / Church is school

2. Writing for 1 line / 2 lines / 3 etc. ----The staff is born.

string era

3. Scarlatti, Vivaldi, Handel, Bach- The baroque era.

4. Haydn, J.C.Bach, Mozart, Beethoven- Classical era

5. Chopin, liszt, Mendelssohn ---- Romantic era

6. Debussy, Ravel, -- The whole-tone impressionist era

piano

Entertainment Era
7. Joplin, Waller, Girshwin- Rag / stride / tune / dance era.

Rubinstein, Horowitz, Van Cliburn - Jimmy Durante, Louis Armstrong, Tatum & Garner
8. Hyman, Hanckock, Jarrod-- Jazz era is born

Sarah Vaughan / Carmen Mcrae / Ella / Frank Sinatra : are the singers of this era

electronic

9. Beatles, Rock, Country-- strictly song writing era

Elvis (singer) / Paul McCartney (writer, singer, performer) & Faith Hill (singer) Dominates
10. The computer era. 1985 - The service of a musician is no longer needed. As far as commercialism & Money. It's equivalent to the snap shot Camera to the artists of past century. The Painters.

Keyboard matured

The Classical Era —— Performed ← Theory is used — Tonal Concrete / Improvisation

The Jazz Era —— Wholetone Abstract / Improvisation

The Song writing Era — Performed / Studio — Achieved by ear at most part, from Classical & Jazz — Tonal Vocals / Abstract musical poems

The Computer Era — Studio — Machine generated — Tonal Vocals / Abstract mossaic collage

175

Final Thoughts from a Whole-tone era and the Wealth of Song-Writing

In my life-time, the Electronic recording song writing era was the procurement of my generation. The new sound of an ampped voicings. The stereo generation. The creation with electronic sounds and voicings. The sound is bigger with an unimaginative imagination. The new world of sounds. Overdubbing. Careful well sought out recordings. Trial and error. Two sides of a new way of recording. Engineering and pre-amplification. A sound bigger than life. And a new generation of musicians that accomidate a new style of playing. Called the pop songwriters. Rock, Country, R & B.

Not to be confused with the past blues show tune songwriters: Mercer, Arlen, Ellington, Girshwin..The great Jerry Harman or the great Leonard Bernstein, etc.. Hence: The best song writers that emerged in my opinion and many others are: World wide and Living ; Paul McCartney and in the US: Roger Nichols & Burt Bacharach. Carol King, Brian Wilson & Stevie Wonder, B.Dylan whose poetic lyrics and body of works are unmatched for a cause and a generation in which he gave birth to theatrical rock stars. As CSNY did almost a generation later. *P.Williams, N.Sedaka, B.Manilow, T.Rundgren, J.Taylor, Costello, H-Dozier, Anka, Gibbs, John-Taupin, Hall-Oats, J.Webb, A.Webber, B.Joel, The Bergmans, R.Flack, L.Richie, D.Foster, D.Warren, Sting, J. Mellencamp, M. Hamlish, Paul & Carly, M.Ethridge, Simon, J.Mitchell, B.Withers, S.Crow, B.Springsteen, The "Heart" wilson sisters, Santana, Frye & Henley, T.Petty, Ashford & Simpson, D. Mclean,G.Campbell, Isley brothers, D.Gates,* Motown-Filly, Muscle Shoals, Atlanta or Texas, Carolina Beach Music..

Nashville & LA are the songwriting capitals of the world. And has too numerous writers to even fit on this page. One can go on and on. Because the song writing generation has just closed recently as the machine track generated era just began. (1985). Also the country rock era and the rock soul era has just Launched. But It is not of any wonder that Paul McCartney and Roger Nichols had affiliation with the classical and the modern. McCartney's father was a jazz musician who played up and down the english coast. And the producer who produced the Beatles is George Martin whom is known for his classical background. And for Roger Nichols; His mother was a music teacher and his father a jazz musician also. Therefore it is of no wonder the chemistry of these well sought out proven song writers yielded them a great emphasis on a bilingual metamorphous from both fields. It is the education or experience and the exposer that foreshadows the final coincidental. And not some sort of a gift of wonder. It is hard work that goes along, and nothing but. Entertaining, night after night. Show business. The love of creation in music.

Among other grates in my generation were: Bacharach & David. Here Bacharach is a good example of a well read songwriter, Arranger, Orchestrator amongst others who don't read music. Songwriting can be achieved by both, read & unread musicians. Because of the three minute duration of music which in turn can be kept to memory, and not written down on a staff. But is time consuming ! Because of the well drawn Ideas and poetic interim that come from somewhere that is not of control of the songwriter.

The bands were Chicago: Music graduates. Earth Wind & Fire & The Allman Brothers well produced. The Beatles; Lennon & McCartney mentioned here and for-most. Their body of songs are un-matched by anyone. For the diversified number, the taste, the arranged three part harmonies, the well structured fresh up tempo, forward moving, spark and tonal sound from a binary changing era & artistic tasteful understanding of their innocent genuine gullible life being mirrored by their music. And the Mystery of the un-known of wealth drawing. What is it ? There are many gifted people in society that have had some notoriety. And one that comes to mind is the late" rain man " of a Hollywood picture depiction. While they are truly and remarkably unbelievably immortally gifted with a built in calculator and an encyclopedia to boot, not to mention the reading and memory excels. Not any of these gifts are of use without the right direction and hard work. So its to my best and final interest to point out: *The educational and experienced theoretical elements in achieving what is of a resolute. And the direction of a must and an imperative, that derives education in Geometrical Theory, in Tonal Innovation, in Abstract Harmony, with Science & Emotion at one persisting history in repeating itself correctly.*

Final Thoughts

When composing or improvising, imagine the piano as a scale, and you are the judge. What you want is to use the entire piano. But not in one place all the time, although sometimes I still do because of body position and age. But what you want is to use it justifiably or accordingly, otherwise your music becomes monotones and boring. You want to keep it alive, fresh, focused, interesting, honest and in charge of it all. You don't want it to take charge of you. Although sometimes that's the way music is written. Sometimes it does pour out. And if you notice it will be even and justifiable. It's great when it writes itself. But most of the time one has to be in-charge of it, because it doesn't always pour out, especially when age steps in. Also a lot of times you are in a different domain as of instruments ranges. Or in the jazz venues, we had to perform on piano's that were out of tune or had missing keys. This is how I learned to tune pianos.

All of pianos are different. They each have their own characteristics. Some have octaves that sound better than others. So you would want to play in those octaves to keep interest in your sound. A good example would be the Steinway D verses the Bossendorfer imperial. While the Steinway has more bass or timber at the bottom, it's by far more clearer and evenly built than any other piano remotely available at any given time. But the Imperial Bossendorfer is the only one that has less bass or timber at the bottom. It's acoustically built for further clarity. To play solo jazz piano on it is a whole new experience. The Steinway has a mid upper tenor octave, which to me sounds like a rainbow, or has a bell sweet crispy soft spot, which is immediately recognizable. It often reminds me of the rare honeysuckle smell, a seasonal delicate sound. It's the only one with that trait. So all instruments have their own characteristics, and you have to be the judge of where and how to play them. This is where you can use the different theoretical tools to find the right spot for the right time and area to play with. And remember the (5-1-3) triads are a split position, which allows you to play it all the way down to the bottom with exceptional voicings. Another words if you use the normal first position triads (1-3-5), you will lose clarity down in the lower register. Often one would be taught at jazz schools to use a split 1-5-7 triads to justify for clarity. *(Bill Evans style). (Bach also suspended the 3rd's because of the harpsichords, and used it on the bass). (I call those bombs to drop in the bass. Try dropping the 3rd. bombs in the bass while improvising. They're not hard to find, if you're using 5-1-3's < there they are.)* Because most of the pianos used from that era were not Bossendorfer's or Steinway's. And so using the Classical method with 5-1-3's allows you to go all the way to the bottom with any keyboard. And also they are split for clearity of harmony for orchestra's. Their folds are also.

The primary use of the 5-1-3's is of-course the fingering ability. It's the only position allowable for fluid improvisations on the keyboard. Once you get the idea of how to use these elements, you will have the power to switch from one to the other if it starts sounding too much of the same to you.

There are enough different theoretical elements in this book to circle around from one to the other. Everyday has its own element, and you have to be the judge of it all in a balanced scale of the mind. The better the judge you are the better you are of this scale system. The better on how to please the listener, and keep the music at an honest level, which will keep you amused as well. I refer to this judicial scale system as the gift. Could it be the gift from God that everybody talks about? Perhaps. What we do know is there is a 12 man jury in court. That there are 12 key's involved with it, much the same as the clock which has 12 hours in it. Hum, music deals with timing. Music is time defined by sound. There is also a correlation in the tempo timing used and the tempo in a clock. We mostly use 4/4 or ¾. Rarely use 5/4 or extremely rare 7/8, or the seventh which is unorthodox, and does not flow. Eight repeats at an octave, so from eight up one can reduce the fractions back to 1 or 2 or 3 or 4 or 5 or 6. Example: 9/16 is reduced down to ¾. If divided by ¾. Or 3/8 if divided by 3/2. The clock has the exact same timing as we use in any key. The seven degrees and the multiple of fractions divided by twelve, in which the seventh is obsolete.

A low G is a fourth in relation to middle C, and a fifth from an upper. It's the same note. Is this the fraction that our minds are programmed to create with? Is this the seventh circulating back? Is this the step in which the mathematical poetry is created from? Who invented the clock? Is poetry invented or created from this wind up of geometric or mathematical programming of our brains in conjunction of the heart in which we use everyday?

The twelve month calendar is dated from day one, which is jesus' birthday. Here we see the religious element at play also. Didn't music and notation begin from the church? Didn't it start after the Greeks time and thrive through the Vatican and pass up through Germany? In which Bach set the temperament for the keyboard, whom is considered the father of music. And Haydn, Handel, JC Bach and others were eventually lured to England. Even Beethoven was asked.

The height of this era was the enlightenment era, 1776. The classical heart of an era in which Joseph Haydn and George Washington were identically matched by looks, as well as born on the same year. 1732. Both witnessed an invention of a well thought out system in which the binary or harmonious mathematical poetically effective element is to be used for the betterment of mankind. This system which involves timing, the courts, religion, music, math, physics, politics, God, government and the stars, all co-exist with a programming that we really do not have a grasp or an understanding of to this day. But what we do know is that, if we follow this path, our minds will be free to use in harmony and we shall enforce throughout the world in order to keep man from extinction. So we have all these facts math and music to prove it with.

One would think the mathematicians or the physicist have their own theoretical studies to prove this system. I would add that there is even more difficulty there from the lack of sound to reproof it with, but the less physical ability to content or haggle with in which composers experience.

Dr. Michio Kaku is a theoretical physicist whom have spent his entire life working on just this theory, in which is called " String theory ". He picks it up from where Einstein left it in describing the free mind, free expression, free thought is necessary for creativity, and Imagination is more important than knowledge. Einstein would also answer the question of ; Is there a God? Einstein states there are two answers of the mind of God. First – there's a personal God that answers prayers, the God of Mosses, Jacob etc. The God that does magical tricks. And second - He himself believed in the God of Spinoza, the God of design that says; The universe is gorgeous, beautiful, elegant and simple. A handful of equations that govern the stars and the universes. The laws of physics. Einstein believed in the God of harmony. The God of order, simplicity and elegance.

Dr. Kaku theorizes that subatomic particles are notes on a vibrating string. Physics is the laws of harmony of the string. Chemistry is the melody you can play by interacting strings. The universe is a symphony of strings. And the mind of God that Einstein would eloquently write about is cosmic music resonating through eleven dimensional hyperspace. And that is the best candidate of the mind of God.

Naturally the physical ability is of physics. So here we realize a good healthy physical ability is essential. We also realize that time co-exist with sound. The two are intermittingly indigenous components. We know of this, but we still are at a relatively young stage of understanding. And I can only theorize from the use of my theories by composing on daily basis. They free my mind for a creative composition in contentedness with a mathematical sound proof. We are getting smarter with all the new technology, but we're still along way from understanding our complexity. I can play jazz in any condition, loud audiences, what have you, but I find classical improvisation a bit more tenuous. Quieter conditions help against concentration break ups. And of-course age and the physical ability can play a role. Age and the loss of a physical ability has to rely on theory and reason. So here we're back from were we started from again, and it goes on forever…

I do not mention about Bach's point counterpoint in fifth's. The pentatonics in which Revel used in fourth's, as well as the jazz theories, Schillinger's four part harmony lines or such tools as the modes. Its because there have been enough books published that discuss those topics. R.Kaye plays on a Steinway Exclusively

"Exercise Nocturne"

R.Kaye

This is basic minor folding of Cm to G7, after a while the normal positions sound too glib
so you will substitute and or split the chords and their positions for better voicings. if you play everyday, you'll naturally substitute different voicings. So get sick of the original sonata form folding and substitute naturally. Here an arpeggio is added in bar 1 .

The melody line is using C harmonic minor scale and you can go to c major in the G7 bars, if you prefer to make it easy

. Generaly the melody line will make the difference where your music goes. So be conscious of it as you're writing.

The Cm-G7 folding to Fm-C7 folding which is the circular fourth's. Take its fourth also once
again on the next line to Bbm-F7 folding.

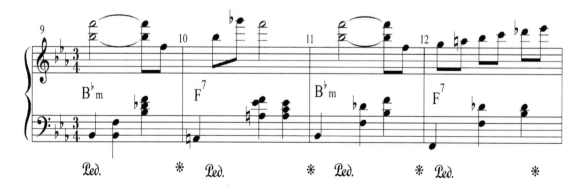

You can take any of these folding sets and switch them around with each other and they will work with each other inspite.
This is the true meaning of harmonics and how they relate to each other. You can play them in any style or composer.
Even Jazz, Bebop, Latin ect...

179

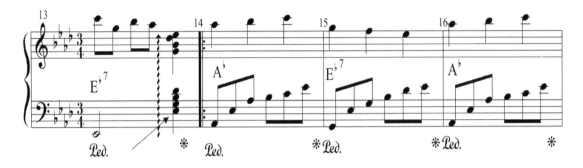

This is a tag bar made of a diminished 7 flattened first., you can call it Eb7 but I call it a diminished flattened first.

That throws it to (Ab-Eb7) folding and from here use a normal progression chopin would use.

It doesn't have to be chopin style, it can be anybody else, but I like the chopin style, as you can tell.

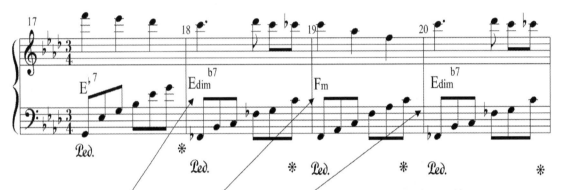

Notice the choice of notes used here, I'm using my electric piano on this exercise , so these notes are what sound best.

If you notice I'm not following the progression as it is exactly, There is plenty of room to play with it. I'm immediately

flattening the diminished 7th then going up to the minor then going back down to the diminished b7 and then going up

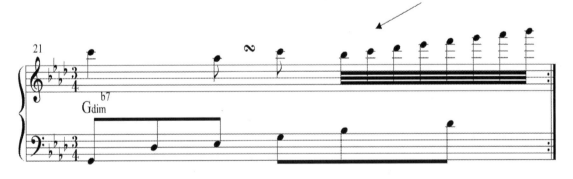

This split run of the last chord sounds OK to me. Of course you can use anything you prefer. You can repeat to bar 14

or you can repeat to the begining or any place that fits anywhere in the middle what have you ect...

I hope I didn't complicate this short Nocturne exercise too much. One can use the original positions if need be.

It will still sound OK . And I hope you get the Idea of what one is supposed to do with all that we have covered.

Pick another theory out from another page and add on.

Finale Nocturne

R. Kaye

This Waltz Nocturne is the basses used for the Impromptu Video on web sight
the Impromptu Video is an Improvisation bassed from this Nocturne. For ref.

Robert Kaye

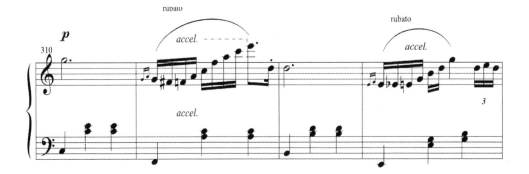

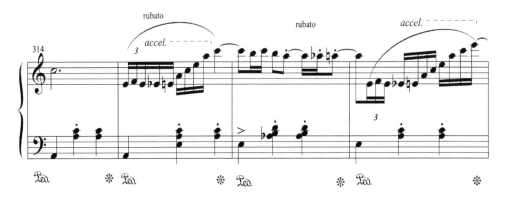

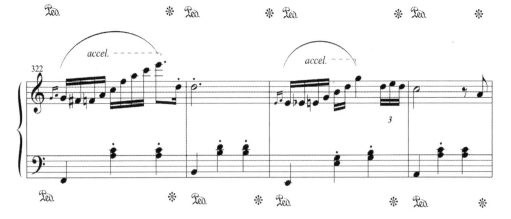

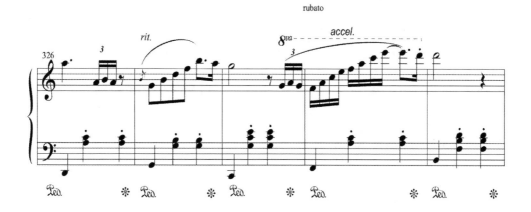

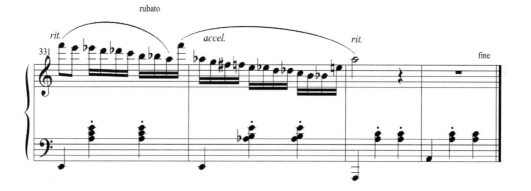

THE THREE STEPS OF THE CLASSICAL METHOD

1. THE 5-1-3 FOLDING OF THE TRIADS

1. The 5-1-3 Triads. Others have called them the 6 / 4 Chords. Some call them the third position. Some call them the 2nd. Inversion. But I call them 5-1-3. Because they suggests what key you are in and it's the Inversion of a major system that is based on Improvisation. Improvisation because of fingering. The fingering is what gives the fluent creation that is even overwhelmed by the composer as well. It's the fluent improvisation that gives one the quick creation of music. There is a difference between the composers of 500 to 1200 pieces of music and the composers of 1 to 3 books. That is the difference of the technique or method. Lots of compositions. And its Because of the 5-1-3 is in the third position triad. Or the 2nd. Inversion technique. All the same.

2. In this segment of the "Classical Method". You would fold to its dominant family back and forth. You are folding to its fifth. So Theoretically this system also makes sense if you do not use the 5-1-3's and use any other dominant 7th. but it will not work for fluent Improvisations. That is the Difference. Later on when you master this method then you might want to experiment with others just to keep in tune. As you are folding to its family dominant 7th. You would start creating scale melody line with the right hand. Major, Minor, Harmonic minor, All depends of what mood you are in at the moment. These differences would stipulate what style of music it would sound like. The mediant and the submediant
    are targeted for additional harmonies and construction of form and
    melody line. Sometimes you let the harmonies pick your melody line
    (Left Hand) and sometimes you would let the (Right Hand) scale find the path in
    which the Composition writes itself. The melody will let you know
    automatically.

3. Also at this point of Improvisational Composition you will use the circular 4th and 5th alternating back and forth. And also alternating between the majors and the minors. Listening al-along and making sure it sounds fresh and not monotonous or a cliché'. It will also keep you interested and amused. And will find its way for you.

2. THE DIMINISHED

1. The diminished. At this point you are in creation land of wizardry. You are obligated to create in whatever style or creative process you choose to take. You can start resolving if you wish. Or you can build timber if you wish. You are basically in the loin or thick of things. You can wallow as long as you like or harmonize in the minors or diminished both the same, or can be. You have an option to build and resolve the diminished by using the golden rule of fingering. Thus exploring all key's and then some. Al-along building on and creating melodies in conjunction with. This is where creating classical music becomes in composition and endless. Never in loss or block of ideas. You can even use your rules and create in your mind. Hear it in your mind.. You will know what

formulas to use from the mind. Targeting and resolve. You will learn it sounds, and even if you don't completely mirror the sound in your mind. The rules will work for you in spite. The Diminished is the Harmonic wild card. I've created certain formulas such as the romantic diminished. The diminished b7th. The most and widely used because of their key entrance to the circular fifth's. The diminished is the key to a new key. Any dominant 7th. Has a diminished in it. Any Folding Family of Triad has a diminished in it. Therefore it connects between the Triads and the dominants.

It also is used with the modern modal elements. It connects with the modern sound. It stresses the 7th, b9, #9, #11, 13th. of the dominant. Its scale I do not use in the "Classical Method". But I tend to stay in the classical element. And use the harmonic minor scale and thus relegating and targeting true harmonics and composition and not abstract. But eternal minors or diminished in poetic harmony. " The "Classical Method". It is also worth exploring in the modern for educational purposes. As well as enjoyment of different styles or types of music. It is essential to learn the indigenous diminished scale. Which is ½ step whole step. ½ step whole step ect. You do inter the world of symmetric here. Maybe one day someone will study and write a book on symmetric poetry as apposed to Classical poetry as I have written. Although if you use the method I suggest here you can create modern poetry.

3. THE DOMINANTS

1. The dominants. They are just what they are. The domineering sound. The tension go getters. The bridge. The build ups. The point makers. The resolvents. The one step before the calm. The bridge to the other side.

2. They tend to resolve to a 4th. Of-course the leading pure tones are the 4th. & the 5th. So theoretically that's the harmonies for the dominant resolve. The # keys tend to be more aggressive on the upper tension and the b Keys tend to be more sweeter or mellow in tension. The dominant is the carrying bridal element to these key resolves. They resolve the diminished. They resolve the 5-1-3 folding families by building the tension. Therefore they are one of the tools used anywhere and add to the essential eternal improvisational element. The 12 bar blues in which Jazz was created from. Uses the dominant 7th. for eternal improvisation. It is also referred to as the turnaround resolving back to the top or the root or the One. The Tonic.

3. The Descending Circular 4th's. These are all resolves in fourth's therefore can be interred from any dominant anywhere in any key. Thus opens an enormous world of improvisation in harmonic poetry. Lyrical as well as melodic. The modern fourth's in Pattern is another resolve to the dominants of a modern abstract sounds.

4. The diminished golden rule of thumb. Is the resolve of the Dominant.
   This is the way to know all the Dominants and their use in any key. And the diminished dominant. Which is the improvisational essencial element in harmony. The harmonic wild card. Improvisation in composition.

5. " Dominant is the art of keeping everything under control ". (Dog Whisperer)

Robert Kaye

The Building of the Musical Concept

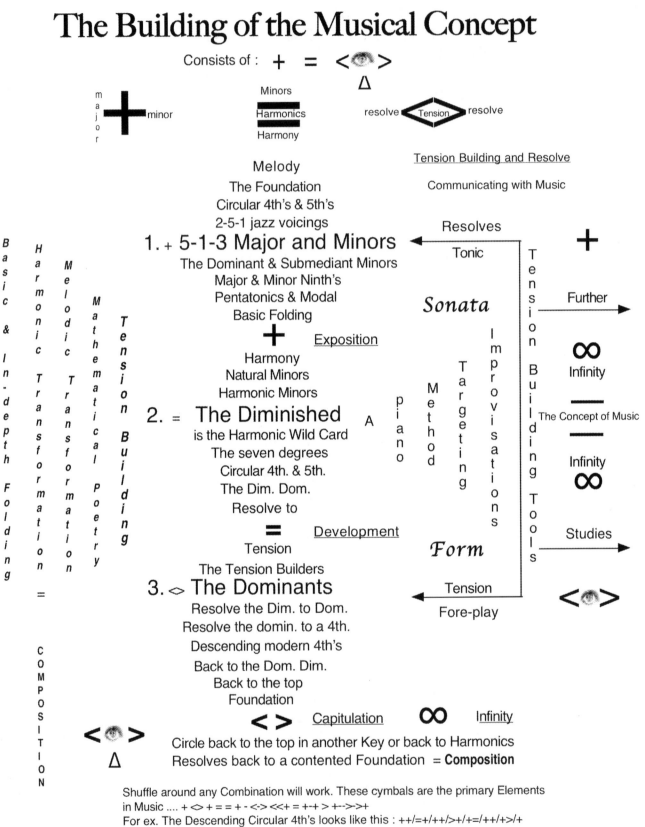

Consists of :   + = <👁> >
Δ

major | +minor
minor

Minors
Harmonics
Harmony

resolve <Tension> resolve

Tension Building and Resolve

Communicating with Music

Melody
The Foundation
Circular 4th's & 5th's
2-5-1 jazz voicings

Resolves

Tonic

1. + 5-1-3 Major and Minors
The Dominant & Submediant Minors
Major & Minor Ninth's
Pentatonics & Modal
Basic Folding

Sonata

Further

+

+ Exposition
Harmony
Natural Minors
Harmonic Minors

∞

Infinity

2. = The Diminished   A
is the Harmonic Wild Card
The seven degrees
Circular 4th. & 5th.
The Dim. Dom.
Resolve to

The Concept of Music

Infinity
∞

= Development
Tension
The Tension Builders

Form

Studies

3. ◇ The Dominants
Resolve the Dim. to Dom.
Resolve the domin. to a 4th.
Descending modern 4th's
Back to the Dom. Dim.
Back to the top
Foundation

Tension
Fore-play

<👁>

<👁 > Capitulation   ∞   Infinity
Δ   Circle back to the top in another Key or back to Harmonics
Resolves back to a contented Foundation = **Composition**

Left vertical labels: Basic & In-depth Folding = COMPOSITION | Harmonic Transformation | Melodic Transformation | Mathematical Poetry | Tension Building

Right vertical label: Tension Building Tools

Middle vertical labels: piano | Method | Targeting | Improvisations

Shuffle around any Combination will work. These cymbals are the primary Elements
in Music .... + <> + = = + - <-> <<+ = +-+ > +--->>+
For ex. The Descending Circular 4th's looks like this : ++/=+/++/>+/+=/++/+>/+

* Please do not be fooled by symbolism, for anyone can create their own, and there are many out there.
Symbolism's are deceiving. The overall picture with exercising, experience is the proper way to see it.

* Rated PG 14

<u>COMPOSING and composers</u>

-The creative Element of Using all the Keys on daily basis is more enriching and rewarding than any other form or style of music present. The artistic structure is unlimited with infinity.

The sonata form in theory is the same from J.C.Bach, Haydn, Mozart, Beethoven to Chopin. It's the classical style that changed as the keyboard matured with the industrial revolution. The cadenza is the sonata form which changed with styles as the piano changed but remained the same scientific fingering theory. Chopin's style is the same as J.S. Bach, Haydn, Mozart, Beethoven. But the piano changed in his era, so "Chopin was the first pianist to make the piano sing" (Arthur Rubinstein).

Chopin was in the middle of the musical concept as it was created. He played Bach's music as well as composed ecossaise which is stride piano notated. He represents the evolution of the musical concept. From the baroque to the classical to the romantic to rhythm. Science and poetry. The central figure in music using both at the piano. Beethoven was actually first to explore the theory, but didn't have the grand piano as it was improved.

Mozart got his classical style from J.C.Bach and Haydn of-course. Beethoven played Bach as a child also and from all came his compositioning efforts or ideas, motifs or themes as well as Clemente's keyboard theories and Haydn's important last works of the symphony style.

Chopin played Bach as a child also, as well as practiced it before he gave his concerts. It helped him focus on his style as well as restrict bad habits or defer mind spending of his own style and sharpen up before his performances.

Vladimir Packman, a student of Chopin remembers Chopin's playing one of his Impromptu. Packmann recorded it in the 1920's. It sounds like Art Tatum. Therefore Tatum's improvisation of the piano is equivalent of the great composers skills, as well as the great pianists skills.   (interpretive performers), But lacks the compositional cadenzal theory. Tatum used the American standards as the theoretical chart to follow and improvise on..

Chopin performed 30 times in his whole lifetime. But wrote compositions that accumulated the essence of the best pianist ever. Poetic, euphoric, great knowledge and understanding of composition as well as the virtuous physical ability of playing the piano in which mesmerized everyone. He himself said he was the king of the piano.

Both Tatum & Chopin were recognized as having god's ability. Tatum was recognized as the premier virtuous jazz pianist that had the likes of Rubinstein and Horowitz attend his gigs. He has no music under his name, but the constant playing from club to club and the records that are the aftermath and culmination of one of the best Jazz artist if not the best.

Both Tatum and Chopin died at 40 years old. While Rubinstein and Horowitz lived a long fruitful life. And with a career all the way to the end.

Composing from the mind is Composing by understanding already the musical concept. The mind is capable of producing music as imagined in an orderly fashion. It hears it, accurate, consistent, enjoyable and tasteful. Not bothersome of current events occurring on constant basis.

String music, as in chamber music is preferably heard in the mind because of its inability to duplicate from the keyboard. Mozart was the primary example of chamber music heard in the mind. And during his lifetime the orchestra was nothing but a chamber size. And the Stradivarius purity in harmony of the strings is unparallel in music and the primary essential sound of classical music at its birth. That is the Classical tone in real sense. Built from the structure of the cadenza.

Because the piano didn't exist at that time. The violin is considered the most tasteful instrument in music still to this day. Frank Sinatra said he fell in love with music when he heard his first violin. And what Mozart heard in his head was the sonata style. Which is the cadenza. In which he was a master at the theory and fingering of. He lacked the keyboard or the piano of Chopin's day. Therefore his music sounded as it did. But Mozart also was a virtuoso like all the others in which after writing the main theme or melody heard in his head or turned up from fingering and improvisations, he then continued and expanded or developed the theoretical composition at length. As well as Beethoven and the rest that followed. This is the symphony form.

Played pieces as opposed to heard pieces in the mind can get complex to the point of playing with harmonics in rhythm and cohesive order of an unimaginative proportions. Manipulative techniques can emerge. As well as innovative styles.

A composer is a spiritual scientist working in his laboratory conducting musical theoretical and theatrical story telling and experimentations continuously. By playing the Piano as its heard in the mind. Or being surprised as all great creative artists strive for on daily basis. This is the reward or treat of everyday life.

The average jazz pianist or classical composer has explored and experimented with his instrument much more than an ordinary musician would. This is also time consuming, a physical nightmare, and a derivative relinquishing from interpretative performances. Where interpretative performers experience excellence and great profound music at the highest level.

Bach is the father of music, for his contribution to the temperament of the keyboard. All keyboards were measured by his organ in Europe. At 88A was the pitch and his standard, but 44A compared to the modern. He created complexity in baroque music. Again because of his keyboard skill. His style is so powerful, that it burns in the mind indelibly. And is recognized immediately over any other baroque composer. Most of his music is sacred of-course. As well as his touch and style in which one can still emulate in reverence and respect. It represents science and virtuosity, the divinity and sacredness at the highest form or level in keyboard and chamber orchestra. He was the first to create the concerto. And very much Poetic as well as Scientific. ∞

Mozart is best describes as the eloquent, delicate geometrical purist and strictly harmonic classicalist. He was the heart and soul of the classical style. He represents classical music for its fine refinement, restraint and good taste. The rhythmic flexibility makes it humanisticly complex.

Beethoven is considered the strength and power of classical music. He single handedly shook the earth's axis with his music. Geometrically and later slightly romantic as the piano was improved. He was the first defined pianist. And represent the power of music.

Chopin was considered as the heart of music were both geometrical and poetical meet. His heart was buried under a church. And a harp represents his music. His style is considered the incidental piano music. Mysterious and refined and can explode at any moment. As well as can be delicate as walking on egg shells. He understood what Beethoven was trying to achieve. And was pegged as the new Mozart in his early childhood. Again he's considered as the king of the piano.

Rhachmaninov's style is considered geometrically and abstractly romantic. He is another great pianist that put most of his effort in his piano concertos. And represents the style to win a piano competition with.

Schumann is considered the romantic pianist with the geometric Bethoovian symphonies and orchestral work. He mixed styles to achieve power from all.. Evident from his oratorial baroque composition. Which is what everyone would want to do as a composer. And still is the goal.

Mendelssohn's style is considered geometrically romantic also. His music demonstrates the structural clarity of Mozart invested with generalized emotional expressive control, more typical with the nineteen century romanticism. As well as Tchaikovsky's Romantic expression and classical structure. Modeled after Mendelssohn. But between Russian emotion and German intellect and control..

The great composers would have given their toes if they only would have had the computerized equipment of today. For multiple printings of the orchestral parts.

A slightly out of tune piano can still be played hard, thus is covered up in that manner. And improvisations is advantageous and useful for those exemptions. But if a piano is badly out of tune, no matter how much it costs, a cheep $50 dollar keyboard will be much of use and overcome it.

Notation of a piano piece is impossible without the knowledge of the musical concept. Or the structure of the Cadenza. Because of the separation of hands for the notation staff.

Chopin used a copyist at the end of his life. And without him seeing Chopin's fingers and hands. He would have had to be a knowledgeable composer in classical structure and the cadenza or sonata form and the romantically poetical style as well as to separate the notes with respect of hands in the proper staffs.

The Essential <u>Target Notes</u> to Memorize
and in the proper Order of a Compositional path.
The Classical Construct as it's heard.

It's very Important to use these Target notes as the Symbols in memory. They Should be the language for your Conversation. This is the Terminology to memorize. And should not be confused by using other Symbols, methods or the Standard Terminology to distract. These Targets are in essence and equivalent to one Composition to Memorize. Yet yielding for you eternal Compositions with Improvisations. This is an Arguable point that is discussed often by Scholars. Is Composition an Improvisation ? That all depends if you're a Good Pianist perhaps.Test yourself by taking any Song and figuring it out by using the target notes to decipher with. Analyze any Music by following your Target notes. They are the guide to follow. The Musical Maze is no longer a Maze. But a playground for the Heart and Soul. With your hands at work. The Freedom to Communicate at any level musically. And at the speed of thought in Time.....

1. The first of Importance is the Circular 4th.& 5th. of the 5-1-3 with their proper basic Folds
    These can be used for Symphonies as well as solo piano compositions. Geometrically. <u>Improvisation.</u>
2. Next comes the Diminished rule of thumb Target notes / The Dominant Diminished
    Poetically following the rules or Geometrically at random. These are most important for <u>Improvisation.</u>
3. Next are the target notes of the scales of the 5-1-3. (These targets will Compose & Guide you.)
    These are the most important positions in regard to <u>Improvisations.</u>
4. Next are the Target Notes for the Natural & Dominant Minors.
    These are the door going to the outside world. Essential for <u>Improvisations.</u>
5. Next are the Target notes and pattern for the 7 Degrees. One assumes that's standard. These may not be the
    improvisational tools for some other than the key of C, but they need to be learned. As well as the 3-5-1 degrees.
6. Next are the Second position Target notes, Major & Minor, Their Folds, Scales & Patterns.
    These patterns are ideal for Improvisations. Going from 5-1-3 to the 3-5-1 Patterns are essential. <u>Improvisations.</u>
7. Next are the Neapolitan Targets especially for Strict Classical style. And piano.
    The Neapolitans in Circular 4th. and 5th. for strict piano virtuos compositions. As well as the Descends.
8. Next are the Descending & Ascending Circular 4th's. And their Entrances. The many different approaches.
    For such compositions as Bach's goldberg variations. The Descends for all positions are Important. p. 87 is for Improvisations
9. Next are the Target notes for the Diminished flattened 7th in Circular 4th & 5th.
    Again these are the essential tools for piano Improvisations. The Chopin method or all else. <u>Improvisations.</u>
10. Next and for-most : The final full Classical Harmonic Minor prog. The 7 Degrees (Pattern). As well as pages 101, 118
    Mix the following pages for theoretical infinite <u>Improvisations</u>: (90,93,98) - (19, 26, 88, 89,101,125,133) - (125,126,127,129,133,192)
11. Next are the Delicate piano Magic extended folds.... Timber Improvisational Arpeggiations.
    (Schumann...Mendelssohn..Chopin.) These are essential in fluent modern romantic <u>Improvisations.</u> pages 127 - 118
12. And etc....... What order matters what style of music you are composing for also. So you pick from here on......
    for example: if you used the improvisational path above in a Baroque session you would maybe end up with a Courante
    or a Fantasia in the Baroque style. If you used it in a Romantic style, you would end up with Chopin's style. If you
    use it in a Classical style, of-course that would be Mozart or Beethoven. A march maybe, or a Symphonic Sonate.

∞

And the infinite page 101 with page 88 and 133 should be the essential and first learned to picture to move further on.The descends pages (55 thru 78) &
(p. 87) will merge onto automatically as these groupings are learned in these order. Descends in C will make it easier to grasp first and fluent with dexterity to play live
without much preparations but full creativity keeping oneself amused interested and enjoying the process. As the other keys will be apprehended and grasped to Improvise
with live eventually as the next two pages are the witness to your hard work (190-191). But attentively understanding what to handle first and how much physical
availability is at hand and can be used at will and in a relaxed calm or vivacious mode with virtuos creative applications at the speed of thought.

∞

An Important rule to follow is: You are hiking in the woods. You have to memorize the markers laid out for you in order not to get lost.
There is a path there, worn out for you to follow if you wish. In which you can jog home if you wish, run, or even sprint. Its what i call the 5-1-3
fingering Triangle. The build itself. Stay in this path and use page 101 as the map to chart the journey through the woods on daily basis. The 5-
1-3 minors or the 5-1-3 majors in the infinite triangle circle. First, recognize that certain theories will slow you down or even get you lost. So
know the primary path right away to use: For example: You focus on 1 key right away. This key has two neighbors, one on the right and one on
the left. The central major key will have the natural minor to master link to the other keys. Take the natural minor and sharpen its top finger, 1/2
step. Now you have the three minors of the central key and the three harmonic minor scales to use for the three keys. Each minor 5-1-3 folds
up 1/2 step to give you the diminished of it. Now you know the three diminished for each key, and its harmonic minor scale to use for each key
also. You now can weave from key to key by jumping from diminished to diminished and switch scale to scale, key to key. And they will
harmonize. The majors are also there to use with the diminished and their major, harmonic minor, dominant folds as well. Knowing how to weave
from key to key, diminished to diminished, scale to scale, minor to minor, fold to fold. Knowing which diminished belongs to which key is the
trick. And which harmonic minor scale belongs to which key and minor is another trick. This is why you use the target notes to identify them
with. One has to use 75 % of the brain in classical theory, and 25% feel from the heart. They will switch on you at those sub conscience
moments when you need a breather for the next idea to come to you. You have to have a sense of direction or a feel to rely on, to see the
worn-out path. So you do have to use both Science & Sense, Feel & Structure to rely on, as assurance, this is the path to follow because, you
will know it from the brain. Using both gives you the infinite timeless tear through space, and defies gravity, at the speed of thought..One or two
hours can pass by in five or ten minutes..This is the page, or the course (101) to practice on daily basis, in order to know the path in the woods to use on daily basis. How
well you know it, assures how well you can absorb nature, find your way and continuously understand where you're at...

Δ Classical ∞   ∞ Jazz Δ

Baroque   **My Improvisational golden rule of thumb of the build of Composition in One Glance**   Modal

1. You can start from any minor or Major. If i start from a minor. I choose a 5-1-3 minor. Then i look at the notes of it. Immediately i recognize that the lower notes are going to be my minors to use with the top note being a major, in which is going to be my overall Major key to use and the key i'm in at the moment. And immediately I also sharpen the top note 1 step <u>in my mind</u> and know its become now the third minor of my key. Each key has 3 minors, right? Ok. If I'm improvising jazz, then this top note sharpened 1 step, will also give me the 2-5-1 jazz voicing to use. (page 157). I now have the three minors of my key immediately in mind. The reason is because immediately one can start folding with the 5-1-3 minors into a dominant 7th. Or into a diminished 7th. one step up.(And that will be the diminished for that minor, thus giving you the three diminished to use also, three minors three diminished) Or fold into 4th.'s one step up on page 87. As well as the other more involved parallels if wished upon. (outside-inside/outside-inside fingers crawling up and down). Now with these three minors, the top notes of all of them can also be sharpened 1 step to give you all the 2-5-1 of that key just the same, for jazz. The top finger is usually the stronger to improvise with, even though its first looked at in the mind. Its actually the stronger minor to use out of the rest of the minors. Now once you see this 3 sided pyramid of minors, diminished, neapolitan keys to use. You can branch out from any of these minors to start another pyramid. Or you can branch out from any of these major keys also.

--- Each minor 5-1-3 gives you 2 harmonic minor scales to use immediately, and when sharpening the top finger then its 3 harmonic minor scales to use. And a major scale which is the key you're in.Which is the top finger that was sharpened. So immediately its 3 harmonic minors and one major scale. All seen in a glance.

2. If I start on a major. Or in a major in the middle of an improvisational session. Then i immediately also sharpen the top finger of the 5-1-3 Major, 1/2 step this time, and in the mind. In-which it will give me the three key's that i will use and that will be the neapolitan keys harmonizing close together. It will also be the 2-5-1 jazz voicing that i will use.. The majors also will fold to dominants and diminished just as the minors. And with the majors you have the dominant and natural minors which are the branch outs into the minors. (page 82).

After which one will circle eternally in an infinite geometric cycle forever. And after seeing this Geometric triangles, then one can use the other theories with the second position and tonic 1-3-5. And using the 5-1-3 and 3-5-1 minors in conjunction will enrich your composition, as well as keep one amused. But know that the 5-1-3's are the home for the Improvisational fingering at whole. Example:

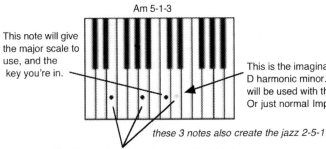

Am 5-1-3

This note will give the major scale to use, and the key you're in.

This is the imaginary sharpened top finger in which will also be used, D harmonic minor. Or for jazz, it is the creation of the 2-5-1, in which will be used with the pentatonics or the modern 4th's on page 158. Or just normal Improvisations. Classical & Jazz

these 3 notes also create the jazz 2-5-1

The 3 harmonic minor scales to use - Em 5-1-3, Am 5-1-3, Dm 5-1-3... as well as you can take any of these notes and start a new 5-1-3 minor out of them as well in which will branch out and multiplies in 3's.

Both of these can fold into a multiple of 3's. Weather they are diminished, Dominants, or Descends.

To find the 3 minors from C major 5-1-3 or any 5-1-3 major: Find the natural minor of the major 5-1-3. Which is Am here. And follow the proceeder above for the minors. immediately sharpen the top finger in your mind. And that will give you the 3 minors of any major 5-1-3. Then proceed to continue to draw more info, as stated above etc...

Or can branch out to 3 new keys from any of these 3 notes

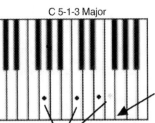

C 5-1-3 Major

This is the imaginary sharpened top finger in which will give the key of F to use with the keys of G and C. It also creates the 2-5-1 jazz voicing as well. And will be used with the pentatonics as well as the modern 4th and other jazz tools. If used in jazz.

these 3 notes also create the jazz 2-5-1

The three keys that are close to each other that will be used in this improvisational session or episode, as Bach called them. From these keys one branches out to the dominant and natural minors to fall in the infinite cycle of geometric harmonies. (page 82)

3. After the exposition above; You then take the pattern from page 133 and apply to whatever key you wind up on. Moving from key to key as the development. And i remember the pattern of page 133 in my mind and apply it to all the other keys by the picture of the F minor key in particular as the mnemonic key to use on page 133. Ther's something about the F minor key that stays in the mind.* All the great composers did this. They had this routine in their minds. Oh and this is also applied to Jazz, by using the 2-5-1's for Jazz Improvisations.

My Diminished Improvisational golden rule of thumb

The seventh

<u>Reference chart</u>
The twelve commandments

Roll the dice - 7 / 11

Where the compositional creativity of **Beethoven** thrived and for all those that came afterwards

The Harmonic wild card

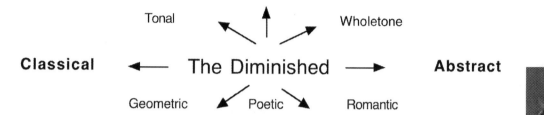

```
              Tonal      ↑      Wholetone
                    ↖    |    ↗
Classical  ←————  The Diminished  ————→  Abstract
                    ↙         ↘
          Geometric   Poetic      Romantic
```

1. From any Diminished 1/2 step above any note can play major or minor 1-3-5 or 5-1-3.
   And minor 3-5-1 which is 5-b1-3 from the fifth.

2. From any Diminished 1/2 step under any note can play minor #5. The major 3-5-1. And can flatten
   the 3 of it to turn it into 3-5-1 minor. The 3-5-1 major is always looked at as an ordinary minor #5

3. From any Diminished If any note is flattened then its the dominant of that note
   and take next finger up and 1/2 step up can play major or minor 1-3-5 or 5-1-3.

4. From any Diminished If any note is sharpened then its the harmonic minor of that note
   and the next finger up 1/2 step up can play major or minor 1-3-5 or 5-1-3 or 5-b1-3.
   The 5-b1-3 is from the 5. (minor 3-5-1) And if you sharpen the bottom note it turns into a major 3-5-1.

5. From any Diminished If any note is flattened then take the next finger down and 1/2 step
   under play 3-5-1 major from the 3. Which is an ordinary minor #5 of-course and can also flatten the 3 to make it
   3-5-1 minor.

6. From any Diminished If any note is sharpened then go down to next finger and 1/2 step
   down can play 3-5-1 from the 3. And you can flatten the 3 to turn it into a 3-5-1 minor also.

7. From any Diminished If any note is flattened then go up or down **2** fingers and 1/2 step up play
   3-5-1 minor from the 3 or 5-b1-3 from the fifth. The same. (Also you can play 5-1-3 major. But its for harmony and the rules go out)

8. From any Diminished If any note is flattened then any finger and 1/2 step up can be a harmonic. Or
   5-b1-3 from the 5 or ordinary major 7th (these are a harmony , door opener and not a resolve as the others.)

9. From any Diminished 1/ 2 step under any note can be another Diminished b7th.

10. From any Diminished 1/2 step under any note can be a Dominant 7th.

11. From any Diminished 1/2 step under the second finger play octaved notes with left
    hand. As the ninth.

12. From any Diminished 1/2 step above any note can play the harmonic minor scale of that note.
    And at any time if you use or resolve to a minor from any of the above, you can use the harmonic minor
    scales of that note for the poetic rule. (Or use the modal harmonic minor. 5th. p.129 etc..) To keep interest...
    Follow the rules and tonality will insue automatically. If the rules go out then its abstract and it has to have rhythm , bass
    or a beat to keep one's interest.
    -- if you take 1/2 step up or down from all fingers, play major or minor, its harmonies also. Geometric, Symmetric and Universal for all others !
    But Follow my rules -   Follow my rules -   Follow my rules -   Follow my rules -   Follow my rules -   Follow my rules -
    For it will culminate the proper path for a Classical or Romantic path to follow. Geometric or Poetic. Poetry in motion. A binary construct.

Piano Sonata

4th. Mvt. - Andante

Jun 16, 2011

Excerpt for Piano -

From Piano string Quintet

R.Kaye

Art is: Paradoxal

A game whose rules are constantly changing.

That's what makes it interesting

The representation or imitation

of the objects of the world around us

OR

You paint what is there

not what you can see

pablo Picasso

It is not the form we respond to in art

but the geometric shapes beneath the forms

SO   Paul Klee

How do you define art?

After M. Duchamp no one is sure

" Creativity is the residue of wasted time "

" The answer will only arrive when you stop searching for it "

A.Einstein

Artists search for their own sense of truth

The Modern Virtual Studio

&
Orchestra

Creativity is our most important mental talent and can arrive in a split second

And the producing, engineering, notating, programing, practicing can take decades to learn and execute

Unless its handed down from those that have created it !

A short note to the readers, academics and purchasers of this book:

May I rephrase and point out clearly to all of those that have studied and or earned a degree in music. I'm well aware of the proper proceeder attuned in going about or following the proper path to a well explanatory descriptive dilatory emphasis, analogous or analysis of the musical concept. Be it the notated correct enharmonics or the descriptive symbolism of the standard academically used methods. This method breaks the standard path or proceeder of the popularly common school reformation. It is the simplification of thought. This is the first book written on classical improvisations and taken from a complete different angle of sight. I have rewritten or edited it from the first few copies in which were left alone and kept in simplified form and in the proper path and methodology in which the speed of thought is at hand at an instant. I wish I hadn't done so. So I do need to emphasis here for the most part, that as I have edited this copy in the common format of enharmonic standard school coherence, may I emphasis and yell out loud, that this defeats the purpose of simplifying very difficult structural harmony that no one has documented and one should rewrite or look at this book from that angle of:

Where a C# is a Db only. Where a G# is an Ab only. Where an Eb minor is not a D# minor. A Bb minor is not an A# minor. Look at these keys in flats to relinquish the extra enharmonically minored keys for the speed of thought. I use all flat keys to quickly linguist a picture in thought in my mind. Cb major is an ordinary old B. Gb is an F#. So to look at these keys in two, three or however as many different motifs is an irony in defeat in learning the sound that the mind is trying to grasp with the structural shape of one position only and accomplish at the speed of thought. To relinquish these 18 enharmonic keys is to use 12 keys at hand at all times in improvisations in which I think the mind is attuned to in geometrical patterns of twelve only. Twelve keys is the magic number to use mathematically. To add the extra keys would only complicate a notated descriptive hash to content with that is unnecessary and will confuse and brake down the speed of thought. Only afterwards do you notate accordingly. These twelve keys have their mode of minors as well that are automatically used with target notes that are important and created from only those that have the experience of playing live professionally. As the great composers did themselves. Notation is simple, but it's what causes the difficulty and the surrealism in music. It is a pejorative not idealistically a correct path to use. But is idealistically used for communication, interpretation and at times may draw ideas with as the enharmonic keys to use or the surrealism or minimalism if need be. Notation is derived for keeping the notes in the middle of the staff. That is the main reason the notation path is the standard. The tonal ideas come from the structure of sight from the keyboard. A methodology that suits the player. That delivers infinite composition.

To all of those that have studied and have gained degrees in this descriptive analogy. May I remind you, this is the first book on classical improvisations. I have heard my work echoed by distinguished lecturers already. And given a clean bill of health. If you're wondering why all the misspelling, incompletions from the previous copies?. Its because I sent my notes to the publishers over the years while I'm working or writing and uncovering this path of Improvisational composition. One produced the other in real time. There is no way around the fermentation time period. Also, I am monitored on daily basis, 24/7 and all my work is distributed before all else without my consent. Therefore I sent all my material to the publishers quickly before anyone can claim it or demean it for their own gains as of the Amazon Ph.D. and his students have contrived for their own gains, publicly with venomous hate.

Let me repeat once again: I do not care of the past misspelling or improper paragraphing, paraphrasing of previous versions, nor do I care what anyone really thinks. For I have reproofed my theories of the great classical composers and use them on daily basis. That is of utter importance and first priority to anyone serious about music. And not all else after the fact of trying to gain for their own fifteen minutes of fame.

I do not care what any academic thinks or his or her opinion. I have created a method in which is sound and proven to work properly at the speed of thought. This is the first of its kind and the first to the scholastic environment in which no one have been exposed to. So I can understand the first initial reaction but content to emphasis over and over. For it seems that once someone learns an ongoing path of the initial long process of analysis, they will not conform to any other for the time it takes to re emphasis and re-learn. I have used all of the methods and have been around for a long time in this profession. And this is the only way to quickly follow the path the great composers have been on. Or merely play beautiful or powerful music at will and at an improvisational path that have long been paved over.

After my initial release of the first edition of this book. We do now start to hear other PhD's speaking up about classical improvisations. This is the first book uncovering this issue. And long overdue ....

R.Kaye

Telepathy is signature of the divine
&
Luck is the residue in design

∞

Over time, Experience not only gives you more information to
use, but the exposure to the music that is creating the knowledge
that can also spark the imagination in which can lead to a
subjective understanding that can inhibit and bring about our
deepest insights to come from pure reason and not experience.

∞

The Universe is an incomprehensible thing, that it is comprehensible

Albert Einstein

About the Author

To my surprise this book has transcended and I have kept out any incidents to the best of my ability, writing only about what I know best and what my real love has been since childhood that somehow was thwarted from a real education in music to the professional experience of a performing monkey in all the genre's, publicly manifesting to this infinite ∞ methodology and its triangular, geometric and poetic revelations. Δ

I remember faintly attempting to emulate my mother to play an excerpt of a Ravel piano piece as she would have piano teachers trying to teach her this fingering riff over and over, and afterwards I would get so fed up with it that I would play it quickly to get it over with, as the lesson ended and the teacher was on her way out, at the age of 4.

I have played in night clubs, bars, hotels, restaurants, schools, universities, churches, comedy clubs, theaters, concert halls, outdoor concerts, weddings, funerals, parades, malls, shopping centers, private ceremonies, plays, pig-pickings or for dignitaries ….

I Have played professionally in every venue from the classical, jazz, rock, southern rock, and top 40, to the Broadway show tunes, or leisure bossa nova, samba of the hotel venues, or the disco and the country era. I have composed for every venue. And am a songwriter / producer as well. This book is the product of my compilation of notes in which I accumulated in the span of 10 years of studies, compositions and accidental revelations, in-which I use to compose with on daily basis.

Ten years ago, this subject was not even relevant. Nor were any books of this topic available. This is the first. And my acclaim of classical improvisation in the style of Chopin, Bach, Mozart, Beethoven Etc. Should be no different than playing cocktail piano. Or the fact that how did the great composers themselves, write one composition a day, instantly as they improvised live themselves, just the same. Common sense in which I proved. And my years of work unveiling the secrets of the great composers. Theories, patterns and formula's - from experience is the result of my geometrical and poetical methodology. Bound inside :

" The Classical Method "

Reviews

Wow that's really an outstanding Masterpiece !
I think this must be indisputable proof that you have unlocked the secrets of the masters !
I personally think Julliard ought to bestow upon you an honorary Ph.D. !
In the meantime, I am floored by your performance and must go listen again.

Yours Admiringly -Alice Kim Jenkins – Composer / Pianist - Graduate of music / Seattle, Washington

Actually can't wait to get my hands on your book…Classical Improvisation is something not really well known to musicians of other genres, and an in-depth knowledge of the style's techniques is invaluable. Not seen anything of this book's nature before, so it's a revolutionary idea indeed !

I continually study scores for " colours " and rely on my training to reveal the composers " eye " within the piece, so this is more power to my work !

Thanks so much
Brian Cunningham – Oxford / The Royal College of Music.
English Baroque Composer in Residence

Dear Robert Kaye
Thank you for writing your Book. I am sure it was not easy to put all that Information down on paper ! I read your Forward and I have had the exact same feelings…. That writing music down is painful. I am 54 years old and I have played the piano since I was a little boy. I had great teachers. I was groomed to be a concert pianist. Although I did not choose that path for myself. I always wanted to know how to improvise and compose. I did not know how to go about that. I have been reading various books on the subject the past few years. I was a music major in college for two years. I learned music theory there, but it did not seem to help me achieve what I was after… to be able to play my own music. I know intuitively that the masters had some kind of education I was lacking. It is not magic, but it seemed like magic until one has a grasp of at least some ideas that work and make sense. Today I work as a church organist. What I gleaned from your book is the idea of the circle of fifth's and using common tones to go from key to key. I need to just simply sit down now play, play, play and experiment, experiment, experiment. I have made some progress. My thanks to people like yourself who take the time to teach others. God Bless You.

Organist × Roger McCormick

Palm Beach Gardens, Florida

Many thanks to all who made this book happen. All the great musicians that I've worked with throughout the years. All well deserved. Today, many hold prominent teaching positions at popular Universities throughout the Country. UNC, ECU, Duke university, UNCG, UNCC, UCLA, ASU, USC etc.. As well as the many friends that were brought to attention in Hollywood, New york and Nashville. I owe my Gratitude & Respect to all. Active - (1960's – 2000)   **www.robsnob.com**